The Reformed Doctrine Of Predestination

By Loraine Boettner D.D.
Edited by Anthony Uyl

Devoted Publishing
Woodstock, Ontario, 2017

The Reformed Doctrine Of Predestination
By Loraine Boettner D.D.
Edited by Anthony Uyl

Copyright 1932 by Loraine Boettner

The text of The Reformed Doctrine of Predestination is all in the Public Domain. This edition is published by Devoted Publishing a division of 2165467 Ontario Inc.

What kind of philosophies do you have?
Let us know!

Contact us at: devotedpub@hotmail.com
Visit us on Facebook: Devoted Publishing
Get more products via our website: www.devotedpublishing.com
Published in Woodstock, Ontario, Canada 2017.

For bulk educational rates, please contact us at the above email address.

ISBN: 978-1-77356-000-7

Table of Contents

Chapter I - Introduction 5
    Footnotes: 8
Section I 9
Chapter II - Statement of the Doctrine 9
    Footnotes: 11
Chapter III - God Has a Plan 12
    Footnotes: 15
Chapter IV - The Sovereignty of God 16
    Footnotes: 17
Chapter V - The Providence of God 18
    Footnotes: 20
Chapter VI - The Foreknowledge of God 21
    Footnotes: 23
Chapter VII - Outline of Systems 24
    Footnotes: 25
Chapter VIII - The Scriptures Are the Final Authority by Which Systems Are to Be Judged 26
    Footnotes: 27
Chapter IX - A Warning Against Undue Speculation 28
    Footnotes: 28
Section II - The Five Points of Calvinism 29
Chapter X - Total Inability 29
    Footnotes: 38
Chapter XI - Unconditional Election 39
    Footnotes: 64
Chapter XII - Atonement 66
    Footnotes: 70
Chapter XIII - Efficacious Grace 71
    Footnotes: 78
Chapter XIV - The Perseverance of the Saints 80
    Footnotes: 87
Section III 88
Chapter XV 88
    Footnotes: 89
Chapter XVI 90
    Footnotes: 97
Chapter XVII 98
    Footnotes: 107
Chapter XVIII 109
    Footnotes: 112

The Reformed Doctrine Of Predestination

Chapter XIX ... 113
   Footnotes: ... 117
Chapter XX ... 118
   Footnotes: ... 121
Chapter XXI ... 122
   Footnotes: ... 123
Chapter XXII ... 124
   Footnotes: ... 127
Section IV ... 128
Chapter XXIII - Salvation by Grace ... 128
   Footnotes: ... 131
Chapter XXIV - Personal Assurance That One Is Among the Elect ... 132
   Footnotes: ... 134
Chapter XXV - Predestination in the Physical World ... 135
   Footnotes: ... 136
Chapter XXVI - A Comparison with the Mohammedan Doctrine of Predestination ... 137
   Footnotes: ... 139
Section V ... 140
   Footnotes: ... 153
Chapter XXVIII - Calvinism in History ... 154
   Footnotes: ... 178

Loraine Boettner D.D.

Chapter I – Introduction

The purpose of this book is not to set forth a new system of theological thought, but to give a re-statement to that great system which is known as the Reformed Faith or Calvinism, and to show that this is beyond all doubt the teaching of the Bible and of reason.

The doctrine of Predestination receives comparatively little attention in our day and it is very imperfectly understood even by those who are supposed to hold it most loyally. It is a doctrine, however, which is contained in the creeds of most evangelical churches and which has had a remarkable influence both in Church and State. The official standards of the various branches of the Presbyterian and Reformed Churches in Europe and America are thoroughly Calvinistic. The Baptist and Congregational Churches, although they have no formulated creeds, have in the main been Calvinistic if we may judge from the writings and teachings of their representative theologians. The great free church of Holland and almost all the churches of Scotland are Calvinistic. The Established Church of England and her daughter, the Episcopal Church of America, have a Calvinistic creed in the Thirty-nine Articles. The Whitefield Methodists in Wales to this day bear the name of "Calvinistic Methodists."

Among the past and present advocates of this doctrine are to be found some of the world's greatest and wisest men. It was taught not only by Calvin, but by Luther, Zwingli, Melanchthon (although Melanchthon later retreated toward the Semi-Pelagian position), by Bullinger, Bucer, and all of the outstanding leaders in the Reformation. While differing on some other points they agreed on this doctrine of Predestination and taught it with emphasis. Luther's chief work, "The Bondage of the Will," shows that he went into the doctrine as heartily as did Calvin himself. He even asserted it with more warmth and proceeded to much harsher lengths in defending it than Calvin ever did. And the Lutheran Church today as judged by the Formula of Concord holds the doctrine of Predestination in a modified form. The Puritans in England and those who early settled in America, as well as the Covenanters in Scotland and the Huguenots in France, were thorough-going Calvinists; and it is little credit to historians in general that this fact has been so largely passed over in silence. This faith was for a time held by the Roman Catholic Church, and at no time has that church ever openly repudiated it. Augustine's doctrine of Predestination set against him all the half-hearted elements in the Church and arrayed him against every man who belittled the sovereignty of God. He overcame them, and the doctrine of Predestination entered the belief of the universal Church. The great majority of the creeds of historic Christendom have set forth the doctrines of Election, Predestination, and final Perseverance, as will readily be seen by any one who will make even a cursory study of the subject. On the other hand Arminianism existed for centuries only as a heresy on the outskirts of true religion, and in fact it was not championed by an organized Christian church until the year 1784, at which time it was incorporated into the system of doctrine of the Methodist Church in England. The great theologians of history, Augustine, Wycliffe, Luther, Calvin, Zwingli, Zanchius, Owen, Whitefield, Toplady, and in more recent times Hodge, Dabney, Cunningham, Smith, Shedd, Warfield, and Kuyper, held this doctrine and taught it with force. That they have been the lights and ornaments of the highest type of Christianity will be admitted by practically all Protestants. Furthermore, their works on this great subject have never been answered. Then, too, when we stop to consider that among non-Christian religions Mohammedanism has so many millions who believe in some kind of Predestination, that the doctrine of Fatalism has been held in some form or other in several heathen countries, and that the mechanistic and deterministic philosophies have exerted such great influences in England, Germany, and America, we see that this doctrine is at least worthy of careful study.

From the time of the Reformation up until about one hundred years ago these doctrines were boldly set forth by the great majority of the ministers and teachers in the Protestant churches; but today we find far the greater majority holding and teaching other systems. It is only rarely that we now come across those who can be called "Calvinists without reserve." We may quite appropriately apply to our own churches the words of Toplady in regard to the Church of England: "Time has been when the Calvinistic doctrines were considered and defended as the Palladium of our Established Church; by her bishops and clergy, by the universities, and the whole body of the laity. It was (during the reigns of Edward VI, Queen Elizabeth, James I, and the greater part of Charles I) as difficult to meet with a clergyman who did not preach the doctrines of the Church of England, as it is now to find one who does. We have generally forsaken the principles of the Reformation, and Ichabod, or 'the glory is

The Reformed Doctrine Of Predestination

departed,' has been written on most of our pulpits and church-doors ever since." [1]

The tendency in our enlightened age is to look upon Calvinism as a worn-out and obsolete creed. At the beginning of his splendid article on "The Reformed Faith in the Modern World," Prof. F. E. Hamilton says, "It seems to be tacitly assumed by a large number of people in the Presbyterian Church today that Calvinism has been outgrown in religious circles. In fact, the average church member, or even minister of the gospel, is inclined to look upon a person who declares that he believes in Predestination, with a glance of amused tolerance. It seems incredible to them that there should exist such an intellectual curiosity as a real Calvinist, in an age of enlightenment like the present. As for seriously examining the arguments for Calvinism, the idea never enters their heads. It is deemed as out of date as the Inquisition, or the idea of a fiat world, and is looked upon as one of the fantastic schemes of thought that men held before the age of modern science." Because of this present day attitude toward Calvinism, and because of the general lack of information concerning these doctrines, we regard the subject of this book as one of great importance.

It was Calvin who wrought out this system of theological thought with such logical clearness and emphasis that it has ever since borne his name. He did not, of course, originate the system but only set forth what appeared to him to shine forth so clearly from the pages of Holy Scripture. Augustine had taught the essentials of the system a thousand years before Calvin was born, and the whole body of the leaders of the Reformation movement taught the same. But it was given to Calvin with his deep knowledge of Scripture, his keen intellect and systematizing genius, to set forth and defend these truths more clearly and ably than had ever been done before.

We call this system of doctrine "Calvinism," and accept the term "Calvinist" as our badge of honor; yet names are mere conveniences. "We might," says Warburton, "quite as appropriately, and with equally as much reason, call gravitation 'Newtonism,' because the principles of gravitation were first dearly demonstrated by the great philosopher Newton. Men had been fully conversant with the facts of gravitation for long ages before Newton was born. These facts had indeed been visible from the first days of creation, inasmuch as gravitation was one of the laws which God ordained for the governing of the universe. But the principles of gravitation were not fully known, and the far-reaching effects of its power and influence were not understood until they were discovered by Sir Isaac Newton. So, too, was it with what men call Calvinism. The inherent principles of it had been in existence for long ages before Calvin was born. They had indeed been visible as patent factors in the world's history from the time of man's creation. But inasmuch as it was Calvin who first formulated these principles into a more or less complete system, that system, or creed, if you will, and likewise those principles which are embodied in it, came to bear his name." [2]

We may add further that the names Calvinist, Lutheran, Puritan, Pilgrim, Methodist, Baptist, and even the name Christian, were originally nicknames. But usage has established their validity and their meaning is well understood.

The quality which gave such force to Calvin's teaching was his close adherence to the Bible as an inspired and authoritative book. He has been referred to as preeminently the biblical theologian of his age. Where the Bible led, there he went; where it failed him, there he stopped short. This refusal to go beyond what is written, coupled with a ready acceptance of what the Bible did teach, gave an air of finality and positiveness to his declarations which made them offensive to his critics. Because of his keen insight and power of logical development he has often been referred to as merely a speculative theologian. That he was a speculative genius of the first order is, of course, not to be denied; and in the cogency of his logical analysis he possessed a weapon which made him terrible to his enemies. But it was not on these gifts that he depended primarily when forming and developing his theological system.

Calvin's active and powerful intellect led him to sound the depths of every subject which he touched. In his investigations about God and the plan of redemption he went very far, penetrating into mysteries concerning which the average man seldom if ever dreams. He brought to light a side of Scripture which had as yet been very much in the shade and stressed those deep truths which in the ages preceding the Reformation had comparatively escaped notice in the Church. He brought to light forgotten doctrines of the apostle Paul, and fastened them in their full and complete sense upon one great branch of the Christian Church.

This doctrine of Predestination has perhaps raised a greater storm of opposition, and has doubtless been more misrepresented and caricatured, than any other doctrine in the Scriptures. "To mention it before some," says Warburton, "is like shaking the proverbial red flag before an enraged bull. It arouses the fiercest passions of their nature, and brings forth a torrent of abuse and calumny. But, because men have fought against it, or because they hate it, or perhaps misunderstand it, is no reasonable or logical cause why we should turn the doctrine adrift, or cast it behind our backs. The real question, the all-important question, is not: How do men receive it? but, Is it true?" [3]

One reason why many people, even supposedly educated people, are so quick to reject the doctrine of Predestination is because of pure ignorance of what the doctrine really is and of what the Bible teaches in regard to it. This ignorance is not at all surprising when one considers the almost complete

Loraine Boettner D.D.

lack of Bible training in our day. A careful study of the Bible would convince many people that it is a very different book than they assume it to be. The tremendous influence which this doctrine has exerted in the history of Europe and America should at least entitle it to a respectful hearing. Furthermore, we submit that according to all the laws of reason and logic a person has no right to deny the truth of a doctrine without first having studied in an unprejudiced manner the evidence on both sides. This is a doctrine which deals with some of the most profound truths revealed in Scripture and it will abundantly repay careful study on the part of Christian people. If any are disposed to reject it without first making a careful study of its claims, let them not forget that it has commanded the firm belief of multitudes of the wisest and best men that have ever lived, and that there must, therefore, be strong reasons in favor of its truth.

Perhaps a few words of caution should be given here to the effect that while the doctrine of Predestination is a great and blessed Scripture truth and a fundamental doctrine of several churches, it must never be looked upon as the sum and substance of the Reformed Faith. As Dr. Kuyper has said, "It is a mistake to discover the specific character of Calvinism in the doctrine of Predestination, or in the authority of Scripture. For Calvinism all these are logical consequences, not the point of departure-- foliage bearing witness to the luxuriousness of its growth, but not the root from which it is sprouted." If the doctrine is detached from its natural association with other truths and exhibited alone, the effect is exaggerated. The system is then distorted and misrepresented. A statement of any principle, in order to be true, must present it in harmony with all the other elements of the system of which it forms a part. The Westminster Confession of Faith is a balanced statement of this system as a whole, and it gives due prominence to those other doctrines, such as the Trinity, the Deity of Christ, the personality of the Holy Spirit, the Inspiration of the Scriptures, Miracles, the Atonement, Resurrection, the personal return of Christ, and so forth. Furthermore, we do not deny that the Arminians hold many and important truths. But we do hold that a full and complete exposition of the Christian system can be given only on the basis of the truth as set forth in the Calvinistic system.

In the minds of most people the doctrine of Predestination and Calvinism are practically synonymous terms. This. however, should not be the case, and the too close identification of the two has doubtless done much to prejudice many people against the Calvinistic system. The same is true in regard to a too close identification of Calvinism and the "Five Points," as will be shown later. While Predestination and the Five Points are all essential elements of Calvinism, they by no means constitute its whole.

The doctrine of Predestination has been made the subject of almost endless discussion, much of which, it must be admitted, was for the purpose of softening its outlines or of explaining it away. "The consideration of this great doctrine," says Cunningham, "runs up into the most profound and inaccessible subjects that can occupy the minds of men,--the nature and attributes, the purposes and the actings of the infinite and incomprehensible Jehovah,--viewed especially in their bearings upon the everlasting destinies of His intelligent creatures. The peculiar nature of the subject certainly demands, in right reason, that it should ever be approached and considered with the profoundest humility, caution, and reverence, as it brings us into contact, on the one side, with a subject so awful and overwhelming as the everlasting misery of an innumerable multitude of our fellow men. Many men have discussed the subject in this spirit, but many also have indulged in much presumptuous and irreverent speculation regarding it. There is probably no subject that has occupied more of the attention of intelligent men in every age. It has been most fully discussed in all of its bearings, philosophical, theological, and practical; and if there be any subject of speculation with respect to which we are warranted in saying that it has been exhausted, it is this.

"Some, at least, of the topics comprehended under this general head have been discussed by almost every philosopher of eminence in ancient as well as in modern times. * * * All that the highest ability, ingenuity, and acuteness can effect, has been brought to bear upon the discussion of this subject; and the difficulties attaching to it have never been fully solved, and we are well warranted in saying that they never will, unless God gives us either a fuller revelation or greatly enlarged capacities,--although, perhaps, it would be more correct to say that, from the very nature of the case, a finite being can never fully comprehend it since this would imply that he could fully comprehend the infinite mind." [4]

In the development of this book much use has been made of other books in order that this one may contain the very cream and quintessence of the best authors on the subject. Consequently many of the arguments found here are from men very superior to the present writer. Indeed, when he glances at the whole he is inclined to say with a celebrated French writer, "I have culled a bouquet of varied flowers from men's gardens, and nothing is my own but the string that binds them." Yet much is his own, especially as regards the organization and arrangement of materials.

Throughout this book the terms "predestination" and "foreordination" are used as exact synonyms, the choice being deterrained only by taste. If a distinction be desired the word "foreordination" can perhaps better be used where the thing spoken of is an event in history or in nature, while "predestination" can refer mainly to the final destiny of persons. The Scripture quotations have been

The Reformed Doctrine Of Predestination

made from the American Standard Version of the Bible rather than from the King James Version since the former is more accurate.

The author wishes particularly to thank Dr. Samuel G. Craig, Editor of CHRISTIANITY TODAY, Dr. Frank H. Stevenson, President of the Board of Trustees of Westminster Theological Seminary, Dr. Cornelius Van Til, Professor of Apologetics in Westminster Theological Seminary, Dr. C. W. Hodge, Professor of Systematic Theology in Princeton Theological Seminary, under whose supervision this material in much shorter form was originally prepared, and Rev. Henry Atherton, General Secretary of the Sovereign Grace Union, London, England, for valuable assistance.

This book, we repeat, is designed to set forth and defend the Reformed Faith, commonly known as Calvinism. It is not directed against any particular denomination, but against Arminianism in general. The author is a member of the Presbyterian Church, U.S.A., but is well aware of the radical departure which the rank and file of Presbyterians have made from their own creed. The book is sent forth with the hope that those who profess to hold the Reformed Faith may have a better understanding of the great truths which are here treated and may value their heritage more highly; and that those who have not known this system, or who have opposed it, may be convinced of its truth and come to love it.

The question which faces us then, is, Has God from all eternity foreordained all things which come to pass? If so, what evidence do we have to that effect. and how is the fact consistent with the free agency of rational creatures and with His own perfections?

Footnotes:

1. Preface to Zanchius' Predestination, p. 16.
2. Calvinism, p. 2.
3. Calvinism, p. 23.
4. Cunningham, Historical Theology, II, pp. 418, 419.

Loraine Boettner D.D.

Section I

Chapter II – Statement of the Doctrine

In the Westminster Confession, which sets forth the beliefs of the Presbyterian and Reformed Churches and which is the most perfect expression of the Reformed Faith, we read: "God from all eternity did by the most wise and holy counsel of His own will, freely and unchangeably ordain whatsoever comes to pass; yet so as thereby neither is God the author of sin, nor is violence offered to the will of the creatures, nor is the liberty or contingency of second causes taken away, but rather established." And further, "Although God knows whatsoever may or can come to pass upon all supposed conditions; yet hath He not decreed any thing because He foresaw it as future, or as that which would come to pass upon such conditions."

This doctrine of Predestination represents the purpose of God as absolute and unconditional, independent of the whole finite creation, and as originating solely in the eternal counsel of His will. God is seen as the great and mighty King who has appointed the course of nature and who directs the course of history even down to its minutest details. His decree is eternal, unchangeable, holy, wise, and sovereign. It extends not merely to the course of the physical world but to every event in human history from the creation to the judgment, and includes all the activities of saints and angels in heaven and of reprobates and demons in hell. It embraces the whole scope of creaturely existence, through time and eternity, comprehending at once all things that ever were or will be in their causes, conditions, successions, and relations. Everything outside of God Himself is included in this all-embracing decree, and that very naturally since all other beings owe their existence and continuance in existence to His creative and sustaining power. It provides a providential control under which all things are hastening to the end of God's determining; and the goal is,

> "One far-off divine event
> Toward which the whole creation moves.

Since the finite creation through its whole range exists as a medium through which God manifests His glory, and since it is absolutely dependent on Him, it of itself could originate no conditions which would limit or defeat the manifestation of that glory. From all eternity God has purposed to do just exactly what He is doing. He is the sovereign Ruler of the universe and "does according to His will in the army of heaven and among the inhabitants of the earth; and none can stay His hand, or say unto Him, What doest thou?" Daniel 4:35. Since the universe had its origin in God and depends on Him for its continued existence it must be, in all its parts and at all times, subject to His control so that nothing can come to pass contrary to what He expressly decrees or permits. Thus the eternal purpose is represented as an act of sovereign predestination or foreordination, and unconditioned by any subsequent fact or change in time. Hence it is represented as being the basis of the divine foreknowledge of all future events, and not conditioned by that foreknowledge or by anything originated by the events themselves.

The Reformed theologians logically and consistently applied to the spheres of creation and providence those great principles which were later set forth in the Westminster Standards. They saw the hand of God in every event in all the history of mankind and in all the workings of physical nature so that the world was the complete realization in time of the eternal ideal. The world as a whole and in all its parts and movements and changes was brought into a unity by the governing, all-pervading, all-harmonizing activity of the divine will, and its purpose was to manifest the divine glory. While their conception was that of a divine ordering of the whole course of history to the veriest detail, they were especially concerned with its relation to man's salvation. Calvin, the brilliant and systematic theologian of the Reformation, put the matter thus: "Predestination we call the eternal decree of God, by which He has determined in Himself, what He would have to become of every individual of mankind. For they are not all created with a similar destiny; but eternal life is foreordained for some and eternal death for others. Every man, therefore, being created for one or the other of these ends, we say he is predestinated either to life or to death." [5]

The Reformed Doctrine Of Predestination

That Luther was as zealous for absolute predestination as was Calvin is shown in his commentary on Romans, where he wrote: "All things whatever arise from, and depend on, the divine appointment; whereby it was foreordained who should receive the word of life, and who should disbelieve it; who should be delivered from their sins, and who should be hardened in them; and who should be justified and who should be condemned." And Melanchthon, his close friend and fellow-laborer, says: "All things turn out according to divine predestination; not only the works we do outwardly, but even the thoughts we think inwardly"; and again, "There is no such thing as chance, or fortune; nor is there a readier way to gain the fear of God, and to put our whole trust in Him, than to be thoroughly versed in the doctrine of Predestination."

"Order is heaven's first law." From the divine viewpoint there is unbroken order and progress from the first beginnings of the creation to the end of the world and the ushering in of the kingdom of heaven in all its glory. The divine purpose and plan is nowhere defeated nor interrupted; that which in many cases appears to us to be defeat is not really such but only appears to be, because our finite and imperfect nature does not permit us to see all the parts in the whole nor the whole in all its parts. If at one glance we could take in "the mighty spectacle of the natural world and the complex drama of human history," we should see the world as one harmonious unit manifesting the glorious perfections of God.

"Though the world seems to run at random," says Bishop, "and affairs to be huddled together in blind confusion and rude disorder, yet, God sees and knows the concatenation of all causes and effects, and so governs them that He makes a perfect harmony out of all those seeming jarrings and discords. It is most necessary that we should have our hearts well established in the firm and unwavering belief of this truth, that whatever comes to pass, be it good or evil, we may look up to the hand and disposal of all, to God. In respect of God, there is nothing casual nor contingent in the world. If a master should send a servant to a certain place and command him to stay there till such a time, and, presently after, should send another servant to the same place, the meeting of these two is wholly casual in respect to themselves, but ordained and foreseen by the master who sent them. They fall out unexpectedly as to us, but not so as to God. He foresees and He appoints all the vicissitudes of things." [6]

The psalmist exclaimed, "O Jehovah our Lord, How excellent is thy name in all the earth!" And the writer of Ecclesiastes says, "He hath made everything beautiful in its time." In the vision which the prophet Isaiah saw, the seraphim sang, "Holy, holy, holy, is Jehovah of hosts: The whole earth is full of His glory." When seen from this divine view-point every event in the course of human affairs in all ages and in all nations has, no matter how insignificant it may appear to us, its exact place in the development of the eternal plan. It has relations with preceding causes and exerts an ever widening influence through its effects so that it is related to the whole system of things and has its individual part in maintaining the perfect equilibrium of this world-order. Many instances might be given to show that events of the greatest importance have often depended upon what at the time appeared to be the most fortuitous and trivial events. The inter-relation and connection of events is such that if one of these were to be omitted or modified, all that follows soon would be modified or prevented. Hence the certainty that the divine administration rests on the foreordination of God extending to all events both great and small. And, strictly speaking, no event is really small; each one has its exact place in the divine plan, and some are only relatively greater than others. The course of history, then, is infinitely complex, yet a unit in the sight of God. This truth, together with the reason for it, is very beautifully summed up in the Shorter Catechism which states that, "The decrees of God are, His eternal purpose, according to the counsel of His will, whereby for His own glory, He hath foreordained whatsoever comes to pass."

Dr. Abraham Kuyper, of Holland, who is recognized as one of the outstanding Calvinistic theologians in recent years, has given us some valuable thought in the following paragraph: "The determination of the existence of all things to be created, or what is to be camellia or buttercup, nightingale or crow, hart or swine, and equally among men, the determination of our own persons, whether one is to be born as boy or girl, rich or poor, dull or clever, white or colored or even as Abel and Cain, is the most tremendous predestination conceivable in heaven or on earth; and still we see it taking place before our eyes every day, and we ourselves are subject to it in our entire personality; our entire existence, our very nature, our position in life being entirely dependent on it. This all-embracing predestination, the Calvinist places, not in the hands of man, and still less in the hand of blind natural force, but in the hand of Almighty God, sovereign Creator and Possessor of heaven and earth; and it is in the figure of the potter and the clay that Scripture has from the time of the prophets expounded to us this all-dominating election. Election in creation, election in providence, and so election also to eternal life; election in the realm of grace as well as in the realm of nature." [7]

We can have no adequate appreciation of this world-order until we see it as one mighty system through which God is working out His plans. Calvin's clear and consistent theism gave him a keen sense of the infinite majesty of the Almighty Person in whose hands all things lay, and made him a very pronounced predestinarian. In this doctrine of the unconditional and eternal purpose of the omniscient and omnipotent God, he found the program of the history of the fall and redemption of the human race.

Loraine Boettner D.D.

He ventured boldly but reverently upon the brink of that abyss of speculation where all human knowledge is lost in mystery and adoration.

The Reformed Faith, then, offers us a great God who is really the sovereign Ruler of the Universe. "Its grand principle," says Bayne, "is the contemplation of the universe of God revealed in Christ. In all places, in all times, from eternity to eternity, Calvinism sees God." Our age, with its emphasis on democracy, doesn't like this view, and perhaps no other age liked it less. The tendency today is to exalt man and to give God only a very limited part in the affairs of the world. As Dr. A. A. Hodge has said, "The new theology, asserting the narrowness of the old, is discarding the foreordination of Jehovah as a worn-out figment of the schools, discredited by the advanced culture of today. This is not the first time that the owls, mistaking the shadow of a passing eclipse for their native night, have prematurely hooted at the eagles, convinced that what is invisible to them cannot possibly exist." [8]

This, in general, is the broad conception of predestination as it has been held by the great theologians of the Presbyterian and Reformed Churches.

Foreordination is explicitly stated in Scripture.

Acts 4:27, 28: For of a truth in this city against thy holy servant Jesus, whom thou didst anoint, both Herod and Pontius Pilate, with the Gentiles and the peoples of Israel, were gathered together, to do whatsoever thy hand and thy counsel foreordained to come to pass.

Ephesians 1:5: Having foreordained us unto adoption as sons through Jesus Christ unto Himself, according to the good pleasure of His will.

Ephesians 1:11: In whom also we were made a heritage, having been foreordained according to the purpose of Him who worketh all things after the counsel of His will.

Romans 8:29, 30: For whom He foreknew, He also foreordained to be conformed to the image of His Son, that He might be the firstborn among many brethren: and whom He foreordained, them He also called: and whom He called, them He also justified: and whom He justified, them He also glorified.

1 Corinthians 2:7: But we speak God's wisdom in a mystery, even the wisdom that hath been hidden, which God foreordained before the worlds unto our glory.

Acts 2:23: Him (Jesus) being delivered up by the determinate counsel and foreknowledge of God, ye by the hands of lawless men did crucify and slay.

Acts 13:48: And as the Gentiles heard this, they were glad, and glorified the word of God; and as many as were ordained to eternal life believed.

Ephesians 2:10: For we are His workmanship, created in Christ Jesus for good works, which God afore prepared that we should walk in them.

Romans 9:23: That He might make known the riches of His glory upon the vessels of mercy, which He afore prepared unto glory.

Psalm 139:16: Thine eyes did see mine unformed substance; And in thy book they were all written, Even the days that were ordained for me, When as yet there was none of them.

Footnotes:

5. Institutes, Book III, Ch. XXI, sec. 5.
6. Quoted by Toplady in Preface to Zanchius' Predestination.
7. Lectures on Calvinism, p. 272.
8. Popular Lectures on Theological Themes, p. 158.

Chapter III - God Has a Plan

It is unthinkable that a God of infinite wisdom and power would create a world without a definite plan for that world. And because God is thus infinite His plan must extend to every detail of the world's existence. If we could see the world in all its relations, past, present, and future, we would see that it is following a predetermined course with exact precision. Among created things we may search where we will, as far as the microscope and the telescope will enable the eye to see, we find organization everywhere. Large forms resolve themselves into parts, and these parts in their turn are but organized of other parts down as far as we can see into infinity.

Even man, who is but the creature of a day and subject to all kinds of errors, develops a plan before he acts; and a man who acts without design or purpose is accounted foolish. Before we make a trip or undertake a piece of work all of us set our goal and then work to attain that goal in so far as we are able. Regardless of how some people may oppose Predestination in theory, all of us in our every-day lives are practical predestinarians. As E. W. Smith says, a wise man "first determines upon the end he desires to attain, and then upon the best means of attaining it. Before the architect begins his edifice, he makes his drawings and forms his plans, even to the minutest details of construction. In the architect's brain the building stands complete in all its parts before a stone is laid. So with the merchant, the lawyer, the farmer, and all rational and intelligent men. Their activity is along the line of previously formed purposes, the fulfillment, so far as their finite capacities will allow, Of preconceived plans." [9]

The larger our enterprise is, the more important it is that we shall have a plan; otherwise all our work ends in failure. One would be considered mentally deranged who undertook to build a ship, or a railroad, or to govern a nation without a plan. We are told that before Napoleon began the invasion of Russia he had a plan worked out in detail, showing what line of march each division of his army was to follow, where it was to be at a certain time, what equipment and provisions it was to have, etc. Whatever was wanting in that plan was due to the limitations of human power and wisdom. Had Napoleon's foresight been perfect and his control of events absolute, his plan--or we may say, his foreordination--would have extended to every act of every soldier who made that march.

And if this is true of man, how much more is it true of God! "A universe without decrees," says A. J. Gordon. "would be as irrational and appalling as would be an express train driving on in the darkness without headlight or engineer, and with no certainty that the next moment it might not plunge into the abyss." We cannot conceive of God bringing into existence a universe without a plan which would extend to all that would be done in that universe. As the Scriptures teach that God's providential control extends to all events, even the most minute, they thereby teach that His plan is equally comprehensive. It is one of His perfections that He has the best possible plan, and that He conducts the course of history to its appointed end. And to admit that He has a plan which He carries out is to admit Predestination. "God's plan is shown in its effectuation to be one," says Dabney. "Cause is linked with effect, and what was effect becomes cause; the influences of events on events interlace with each other, and descend in widening streams to subsequent events; so that the whole complex result is through every part. As astronomers suppose that the removal of one planet from our system would modify more or less the balance and orbits of all the rest, so the failure of one event in this plan would derange the whole, directly or indirectly." [10]

If God had not foreordained the course of events but waited until some undetermined condition was or was not fulfilled, His decrees could be neither eternal nor immutable. We know, however, that He is incapable of mistake, and that He cannot be surprised by any unforeseen inconveniences. His kingdom is in the heavens and He rules over all. His plan must, therefore, include every event in the entire sweep of history.

That even the small events have their place in this plan. and that they must be as they are, is easily seen. All of us know of certain "chance happenings" which have actually changed the course of our lives. The effects of these extend throughout all succeeding history in ever-widening influences, causing other "chance happenings." It is said that the quacking of some geese once saved Rome. Whether historically true or not it will serve as a good illustration. Had not the geese awakened the guards who gave the alarm and aroused the defending army, Rome would have fallen and the course of history from that time on would have been radically different. Had those geese remained silent who can imagine what empires might have been in existence today, or where the centers of culture might have been?

Loraine Boettner D.D.

During a battle a bullet misses the general by only an inch. His life is spared, he goes on commanding his troops, wins a decisive victory, and is made the chief ruler of his country for many years,--as was the case with George Washington. Yet what a different course history would have taken had the soldier on the other side aimed the slightest trifle higher or lower! The great Chicago fire of 1871, which destroyed more than 1 half of the city, was started, we are told, when a cow kicked over a lantern. How different would have been the history of Chicago if that one motion had been slightly different! "The control of the greatest must include the control of the less, for not only are great things made up of little things, but history shows how the veriest trifles are continually proving the pivots on which momentous events revolve. The persistence of a spider nerved a despairing man to fresh exertions which shaped a nation's future. The God who predestinated the course of Scotch history must have planned and presided over the movements of that tiny insect that saved Robert Bruce from despair." [11] Examples of this kind could be multiplied indefinitely.

The Pelagian denies that God has a plan; the Arminian says that God has a general but not a specific plan; but the Calvinist says that God has a specific plan which embraces all events in all ages. In recognizing that the eternal God has an eternal plan in which is predetermined every event that comes to pass, the Calvinist simply recognizes that God is God, and frees Him from all human limitations. The Scriptures represent God as a person, like other persons in that His acts are purposeful, but unlike other persons in that He is all-wise in His planning and all-powerful in His performing. They see the universe as the product of His creative power, and as the theater in which are displayed His glorious perfections, and which must in all its form and all its history, down to the least detail, correspond with His purpose in making it.

In a very illuminating article on "Predestination," Dr. Benjamin B. Warfield, who in the opinion of the present writer has emerged as the outstanding theologian since John Calvin, tells us that the writers of Scripture saw the divine plan as "broad enough to embrace the whole universe of things, and minute enough to concern itself with the smallest details, and actualizing itself with inevitable certainty in every event that comes to pass." "In the infinite wisdom of the Lord of all the earth, each event falls with exact precision into its proper place in this unfolding of His eternal plan; nothing, however small, however strange, occurs without His ordering, or without its peculiar fitness for its place in the working out of His purposes; and the end of all shall be the manifestation of His glory, and accumulation of His praise. This is the Old Testament (as well as the New Testament) philosophy of the universe--a world-view which attains concrete unity in an absolute decree, or purpose, or plan of which all that comes to pass is the development in time." [12]

The very essence of consistent theism is that God would have an exact plan for the world, would foreknow the actions of all the creatures He proposed to create, and through His all-inclusive providence would control the whole system. If He fore-ordained only certain isolated events, confusion both in the natural-world and in human affairs would be introduced into the system and He would need to be constantly developing new plans to accomplish what be desired. His government of the world then would be a capricious patch work of new expedients He would at best govern only in a general way, and would be ignorant of much of the future. But no one with proper ideas of God believes that He has to change His mind every few days to make room for unexpected happenings which were not included in His original plan. If the perfection of the divine plan be denied, no consistent stopping place will be found short of atheism.

In the first place there was no necessity that God should create at all. He acted with perfect freedom when He brought this world into existence. When He did choose to create there was before Him an infinite number of possible plans. But as a matter of fact we find that He chose this particular one in which we now are. And since He knew perfectly every event of every kind which would be involved in this particular world-order, He very obviously predetermined every event which would happen when He chose this plan. His choice of the plan, or His making certain that the creation should be on this order, we call His foreordination or His predestination.

Even the sinful acts of men are included in this plan. They are foreseen, permitted, and have their exact place. They are controlled and overruled for the divine glory. The crucifixion of Christ, which is admittedly the worst crime in all human history, had, we are expressly told, its exact and necessary place in the plan (Acts 2:23; 4:28). This particular manner of redemption is not an expedient to which God was driven after being defeated and disappointed by the fall of man. Rather it is "according to the eternal purpose which He purposed in Christ Jesus our Lord," Ephesians 3:11 . Peter tells us that Christ as a sacrifice for sin was "foreknown indeed before the foundation of the world," 1 Peter 1:20. Believers were "chosen in Him before the foundation of the world" (or from eternity), Ephesians 1:4. We are saved not by our own temporary works, "but according to His purpose and grace, which was given us in Christ Jesus before times eternal," 2 Timothy 1:9. And if the crucifixion of Christ, or His offering up Himself as a sacrifice for sin, was in the eternal plan, then plainly the fall of Adam and all other sins which made that sacrifice necessary were in the plan, no matter how undesirable a part of that plan they may have been.

History in all its details, even the most minute, is but the unfolding of the eternal purposes of God. His decrees are not successively formed as the emergency arises, but are all parts of one all-comprehending plan, and we should never think of Him suddenly evolving a plan or doing something which He had not thought of before.

The fact that the Scriptures often speak of one purpose of God as dependent on the outcome of another or on the actions of men, is no objection against this doctrine. The Scriptures are written in the every-day language of men, and they often describe an act or a thing as it appears to be, rather than as it really is. The Bible speaks of "the four corners of the earth," Isaiah 11:12, and of "the foundations of the earth," Psalm 104:5; yet no one understands this to mean that the earth is square, or that it actually rests upon a foundation. We speak of the sun rising and setting, yet we know that it is not the motion of the sun but that of the earth as it turns over on its axis which causes this phenomenon. Likewise, when the Scriptures speak of God repenting, for instance, no one with proper ideas of God understands it to mean that He sees He has pursued a wrong course and changes His mind. It simply means that His action as seen from the human view-point appears to be like that of a man who repents. In other places the Scriptures speak of the hands, or arms, or eyes of God. These are what are known as "anthropomorphisms," instances in which God is referred to as if He were a man. When the word "repent," for instance, is used in its strict sense God is said never to repent: "God is not a man, that He should lie, Neither the son of man, that He should repent." Numbers 23:19; and again, "The Strength of Israel will not lie nor repent; for He is not a man, that He should repent," 1 Samuel 15:29.

The contemplation of this great plan must redound to the praise of the unsearchable wisdom and illimitable power of Him who devised and executes it. And what can give the Christian more satisfaction and joy than to know that the whole course of the world is ordered with reference to the establishment of the Kingdom of heaven and the manifestation of the Divine glory; and that he is one of the objects upon which infinite love and mercy is to be lavished?

SCRIPTURE PROOF

1. God's plan is eternal:

2 Timothy 1:9: (It is God) who saved us, and called us with a holy calling, not according to our works, but according to His own purpose and grace, which was given us in Christ Jesus before times eternal.

Psalm 33:11: The counsel of Jehovah standeth fast for ever, The thoughts of His heart to all generations.

Isaiah 37:26: Hast thou not heard how I have done it long ago, and formed it of ancient times?

Isaiah 46:9, 10: I am God and there is none like me; declaring the end from the beginning, and from ancient times things that are not yet done.

2 Thessalonians 2:13: God chose you from the beginning unto salvation in sanctification of the Spirit and belief of the truth.

Matthew 25:34: Then shall the King say unto them on His right hand, Come, ye blessed of my Father, inherit the kingdom prepared for you from the foundation of the world.

1 Peter 1:20: (Christ) who (as a sacrifice for sin) was foreknown indeed before the foundation of the world.

Jeremiah 31:3: Jehovah appeared of old unto me, saying, Yea, I have loved thee with an everlasting love.

Acts 15:18: Saith the Lord, who maketh these things known from of old.

Psalm 139:16: Thine eyes did see mine unformed substance; And in thy book they were all written, Even the days that were ordained for me, When as yet there was none of them.

2. God's plan is unchangeable:

James 1:17: Every good gift and every perfect gift is from above, coming down from the Father of lights, with whom can be no variation, neither shadow that is cast by turning.

Isaiah 14:24: Jehovah of hosts hath sworn, saying, Surely, as I have thought, so shall it come to pass; and as I have purposed, so shall it stand.

Isaiah 46:10, 11: My counsel shall stand and I will do all my pleasure: . . . yea, I have spoken, and I will also bring it to pass; I have purposed I will also do it.

Numbers 23:19: God is not a man, that He should lie, Neither the son of man, that He should repent; Hath He said, and shall He not do it; Or hath He spoken, and shall He not make It good?

Malachi 3:6: I, Jehovah, change not; therefore, ye, O sons of Jacob, are not consumed.

3. The divine plan includes the future acts of men:

Daniel 2:28: But there is a God in heaven that revealeth secrets, and He hath made known to the King Nebuchadnezzar what shall be in the latter days.

John 6:64: For Jesus knew from the beginning who they were that believed not, and who it was that should betray Him.

Matthew 20:18, 19: Behold, we go up to Jerusalem; and the Son of man shall be delivered unto the chief priests and scribes; and they shall condemn Him to death, and shall deliver Him unto the Gentiles to mock, and to scourge, and to crucify ; and the third day He shall be raised up.

(All the Scripture prophecies which are predictions of future events come under this heading. See especially: Micah 5:2; Cp. with Matthew 2:5, 6 and Luke 2:1-7; Psalm 22:18, Cp. John 19:24; Psalm 69:21, Cp. John 19:29; Zechariah 12:10, Cp. John 19:37; Mark 14:30; Zechariah 11:12, 13 , Cp. Matthew 27:9, 10; Psalm 34:19, 20, Cp. John 19:33, 36.)

4. The divine plan Includes the fortuitous events or chance happenings:

Proverbs 16:33: The lot is cast Into the lap; But the whole disposing thereof Is of Jehovah.

Jonah 1:7: So they cast lots, and the lot fell on Jonah.

Acts 1:24, 26: And they prayed, and said, Thou, Lord, who knowest the hearts of all men, show of these two the one whom thou has chosen . . . And they cast lots for them; and the lot fell on Matthias.

Job 36:32: He covereth His hands with the lightning, And giveth it a charge that it strike the mark.

1 Kings 22:28, 34: And Micaiah said, If thou (Ahab) return at all in peace, Jehovah hath not spoken by me . . . And a certain man drew his bow at a venture, and smote the king of Israel between the joints of the armor.

Job 5:6: For affliction cometh not forth from the dust; Neither doth trouble spring out of the ground.

Mark 14:30: And Jesus said unto him (Peter), Verily I say unto thee, that thou, today, even this night. before the cock crow twice shall deny me thrice.

(Cp. Genesis 37:28 and 45:5; Cp. 1 Samuel 9:15,16 and 9:5-10.)

5. Some events are recorded as fixed or inevitably certain:

Luke 22:22: For the Son of man indeed goeth, as it hath been determined; but woe unto that man through whom He is betrayed.

John 8:20: These words spake He in the treasury, as He taught in the temple; and no man took Him; because His hour was not yet come.

Matthew 24:36: But of that day and hour (the end of the world) knoweth no one, not even the angels in heaven, neither the Son, but the Father only.

Genesis 41:32: And for that the dream was doubled unto Pharoah, it is because the thing is established of God, and He will shortly bring it to pass.

Habakkuk 2:3: For the vision is yet for the appointed time, and it hasteneth toward the end, and shall not lie; though it tarry, wait for it; because it will surely come, it will not delay.

Luke 21:24: And Jerusalem shall be trodden down of the Gentiles until the times of the Gentiles be fulfilled.

Jeremiah 15:2: And it shall come to pass when they say unto thee, Whither shall we go forth? then thou shalt tell them. Thus saith Jehovah: Such as are for death, to death; and such as are for the sword, to the sword; and such as are for famine, to the famine; and such as are for captivity, to captivity.

Job 14:5: Seeing that his days are determined, And the number of his months is with thee, And thou has appointed bounds that he cannot pass.

Jeremiah 27:7: And all nations shall serve him (Nebuchadnezzar), and his son, and his son's son, until the time of his own land come; and then many nations and great kings shall make him their bondman.

6. Even the sinful acts of men are included in the plan and are overruled for good.

Genesis 50:20: As for you, ye meant evil against me (Joseph), but God meant it for good.

Isaiah 45:7: I form the light, and create darkness: I make peace, and create evil: I am Jehovah that doeth all these things.

Amos 3:6: Shall evil befall a city and Jehovah hath not done it?

Acts 3:18: The things which God foreshowed by the mouth of all the prophets, that His Christ should suffer, He thus fulfilled.

Matthew 21:42: The stone which the builders rejected, the same was made the head of the corner.

Romans 8:28: To them that love God all things work together for good, even to them that are called according to His purpose.

Footnotes:

9. The Creed of Presbyterians, p. 159.
10. Theology, p. 214.
11. The Creed of Presbyterians, p. 160.
12. Biblical Doctrines, pp. 13, 22.

Chapter IV - The Sovereignty of God

Every thinking person readily sees that some sovereignty rules his life. He was not asked whether or not he would have existence; nor when, where, or what he would be born; whether in the twentieth century or before the flood; whether white or Negro; whether in America or in China. It has been recognized by Christians in all ages that God is the Creator and Ruler of the universe, and that as the Creator and Ruler of the universe He is the ultimate source of all the power that is found in the creatures. Hence nothing can come to pass apart from His sovereign will; and when we dwell upon this truth we find that it involves considerations which establish the Calvinistic and disprove the Arminian position.

By virtue of the fact that God has created every thing which exists, He is the absolute Owner and final Disposer of all that He has made. He exerts not merely a general influence, but actually rules in the world which He has created. The nations of the earth, in their insignificance, are as the small dust of the balance when compared with His greatness; and far sooner might the sun be stopped in his course than God be hindered in His work or in His will. Amid all the apparent defeats and inconsistencies of life God actually moves on in undisturbed majesty. Even the sinful actions of men can occur only by His permission. And since he permits not unwillingly but willingly, all that comes to pass--including the actions and ultimate destiny of men--must be, in some sense, in accordance with what He has desired and purposed. Just in proportion as this is denied God is excluded from the government of the world. Naturally some problems arise here which we in our present state of knowledge are not fully capable of solving; but that is no sufficient ground for rejecting what the Scriptures and the plain dictates of reason affirm to be true.

If the power of an earthly king Is law in his kingdom, how much more shall the word of God be in His! For example, the Christian knows that the day is certainly coming when, willingly or unwillingly, every knee shall bow and every tongue confess that Christ is Lord, to the glory of God the Father. In the Scriptures He is represented to us as God ALMIGHTY, who sits upon the throne of universal dominion. He knows the end from the beginning and the means to be used in attaining that end. He is able to do for us exceedingly abundantly above all that we ask or even think. The category of the impossible has no existence for Him "with whom all things are possible," Matthew 19:26; Mark 10:27. This, however, does not mean that God has power to do that which is contrary to His nature, or to work contradictions. It is impossible for God to lie, or to do anything which is morally wrong. He cannot make two and two equal five, nor can He make a wheel turn around and stand still at the same time. His omnipotence is as sure a guarantee that the course of the world will conform to His plan as is His holiness a guarantee that all His works will be right.

Not only in the New Testament but In the Old Testament as well we find this doctrine of God's sovereignty consistently developed. Dr. Warfield says concerning the doctrine as it is found there: "The Almighty Maker of all that is represented equally as the irresistible Ruler of all that He has made; Jehovah sits as King for ever (Psalm 29:10). " He goes on to say that the writers rarely use such expressions as "it rains;" they instinctively speak of God sending rain, etc. The possibility of accident and chance are excluded and even "the lot was an accepted means of obtaining the decision of God (Joshua 7:16; 14:2; 18:6; 1 Samuel 10:19; Jonah 1:7). All things without exception, indeed, are disposed by Him, and His will is the ultimate account of all that occurs. Heaven and earth and all that is in them are the instruments through which He works His ends. Nature, nations, and the fortunes of the individual alike present in all their changes the transcript of His purpose. The winds are His messengers, the flaming fire His servant: every natural occurrence is His act; prosperity is His gift, and if calamity falls upon man it is the Lord that has done it (Amos 3:5, 6; Lamentations 3:33-38; Isaiah 47:7; Ecclesiastes 7:14; Isaiah 54:16). It is He that leads the feet of men, wit they whither or not; He that raises up and casts down; opens and hardens the heart; and creates the very thoughts and intents of the soul." [13]

And shall we not believe that God can convert a sinner when He pleases? Cannot the Almighty, the omnipotent Ruler of the universe, change the characters of the creatures He has made? He changed the water into wine at Cana, and converted Saul on the road to Damascus. The leper said, "Lord, if thou wilt, thou canst make me clean," and at a word his leprosy was cleansed. God is as able to cleanse the soul as the body, and we believe that if He chose to do so He could raise up such a flood of Christian ministers, missionaries, and workers of various kinds that the world would be converted in a very short time. If He actually purposed to save all men He could send hosts of angels to instruct them and to do supernatural works on the earth. He could Himself work marvelously on the heart of every person so that no one would be lost. Since evil exists only by His permission, He could, if He chose, blot it out of existence. His power in this latter respect was shown, for instance, in the work of the destroying angel who in one night slew all the first-born of the Egyptians (Exodus 12:29), and in another night slew 185,000 of the Assyrian army (2 Kings 19:35). It was shown when the earth opened and swallowed Korah and his rebellious allies (Numbers 16:31-33). Ananias and Sapphira were smitten (Acts 5:1-11); Herod was smitten and died a horrible death (Acts 12:23). God has lost none of His power, and it is highly dishonoring to Him to suppose that He is struggling along with the human race doing the best He can but unable to accomplish His purposes.

Although the sovereignty of God is universal and absolute, it is not the sovereignty of blind power. It is coupled with infinite wisdom, holiness and love. And this doctrine, when properly understood, is a most comforting and reassuring one. Who would not prefer to have his affairs in the hands of a God of infinite power, wisdom, holiness and love, rather than to have them left to fate, or chance, or irrevocable natural law, or to short-sighted and perverted self? Those who reject God's sovereignty should consider what alternatives they have left.

The affairs of the universe, then, are controlled and guided, how? "According to the purpose of Him who worketh all things after the counsel of His will." The present day tendency is to set aside the doctrines of Divine Sovereignty and Predestination in order to make room for the autocracy of the human will. The pride and presumption of man, on the one hand, and his ignorance and depravity on the other, lead him to exclude God and to exalt himself so far as he is able; and both of these tendencies combine to lead the great majority of mankind away from Calvinism.

The Arminian idea which assumes that the serious intentions of God way in some cases at least be defeated, and that man, who is not only a creature but a sinful creature, can exercise veto power over the plans of Almighty God, is in striking contrast with the Biblical idea of His immeasurable exaltation by which He is removed from all the weaknesses of humanity. That the plans of men are not always executed is due to a lack of power, or a lack of wisdom; but since God is unlimited In these and all other resources, no unforeseen emergencies can arise, and to Him the causes for change have no existence. To suppose that His plans fail and that He strives to no effect, is to reduce Him to the level of His creatures.

SCRIPTURE PROOF

Daniel 4:35: He doeth according to His will In the army of heaven, and among the inhabitants of the earth; and none can stay His hand, or say unto Him, What doest thou?

Jeremiah 32:17: Ah Lord Jehovah! behold thou hast made the heavens and the earth by thy great power and by thine outstretched arm; and there is nothing too hard for thee.

Matthew 28:18: All authority bath been given unto me (Christ) in heaven and on earth.

Ephesians 1:22: And He put all things in subjection under His feet, and gave Him to be head over all things to the church.

Ephesians 1:11: In whom we were made a heritage, having been foreordained according to the purpose of Him who worketh all things after the counsel of His will.

Isaiah 14:24, 27: Jehovah of hosts hath sworn, saying, surely as I have thought, so shall it come to pass.... For Jehovah of hosts hath purposed, and who shall annul it? and His hand is stretched out, and who shall turn it back?

Isaiah 46:9, 10, 11: Remember the former things of old; for I am God. and there is none else; I am God and there is none like me; declaring the end from the beginning, and from ancient times things that are not yet done, saying, My counsel shall stand, and I will do all my pleasure.... yea, I have spoken; I will also bring It to pass; I have purposed, I will also do it.

Genesis 18:14: Is anything too hard for Jehovah?

Job 42:2: I know that thou canst do all things, And that no purpose of thine can be restrained.

Psalm 115:3: Our God is in the heavens. He hath done whatsoever He pleased.

Psalm 135:6: Whatsoever Jehovah pleased, that hath He done. In heaven, in earth, in the seas, and in all deeps.

Isaiah 55:11: So shall my word be that goeth forth out of my mouth; it shall not return unto me void, but it shall accomplish that which I please, and it shall prosper in the thing whereto I sent it.

Romans 9:20, 21: Nay but, O man, who art thou that repliest against God? Shall the thing formed say to him that formed it, Why didst thou make me thus? Or hath not the potter a right over the clay, from the same lump to make one part a vessel unto honor, and another unto dishonor?

Footnotes:

13. Biblical Doctrines, art. Predestination, p. 9.

Chapter V - The Providence of God

"God's works of providence are His most holy, wise, and powerful preserving and governing all his creatures and all their actions." (Shorter Catechism, answer to Question 11.) The Scriptures very clearly teach that all things outside of God owe not merely their original creation, but their continued existence, with all their properties and Powers, to the will of God. He upholds all things by the word of His power, Hebrews 1:3. He is before all things, and in Him all things consist, Colossians 1:17. "Thou art Jehovah, even thou alone; thou hast made heaven, the heaven of heavens, with all their hosts, the earth and all things that are therein, the seas and all that is in them, and thou preservest them all," Nehemiah 9:6. "In Him we live, and move and have our being," Acts 17:28. He is "over all, and through all, and in all," Ephesians 4:6.

Throughout the Bible the laws of nature, the course of history, the varying fortunes of individuals, are ever attributed to God's providential control. All things, both in heaven and earth, from the seraphim down to the tiny atom, are ordered by His never-failing providence. So intimate is His relationship with the whole creation that a careless reader might be led toward pantheistic conclusions. Yet individual personalities and second causes are fully recognized,--not as independent of God, but as having their proper place in His plan. And alongside of this doctrine of His Immanence the Scripture writers also present the kindred doctrine of His Transcendence, in which God is distinctly set forth as entirely separate from and above the whole creation.

Yet as regards God's providence we are to understand that He is intimately concerned with every detail in the affairs of men and in the course of nature. "To suppose that anything is too great to be comprehended in His control," says Dr. Charles Hodge, "or anything so minute as to escape His notice; or that the infinitude of particulars can distract His attention, is to forget that God is infinite . . . . The sun diffuses its light through all space as easily as upon any point. God is as much present everywhere, and with everything, as though He were only in one place, and had but one object of attention." And again, "He is present in every blade of grass, yet guiding Arcturus in his course, marshalling the stars as a host, calling them by their names; present also in every human soul, giving it understanding, endowing it with gifts, working in it both to will and to do. The human heart is in His hands; and he turneth it even as the rivers of water are turned." [14]

It is almost universally admitted that God determines when, where, and under what circumstances, each individual of our race shall be born, live, and die, whether it shall be male or female, white or black, wise or foolish. God is no less sovereign in the distribution of His favors. He does what He will with His own. To some He gives riches, to others honor, to others health, to others certain talents for music, oratory, art, finance, statesmanship, etc. Others are poor, unknown, born in dishonor, the victims of disease, and live lives of wretchedness. Some are placed in Christian lands where they receive all the benefits of the Gospel; others live and die in the darkness of heathenism. Some are brought through faith unto salvation; others are left to perish in unbelief. And to a very large extent these external things, which are not the result of individual choice, decide the person's life course and eternal destiny. Both Scripture and every day experience teach us that God gives to some what He withholds from others. If it be asked why He does this, or why he does not save all, the only available answer is found in the words of the Lord Jesus, "Yea, Father, for so it was well-pleasing in thy sight." Only the Scripture doctrine of the fall and redemption will give us any light on what we see about us.

It is to be remembered that those who receive these gifts, whether spiritual or temporal, receive them through pure grace, while in regard to the others God simply withholds those gifts which He was under no obligation to bestow. Nations, as well as individuals, are thus in the hands of God, who appoints the bounds of their habitation, and controls their destiny. He controls them as absolutely as a man controls a rod or a staff. They are in His hands, and He employs them to accomplish His purposes. He breaks them in pieces as a potter's vessel, or He exalts them to greatness, according to His good pleasure. He gives peace and fruitful seasons, property and happiness, or He sends the desolations of war, famine, drought and pestilence. All of these things are of His disposing, and are designed for intelligent ends under His universal providence. God is no mere spectator of the universe He has made, but is everywhere present and active, the all-sustaining ground, and all-governing power of all that is.

Although the price of the sparrow is small, and its flight seems giddy and at random, yet it does not fall to the ground, nor slight anywhere without your Father. "His all-wise providence hath before

Loraine Boettner D.D.

appointed what bough it shall perch upon; what grains it shall pick up; where it shall lodge and where it shall build; on what it shall live and where it shall die." [15]

Every raindrop and every snowflake which falls from the cloud, every insect which moves, every plant which grows, every grain of dust which floats in the air has had certain definite causes and will have certain definite effects. Each is a link in the chain of events and many of the great events of history have turned on these apparently insignificant things.

Throughout the whole course of events there is progress toward a predetermined end. Dr. Warfield has well written: "It was not accident that brought Rebecca to the well to welcome Abraham's servant (Genesis 24), or that sent Joseph into Egypt (Genesis 45:8; 50:20,. 'God meant it for good'), or guided Pharaoh's daughter to the ark among the flags (Exodus 2), or that, later, directed the millstone that crushed Abimelech's head (Judges 9:53), or winged the arrow shot at a venture to smite the king in the joints of the armor (1 Kings 22:34). Every historical event is rather treated as an item in the orderly carrying out of an underlying Divine purpose; and the historian is continually aware of the presence in history of Him who gives even to the lightning a charge to strike the mark (Job 36:32)." [16]

"In the great railroad stations," said Dr. Clarence E. Macartney, "you can see a metallic pencil come out and write in great characters on the wall the time of the arrival or departure of the trains. The metallic pencil seems to write of itself, but we know that hidden in an office somewhere the mind and hand of a man are operating the pencil. So in our own life, we note our own deliberations and choices and decisions, and yet in the fabric of our destiny there seem to be other strands, strands not of our own weaving. Apparently trivial events play their part in great issues." [17]

Man's sense of moral responsibility and dependence, and his instinctive appeal to God in times of danger, show how universal and innate is the conviction that God does govern the world and all human events. But while the Bible repeatedly teaches that this providential control is universal, Powerful, wise, and holy, it nowhere attempts to inform us how it is to be reconciled with man's free agency. All that we need to know is that God does govern His creatures and that His control over them is such that no violence is done to their natures. Perhaps the relationship between divine sovereignty and human freedom can best be summed up in these words: God so presents the outside inducements that man acts in accordance with his own nature, yet does exactly what God has planned for him to do.

This subject, as it relates to human responsibility, will be more fully treated in the chapter on Free Agency.

SCRIPTURE PROOF

That this is the Scripture doctrine of Providence is so plain that it is admitted by many whose philosophical views lead them to reject it for themselves. We shall now present a summary of Scripture proof, showing that all events have a divinely appointed place and purpose, that God's providence is universal, and that He thus secures the complete fulfillment of His plans. God's providential control extends over:

(a) Nature or the physical world. "Jehovah doeth His will in the whirlwind and in the storm, and the clouds are the dust of his feet," Nahum 1:3. "Only in the land of Goshen where the children of Israel were, there was no hail," Exodus 9:26. "He maketh His sun to rise on the evil and the good, and sendeth rain on the just and the unjust," Matthew 5:45. The famine in Egypt appeared to men to be only the result of natural causes; yet Joseph could say, "The thing is established of God, and God will shortly bring it to pass." Genesis 41: 32. "And I also have withholden the rain from you, when there were yet three months before the harvest; and I caused it to rain upon one city, and caused it not to rain upon another city," Amos 4:7. "He gave you from heaven rains and fruitful seasons, filling your heart with food and gladness," Acts 14:17. "Who hath measured the waters in the hollow of his hand, and meted out heaven with the span, and comprehended the dust of the earth in a measure, and weighed the mountains in scales, and the hills in a balance?" Isaiah 40:12.

(b) The animal creation. "Are not two sparrows sold for a penny and not one of them shall fall to the ground without your Father," Matthew 10:29. "Behold the birds of the heavens, that they sow not, neither do they reap, nor gather into barns; and your heavenly Father feedeth them," Matthew 6:26. "My God hath sent His angel and hath shut the lions' months, that they have not hurt me," Daniel 6:22. "The young lions roar after their prey, and seek their meat from God," Psalm 104:21. "Thus God hath taken away the cattle of your father (Laban) and given them to me" (Jacob), Genesis 31:9.

(c) Nations. (Nebuchadnezzar's humiliation was) "to the intent that the living may know that the Most High ruleth in the kingdom of men, and giveth it to whomsoever He will, and setteth up over it the lowest of men," Daniel 4:17. "Behold, the nations are as a drop in the bucket, and are accounted as the small dust of the balance; behold, He taketh up the isles as a very little thing," Isaiah 40:15. "Let them say among the nations, Jehovah reigneth," 1 Chronicles 16:31. "For God Is the King of all the earth," Psalm 47:7. "He changeth the times and the seasons; He removeth kings, and setteth up kings," Daniel 2:21. "Jehovah bringeth the counsel of the nations to naught; He maketh the thoughts of the people to be of none effect," Psalm 33:10. "And Jehovah gave them rest round about .... Jehovah delivered all their

The Reformed Doctrine Of Predestination

enemies into their hands," Joshua 21:44. "And the children of Israel did that which was evil in the sight of Jehovah; and Jehovah delivered them into the hands of Midian seven years," Judges 6:1. 'Shall evil befall a city, and Jehovah hath not done it?" Amos 3:6. "For, lo, I raise up the Chaldeans, that bitter and hasty nation, that march through the breadth of the earth, to possess dwelling places that are not theirs," Habakkuk 1:6.

(d) Individual men. "The king's heart is in the hand of Jehovah as the watercourses; He turneth it whithersoever He will," Proverbs 21:1. "A man's goings are established of Jehovah," Psalm 37:23. "A man's heart deviseth his way, but the Lord directeth his steps," Proverbs 16:9. "For we ought to say, if the Lord will, we shall both live, and do this or that," James 4:15. "Of Him, and through Him, and unto Him are all things," Romans 11:36. "Who maketh thee to differ? And what hast thou that thou didst not receive?" 1 Corinthians 4:7. "The angel of the Lord encampeth round about them that fear Him, And delivereth them," Psalm 34:7. "If it be so our God whom we serve is able to deliver us from the burning fiery furnace; and He will deliver us out of thy hand,O king," Daniel 3:17. "Jehovah is on my side; I shall not fear; What can man do unto me?" Psalm 118:6. But now, O Jehovah, thou art our Father; we are the clay and thou our potter; and we are the work of thy hands," Isaiah 64:8. "And the hand of our God was upon us, and He delivered us (the returning exiles) from the hand of the enemy and the lier-in-wait by the way," Ezra 8:31. "And God brought their counsel to naught," Nehemiah 4:15. "But against any of the children of Israel shall not a dog move his tongue, against man or bent; that ye way know how Jehovah doth make a distinction between the Egyptians and Israel," Exodus 11:7. "And the Lord said unto Paul in the night by a vision, Be not afraid, but speak and hold not thy peace; for I am with thee, and no man shall set on thee to harm thee," Acts 18:9.

(e) The free acts of men. "It is God who worketh in you both to will and to work, for His good pleasure," Philippians 2:13. "And Jehovah gave the people favor in the sight of the Egyptians, so that they let them have what they asked." Exodus 12:36. "And the king (of Persia, Artaxerxes) granted him (Ezra) all his request, according to the hand of Jehovah his God upon him," Ezra 7:6. "For Jehovah had made them joyful, and had turned the heart of the king of Assyria unto them, to strengthen their hands in the work of the house of God" (rebuilding the temple), Ezra 6:22. "And I will put my spirit within you, and cause you to walk in my statutes, and ye shall keep mine ordinances, and do them," Ezekiel 36:27.

(f) The sinful acts of men. "For of a truth in this city against thy holy servant Jesus, whom thou didst anoint, both Herod and Pontius Pilate, and the Gentiles and the people of Israel, were gathered together, to do whatsoever thy hand and thy counsel foreordained to come to pass," Acts 4:27, 28. "Jesus answered him (Pilate), Thou wouldst have no power against me, except it were given thee from above," John 19:11. (David, rebuking Abishai, in regard to Shimei) "Because he curseth, and Jehovah hath said, Curse David.... Let him alone, and let him curse; for Jehovah bath bidden him" II Sam. 16:10, 11. "Surely the wrath of man shall praise thee; and the residue of wrath shalt thou gird upon thee" (or restrain), Ps. 76:10. "And I, behold I will harden the hearts of the Egyptians and they shall go in (the Red Sea) after them; and I will get me honor upon Pharaoh, and upon all his host, and upon his chariots, and upon his horsemen," Ex. 14:17.

(g) To the fortuitous events or "chance happenings. "See section 4 (Ch. III)."

Footnotes:

14. Systematic Theology, II, pp. 583, 585.
15. Toplady, Preface to Zanchius' Predestination, p. 14.
16. Biblical Doctrines, p. 14.
17. Moderator's sermon, on Predestination, preached before the General Assembly of the Presbyterian Church, U.S.A., 1924.

Loraine Boettner D.D.

Chapter VI – The Foreknowledge of God

The Arminian objection against foreordination bears with equal force against the foreknowledge of God. What God foreknows must, in the very nature of the case, be as fixed and certain as what is foreordained; and if one is inconsistent with the free agency of man, the other is also. Foreordination renders the events certain, while foreknowledge presupposes that they are certain.

Now if future events are foreknown to God, they cannot by any possibility take a turn contrary to His knowledge. If the course of future events is foreknown, history will follow that course as definitely as a locomotive follows the rails from New York to Chicago. The Arminian doctrine, in rejecting foreordination, rejects the theistic basis for foreknowledge. Common sense tells us that no event can be foreknown unless by some means, either physical or mental, it has been predetermined. Our choice as to what determines the certainty of future events narrows down to two alternatives--the foreordination of the wise and merciful heavenly Father, or the working of blind, physical fate.

The Socinians and Unitarians, while not so evangelical as the Arminians, are at this point more consistent; for after rejecting the foreordination of God, they also deny that He can foreknow the acts of free agents. They hold that in the very nature of the case it cannot be known how the person will act until the time comes and the choice is made. This view of course reduces the prophecies of Scripture to shrewd guesses at best, and destroys the historic Christian view of the Inspiration of the Scriptures. It is a view which has never been held by any recognized Christian church. Some of the Socinians and Unitarians have been bold enough and honest enough to acknowledge that the reason which led them to deny God's certain foreknowledge of the future acts of men, was, that if this be admitted it would be impossible to disprove the Calvinistic doctrine of Predestination.

Many Arminians have felt the force of this argument, and while they have not followed the Unitarians in denying God's foreknowledge, they have made it plain that they would very willingly deny it if they could, or dared. Some have spoken disparagingly of the doctrine of foreknowledge and have intimated that, in their opinion, it was not of much importance whether one believed it or not. Some have gone so far as to tell us plainly that men had better reject foreknowledge than admit Predestination. Others have suggested that God may voluntarily neglect to know some of the acts of men in order to leave them free; but this of course destroys the omniscience of God. Still others have suggested that God's omniscience may imply only that He can know all things, if He chooses,--just as His omnipotence implies that He can do all things, if He chooses. But the comparison will not hold, for these certain acts are not merely possibilities but realities, although yet future; and to ascribe ignorance to God concerning these is to deny Him the attribute of omniscience. This explanation would give us the absurdity of an omniscience that is not omniscient.

When the Arminian is confronted with the argument from the foreknowledge of God, he has to admit the certainty or fixity of future events. Yet when dealing with the problem of free agency he wishes to maintain that the acts of free agents are uncertain and ultimately dependent on the choice of the person,--which is plainly an inconsistent position. A view which holds that the free acts of men are uncertain, sacrifices the sovereignty of God in order to preserve the freedom of men.

Furthermore, if the acts of free agents are in themselves uncertain, God must then wait until the event has had its issue before making His plans. In trying to convert a soul, then He would be conceived of as working in the same manner that Napoleon is said to have gone into battle-with three or four plans in mind, so that if the first failed, he could fall back upon the second, and if that failed, then the third, and so on,--a view which is altogether inconsistent with a true view of His nature. He would then be ignorant of much of the future and would daily be gaining vast stores of knowledge. His government of the world also, in that case, would be very uncertain and changeable, dependent as it would be on the unforeseen conduct of men.

To deny God the perfections of foreknowledge and immutability is to represent Him as a disappointed and unhappy being who is often checkmated and defeated by His creatures. But who can really believe that in the presence of man the Great Jehovah must sit waiting, inquiring, "What will he do?" Yet unless Arminianism denies the foreknowledge of God, it stands defenseless before the logical consistency of Calvinism; for foreknowledge implies certainty and certainty implies foreordination.

Speaking through the prophet Isaiah the Lord said: "I am God, and there is none like me; declaring the end from the beginning, and from ancient times things that are not yet done; saying, My counsel shall stand, and I will do all my pleasure," Isaiah 46:10. "Thou understandest my thoughts afar off," said the psalmist, 139:2. He "knoweth the heart," Acts 15:8. "There is no creature that is not manifest in His sight; but all things are naked and laid open before the eyes of Him with whom we have to do," Hebrews 4:13.

Much of the difficulty in regard to the doctrine of Predestination is due to the finite character of our mind, which can grasp only a few details at a time, and which understands only a part of the relations between these. We are creatures of time, and often fail to take into consideration the fact that God is not limited as we are. That which appears to us as "past," "present," and "future," is all "present" to His mind. It is an eternal "now." He is "the high and lofty One that inhabits eternity," Isaiah 57:15. "A thousands years in thy sight are but as yesterday when it is past, And as a watch in the night," Psalm 90:4. Hence the events which we see coming to pass in time are only the events which He appointed and set before Him from eternity. Time is a property of the finite creation and is objective to God. He is above it and sees it, but is not conditioned by it. He is also independent of space, which is another property of the finite creation. Just as He sees at one glance a road leading from New York to San Francisco, while we see only a small portion of it as we pass over it, so He sees all events in history, past, present, and future at one glance. When we realize that the complete process of history is before Him as an eternal "now," and that He is the Creator of all finite existence, the doctrine of Predestination at least becomes an easier doctrine.

In the eternal ages back of the creation there could not have been any certainty as to future events unless God had formed a decree in regard to them. Events pass from the category of things that may or may not be, to that of things that shall certainly be, or from possibility to fruition, only when God passes a decree to that effect. This fixity or certainty could have had its ground in nothing outside of the divine Mind, for in eternity nothing else existed. Says Dr. R. L. Dabney: "The only way in which any object can by any possibility have passed from God's vision of the possible into His foreknowledge of the actual, is by His purposing to effectuate it Himself, or intentionally and purposely to permit its effectuation by some other agent whom He expressly purposed to bring into existence. This is clear from this fact. An effect conceived in posse only rises into actuality by virtue of an efficient cause or causes. When God was looking forward from the point of view of His original infinite prescience, there was but one cause, Himself. If any other cause or agent is ever to arise, it must be by God's agency. If effects are embraced in God's infinite prescience, which these other agents are to produce, still, in willing these other agents into existence, with infinite prescience, God did virtually will into existence, or purpose, all the effects of which they were to be efficients." [18]

And to the same effect the Baptist theologian, Dr. A. B. Strong, who for a number of years was President and Professor in the Rochester Theological Seminary, writes: "In eternity there could have been no cause of the future existence of the universe, outside of God Himself, since no being existed but God Himself. In eternity God foresaw that the creation of the world and the Institution of its laws would make certain its actual history even to the most insignificant details. But God decreed to create and to institute these laws. In so decreeing He necessarily decreed all that was to come. In fine, God foresaw the future events of the universe as certain, because He had decreed to create; but this determination to create involved also a determination of all the actual results of that creation; or, in other words, God decreed those results." [19]

Foreknowledge must not be confused with foreordination. Foreknowledge presupposes foreordination, but is not itself foreordination. The actions of free agents do not take place because they are foreseen, but they are foreseen because they are certain to take place. Hence Strong says, "Logically, though not chronologically, decree comes before foreknowledge. When I say, 'I know what I will do,' it is evident that I have determined already, and that my knowledge does not precede determination, but follows it and is based upon it." [20]

Since God's foreknowledge is complete, He knows the destiny of every person, not merely before the person has made his choice in this life, but from eternity. And since He knows their destiny before they are created, and then proceeds to create, it is plain that the saved and the lost alike fulfill His plan for them; for if He did not plan that any particular ones should be lost, He could at least refrain from creating them.

We conclude, then, that the Christian doctrine of the Foreknowledge of God proves also His Predestination. Since these events are foreknown, they are fixed and settled things; and nothing can have fixed and settled them except the good pleasure of God,--the great first cause,-- freely and unchangeably foreordaining whatever comes to pass. The whole difficulty lies in the acts of free agents being certain; yet certainty is required for foreknowledge as well as for foreordination. The Arminian arguments, if valid, would disprove both foreknowledge and foreordination. And since they prove too much we conclude that they prove nothing at all.

Footnotes:
18. Theology, p. 212.
19. Systematic Theology, p. 356.
20. Systematic Theology, p. 357.

Chapter VII - Outline of Systems

There are really only three systems which claim to set forth a way of salvation through Christ. They are:

(1) Universalism,--which holds that Christ died for all men and that eventually all shall be saved, either in this life or through a future probation. This view perhaps makes the strongest appeal to our feelings, but is un-Scriptural, and has never been held by an organized Christian church.

(2) Arminianism,--which holds that Christ died equally and indiscriminately for every individual of mankind, for those who perish no less than for those who are saved: that election is not an eternal and unconditional act of God; that saving grace is offered to every man, which grace he may receive or reject just as he pleases; that man may successfully resist the regenerating power of the Holy Spirit if he chooses to do so; that saving grace is not necessarily permanent, but that those who are loved of God, ransomed by Christ, and born again of the Holy Spirit, may (let God wish and strive ever so much to the contrary) throw away all and perish eternally.

Arminianism in its radical and more fully developed forms is essentially a recrudescence of Pelagianism, a type of self-salvation. In fact, the ancestry of Arminianism can be traced back to Pelagianism as definitely as can that of Calvinism be traced back to Augustinianism. It might, perhaps, be more properly called "Pelagianism," seeing that its principles were brought into existence nearly twelve hundred years before Arminius was born. Pelagianism denied human depravity, and the necessity of efficacious grace, and exalted the human will above the divine. "Its doctrines pleased the natural palate of man, hating, as all men do hate, the doctrine of universal depravity. To say that man could grow holy and spotless, that he could secure God's grace, and attain to salvation by an act of his own free will, was teaching that attracted, as it still does attract, thousands." [21]

Arminianism at its best is a somewhat vague and indefinite attempt at reconciliation, hovering midway between the sharply marked systems of Pelagius and Augustine, taking off the edges of each, and inclining now to the one, now to the other. Dr. A. A. Hodge refers to it as a "manifold and elastic system of compromise." Its leading idea is that divine grace and human will jointly accomplish the work of conversion and sanctification, and that man has the sovereign right of accepting or rejecting. It affirms that man is weak as a result of the fall, but denies that all ability has been lost. Man therefore merely needs divine grace to assist his personal efforts. Or, to put it another way, he is sick, but not dead; he indeed cannot help himself, but he can engage the help of a physician, and can either accept or reject the help when it is offered. He thus has power to co-operate with the grace of God in the matter of salvation. This view exalts man's freedom at the expense of God's sovereignty. It has some apparent, but no real, Scripture authority, and is plainly contradicted by other parts of Scripture.

History shows plainly that the tendency of Arminianism is to compromise and to drift gradually from an evangelical basis. Hence it is that to this day there has never been developed a logical and systematic body of Arminian theology. It has, in the Methodist Church for instance, a brief and informal creed in some twenty-five articles; but the contrast between that statement and the carefully wrought-out Westminster Confession is seen at a glance.

(3) The third system setting forth a way of salvation through Christ is Calvinism. Calvinism holds that as a result of the fall into sin all men in themselves are guilty, corrupted, hopelessly lost; that from this fallen mass God sovereignly elects some to salvation through Christ, while passing by others; that Christ is sent to redeem His people by a purely substitutionary atonement; that the Holy Spirit efficaciously applies this redemption to the elect; and that all of the elect are infallibly brought to salvation. This view alone is consistent with Scripture and with what we see in the world about us.

Calvinism holds that the fall left man totally unable to do anything meriting salvation, that he is wholly dependent on divine grace for the inception and development of spiritual life. The chief fault of Arminianism is its insufficient recognition of the part that God takes in redemption. It loves to admire the dignity and strength of man; Calvinism loses itself in adoration of the grace and omnipotence of God. Calvinism casts man first into to supernatural strength. The one flatters natural pride; the other is a gospel for penitent sinners. As that which exalts man in his own sight and tickles his fancies is more welcome to the natural heart than that which abases him, Arminianism is likely to prove itself more popular. Yet Calvinism is nearer to the facts, however harsh and forbidding those facts may seem. "It is not always the most agreeable medicine which is the most healing. The experience of the apostle John is one of frequent occurrence, that the little book which is sweet as honey in the mouth is bitter in the belly. Christ crucified was a stumbling-block to one class of people and foolishness to another, and yet He was, and is, the power of God and the wisdom of God unto salvation to all who believe." [22]

Men constantly deceive themselves by postulating their own peculiar feelings and opinions as moral axioms. To some it is self-evidently true that a holy God cannot permit sin; hence they infer that there is no God. To others it is self-evident that a merciful God cannot permit a portion of His rational creatures to be forever the victims of sin and misery, and consequently they deny the doctrine of eternal punishment. Some assume that the innocent cannot justly be punished for the guilty, and are led to deny the vicarious and substitutionary suffering and death of Christ. And to others it is an axiom that the free acts of a free agent cannot be certain and under the control of God, so they deny the foreordination, or even the foreknowledge, of such acts.

We are not at liberty, however, to develop a system of our own liking. "The question which of these systems is true," says Dr. Charles Hodge, a zealous and uncompromising advocate of Calvinism, "is not to be decided by ascertaining which is the more agreeable to our feelings or the more plausible to our understanding, but which is consistent with the doctrines of the Bible and the facts of experience." "It is the duty of every theologian to subordinate his theories to the Bible, and teach not what seems to him to be true or reasonable, but simply what the Bible teaches," And again, "There would be no end of controversy, and no security for any truth whatever, if the strong personal convictions of individual minds be allowed to determine what is, or what is not true, what the Bible may, and what it may not be allowed to teach." [23]

As in the case of the other doctrines which are common to the Christian system, there is no place in the Bible where these distinctive Calvinistic doctrines are set forth in a systematic and complete form. The Bible is not a work on Systematic Theology, but only the quarry out of which the stone for such a temple can be obtained. Instead of giving us a formal statement of a theological system it gives us a mass of raw materials which must be organized and systematized and worked up into their organic relations. Nowhere, for instance, do we find a formal statement of the doctrine of the Trinity, or of the person of Christ, or of the inspiration of the Scriptures. It gives us an account of the origin and development of the Hebrew people and of the founding of Christianity, and the doctrinal facts are given with little regard to their logical relations. These facts need to be classified and arranged in a logical system and thus transformed into theology. This fact, that the material in the Bible is not arranged in a theological system, is in accordance with God's procedure in other realms. He has not given us a fully developed system of biology, or astronomy, or politics. We simply find the unorganized facts in nature and in experience and are left to develop them into a system as best we may. And since the doctrines are not thus presented in a systematic and formal way it is much easier for false interpretations to arise.

Footnotes:

21. Warburton, Calvinism, p. 11.
22. McFetridge, Calvinism in History, p. 136.
23. Systematic Theology, II, pp. 356, 559, 531.

Chapter VIII – The Scriptures Are the Final Authority by Which Systems Are to Be Judged

In all matters of controversy between Christians the Scriptures are accepted as the highest court of appeal. Historically they have been the common authority of Christendom. We believe that they contain one harmonious and sufficiently complete system of doctrine; that all of their parts are consistent with each other; and that it is our duty to trace out this consistency by a careful investigation of the meaning of particular passages. [24]

"The Word of God," says Warburton, concerning these doctrines, "is the great and final tribunal before which they must be brought, and by which they must be tried. And the truth or falsity of our belief is measured by the corresponding agreement with, or diversity from, that form of doctrine which is set forth in the unerring revelation that God has given to us in His inspired Word. It is by this criterion that Calvinism must be tried. It is by this criterion that Arminianism or Pelagianism must be tried. It is by this criterion, and by this criterion alone, that every form of belief, be it religious, or be it scientific, must be tried; and if they speak not according to this Word, it is because there is no light in them . . . We believe in the full, verbal inspiration of the Word of God. We hold it to be the only authority in all matters and assert that no doctrine can be true, or essential, if it does not find a place in this Word." [25]

It is obvious that the truth or falsity of this profound doctrine of Predestination can be decided only by divine revelation. No person, acting merely on his own observations and judgments, can know what are the basic principles of the plan which God is following. Philosophical speculation and all abstract reasoning should be held in abeyance until we have first heard the testimony of Scripture,--and when we have heard that testimony, we should humbly submit. Would that we had more people with that noble character of the Bereans who searched the Scriptures daily to see whether or not these things were so.

In connection with each of the doctrines discussed in this book we have presented a large mass of Scripture evidence--evidence both direct and inferential--evidence which cannot be answered or explained away--evidence greatly superior in strength, extent and explicitness, to any that can be adduced on the other side. The Bible unfolds a scheme of redemption which is Calvinistic from beginning to end. and these doctrines are taught with such inescapable clearness that the question is settled for all those who accept the Bible as the Word of God. These doctrines are set forth in the most impressive way; and the unstudied naturalness and simplicity with which they are given makes them all the more impressive. Should any one ask us the question, Are there any stars in the heavens? Our answer would be, The heavens are full of stars, Psalm 8:3, 4. Or again, Are there any fishes in the sea? Our answer would be, The sea is full of fishes, Psalm 104:25, 27. Or again, Are there any trees in the forest? We would again reply, The forest is full of trees. And in like manner should we be asked the question, Is the doctrine of Predestination in the Bible? Our answer should be, The Bible is full of it from Genesis to Revelation.

That such doctrines as the Trinity, the Deity of Christ, the personality of the Holy Spirit, the sinfulness of man, and the reality of future punishments, are Scriptural is not denied even by those who refuse to accept them as true. It is a common thing for rationalists and so-called higher critics to admit that the apostles believed and taught the evangelical and Calvinistic doctrines, and that with a strict application of the rules of exegesis their statements cannot admit of any other interpretation; but of course they do not consider themselves bound to accept the authority of any apostle. They ascribe the apostles' belief in these doctrines, for instance, to "the erroneous notions of a crude and uncivilized age." This, however, does not detract from the value of their testimony that these passages, critically interpreted, can have no other meaning. Furthermore, we would prefer to say with the rationalists that the Scriptures teach these doctrines but that the Scriptures are no authority for us, rather than to profess acceptance of their teaching while ingeniously evading the force of their argument.

We shall show that there is no great difficulty--no undue violence or straining required--to interpret consistently with our doctrine the passages which are brought forth by Arminians, while it is impossible, without the most unwarrantable and unnatural forcing and straining, to reconcile their doctrine with our passages. Furthermore, our doctrine could not be overthrown merely by bringing forth other passages which would contradict it, for that at most would only give us a self-contradictory Bible.

In the light of modern scientific exegesis, it is quite evident that the objections which are raised against the Reformed Theology are emotional or philosophical rather than exegetical. And had men been content to interpret the language of Scripture according to the acknowledged principles of interpretation, the faith of Christians might have been far more harmonious. Our opponents, says Cunningham, are able to "argue with some plausibility only when they are dealing with single passages, or particular classes of passages, but keeping out of view, or throwing into the background, the general mass of Scripture evidence bearing upon the whole subject. When we take a conjunct view of the whole body of Scripture statements, manifestly intended to make known to us the nature, causes, and consequences of Christ's death, literal and figurative--view them in combination with each other--and fairly estimate what they are fitted to teach, there is no good ground for doubt as to the general conclusions which we should feel ourselves constrained to adopt." [26]

So long as we hold to the Reformed principle that the Scriptures are to be accepted as the sole authority in matters of doctrine the Calvinistic system will stand as the only one which adequately treats of God, man, and redemption.

Footnotes:

24. For the most exhaustive and scholarly treatment of the doctrines of Revelation and Inspiration, see Warfield, "Revelation and Inspiration."

25. Calvinism, p. 21.

26. Historical Theology, II, p. 298.

Chapter IX - A Warning Against Undue Speculation

Just at this point we shall give a few words of warning against undue speculation and curiosity in dealing with this lofty doctrine of Predestination. Perhaps we can do no better than to quote the words of Calvin himself which are found in the first section of his treatment of this subject: "The discussion of Predestination--a subject of itself rather intricate--is made very perplexed, and therefore dangerous, by human curiosity, which no barriers can restrain from wandering into forbidden labyrinths, and from soaring beyond its sphere, as if determined to leave none of the Divine secrets unscrutinized or unexplored . . . First, then, let them remember that when they inquire into Predestination, they penetrate into the inmost recesses of divine wisdom, where the careless and confident intruder will obtain no satisfaction to his curiosity . . . For we know that when we have exceeded the limits of the word, we shall get into a devious and irksome course, in which errors, slips, and falls will be inevitable. Let us then, in the first place bear in mind, that to desire any more knowledge of Predestination than that which is unfolded in the Word of God, indicates as great folly as to wish to walk through impassible roads, or to see in the dark. Nor let us be ashamed to be ignorant of some things relative to a subject in which there is a kind of learned ignorance." [27]

We are not under obligation to "explain" these truths; we are only under obligation to state what God has revealed in His word, and to vindicate these statements as far as possible from misconception and objections. In the nature of the case all that we can know concerning such profound truths is what the Spirit has seen fit to reveal concerning them, being confident that whatever God has revealed is undoubtedly true and is to be believed although we may not be able to sound its depths with the line of our reason. In our ignorance of His inter-related purposes, we are not fitted to be His counselors. "Thy judgments are a great deep," said the psalmist. As well might man attempt to swim the ocean as to fathom the judgments of God. Man knows far too little to justify him in attempting to explain the mysteries of God's rule.

The importance of the subject discussed should lead us to proceed only with profoundest reverence and caution. While it is true that mysteries are to be handled with care, and while unwarranted and presumptuous speculations concerning divine things are to be avoided, yet if we would declare the Gospel in its purity and fullness we must be careful not to withhold from believers what is declared in the Scriptures concerning Predestination. That some of these truths will be perverted and abused by the ungodly is to be expected. No matter how plainly it is taught in Scripture, the unenlightened mind considers it as absurd, for instance, that one God should exist in three persons, or that God should foreknow the entire course of world events, as that His plan should include the destiny of every person. And while we can know only as much about Predestination as God has seen fit to reveal, it is important that we shall know that much; otherwise it would not have been revealed. Where Scripture leads we may safely follow.

Footnotes:

27. Institutes, Ch. XXI, sect. I, II.

Section II – The Five Points of Calvinism

The Calvinistic system especially emphasizes five distinct doctrines. These are technically known as "The Five Points of Calvinism," and they are the main pillars upon which the superstructure rests. In this section we shall examine each of these, giving the Scripture basis and the arguments from reason which support them. We shall then consider the objections which are commonly brought against them.

As will be shown, the Bible contains an abundance of material for the development of each of these doctrines. Furthermore, these are not isolated and independent doctrines but are so inter-related that they form a simple, harmonious, self-consistent system; and the way in which they fit together as component parts of a well-ordered whole has won the admiration of thinking men of all creeds. Prove any one of them true and all the others will follow as logical and necessary parts of the system. Prove any one of them false and the whole system must be abandoned. They are found to dovetail perfectly one into the other. They are so many links in the great chain of causes, and not one of them can be taken away without marring and subverting the whole Gospel plan of salvation through Christ. We cannot conceive of this agreement arising merely by accident, nor even being possible, unless these doctrines are true.

Let it be borne in mind that in this book we do not propose to discuss in detail those other doctrines of the Scriptures which are accepted by evangelical Christendom, but to set forth and defend those which are peculiar to the Calvinistic system. Unless this be kept in mind much of the real strength and beauty of generic Calvinism will be lost and the so-called "Five Points of Calvinism,"--which historically and in reality are the obverse of what might be called the "Five Points of Arminianism,"-- will assume undue prominence in the system. Let the reader, then, guard against a too close identification of the Five Points and the Calvinistic system. While these are essential elements, the system really includes much more. As stated in the Introduction, the Westminster Confession is a balanced statement of the Reformed Faith or Calvinism, and it gives due prominence to the other Christian doctrines.

The Five Points may be more easily remembered if they are associated with the word T-U-L-I-P; T, Total Inability ; U, Unconditional Election; L, Limited Atonement; I, Irresistible (Efficacious) Grace; and P, Perseverance of the Saints.

Chapter X – Total Inability

1. Statement of the Doctrine. 2. The Extent and Effects of Original Sin. 3. The Defects in Man's Common Virtues. 4. The Fall of Man. 5. The Representative Principle. 6. The Goodness and Severity of God. 7. Scripture Proof.

In the Westminster Confession the doctrine of Total Inability Is stated as follows: -- "Man, by his fall Into a state of sin, hath wholly lost all ability of will to any spiritual good accompanying salvation; so as a natural man, being altogether averse from good, and dead in sin, is not able, by his own strength, to convert himself, or to prepare himself thereunto." [28]

Paul, Augustine, and Calvin have as their starting point the fact that all mankind sinned in Adam and that all men are "without excuse," Rom. 2:1. Time and again Paul tells us that we are dead in trespasses and sins, estranged from God, and helpless. In writing to the Ephesian Christians he reminded them that before they received the Gospel they were "separate from Christ, alienated from the common. wealth of Israel, and strangers from the covenants of the promise, having no hope and without God in the world," 2:12. There we notice the five-fold emphasis as he piles phrase on top of phrase to stress this truth.

2. THE EXTENT AND EFFECTS OF ORIGINAL SIN

This doctrine of Total Inability, which declares that men are dead in sin, does not mean that all men are equally bad, nor that any man is as bad as he could be, nor that any one in entirely destitute of virtue, nor that human nature is evil In Itself, nor that man's spirit is inactive, and much less does it mean that the body is dead. What it does mean is that since the fall man rests under the curse of sin, that he is actuated by wrong principles, and that he is wholly unable to love God or to do anything meriting salvation. His corruption is extensive but not necessarily intensive.

It is in this sense that man since the fail "is utterly indisposed, disabled, and made opposite to all good, and wholly inclined to all evil." He possesses a fixed bias of the will against God, and instinctively and willingly turns to evil. He is an alien by birth, and a sinner by choice. The inability under which he labors is not an inability to exercise volitions, but an inability to be willing to exercise holy volitions. And it is this phase of it which led Luther to declare that "Free-will is an empty term, whose reality is lost. And a lost liberty, according to my grammar, is no liberty at all." [29] In matters pertaining to his salvation, the unregenerate man is not at liberty to choose between good and evil, but only to choose between greater and lesser evil, which is not properly free will. The fact that fallen man still has ability to do certain acts morally good in themselves does not prove that he can do acts meriting salvation, for his motives may be wholly wrong.

Man is a free agent but be cannot originate the love of God in his heart. His will is free in the sense that it is not controlled by any force outside of himself. As the bird with a broken wing is "free" to fly but not able, so the natural man is free to come to God but not able. How can he repent of his sin when he loves it? How can he come to God when he hates Him? This is the inability of the will under which man labors. Jesus said, "And this is the judgment, that light is come into the world, and men loved the darkness rather than the light; for their works were evil," John 3:19; and again, "Ye will not come to me, that ye may have life," John 5:40. Man's ruin lies mainly in his own perverse will. He cannot come because he will not. Help enough is provided if he were only willing to accept it. Paul tells us, "The carnal mind is enmity against God; for it is not subject to the law of God, neither indeed can it be. So they that are in the flesh cannot please God:" Romans 8:7.

To assume that because man has ability to love he therefore has ability to love God, is about as wise as to assume that since water has the ability to flow, it therefore has the ability to flow up hill; or to reason that because a man has power to cast himself from the top of a precipice to the bottom, he therefore has equal power to transport himself from the bottom to the top.

Fallen man sees nothing desirable in "the One who is altogether lovely, the fairest among ten thousand." He may admire Jesus as a man, but he wants nothing to do with Him as God, and he resists the outward holy influences of the Spirit with all his power. Sin, and not righteousness, has become his natural element so that he has no desire for salvation.

Man's fallen nature gives rise to a most obdurate blindness, stupidity, and opposition concerning the things of God. His will is under the control of a darkened understanding, which puts sweet for bitter, and bitter for sweet, good for evil, and evil for good. So far as his relations with God are concerned, he wills only that which is evil, although he wills it freely. Spontaneity and enslavement actually exist together.

In other words, fallen man is so morally blind that he uniformly prefers and chooses evil instead of good, as do the fallen angels or demons. When the Christian is completely sanctified he reaches a state in which he uniformly prefers and chooses good, as do the holy angels. Both of these states are consistent with freedom and responsibility of moral agents. Yet while fallen man acts thus uniformly he is never compelled to sin, but does it freely and delights in it. His dispositions and desires are so inclined, and he acts knowingly and willingly from the spontaneous motion of the heart. This natural bias or appetite for that which is evil is characteristic of man's fallen and corrupt nature, so that, as Job says, he "drinketh iniquity like water," 15:16.

We read that "The natural man receiveth not the things of the Spirit, for they are foolishness to him; neither can he know them, for they are spiritually discerned," 1 Corinthians 2:14. We are at a loss to understand how any one can take a plain common sense view of this passage of Scripture and yet contend for the doctrine of human ability. Man in his natural state cannot even see the kingdom of God, much less can he get into it. An uncultured person may see a beautiful work of art as an object of vision, but he has no appreciation of its excellence. He may see the figures of a complex mathematical equation, but they have no meaning for him. Horses and cattle may see the same beautiful sunset or other phenomenon in nature that men see, but they are blind to all of the artistic beauty. So it is when the Gospel of the cross is presented to the unregenerate man. He may have an intellectual knowledge of the facts and doctrines of the Bible, but he lacks all spiritual discernment of their excellence, and finds no delight in them. The same Christ is to one man without form or comeliness that he should desire Him; to another He is the Prince of life and the Savior of the world, God manifest in the flesh, whom it is impossible not to adore, love and obey.

This total inability, however, arises not merely from a perverted moral nature, but also from ignorance. Paul wrote that the Gentiles "walk in the vanity of their mind, being darkened in their understanding, alienated from the life of God, because of the ignorance that is in them, because of the hardening of their heart," Ephesians 4:17, 18. And again, "The word of the cross is to them that perish foolishness; but unto us who are saved it is the power of God," 1 Corinthians 1:18. When he wrote of "Things which eye saw not, and ear heard not, And which entered not into the heart of man, Whatsoever things God hath prepared for them that love Him," he had reference, not to the glories of the heavenly state as is commonly supposed, but to the spiritual realities in this life which cannot be seen by the unregenerate mind, as is made plain by the words of the following verse: "But unto us God revealed them through the Spirit," 1 Corinthians 2:9, 10. On one occasion Jesus said, "No one knoweth the Son, save the Father; neither doth any know the Father save the Son, and he to whomsoever the Son willeth to reveal Him," Matthew 11:27. Here we are plainly told that man in his unregenerate, unenlightened nature does not know God in any sense worthy the name, and that the Son is sovereign in choosing who shall come into this saving knowledge of God.

Fallen man then lacks the power of spiritual discernment. His reason or understanding is blinded, and the taste and feelings are perverted. And since this state of mind is innate, as a condition of man's nature, it is beyond the power of the will to change it. Rather it controls both the affections and volitions. The effect of regeneration is clearly taught in the divine commission which Paul received at his conversion when he was told that he was to be sent to the Gentiles "to open their eyes, that they might turn from darkness to light and from the power of Satan unto God," Acts 26:18.

Jesus taught the same truth under a different figure when He said to the Pharisees, "Why do ye not understand my speech? Even because ye cannot hear my word. Ye are of your father the Devil, and the lusts of your father it is your will to do," John 8:43, 44. They could not understand, nor even hear His words in any intelligible way. To them His words were only foolishness, madness; and they accused Him of being demon possessed (vss. 48, 52). Only His disciples could know the truth (vss. 31, 32); the Pharisees were children of the Devil (vss. 42, 44), and bondservants of sin (vs. 34). although they thought themselves free (vs. 33).

At another time Jesus taught that a good tree could not bring forth evil fruit, nor an evil tree good fruit. And since in this similitude the good and evil trees represent good and evil men, what does It mean but that one class of men is governed by one set of basic principles, while the other class is governed by another set of basic principles? The fruits of these two trees are acts, words, thoughts, which if good proceed from a good nature, and if evil proceed from and evil nature. It is impossible, then, for one and the same root to bring forth fruit of different kinds. Hence we deny the existence in man of a power which may act either way, on the logical ground that both virtue and vice cannot come out of the same moral condition of the agent. And we affirm that human actions which relate to God proceed either out of a moral condition which necessarily produces good actions or out of a moral condition which necessarily produces evil actions.

"In the Epistle to the Ephesians Paul declares that Prior to the quickening of the Spirit of God each individual soul lies dead in trespasses and sins. Now it will surely be admitted that to be dead, and to be dead in sin, is clear and positive evidence that there is neither aptitude nor Power remaining for the performance of any spiritual action. If a man were dead, in a natural and physical sense, it would at once be readily granted that there is no further Possibility of that man being able to perform any physical actions. A corpse cannot act in any way whatever, and that man would be reckoned to have taken leave of his senses who asserted that it could. If a man is dead spiritually, therefore, it is surely equally as evident that he is unable to perform any spiritual actions, and thus the doctrine of man's moral inability rests upon strong Scriptural evidence." [30]

"On the principle that no clean thing can come out of what is unclean (Job 14:4), all that are born of woman are declared 'abominable and corrupt,' to whose nature iniquity alone is attractive (Job 15:14-16). Accordingly, to become sinful, men do not wait until the age of accountable action arrives. Rather, they are apostates from the womb, and as soon as they are born go astray, speaking lies (Psalm 58:3); they are even shapen in iniquity, and conceived in sin (Psalm 51:5). The propensity of their heart is evil from their youth (Genesis 8:21), and it is out of the heart that all the issues of life proceed (Proverbs 4: 23; 20: 11). Acts of sin are therefore but the expression of the natural heart, which is deceitful above all things and exceedingly corrupt (Jeremiah 17:9)." [31]

Ezekiel presents this same truth in graphic language and gives us the picture of the helpless infant which was cast out in its blood and left to die, but which the Lord graciously found and cared for (Chapter 16).

This doctrine of original sin supposes that fallen men have the same kind and degree of liberty in sinning under the influence of a corrupt nature as have the Devil and the demons, or that the saints in glory and the holy angels have in acting rightly under the influence of a holy nature. That is, men and angels act according to their natures. As the saints and angels are confirmed in holiness,--that is, possessed of a nature which is wholly inclined to righteousness and adverse to sin,--so the nature of fallen men and of demons is such that they cannot perform a single act with right motives toward God. Hence the necessity that God shall sovereignly change the person's character in regeneration.

The Old Testament ceremonies of circumcision of the new-born child, and of purification of the mother, were designed to teach that man comes into the world sinful that since the fall human nature is corrupt in its very origin. Paul stated this truth in another and, if possible, even stronger way in 2 Corinthians 4: 3, 4: "And if our Gospel is veiled it is veiled to them that perish; in whom the god of this world (by which he means the Devil) hath blinded the minds of the unbelieving, that the light of the

Gospel of the glory of Christ who is the image of God, should not dawn upon them." In a word, then, fallen men without the operations of The Spirit of God, are under the rule of Satan. They are led captive by him at his will, 2 Timothy 2:26. So long as this "strong man fully armed" is not molested by the "stronger than he." he keeps his kingdom in peace and his captives willingly do his bidding. But the "stronger than he" has overcome him, has taken his armor from him, and has liberated a part of his captives (Luke 11:21, 22). God now exercises the right of releasing whom He will; and all born again Christians are ransomed sinners from that kingdom.

The Scriptures declare that fallen man is a captive, a willing slave to sin, and entirely unable to deliver himself from its bondage and corruption. He is incapable of understanding, and much less of doing, the things of God. There is what we might term "the freedom of slavery,"--a state in which the subject is free only to do the will of his master, which in this case is sin. It was this to which Jesus referred when He said, "Every one that committeth sin is the bondservant of sin," John 8:34.

And such being the depth of man's corruption it is wholly beyond his own power to cleanse himself. His only hope of an amendment of life lies accordingly in a change of heart, which change is brought about by the sovereign re-creative power of the Holy Spirit who works when and where and how He pleases. As well might one attempt to pump a leaking ship while the leak is still unmended, as to reform the unregenerate without this inward change. Or as well might the Ethiopian change his skin, or the leopard his spots, as he who is accustomed to do evil correct his ways. This transfer from spiritual death to spiritual life we call "regeneration." It is referred to in Scripture by various terms: "regeneration," a "making alive," a "calling out of darkness into light," a "quickening," a "renewing," a taking away of the heart of stone and giving the heart of flesh, etc., which work is exclusively that of the Holy Spirit. As a result of this change a man comes to see the truth and gladly accepts it. His very instincts and intimate impulses are transferred to the side of law, obedience to which becomes but the spontaneous expression of his nature. Regeneration is said to be wrought by that same supernatural power which God wrought in Christ when He raised Him from the dead (Ephesians 1:18-20). Man does not possess the power of self-regeneration, and until this inward change takes place, he cannot be convinced of the truth of the Gospel by any amount of external testimony. "If they hear not Moses and the prophets, neither will they be persuaded if one rise from the dead."

3. THE DEFECTS IN MAN'S COMMON VIRTUES

The unregenerate man can, through common grace, love his family and he may be a good citizen. He may give a million dollars to build a hospital, but he cannot give even a cup of cold water to a disciple in the name of Jesus. If a drunkard, he may abstain from drink for utilitarian purposes, but he cannot do it out of love for God. All of his common virtues or good works have a fatal defect in that his motives which prompt them are not to glorify God, -- a defect so vital that it throws any element of goodness as to man wholly into the shade. It matters not how good the works may be in themselves, for so long as the doer of them in out of harmony with God, none of his works are spiritually acceptable. Furthermore, the good works of the unregenerate have no stable foundation, for his nature is still unchanged: and as naturally and as certainly as the washed sow returns to her wallowing in the mire, so he sooner or later returns to his evil ways.

In the realm of morals it is a rule that the morality of the man must precede the morality of the action. One may speak with the tongues of men and of angels; yet if he Is lacking that inward principle of love toward God, he is become as sounding brass, or a clanging cymbal. He may give all his goods to feed the poor, and may give his body to be burned; yet if he lacks that inward principle. it profits him nothing. As human beings we know that an act of service rendered to us (by whatever utilitarian motives prompted) by someone who is at heart our enemy, does not merit our love and approbation. The Scripture statement that "Without faith it is impossible to be well-pleasing unto God," finds Its explanation in this, that faith is the foundation of all the other virtues, and nothing is acceptable to God which does not flow from right feelings.

A moral act is to be judged by the standard of love to God, which love is, as it were, the soul of all other virtue, and which is bestowed upon us only through grace. Augustine did not deny the existence of natural virtues, such as moderation, honesty, generosity, which constitute a certain merit among men; but be drew a broad line of distinction between these and the specific Christian graces (faith, love and gratitude to God, etc.), which alone are good in the strict sense of the word, and which alone have value before God. This distinction is very plainly illustrated in an example given by W. D. Smith. Says he: "In a gang of pirates we may find many things that are good in themselves. Though they are in wicked rebellion against the laws of the government, they have their own laws and regulations, which they obey strictly. We find among them courage and fidelity, with many other things that will recommend them as pirates. They may do many things, too, which the laws of the government require, but they are not done because the government has so required, but in obedience to their own regulations. For instance the government requires honesty and they may be strictly honest, one with another, In their transactions, and the division of all their spoil. Yet, as respects the government, and the general principle, their whole life is one of the most wicked dishonesty. Now, it is plain, that while they continue in their rebellion they can do nothing to recommend them to the government as citizens. Their first step must be to give up their rebellion, acknowledge their allegiance to the government, and sue for mercy. So all men, in their natural state, are rebels against God, and though they may do many things which the law of God requires, and which will recommend them as men, yet nothing is done with reference to God and His law. Instead, the regulations of society, respect for public opinion, self-interest, their own character in the sight of the world, or some other worldly or wicked motive, reigns supremely; and God, to whom they owe their heart and lives, is forgotten; or, if thought of at all, His claims are wickedly rejected, His counsels spurned, and the heart, in obstinate rebellion, refuses obedience. Now it is plain that while the heart continues in this state the man is a rebel against God, and can do nothing to recommend him to His favor. The first step is to give up his rebellion, repent of his sins, turn to God, and sue for pardon and reconciliation through the Savior. This he is unwilling to do, until he is made willing. He loves his sins, and will continue to love them, until his heart is changed."

The good actions of unregenerate men, Smith continues, "are not positively sinful in themselves, but sinful from defect. They lack the principle which alone can make them righteous in the sight of God. In the case of the pirates it is easy to see that all their actions are sin against the government. While they continue pirates, their sailing, mending, or rigging the vessel and even their eating and drinking, are all sins in the eyes of the government, as they are only so many expedients to enable them to continue their piratical career, and are parts of their life of rebellion. So with sinners. While the heart is wrong, it vitiates everything in the sight of God, even their most ordinary occupations; for the plain, unequivocal language of God is, 'Even the lamp of the wicked, is sin,' Proverbs 21:4." [32]

It is this inability which the Scriptures teach when they declare that "They that are in the flesh cannot please God," Romans 8:8; "Whatsoever Is not of faith in sin," Romans 14:23; and "Without faith it is impossible to be well-pleasing to Him," Hebrews 11:6. Hence even the virtues of the unregenerate man are but as plucked and fading flowers. It was because of this that Jesus said to His disciples, "Except your righteousness shall exceed the righteousness of the scribes and Pharisees, ye shall in no wise enter into the kingdom of heaven." And because those virtues are of this nature, they are only temporary. The one who possesses them is like the seed which falls on the stony soil, which perhaps springs up with promise of fruitage, but soon withers in the sun because it has no root in itself.

It follows also from what has been said that salvation to ABSOLUTELY AND SOLELY OF GRACE,--that God Is free, in consistency with the infinite perfections of His nature, to save none, few, many, or all, according to the sovereign good pleasure of His will. It also follows that salvation is not based on any merits in the creature, and that it depends on God, and not on men, who are, and who are not, to be made partakers of eternal life. God acts as a sovereign in saving some and passing by others who are left to the just recompense of their sins. Sinners are compared to dead men, or even to dry bones in their entire helplessness. In this they are all alike. The choice of some to eternal life is as sovereign as if Christ were to pass through a graveyard and bid one here and another there to come forth, the reason for restoring one to life and leaving another in his grave could be found only in His good pleasure, and not in the dead themselves. Hence the statement that we are foreordained according to the good pleasure of His will, and not after the good inclinations of our own; and in order that we might be holy, not because we were holy (Ephesians 1:4, 5). "Since all men alike deserved only God's wrath and curse the gift of His only begotten Son to die in the stead of malefactors, as the only possible method of expiating their guilt, is the most stupendous exhibition of undeserved favor and personal love that the universe has ever witnessed." [33]

4. THE FALL OF MAN

The fall of the human race into a state of sin and misery is the basis and foundation of the system of redemption which is set forth in the Scriptures, as it is the basis and foundation of the system which we teach. Only Calvinists seem to take the doctrine of the fall very seriously. Yet the Bible from beginning to end declares that man is ruined--totally ruined--that he is in a state of guilt and depravity from which he is utterly unable to deliver himself, and that God might in justice have left him to perish. In the Old Testament the narrative concerning the fall is found in the third chapter of Genesis; and in the New Testament direct references are made to it in Romans 5:12-21; 1 Corinthians 15:22; 2 Corinthians 11:3; 1 Timothy 2:13, 14, etc., although the New Testament emphasizes not the historic fact that man fell, but the ethical fact that he is fallen. The New Testament writers interpreted it literally and based their theology upon it. To Paul Adam was as real as Christ, the fall as real as the atonement. It may be maintained that the apostles were in error, but that this was their position cannot be denied.

Dr. A. A. Hodge has given us a very good statement of the doctrine of the fall which we shall take the privilege of quoting:--"As a fair probation could not, in the nature of the case, be given to every new member in person as it comes into existence an undeveloped infant, God, as guardian of the race and for its best interests, gave all its members a trial in the person of Adam under the most favorable circumstances--making him for that end the representative and personal substitute of each one of his natural descendants. He formed with him a covenant of works and of life; i. e., He gave to him for himself, and in behalf of all whom he represented, a promise of eternal life, conditioned upon perfect obedience,--that is, upon works. The obedience demanded was a specific test for a temporary period, which period of trial must necessarily be closed either by the reward consequent upon obedience, or the death consequent upon disobedience. The 'reward' promised was eternal life, which was a grace including far more than was originally bestowed upon Adam at his creation, the grant of which would have elevated the race into a condition of indefeasible holiness and happiness for ever. The 'penalty' threatened and executed was death; 'The day thou eatest thereof thou shalt surely die.' The nature of the death threatened can be determined only from a consideration of all that was involved in the curse actually inflicted. This we know to have included the instant withdrawal of the divine favor and spiritual intercommunion upon which man's life depended. Hence the alienation and curse of God; the sense of guilt and corruption of nature; consequent actual transgressions, the miseries of life, the dissolution of the body, the pains of hell." [34]

The consequences of Adam's sin are all comprehended under the term death, in its widest sense. Paul gives us the summary statement that "The wages of sin is death." The full import of the death which was threatened to Adam can only be seen by considering all the evil consequences which have since befallen man. It was primarily spiritual death, or eternal separation from God, which was threatened; and physical death, or the death of the body, is but one of the first fruits and relatively unimportant consequences of that greater penalty. Adam did not die physically for 930 years after the fall, but he did die spiritually the very moment he fell into sin. He died just as really as the fish dies when taken from the water, or as the plant dies when taken from the soil.

"In general we cherish a very wrong idea as to how Adam fell . . . . Adam was not tempted by Satan in a direct way . . . . Eve was tempted by Satan, and Eve fell being deceived. But we have inspired evidence to prove that Adam was not deceived (1 Timothy 2:14). He was caught by no wiles of Satan, but that which he did, he did wilfully and deliberately. And in the full consciousness of what he was doing, and with a perfect realization of the solemn consequences which were involved, he deliberately chose to follow his wife in her act of sinful disobedience. It was this deliberate wilfulness of man's sin which constituted its heinous character. Had he been attacked by Satan, and forced to yield through some overwhelming power being brought against him, we might have tried to find some excuse for his fall. But when, with eyes wide open, and with mind perfectly conscious and fully aware of the awful nature of his act, he used his free will to respond to the claims of the creature in defiance of the Creator, no excuse can he found for his fall. His act, in reality, was wilful, defiant rebellion, and by it he openly transferred his allegiance from God to Satan." [35]

And has there not been a fall--a fearful fall? The more we see of human nature as it is manifested in the world about us, the easier it is to believe in this great doctrine of original sin. Consider the world as a whole, filled as it is with murders, robberies, drunkenness, wars, broken homes, and crimes of all kinds. The thousand ingenious forms which crime and vice have assumed in the hands of regular practitioners are all tokens telling a fearful tale. A large portion of the human race today, as in all past ages, is left to live and die in the darkness of heathenism, hopelessly astray from God. Modernism and denial of every kind is rampant even in the Church. Even the religious press, so called, is strongly tinged with unbelief. Observe the general disinclination to pray, or to study the Bible, or to speak of spiritual things. Is not man now, as his progenitor Adam, fleeing from the presence of God, not wanting communion with Him, and with enmity in his heart for his Creator? Surely man's nature is radically wrong. The daily newspaper accounts of events, even in such an enlightened land as America, show that man is sinful, lost from God, and actuated by unholy principles. And the only adequate explanation of all this is that the penalty of death, which was threatened on man before the fall, now rests on the human race.

We live in a lost world, a world which if left to itself would fester in its corruption from eternity to eternity,--a world reeking with iniquity and blasphemy. The effects of the fall are such that man's will in itself tends only downward to sets of sin and folly. As a matter of fact God does not permit the race to become as corrupt as it naturally would if left to itself. He exercises restraining influences, inciting men to love one another, to be honest, philanthropic, and considerate of each others welfare. Unless God exercised these influences, wicked men would become worse and worse, overlapping conventions and social barriers, until the very zenith of lawlessness would soon be reached, and the earth would become so utterly corrupt that the elect could not live on it.

5. THE REPRESENTATIVE PRINCIPLE

It is easy for us to understand how a person may act through a representative, The people of a state act in and through their representatives in the Legislature, If a country has a good president or king, all of the people share the good results; if a bad president or king, all suffer the consequences. In a very real sense parents stand representative for, and to a large extent decide the destinies of, their children. If the parents are wise, virtuous, thrifty, the children reap the blessings; but if they are indolent and immoral the children suffer. In a thousand ways the well-being of individuals is conditioned by the acts of others, so inwrought is this representative principle into our human life. Hence in the Scripture doctrine that Adam stood as the official head and representative of his people we have only the application of a principle which we see at work all about us.

Dr. Charles Hodge has very ably treated this subject in the following section:--

"This representative principle pervades the whole Scriptures. The imputation of Adam's sin to his posterity is not an isolated fact. It is only an illustration of a general principle which characterizes the dispensations of God from the beginning of the world. God declared Himself to Moses as one who visits the iniquity of the fathers upon the children, and upon the children's children unto the third and to the fourth generation, Exodus 34:6, 7 . . . . The curse pronounced on Canaan fell on his posterity. Esau's selling his birthright, shut out his descendants from the covenant of promise. The children of Moab and Ammon were excluded from the congregation of the Lord forever, because their ancestors opposed the Israelites when they came out of Egypt. In the case of Dathan and Abiram, as in that of Achan, 'their wives, and their sons, and their little children perished for the sins of their parents. God said to Eli, that the iniquity of his house should not be purged with sacrifice and offering for ever. To David it was said, 'The sword shall never depart from thy house; because thou hast despised me, and hast taken the wife of Uriah the Hittite to be thy wife.' To the disobedient Gehazi it was said: 'The leprosy of Naaman shall cleave unto thee and unto thy seed forever.' The sin of Jeroboam and of the men of his generation determined the destiny of the ten tribes for all time. The imprecation of the Jews, when they demanded the crucifixion of Christ, 'His blood be on us and on our children,' still weighs down the scattered people of Israel .... This principle runs through the whole Scriptures. When God entered into covenant with Abraham, it was not for himself only but also for his posterity. They were bound by all the stipulations of the covenant. They shared its promises and its threatenings, and in hundreds of cases the penalty of disobedience came upon those who had no personal part in the transgressions. Children suffered equally with adults in the judgments, Whether famine, pestilence, or war, which came upon the people for their sins . . . . And the Jews to this day are suffering the penalty of the sins of their fathers for their rejection of Him of whom Moses and the prophets spoke. The whole plan of redemption rests on this same principle. Christ is the representative of His people, and on this ground their sins are imputed to Him and His righteousness to them . . . . No man who believes the Bible, can shut his eyes to the fact that it everywhere recognizes the representative character of parents, and that the dispensations of God have from the beginning been founded on the principle that the children bear the iniquities of their fathers. This is one of the reasons which infidels assign for rejecting the divine origin of the Scriptures. But infidelity furnishes no relief. History is as full of this doctrine as the Bible is. The punishment of the felon involves his family in his disgrace and misery. The spendthrift and drunkard entail poverty and wretchedness upon all connected with them. There is no nation now existing on the face of the earth, whose condition for weal or woe is net largely determined by the character and conduct of their ancestors . . . The idea of the transfer of guilt or of vicarious punishment lies at the foundation of all the expiatory offerings under the Old Testament, and of the great atonement under the new dispensation. To bear sin, is in Scriptural language to bear the penalty of sin. The victim bore the sin of the offerer. Hands were imposed upon the head of the animal about to be slaughtered, to express the transfer of guilt. That animal must be free from all defect or blemish to make it the more apparent that its blood was shed not for its own deficiencies but for the sin of another. All this was symbolical and typical . . . . And this is what the Scriptures teach concerning the Atonement of Christ. He bore our sins; He was made a curse for us; He suffered the penalty of the law in our stead. All this proceeds on the ground that the sins of one man can be justly, on some adequate ground, imputed to another." [36]

The Scriptures tell us that, "By one man's disobedience the many were made sinners," Romans 5:19. "Through one man sin entered into the world, and death through sin; and so death passed unto all men, for that all sinned," Romans 5:12. "Through one trespass the judgment came unto all men to condemnation" Romans 5:18. It is as if God had said: If sin is to enter, let it enter by one man, so that righteousness also may enter by one man.

Adam was made not only the father but also the representative of the whole human race. And if we fully understood the closeness of the relation between him and them we would fully realize the justice of the transmission of his sin to them. Adam's sin is imputed to his descendants in the same way that Christ's righteousness is imputed to those who believe in Him. Adam's descendants are, of course, no more personally guilty of his sin than Christ's redeemed are personally meritorious of His righteousness.

Suffering and death are declared to be the consequence of sin; and the reason that all die is that "all sinned." Now we know that many suffer and die in infancy, before they have committed any sin themselves. It follows that either God is unjust in punishing the innocent, or that those infants are in some way guilty creatures. And if guilty, how have they sinned? It is impossible to explain it on any other supposition than that they sinned in Adam (1 Corinthians 15:22; Romans 5:12, 18); and they could not have sinned in him in any other way than by representation.

The Reformed Doctrine Of Predestination

But while we are not personally guilty of Adam's sin, we are, nevertheless, liable to punishment for it. "The guilt of Adam's public sin," says Dr. A. A. Hodge, "is by a judicial act of God immediately charged to the account of each and every one of his descendants from the moment he begins to exist, and antecedently to any act of his own. Hence all men come into existence deprived of all those influences of the Holy Spirit upon which their moral and spiritual life depends . . . . and with an antecedent prevailing tendency in their natures to sin; which tendency in them is itself of the nature of sin, and worthy of punishment. Human nature since the fall retains its constitutional faculties of reason, conscience and free agency, and hence man continues to be a responsible moral agent. Yet he is spiritually dead, and totally averse to and incapable of the discharge of any of these duties which spring out of his relation to God, and entirely unable to change his own evil dispositions or innate moral tendencies, or to dispose himself to such a change, or to co-operate with the Holy Spirit in effecting such a change." [37]

And to the same general effect, Dr. R. L. Dabney, the outstanding theologian of the southern Presbyterian Church, says. "The explanation presented by the doctrine of imputation is demanded by all except Pelagians and Socinians. Man's is a spiritually dead and a condemned race. See Ephesians 2:1-5, et passim. He is obviously under a curse for something, from the beginning of his life. Witness the native depravity of infants, and their inheritance of woe and death. Now, either man was tried and fell in Adam, or he has been condemned without trial. He is either under the curse (as it rests on him at the beginning of his existence) for Adam's guilt, or for no guilt at all. Judge which is most honorable to God, a doctrine which, although a profound mystery, represents Him as giving man an equitable and most favored probation in his federal head; or that which makes God condemn him untried, and even before he exists." [38]

6. THE GOODNESS AND SEVERITY OF GOD

A survey of the fall and its extent is humiliating work. It proves to man that all his claims of goodness are unfounded, and it shows him that his only hope is in the sovereign grace of Almighty God. The "graciously restored ability" of which the Arminian talks is not consistent with the facts. The Scriptures, history, and Christian experience by no means warrant such a favorable view of the natural moral condition of man as the Arminian system teaches. On the contrary each of these gives us a very gloomy picture of a fearful corruption and universal inclination to evil, which can only be overcome by the intervention of divine grace. The Calvinistic system teaches a far deeper fall into sin and a far more glorious manifestation of redeeming grace. From these depths the Christian is led to despair of himself, to throw himself unconditionally into the arms of God, and to lay hold on unmerited grace, which alone can save him.

We should see God's mercy and also His severity in the spiritual and physical realms. Life is full of hard facts which, unpleasant though they may be, must simply be faced and admitted. Throughout the Scriptures, and especially in the words of Christ Himself, the final torments of the wicked are described in such ways as to show us that they are indescribably awful. In the gospel of Matthew alone see 5:29, 30; 7:19; 10:28; 11:21-24; 13:30, 41, 42, 49, 50; 18:8, 9, 34; 21:41; 22:14; 24:51; 25:12, 30, 41; and 26:24. Surely a doctrine which received such emphasis from the lips of Christ Himself cannot be passed over in silence distasteful though it may be. In the next world the wicked, with all restraint removed, will go headlong into sin, blaspheming and cursing God, growing worse and worse as they sink deeper and deeper into the bottomless pit. Endless punishment is the penalty of ENDLESS sinning. Furthermore, it is as much the glory of God that He punishes the wicked as that He rewards the righteous. Much of the easy-going indifference toward Christianity in our day is due to the failure of Christian ministers to emphasize these doctrines which Christ taught so repeatedly.

In the physical realm we see God's severity in wars, famines, floods, disasters, diseases, sufferings, deaths, and crimes of all kind which come upon the just and the unjust alike. All of these exist in a world which is under the complete control of a God who is infinite in His perfections.

"Behold then the goodness and severity of God," Romans 11:22. Naturalism does justice to neither of these. Arminianism magnifies the first but neglects the second. Calvinism is the only system which does justice to both. It alone adequately sets forth the facts in regard to the eternal and infinite love of God which caused Him to provide redemption for His people, even at the great cost of sending His only-begotten Son to die on the cross; and also in regard to the awful abyss which exists between sinful man and the holy God. It is true that "God is love," but along with this must be placed the other statement that "our God is a consuming fire," Hebrews 12:29. Any system which omits or under-emphasizes either of these truths will be a mutilated system, no matter how plausible it way sound to men.

This doctrine of the Total Inability of man is terribly stern, severe, forbidding. But it is to be remembered that we are not at liberty to develop a new system suited to our liking. We must take the facts as we find them. Such exhibitions of the true state of mankind are, of course, offensive to unregenerate men generally; and many have tried to find out a system of doctrines more palatable to the popular mind. The state of fallen man is such that he readily listens to any theory which makes him even partly independent of God; he wishes to be the master of his fate and the captain of his soul. The lost, ruined, and helpless state of the sinner needs to be constantly set before him; for until be is brought to feel it, he will never seek help where alone it is to be found. Poor man! truly carnal and sold under sin, not only without power but without inclination to move toward God; and what is more awful still, an actual rebel a presumptuous, blasphemous rival of the Great Jehovah.

This doctrine of Total Inability, or Original Sin, has been treated at some length in order to set forth the fundamental basis upon which the doctrine of Predestination rests. This side of the picture is dark, very dark indeed; but its supplement is the glory of God in redemption. Each of these truths must be seen in its true light before the other can be adequately appreciated.

7. SCRIPTURE PROOF

1 Corinthians 2:14: The natural man receiveth not the things of the Spirit of God: for they are foolishness unto him; and he cannot know them, because they are spiritually judged.

Genesis 2:17: But of the tree of knowledge of good and evil, thou shalt not eat of it; for in the day that thou eatest thereof thou shalt surely die.

Romans 5:12: Therefore, as through one man sin entered into the world, and death through sin; and so death passed unto all men, for that all sinned.

2 Corinthians 1:9: Yea, we ourselves had the sentence of death within ourselves, that we should not trust in ourselves, but in God who raiseth the dead.

Ephesians 2:1-3: And you did He make alive, when ye were dead through your trespasses and sins, wherein ye once walked according to the course of this world, according to the prince of the powers of the air, of the spirit that now worketh in the sons of disobedience; among whom ye also all once lived in the lusts of your flesh, doing the desires of the flesh and of the mind, and were by nature children of wrath, even as the rest.

Ephesians 2:12: Ye were at that time separate from Christ, alienated from the commonwealth of Israel, and strangers from the covenants of promise, having no hope and without God in the world.

Jeremiah 13:23: Can the Ethiopian change his skin or the leopard his spots? Then may ye also do good, that are accustomed to do evil.

Psalm 51:5: Behold, I was brought forth in iniquity; And in sin did my mother conceive me.

John 3:3: Jesus answered and said unto him, Verily, verily, I say unto thee, Except one is born anew, he cannot see the kingdom of God.

Romans 3:10-12: As it is written, There is none righteous, no not one; There is none that understandeth, There is none that seeketh after God; They have all turned aside, they are together become unprofitable; There is none that doeth good. no, not so much as one.

Job 14:4: Who can bring a clean thing out of an unclean? not one.

1 Corinthians 1:18: For the word of the cross is to them that perish foolishness; but unto us who are saved it is the power of God.

Acts 13:41: Behold, ye despisers, and wonder and perish; For I work a work in your days, A work which ye shall in no wise believe, if one declare it unto you.

Proverbs 30:12: There is a generation that are pure in their own eye, And yet are not washed from their filthiness.

John 5:21: For as the Father raiseth the dead and giveth them life, even so the Son also giveth life to whom He will.

John 6:53: Except ye eat the flesh of the Son of man and drink His blood, ye have not life in yourselves.

John 8:19: They said therefore unto Him, Where is thy Father? Jesus answered, Ye know neither me, nor my Father; if ye knew me, ye would know my Father also.

Matthew 11:25: I thank thee, O Father Lord of heaven and earth, that thou didst hide these things from the wise and understanding, and didst reveal them unto babes.

2 Corinthians 5:17: If any man is in Christ, he is a new creature.

John 14:16: (And I will pray the Father, and He shall give you another Comforter, that He may be with you forever,) even the Spirit of truth: whom the world cannot receive; for it beholdeth Him not, neither knoweth Him; ye know Him; for He abideth with you, and shall be in you.

John 3:19: And this is the judgment, that light is come unto the world, and men loved the darkness rather than the light; for their works were evil.

Footnotes:

28. Ch. IX, sec. III
29. Bondage of the Will, p. 125.
30. Warburton, Calvinism, p. 48.
31. Warfield, Biblical Doctrines, p. 440.
32. What is Calvinism, pp. 125-127.
33. A. A. Hodge, pamphlet, Presbyterian Doctrine, p. 23.
34. A. A. Hodge, pamphlet, Presbyterian Doctrine, pp. 19, 20.
35. Warburton, Calvinism, p. 34.
36. Systematic Theology, II, pp. 198, 199, 201.
37. Presbyterian Doctrine, p. 21.
38. Theology, p. 330.

Loraine Boettner D.D.

Chapter XI – Unconditional Election

1. Statement of the Doctrine. 2. Proof from Scripture. 3. Proof from Reason. 4. Faith and Good Works are the Fruits and Proof, not the Basis, of Election. 5. Reprobation. 6. Infralapsarianism and Supralapsarianism. 7. Many are Chosen. 8. A Redeemed World or Race. 9. Vastness of the Redeemed Multitude. 10. The World is Growing Better. 11. Infant Salvation. 12. Summary.

1. STATEMENT OF THE DOCTRINE

The doctrine of Election is to be looked upon as only a particular application of the general doctrine of Predestination or Foreordination as it relates to the salvation of sinners; and since the Scriptures are concerned mainly with the redemption of sinners, this part of the doctrine is naturally thrown up into a place of special prominence. It partakes of all the elements of the general doctrine; and since it is the act of an infinite moral Person, it is represented as being the eternal, absolute, immutable, effective determination by His will of the objects of His saving operations. And no aspect of this elective choice is more constantly emphasized than that of its absolute sovereignty.

The Reformed Faith has held to the existence of an eternal, divine decree which, antecedently to any difference or desert in men themselves separates the human race into two portions and ordains one to everlasting life and the other to everlasting death. So far as this decree relates to men it designates the counsel of God concerning those who had a supremely favorable chance in Adam to earn salvation, but who lost that chance. As a result of the fall they are guilty and corrupted; their motives are wrong and they cannot work out their own salvation. They have forfeited all claim upon God's mercy, and might justly have been left to suffer the penalty of their disobedience as all of the fallen angels were left. But instead the elect members of this race are rescued from this state of guilt and sin and are brought into a state of blessedness and holiness. The non-elect are simply left in their previous state of ruin, and are condemned for their sins. They suffer no unmerited punishment, for God is dealing with them not merely as men but as sinners.

The Westminster Confession states the doctrine thus: "By the decree of God, for the manifestation of His glory, some men and angels are predestinated to everlasting life, and others are foreordained to everlasting death.

"These angels and men, thus predestinated and foreordained, are particularly and unchangeably designed; and their number is so certain and definite that it cannot be either increased or diminished.

"Those of mankind that are predestinated unto life, God, before the foundation of the world was laid, according to His eternal and immutable purpose, and the secret counsel and good pleasure of His will, hath chosen in Christ, unto everlasting glory, out of His mere grace and love, without any foresight of faith or good works, or perseverance in either of them, or any other thing in the creature, as conditions, or causes moving Him thereunto; and all to the praise of His glorious grace.

"As God hath appointed the elect unto glory, so hath He, by the eternal and most free purpose of His will, foreordained all the means thereunto. Whereby they who are elected, being fallen in Adam, are redeemed by Christ, are effectually called unto faith in Christ by His Spirit working in due season; are justified, adopted, sanctified, and kept by His power through faith unto salvation. Neither are any other redeemed by Christ, effectually called, justified, adopted, sanctified, and saved, but the elect only.

"The rest of mankind, God was pleased, according to the unsearchable counsel of His will, whereby He extendeth or withholdeth mercy as He pleaseth, for the glory of His sovereign power over His creatures, to pass by, and to ordain them to dishonor and wrath for their sin, to the praise of His glorious justice." [39]

It is important that we shall have a clear understanding of this doctrine of divine Election, for our views in regard to it determine our views of God, man, the world, and redemption. As Calvin rightly says, "We shall never be clearly convinced as we ought to be that our salvation flows from the fountain of God's free mercy, till we are acquainted with this eternal election, which illustrates the grace of God by this comparison, that He adopts not all promiscuously to the hope of salvation but gives to some what he refuses to others. Ignorance of this principle evidently detracts from the divine glory, and diminishes real humility." [40] Calvin admits that this doctrine arouses very perplexing questions in the minds of some, for, says he, "they consider nothing more unreasonable than that of the common mass of mankind, some should be predestinated to salvation; and others to destruction."

The Reformed Doctrine Of Predestination

The Reformed theologians consistently applied this principle to the actual experience of spiritual phenomena which they themselves felt and saw in others about them. The divine purpose, or Predestination, alone could explain the distinction between good and evil, between the saint and the sinner.

2. PROOF FROM SCRIPTURE

The first question which we need to ask ourselves then, is, Do we find this doctrine taught in the Scriptures? Let us turn to Paul's letter to the Ephesians. There we read: "He chose us in Him before the foundation of the world, that we should be holy and without blemish before Him in love; having foreordained us unto adoption as sons through Jesus Christ unto Himself, according to the good pleasure of His will," 1:4, 5. In Romans 8:29, 30 we read of that golden chain of redemption which stretches from the eternity that is past to the eternity that is to come,--"For whom He foreknew, He also foreordained to be conformed to the image of His Son, that He might be the first-born among many brethren; and whom He foreordained, them He also called: and whom He called, them He also justified: and whom He justified, them He also glorified." Foreknown, foreordained, called, justified, glorified, with always the same people included in each group; and where one of these factors is present, all the others are in principle present with it.

Paul has cast the verse in the past tense because with God the purpose is in principle executed when formed, so certain is it of fulfillment. "These five golden links," says Dr. Warfield, "are welded together in one unbreakable chain, so that all who are set upon in God's gracious distinguishing view are carried on by His grace, step by step, up to the great consummation of that glorification which realizes the promised conformity to the image of God's own Son. It is 'election,' you see, that does all this; for 'whom He foreknew, ... them He also glorified'." [41]

The Scriptures represent election as occurring in past time, irrespective of personal merit, and altogether sovereign,--"The children being not yet born, neither having done anything good or bad, that the purpose of God according to election might stand, not of works, but of Him that calleth, it was said to her, The elder shall serve the younger. Even as it is written, Jacob I loved, but Esau I hated," Romans 9:11, 12. Now if the doctrine of election is not true, we may safely challenge any man to tell us what the apostle means by such language. "We are pointed illustratively to the sovereign acceptance of Isaac and rejection of Ishmael, and to the choice of Jacob and not of Esau before their birth and therefore before either had done good or bad; we are explicitly told that in the matter of salvation it is not of him that wills, or of him that runs, but of God that shows mercy, and that He has mercy on whom He will, and whom He will He hardens; we are pointedly directed to behold in God the potter who makes the vessels which proceed from His hand each for an end of His appointment, that He may work out His will upon them. It is safe to say that language cannot be chosen better adapted to teach Predestination at its height." [42]

Even if we were without any other inspired utterances than those quoted from Paul, so clear and unambiguous are those that we should be constrained to admit that the doctrine of Election finds a place in Scripture. By looking at the Scripture references in the Confession of Faith, we find that it is abundantly sustained in the Bible. If we admit the inspiration of the Bible; if we admit that the writings of the prophets and apostles were breathed by the Spirit of God, and are thus infallible, then what we find there will be sufficient; and thus on the irrefutable testimony of the Scriptures we must acknowledge Election, or Predestination, to be an established truth, and one which we must receive if we are to possess the whole counsel of God. Every Christian must believe in some kind of election; for while the Scriptures leave unexplained many things about the doctrine of Election, they make very plain the FACT that there has been an election.

Christ explicitly declared to His disciples, "Ye did not choose me, but I chose you, and appointed you, that ye should go and bear fruit," John 15:16, by which He made God's choice primary and man's choice only secondary and a result of the former. The Arminian, however, in making salvation depend upon man's choice to use or abuse proffered grace reverses this order and makes man's choice the primary and decisive one. There is no place in the Scriptures for an election which is carefully adjusted to the foreseen actions of the creature. The divine will is never made dependent on the creaturely will for its determinations.

Again the sovereignty of this choice is clearly taught when Paul declares that God commended His love toward us in that while we were yet sinners Christ died for us (Romans 5:8), and that Christ died for the ungodly (Romans 5:6). Here we see that His love was not extended toward us because we were good, but in spite of the fact that we were bad. It is God who chooses the person and causes him to approach unto Him (Psalm 65:4). Arminianism takes this choice out of the hands of God and places it in the hands of man. Any system which substitutes a man-made election falls below the Scripture teaching on this subject.

In the darkest days of Israel's apostasy, as in every other age, it was this principle of election which made a difference between mankind and kept a remnant secure. "Yet will I leave me seven

Loraine Boettner D.D.

thousand in Israel, all the knees which have not bowed unto Baal, and every mouth which hath not kissed him," 1 Kings 19:18. These seven thousand did not stand by their own strength; it is expressly said that God reserved them to Himself, that they might be a remnant.

It is for the sake of the elect that God governs the course of all history (Mark 13:20). They are "the salt of the earth," and "the light of the world;" and so far at least in the world's history they are the few through whom the many are blessed,--God blessed the household of Potiphar for Joseph's sake; and ten righteous people would have saved the city of Sodom. Their election, of course, includes the opportunity of hearing the gospel and receiving the gifts of grace, for without these means the great end of election would not be attained. They are, in fact, elected to all that is included in the idea of eternal life.

Apart from this election of individuals to life, there has been what we may call a national election, or a divine predestination of nations and communities to a knowledge of true religion and to the external privileges of the Gospel. God undoubtedly does choose some nations to receive much greater spiritual and temporal blessings than others. This form of election has been well illustrated in the Jewish nation, in certain European nations and communities, and in America. The contrast is very striking when we compare these with other nations such as China, Japan, India, etc.

Throughout the Old Testament it is repeatedly stated that the Jews were a chosen people. "You only have I known of all the families of the earth," Amos 3:2. "He hath not dealt so with any (other) nation; And as for His ordinances, they have not known them," Psalm 147:20. "For thou art a holy people unto Jehovah thy God: Jehovah thy God hath chosen thee to be a people for His own possession, above all the peoples that are upon the face of the earth," Deuteronomy 7:6. It is made equally plain that God found no merit or dignity in the Jews themselves which moved Him to choose them above others. "Jehovah did not set His love upon you, nor choose you, because ye were more in number than any other people; for ye were the fewest of all peoples: but because Jehovah loveth you, and because He would keep the oath which He sware unto your fathers, hath Jehovah brought you out with a mighty hand, and redeemed you out of the house of bondage from the hand of Pharaoh king of Egypt." Deuteronomy 7:7, 8. And again, "Only Jehovah had a delight in thy fathers to love them, and He chose their seed after them, even above all peoples," Deuteronomy 10:15. Here it is carefully explained, that Israel was honored with the divine choice in contrast with the treatment accorded all the other peoples of the earth, that the choice rested solely on the unmerited love of God, and that It had no foundation in Israel itself.

When Paul was forbidden by the Holy Spirit to preach the Gospel in the province of Asia, and was given the vision of a man in Europe calling across the waters, "Come over into Macedonia, and help us," one section of the world was sovereignly excluded from, and another section was sovereignly given, the privileges of the Gospel. Had the divinely directed call been rather from the shores of India, Europe and America might today have been less civilized than the natives of Tibet. It was the sovereign choice of God which brought the Gospel to the people of Europe and later to America, while the people of the east, and north, and south were left in darkness. We can assign no reason, for instance, why it should have been Abraham's seed, and not the Egyptians or the Assyrians, who were chosen; or why Great Britain and America, which at the time of Christ's appearance on earth were in a state of such complete ignorance, should today possess so largely for themselves, and be disseminating so widely to others, these most important spiritual privileges. The diversities in regard to religious privileges in the different nations is to be ascribed to nothing else than the good pleasure of God.

A third form of election taught in Scripture is that of individuals to the external means of grace, such as hearing and reading the Gospel, association with the people of God, and sharing the benefits of the civilization which has arisen where the Gospel has gone. No one ever had the chance to say at what particular time in the world's history, or in what country, he would be born, whether or not he would be a member of the white race, or of some other. One child is born with health, wealth, and honor, in a favored land, in a Christian home, and grows up with all the blessings which attend the full light of the Gospel. Another is born in poverty and dishonor, of sinful and dissipated parents, and destitute of Christian influences. All of these things are sovereignly decided for them. Surely no one would insist that the favored child has any personal merit which could be the ground for this difference. Furthermore, was it not of God's own choosing that He created us human beings, in His own image, when He might have created us cattle or horses or dogs? Or who would allow the dumb brutes to revile God for their condition in life as though the distinction was unjust? All of these things are due to God's overruling providence, and not to human choice. "Arminians have labored to reconcile all this, as a matter of fact, with their defective and erroneous views of the Divine sovereignty, and with their unscriptural doctrines of universal grace and universal redemption; but they have not usually been satisfied themselves with their own attempts at explanation, and have commonly at last admitted, that there were mysteries in this matter which could not be explained, and which must just be resolved into the sovereignty of God and the unsearchableness of His counsels." [43]

We may perhaps mention a fourth kind of election, that of individuals to certain vocations,--the

The Reformed Doctrine Of Predestination

gifts of special talents which fit one to be a statesman, another to be a doctor, or lawyer, or farmer, or musician, or artisan, gifts of personal beauty, intelligence, disposition, etc. These four kinds of election are in principle the same. Arminians escape no real difficulty in admitting the second, third, and fourth, while denying the first. In each instance God gives to some what He withholds from others. Conditions in the world at large and our own experiences in every day life show us that the blessings bestowed are sovereign and unconditional, irrespective of any previous merit or action on the part of those so chosen. If we are highly favored, we can only be thankful for His blessings; if not highly favored, we have no grounds for complaint. Why precisely this or that one is placed in circumstances which lead to saving faith, while others are not so placed, is indeed, a mystery. We cannot explain the workings of Providence; but we do know that the Judge of all the earth shall do right, and that when we attain to perfect knowledge we shall see that He has sufficient reasons for all His acts.

Furthermore, it may be said that in general the outward conditions with which the individual is surrounded do determine his destiny,--at least to this extent, that those from whom the Gospel is withheld have no chance for salvation. Cunningham has stated this very well in the following paragraph:--"There is an invariable connection established in Gods government of the world, between the enjoyment of outward privileges, or the means of grace, on the one hand, and faith and salvation on the other; in this sense, and to this extent, that the negation of the first implies the negation of the second. We are warranted by the whole tenor of Scripture, in maintaining that where God, in His sovereignty, withholds from men the enjoyment of the means of grace,--an opportunity of becoming acquainted with the only way of salvation,--He at the same time, and by the same means, or ordination, withholds from them the opportunity and power of believing and being saved." [44]

Calvinists maintain that God deals not only with mankind in the mass but with the individuals who are actually saved, that He has elected particular persons to eternal life and to all the means necessary for attaining that life. They admit that some of the passages in which election is mentioned teach only an election of nations, or an election to outward privileges, but they maintain that many other passages teach exclusively and only an election of individuals to eternal life.

There are some, of course, who deny that there has been any such thing as an election at all. They start at the very word as though it were a spectre just come from the shades and never seen before. And yet, in the New Testament alone, the words eklektos, ekloga, and eklego, elect, election, choose, are found some forty-seven or forty-eight times (see Young's Analytical Concordance for complete lists). Others accept the word but attempt to explain away the thing. They profess to believe in a "conditional election," based, as they suppose, upon foreseen faith and evangelical obedience in its objects. This, of course, destroys election in any intelligible sense of the term, and reduces it to a mere recognition or prophecy that at some future time certain persons will be possessed of those qualities. If based on faith and evangelical obedience, then, as it has been cynically phrased, God is careful to elect only those whom He foresees will elect themselves. In the Arminian system election is reduced to a mere word or name, the use of which only tends to involve the subject in greater obscurity and confusion. A mere recognition that those qualities will be present at some future time is, of course, an election falsely so-called, or simply no election at all. And some Arminians, consistently carrying out their own doctrine that the person may or may not accept, and that if he does accept he may fall away again, identify the time of this decree of election with the death of the believer, as if only then his salvation became certain.

Election extends not only to men but also and equally to the angels since they also are a part of God's creation and are under His government. Some of these are holy and happy, others are sinful and miserable. The same reasons which lead us to believe in a predestination of men also lead us to believe in a predestination of angels. The Scriptures confirm this view by references to "elect angels," 1 Timothy 5:21, and "holy angels," Mark 8:38, which are contrasted with wicked angels or demons. We read that God "spared not angels when they sinned, but cast them down to hell, and committed them to pits of darkness to be reserved unto judgment," 2 Peter 2:4; of the "eternal fire which is prepared for the Devil and his angels," Matthew 25:41; of "angels that kept not their own principality, but left their former habitation, He hath kept in everlasting bonds under darkness unto the Judgment of the great day," Jude 6; and of "Michael and his angels going forth to war with the dragon; and the dragon warred and his angels," Revelation 12:7. A study of these passages shows us that, as Dabney says, "there are two kinds of spirits of that order; holy and sinful angels, servants of Christ and servants of Satan; that they were created in an estate of holiness and happiness, and abode in the region called Heaven (God's holiness and goodness are sufficient proof that He would never have created them otherwise); that the evil angels voluntarily forfeited their estate by sinning, and were excluded forever from heaven and holiness; that those who maintained their estate were elected thereto by God, and that their estate of holiness and blessedness is now forever assured." [45]

Paul makes no attempt to explain how God can be just in showing mercy to whom He will and in passing by whom He will. In answer to the objector's question, "Why doth He still find fault?" (with those to whom He has not extended saving mercy), he (Paul) simply resolves the whole thing into the sovereignty of God, by replying, "Nay but, O man, who art thou that repliest against God? Shall the thing formed say to him that formed it, Why hast thou made me thus? Or hath not the potter a right over the clay, from the same lump to make one part a vessel unto honor, and another unto dishonor?" Romans 9:19-21. (And let it be noticed here that Paul says that it is not from different kinds of clay, but "from the same lump," that God, as the potter, makes one vessel unto honor and another unto dishonor.) Paul does not drag God from His throne and set Him before our human reason to be questioned and examined. These secret counsels of His, which even the angels adore with trembling and desire to look into, are left unexplained, except that they are said to be according to His own good pleasure. And after Paul has stated this, he puts forth his hand, as it were, to forbid us from going any further. Had the Arminian assumption been true, namely, that all men are given sufficient grace and that each one is rewarded or punished according to his own use or abuse of this grace, there would have been no difficulty for which to account.

FURTHER SCRIPTURE PROOF

2 Thessalonians 2:13: God chose you from the beginning unto salvation in sanctification of the Spirit and belief of the truth.

Matthew 24:24: There shall arise false Christs, and false prophets, and shall show great signs and wonders; so as to lead astray, if possible, even the elect.

Matthew 24:31: And they (the angels) shall gather together His elect from the four winds, from one end of heaven to the other.

Mark 13:20: For the elect's sake, whom He chose, He shortened those days (at the destruction of Jerusalem).

1 Thessalonians 1:4: Knowing, brethren, beloved of God, your election.

Romans 11:7: The election obtained it, and the rest were hardened.

1 Timothy 5:21: I charge thee in the sight of God, and Jesus Christ, and the elect angels.

Romans 8:33: Who shall lay anything to the charge of God's elect?

Romans 11:5: (In comparison with Elijah's time) Even so at the present time also there is a remnant according to the election of grace.

2 Timothy 2:10: I endure all things for the elect's sake.

Titus 1:1: Paul, a servant of God, and an apostle of Jesus Christ, according to the faith of God's elect.

1 Peter 1:1: Peter, an apostle of Jesus Christ, to the elect.

1 Peter 5:13: She that is in Babylon, elect together with you.

1 Peter 2:9: But ye are an elect race.

1 Thessalonians 5:9: For God appointed us not unto wrath, but unto the obtaining of salvation through our Lord Jesus Christ.

Acts 18:48: And as the Gentiles heard this, they were glad, and glorified the word of God; and as many as were ordained to eternal life believed.

John 17:9: I (Jesus) pray not for the world, but for those whom thou hast given me; for they are thine.

John 6:37: All that the Father giveth me shall come unto me.

John 6:65: No man can come unto me. except it be given unto him of the Father.

John 13:18: I speak not of you all; I know whom I have chosen.

John 15:16: Ye did not choose me, but I chose you.

Psalm 105:6: Ye children of Jacob, His chosen ones.

Romans 9:23: Vessels of mercy, which He afore prepared unto glory. (See also references already quoted in this chapter; Ephesians 1:4, 5, 11; Romans 9:11-13; 8:29, 30; etc.)

3. PROOF FROM REASON

If the doctrine of Total Inability or Original Sin be admitted, the doctrine of unconditional Election follows by the most inescapable logic. If, as the Scriptures and experience tell us, all men are by nature in a state of guilt and depravity from which they are wholly unable to deliver themselves and have no claim whatever on God for deliverance, it follows that if any are saved God must choose out those who shall be the objects of His grace. His love for fallen men expressed itself in the choice of an innumerable multitude of them for salvation, and in the provision of a redeemer, who, acting as their federal head and representative, assumed their guilt, paid their penalty, and earned their salvation. It is always to the love of God that the Scriptures ascribe the elective decree, and they are never weary of raising our eyes from the decree itself to the motive which lay behind it. The doctrine that men are saved only through the unmerited love and grace of God finds its full and honest expression only in the doctrines of Calvinism.

Through the election of individuals the truly gracious character of salvation is most clearly shown. Those who declare that salvation is entirely by the grace of God, and yet deny the doctrine of election, hold an inconsistent position. The inspired writers leave no means unused to drive home the fact that

The Reformed Doctrine Of Predestination

God's election of men is an absolutely sovereign one, founded solely upon His unmerited love, and designed to exhibit before men and angels His grace and saving mercy.

As Ruler and Judge, God is at liberty to deal with a world of sinners according to His own good pleasure. He can rightfully pardon some and condemn others; can rightfully give His saving grace to one and not to another. Since all have sinned and come short of His glory, He is free to have mercy on whom He will have mercy. It is not of him that willeth, nor of him that runneth, but of God who showeth mercy; and the reason why any are saved, and why one rather than another is saved, is to be found alone in the good pleasure of Him who ordereth all things after the counsel of His own will. It is for this reason that before God created the world He chose all those to whom He would freely give the inheritance of eternal blessedness, and the Biblical writers take special pains to give each individual believer in all the enormous multitude of the saved the assurance that from all eternity he has been the peculiar object of the divine choice, and is only now fulfilling the high destiny designed for him from the foundation of the world.

This doctrine of eternal and unconditional election has sometimes been called the "heart" of the Reformed Faith. It emphasizes the sovereignty and grace of God in salvation, while the Arminian view emphasizes the work of faith and obedience in the man who decides to accept the offered grace. In the Calvinistic system it is God alone who chooses those who are to be the heirs of heaven, those with whom He will share His riches in glory; while in the Arminian system it is, in the ultimate analysis, man who determines this,--a principle somewhat lacking in humility to say the least.

It may be asked, Why does God save some and not others? But that belongs to His secret counsels. Precisely why this man receives, and that man does not receive, when neither deserves to receive, we are not told. That God was pleased to set upon us in this His electing grace must ever remain for us a matter of adoring wonder. Certainly there was nothing in us, whether of quality or deed, which could attract His favorable notice or make Him partial to us; for we were dead in trespasses and sins and children of wrath even as others (Ephesians 2:1-3). We can only admire, and wonder, and exclaim with Paul, "O the depth of the riches both of the wisdom and knowledge of God! how unsearchable are His judgments, and His ways past tracing out!" The marvel of marvels is not that God, in His infinite love and justice, has not elected all of this guilty race to be saved, but that He has elected any. When we consider, on the one hand, what a heinous thing sin is, together with its desert of punishment, and on the other, what holiness is, together with God's perfect hatred for sin, the marvel is that God could get the consent of His holy nature to save a single sinner. Furthermore, the reason that God did not choose all to eternal life was not because He did not wish to save all, but that for reasons which we cannot fully explain a universal choice would have been inconsistent with His perfect righteousness.

Nor may any one object that this view represents God an acting arbitrarily and without reason. To assert that is to assert more than any man knows. His reasons for saving particular ones while passing others by have not been revealed to us. "He doeth according to His will in the armies of heaven, and among the inhabitants of the earth," Daniel 4:35. Some are foreordained as sons, "according to the good pleasure of His will," Ephesians 1:5; but that does not mean that He has no reasons for choosing one and leaving another. When a regiment is decimated for insubordination, the fact that every tenth man is chosen for death is for reasons; but the reasons are not in the men.

Undoubtedly God has the best of reasons for choosing one and rejecting another, although He has not told what they are.

"May not the Sov'reign Lord on high Dispense His favors as He will; Choose some to life, while others die, And yet be just and gracious still? Shall man reply against the Lord, And call his Maker's ways unjust? The thunder whose dread word Can crush a thousand worlds to dust.

But, O my soul, if truths so bright Should dazzle and confound thy sight, 'Yet still His written will obey, And wait the great decisive day!" [46]

4. FAITH AND GOOD WORKS ARE THE FRUITS AND PROOF, NOT THE BASIS, OF ELECTION

Neither predestination in general, nor the election of those who are to be saved, is based on God's foresight of any action in the creature. This tenet of the Reformed Faith has been well stated in the Westminster Confession, where we read: "Although God knows whatsoever may or can come to pass upon all supposed conditions; yet hath He not decreed any thing because He foresaw it as future, or as that which would come to pass upon such conditions." And again, "These good works, done in obedience to God's commandments, are the fruits and evidences of a true and lively faith; and by them believers manifest their thankfulness, strengthen their assurance, edify their brethren, adorn the profession of the gospel, stop the mouths of the adversaries, and glorify God, whose workmanship they are, created in Christ Jesus thereunto; that, having their fruit unto holiness, they may have the end, eternal life.

"Their ability to do good works is not at all of themselves, but wholly from the Spirit of Christ. And that they may be enabled thereunto, besides the graces they already received, there is required an actual influence of the same Holy Spirit to work in them to will and to do of His good pleasure; yet are

Loraine Boettner D.D.

they not hereupon to grow negligent, as if they were not bound to perform any duty unless upon a special motion of the Spirit; but they ought to be diligent in stirring up the grace of God that is in them."
47

Foreseen faith and good works, then, are never to be looked upon as the cause of the Divine election. They are rather its fruits and proof. They show that the person has been chosen and regenerated. To make them the basis of election involves us again in a covenant of works, and places God's purposes in time rather than in eternity. This would not be pre-destination but post-destination, an inversion of the Scripture account which makes faith and holiness to be the consequents, and not the antecedents, of election (Ephesians 1:4; John 15:16; Titus 3:5). The statement that we were chosen in Christ "before the foundation of the world," excludes any consideration of merit in us; for the Hebrew idiom, "before the foundation of the world," means that the thing was done in eternity. And when to Paul's statement that it is "not of works, but of Him that calleth," the Arminian replies that it is of future works, he flatly contradicts the apostle's own words.

That the decree of election was in any way based on foreknowledge is refuted by Paul when he says that its purpose was "that we should be holy," Ephesians 1:4. He insists that salvation is "not of works, that no man should glory." In 2 Timothy 1:9 we read that it is God "who saved us, and called us with a holy calling, not according to our works, but according to His own purpose and grace, which was given us in Christ Jesus before times eternal." Calvinists therefore hold that election precedes, and is not based upon, any good works which the person does. The very essence of the doctrine is that in redemption God is moved by no consideration of merit or goodness in the objects of His saving mercy. "That it is not of him that runs, nor of him that wills, but of God who shows mercy, that the sinner obtains salvation, is the steadfast witnesses of the whole body of Scripture, urged with such reiteration and in such varied connections as exclude the possibility that there may lurk behind the act of election consideration of foreseen characters or acts or circumstances--all of which appear as results of election."
48

Foreordination in general cannot rest on foreknowledge; for only that which is certain can be foreknown, and only that which is predetermined can be certain. The Almighty and all-sovereign Ruler of the universe does not govern Himself on the basis of a foreknowledge of things which might haply come to pass. Through the Scriptures the divine foreknowledge is ever thought of as dependent on the divine purpose, and God foreknows only because He has pre-determined. His foreknowledge is but a transcript of His will as to what shall come to pass in the future, and the course which the world takes under His providential control is but the execution of His all-embracing plan. His foreknowledge of what is yet to be, whether it be in regard to the world as a whole or in regard to the, detailed life of every individual, rests upon His pre-arranged plan (Jeremiah 1:5; Psalm 139:14-16; Job 23:13, 14; 28:26, 27; Amos 3:7).

There is, however, one Scripture passage which is often pointed out as teaching that election or even fore-ordination in general is based on foreknowledge, and we shall now give our attention to it. In Romans 8:29, 30 we read: "For whom He foreknew, He also foreordained to be conformed to the image of His Son, that He might be the firstborn among many brethren; and whom He foreordained, them He also called; and whom He called, them He also justified; and whom He justified, them He also glorified." The word "know" is sometimes used in a sense other than that of having merely an intellectual perception of the thing mentioned. It occasionally means that the persons so "known" are the special and peculiar objects of God's favor, as when it was said of the Jews, "You only have I known of all the families of the earth," Amos 3:2. Paul wrote, "If any man loveth God, the same is known of Him," 1 Corinthians 8:3. Jesus is said to "know" His sheep, John 10:14, 27; and to the wicked He is to say, "I never knew you," Matthew 7:23. In the first Psalm we read, "Jehovah knoweth the way of the righteous, But the way of the wicked shall perish."

In all of these passages more than a mental recognition is involved, for God has that of the wicked as well as of the righteous. It is a knowing which has as its objects the elect only, and it is connected with, or is rather the same as love, favor, and approbation. Those in Romans 8:29 are foreknown in the sense that they are fore-appointed to be the special objects of His favor. This is shown more plainly in Romans 11:2-5, where we read, "God did not cast off His people whom He foreknew." A comparison is made with the time of Elijah when God "left for Himself" seven thousand who did not bow the knee to Baal. And then in the fifth verse he adds, "Even so then at this present time also there is a remnant according to the election of grace." Those who were foreknown in verse two and those who are of the election of grace are the same people; hence they were foreknown in the sense that they were fore-appointed to be the objects of His gracious purposes. Notice especially that Romans 8:29 does not say that they were foreknown as doers of good works, but that they were foreknown as individuals to whom God would extend the grace of election. And let it be noticed further that if Paul had here used the term "foreknow" in the sense that election was based on mere foreknowledge, it would have contradicted his statement elsewhere that it is according to the good pleasure of God.

The Arminian view takes election out of the hands of God and puts it into the hands of man. This

The Reformed Doctrine Of Predestination

makes the purposes of Almighty God to be conditioned by the precarious wills of apostate men and makes temporal events to be the cause of His eternal acts. It means further that He has created a set of sovereign beings upon whom to a certain extent His will and actions are dependent. It represents God as a good old father who endeavors to get his children to do right, but who is usually defeated because of their perverse wills; nay, it represents Him as having evolved a plan which through the ages has been so generally defeated that it has sent innumerably more persons to hell than to heaven. A doctrine which leads to such absurdities is not only un-Scriptural but unreasonable and dishonoring to God. In contrast to all this, Calvinism offers us a great God who is infinite in His perfections, who dispenses mercy and justice as He sees best, and who actually rules in the affairs of men.

The Scriptures and Christian experience teach us that the very faith and repentance through which we are saved are themselves the gifts of God. "By grace have ye been saved through faith, and that not of yourselves, it is the gift of God," Ephesians 2:8. The Christians in Achaia had "believed through grace," Acts 18:27. A man is not saved because he believes in Christ; he believes in Christ because he is saved. Even the beginning of faith, the disposition to seek salvation, is itself a work of grace and the gift of God. Paul often says that we are saved "through" faith (that is, as the instrumental cause), but never once does he say that we are saved "on account of" faith (that is, as the meritorious cause). And to the same effect we may say that the redeemed shall be rewarded in proportion to their good works, but not on account of them. And in accordance with this, Augustine says that "The elect of God are chosen by Him to be His children, in order that they might be made to believe, not because He foresaw that they would believe."

Repentance is equally declared to be a gift. "Then to the Gentiles also hath God granted repentance unto life," Acts 11:18. "Him did God exalt with His right hand to be a Prince and Savior, to give repentance to Israel and remission of sins," Acts 5:31. Paul rebuked those who did not realize that it was the goodness of God which led them to repentance, Romans 2:4. Jeremiah cried, "Turn thou me and I shall be turned; for thou art Jehovah my God. Surely after that I was turned, I repented; and after that I was instructed," Jeremiah 31:18, 19. What, for instance, had the infant John the Baptist to do with his being "filled with the Holy Spirit even from his mother's womb?" Luke 1:15. Jesus told His disciples that to them it was given to know the mysteries of the kingdom of heaven, but that to others it was not given (Matthew 13:11). To base election on foreseen faith is to say that we are ordained to eternal life because we believe, whereas the Scriptures declare the contrary: "As many as were ordained to eternal life believed," Acts 13:48.

Our salvation is "not by works done in righteousness which we did ourselves. but according to His mercy He saved us, through the washing of regeneration, and renewing of the Holy Spirit," Titus 3:5. We are encouraged to work out our own salvation with fear and trembling, for it is God who worketh in us, both to will and to do of His good pleasure. And just because God is working in us, we strive to develop and to work out our own salvation (Philippians 2:12, 13). The Psalmist tells us that the Lord's people offer themselves willingly in the day of His power (110:3). Hence conversion is a peculiar and sovereign gift of God. The sinner has no power to turn himself unto God, but is turned or renewed by divine grace before he can do anything spiritually good. In accordance with this Paul teaches that love, joy, peace, goodness, faithfulness. self-control, etc., are not the meritorious basis of salvation, but rather "the fruits of the Spirit," Galatians 5:22, 23. Paul himself was chosen that he might know and do the will of God, not because it was foreseen that he would do it, Acts 22:14, 15. Augustine tells us that, "The grace of God does not find men fit to be elected, but makes them so"; and again, "The nature of the Divine goodness is not only to open to those that knock, but also to cause them to knock and ask." Luther expressed the same truth when he said, "God alone by His Spirit works in us the merit and reward." John tells us that, "We love because He first loved us," 1 John 4:19. These passages unmistakably teach that faith and good works are the fruits of God's work in us. We were not chosen because we were good, but in order that we might become good.

But while good works are not the ground of salvation, they are absolutely essential to it as its fruits and evidences. They are produced by faith as naturally as grapes are produced by the grape vine. And while they do not make us righteous before God, yet they are so united with faith that true faith cannot be found without them. Nor can good works, in the strict sense, be found anywhere without faith. Our salvation is not "of works," but "for good works," Ephesians 2:9, 10; and the genuinely saved Christian will feel himself in his natural element only when producing good works, James points out that a man's faith is spurious if it does not issue in good works. This is the same principle which Jesus set forth when He declared that the character of a tree is shown by its fruits, and that a good tree could not bear evil fruits. Good works are as natural for the Christian as is breathing; he does not breathe to get life; he breathes because he has life, and for that reason cannot help breathing. Good works are his glory; hence Jesus says, "Let your light so shine before men that they may see your good works and glorify (not you, but) your Father who is in heaven," to whom the credit is really due.

The Calvinistic view is the only logical one if we accept the Scriptural declaration that salvation is by grace. Any other involves us in a hopeless chaos of views which are contradictory to the Scriptures.

Loraine Boettner D.D.

There are, of course, mysteries connected with this view; and it is certainly not the view which the natural man would have hit upon if he had been called upon to suggest a plan. But to throw overboard the Scripture doctrine of Predestination simply because it does not fit in with our prejudices and preconceived notions is to act foolishly. To do this is to arraign the Creator at the bar of human reason, to deny the wisdom and righteousness of His dealings just because we cannot fathom them, and then to declare His revelation to be false and deceptive.

"It is a dangerous presumption for men to take upon themselves, with unwashed hands, to unriddle the deep mysteries of God with their carnal reason, where the great apostle stands at the gaze, crying, 'O the depth, how unsearchable' and, 'Who knoweth the mind of the Lord!' Had Paul been of the Arminian persuasion he would have answered, 'Those are elected that are foreseen to believe and persevere!'" [49] There would have been no mystery at all if salvation had been based on their good works.

Here we have a system in which all boasting is excluded, and in which salvation in all of its parts is seen to be the product of unalloyed grace, not founded on, but issuing in, good works.

5. REPROBATION

Statement--Comments by Calvin, Luther, and Warfield--Proof from Scripture--Based on the Doctrine of Original Sin--No Injustice is Done to the Non-Elect--State of the Heathens--Purposes of the Decree of Reprobation--Arminians Center Attack on this Doctrine--Under no Obligation to Explain all These Things.

The doctrine of absolute Predestination of course logically holds that some are foreordained to death as truly as others are foreordained to life. The very terms "elect" and "election" imply the terms "non-elect" and "reprobation." When some are chosen out others are left not chosen. The high privileges and glorious destiny of the former are not shared with the latter. This, too, is of God. We believe that from all eternity God has intended to leave some of Adam's posterity in their sins, and that the decisive factor in the life of each is to be found only in God's will. As Mozley has said, the whole race after the fall was "one mass of perdition," and "it pleased God of His sovereign mercy to rescue some and to leave others where they were; to raise some to glory, giving them such grace as necessarily qualified them for it, and abandon the rest, from whom He withheld such grace, to eternal punishments." [50]

The chief difficulty with the doctrine of Election of course arises in regard to the unsaved; and the Scriptures have given us no extended explanation of their state. Since the mission of Jesus in the world was to save the world rather than to judge it, this side of the matter is less dwelt upon.

In all of the Reformed creeds in which the doctrine of Reprobation is dealt with at all it is treated as an essential part of the doctrine of Predestination. The Westminster Confession, after stating the doctrine of election, adds: "The rest of mankind, God was pleased, according to the inscrutable counsel of His own will, whereby He extendeth or withholdeth mercy as He pleaseth, for the glory of His sovereign power over His creatures, to pass by, and to ordain them to dishonor and wrath for their sin, to the praise of His glorious justice." [51]

Those who hold the doctrine of Election but deny that of Reprobation can lay but little claim to consistency. To affirm the former while denying the latter makes the decree of predestination an illogical and lop-sided decree. The creed which states the former but denies the latter will resemble a wounded eagle attempting to fly with but one wing. In the interests of a "mild Calvinism" some have been inclined to give up the doctrine of Reprobation, and this term (in itself a very innocent term) has been the entering wedge for harmful attacks upon Calvinism pure and simple. "Mild Calvinism" is synonymous with sickly Calvinism, and sickness, if not cured, is the beginning of the end.

Comments by Calvin, Luther, and Warfield

Calvin did not hesitate to base the reprobation of the lost, as well as the election of the saved, on the eternal purpose of God. We have already quoted him to the effect that "not all men are created with a similar destiny but eternal life is foreordained for some, and eternal damnation for others. Every man, therefore, being created for one or the other of these ends, we say, he is predestinated either to life or to death." And again he says, "There can be no election without its opposite, reprobation." [52] That the latter raises problems which are not easy to solve, he readily admits, but advocates it as the only intelligent and Scriptural explanation of the facts.

Luther also as certainly as Calvin attributes the eternal perdition of the wicked, as well as the eternal salvation of the righteous, to the plan of God. "This mightily offends our rational nature," he says, "that God should, of His own mere unbiased will, leave some men to themselves, harden them and condemn them; but He gives abundant demonstration, and does continually, that this is really the case; namely, that the sole cause why some are saved, and others perish, proceeds from His willing the salvation of the former, and the perdition of the latter, according to that of St. Paul, 'He hath mercy on whom He will have mercy, and whom He will He hardeneth.'" And again, "It may seem absurd to human wisdom that God should harden, blind, and deliver up some men to a reprobate sense; that He should first deliver them over to evil, and condemn them for that evil; but the believing, spiritual man sees no absurdity at all in this; knowing that God would be never a whit less good, even though He

The Reformed Doctrine Of Predestination

should destroy all men." He then goes on to say that this must not be understood to mean that God finds men good, wise, obedient, and makes them evil, foolish, and obdurate, but that they are already depraved and fallen and that those who are not regenerated, instead of becoming better under the divine commands and influences, only react to become worse. In reference to Romans IX, X, XI, Luther says that "all things whatever arise from and depend upon the Divine appointment, whereby it was preordained who should receive the word of life and who should disbelieve it, who should be delivered from their sins and who should be hardened in them, who should be justified and who condemned." [53]

"The Biblical writers," says Dr. Warfield, "are as far as possible from obscuring the doctrine of election because of any seemingly unpleasant corollaries that flow from it. On the contrary, they expressly draw the corollaries which have often been so designated, and make them a part of their explicit teaching. Their doctrine of election, they are free to tell us, for example, does certainly involve a corresponding doctrine of preterition. The very term adopted in the New Testament to express it--eklegomai, which, as Meyer justly says (Ephesians 1:4), 'always has, and must of logical necessity have, a reference to others to whom the chosen would, without the ekloga, still belong'--embodies a declaration of the fact that in their election others are passed by and left without the gift of salvation; the whole presentation of the doctrine is such as either to imply or openly to assert, on its very emergence, the removal of the elect by the pure grace of God, not merely from a state of condemnation, but out of the company of the condemned--a company on whom the grace of God has no saving effect, and who are therefore left without hope in their sins; and the positive just reprobation of the impenitent for their sins is repeatedly explicitly taught in sharp contrast with the gratuitous salvation of the elect despite their sins." [54]

And again he says: "The difficulty which is felt by some in following the apostle's argument here (Romans 11 f), we may suspect, has its roots in part in a shrinking from what appears to them an arbitrary assignment of men to diverse destinies without consideration of their desert. Certainly St. Paul as explicitly affirms the sovereignty of reprobation as election,--if these twin ideas are, indeed, separable even in thought; if he represents God as sovereignly loving Jacob, he represents Him equally as sovereignly hating Esau; if he declares that He has mercy on whom He will, He equally declares that He hardens whom He will. Doubtless the difficulty often felt here is, in part, an outgrowth of an insufficient realization of St. Paul's basal conception of the state of men at large as condemned sinners before an angry God. It is with a world of lost sinners that he represents God as dealing; and out of that world building up a Kingdom of Grace. Were not all men sinners, there might still be an election, as sovereign as now; and there being an election, there would still be as sovereign a rejection; but the rejection would not be a rejection to punishment, to destruction, to eternal death, but to some other destiny consonant to the state in which those passed by should be left. It is not indeed, then, because men are sinners that men are left unelected; election is free, and its obverse of rejection must be equally free; but it is solely because men are sinners that what they are left to is destruction. And it is in this universalism of ruin rather than in a universalism of salvation that St. Paul really roots his theodicy. When all deserve death it is a marvel of pure grace that any receive life; and who shall gainsay the right of Him who shows this miraculous mercy, to have mercy on whom He will, and whom He will to harden?" [55]

Proof from Scripture

This is admittedly an unpleasant doctrine. It is not taught to gain favor with men, but only because it is the plain teaching of the Scriptures and the logical counterpart of the doctrine of Election. We shall find that some Scripture passages do teach the doctrine with unmistakable clearness. These should be sufficient for any one who accepts the Bible as the word of God. "Jehovah hath made everything for its own end; Yea, even the wicked for the day of evil," Proverbs 16:4. Christ is said to be to the wicked, "A stone of stumbling, and a rock of offence; for they stumble at the word, being disobedient; whereunto also they were appointed," 1 Peter 2:8. "For there are certain men crept in privily, even they who were of old written of beforehand to this condemnation, ungodly men, turning the grace of our God into lasciviousness, and denying our only Master and Lord, Jesus Christ," Jude 4. "But these, as creatures without reason, born mere animals to be taken and destroyed, railing in matters whereof they are ignorant, shall in their destroying surely be destroyed," 2 Peter 2:12. "For God did put in their heart to do His mind, and to come to one mind, and to give their kingdom unto the beast, until the word of God should be accomplished," Revelation 17:17. Concerning the beast of St. John's vision it is said, "All that dwell on the earth shall worship him, every one whose name hath not been written from the foundation of the world in the book of life of the lamb that hath been slain," Revelation 13:8. and we may contrast these with the disciples whom Jesus told to rejoice because their names were written in heaven (Luke 10:20), and with Paul's fellow workers. "whose names are in the book of life," Philippians 4:3.

Paul declares that the "vessels of wrath" which by the Lord were "fitted unto destruction," were "endured with much long suffering" in order that He might "show His wrath, and make His power known"; and with these are contrasted the "vessels of mercy, which He afore prepared unto glory" in

Loraine Boettner D.D.

order "that He might make known the riches of His glory" upon them (Romans 9:22, 23). Concerning the heathen it is said that "God gave them up unto a reprobate mind, to do those things which are not fitting," Romans 1:28; and the wicked, "after his hardness and impenitent heart treasures up for himself wrath in the day of wrath and revelation of the righteous judgment of God," Romans 2:5.

In regard to those who perish Paul says, "God sendeth them a working of error, that they should believe a lie," 2 Thessalonians 2:11. They are called upon to behold these things in an external way, to wonder at them, and to go on perishing in their sins. Hear the words of Paul in the synagogue at Antioch in Pisidia: "Behold, ye despisers, and wonder, and perish; For I work a work in your days, A work which ye shall in no wise believe, if one declare it unto you," Acts 13:41.

The apostle John, after narrating that the people still disbelieved although Jesus had done so many signs before them, adds, "For this cause they could not believe, for that Isaiah said again, He hath blinded their eyes, and He hardened their heart; Lest they should see with their eyes, and perceive with their heart, And should turn, And I should heal them," John 12:39, 40.

Christ's command to the wicked in the final judgment, "Depart from me, ye cursed, into the eternal fire which is prepared for the Devil and his angels," Matthew 25:41, is the strongest possible decree of reprobation; and it is the same in principle whether issued in time or eternity. What is right for God to do in time it is not wrong for Him to include in His eternal plan.

On one occasion Jesus Himself declared: "For judgment came I into this world, that they that see not may see; and that they that see may become blind," John 9:39. On another occasion He said, "I thank thee, O Father, Lord of heaven and earth, that thou didst hide these things from the wise and understanding, and didst reveal them unto babes," Matthew 11:25. It Is hard for us to realize that the adorable Redeemer and only Savior of men is, to some, a stone of stumbling and a rock of offence; yet that is what the Scriptures declare Him to be. Even before His birth it was said that He was set (that is, appointed) for the falling, as well as for the rising, of many in Israel (Luke 2:34). And when, in His intercessory prayer in the garden of Gethsemane, He said, "I pray for them; I pray not for the world, but for those whom thou hast given me," the non-elect were repudiated in so many words.

Jesus Himself declared that one of the reasons why He spoke in parables was that the truth might be concealed from those for whom it was not intended. We shall let the sacred history speak for itself: "And the disciples came, and said unto Him, Why speakest thou unto them in parables? And He answered and said unto them, Unto you it is given to know the mysteries of the kingdom of heaven, but unto them it is not given. For whosoever hath, to him shall be given, and he shall have abundance; but whosoever hath not, from him shall be taken away even that which he hath. Therefore speak I unto them in parables; because seeing they see not, and hearing they hear not, neither do they understand. And unto them is fulfilled the prophecy of Isaiah, which saith,

> "By hearing ye shall hear, and shall In no wise understand;
> And seeing ye shall see, and shall in no wise perceive;
> For this people's heart is waxed gross.
> And their ears are dull of hearing.
> And their eyes they have closed;
> Lest haply they should perceive with their eyes,
> And hear with their ears,
> And understand with their heart,
> And, should turn again,
> And I should heal them."
> Matthew 13:10-15; Isaiah 6:9, 10.

In these words we have an application of Jesus' words, "Give not that which is holy unto the dogs, neither cast your pearls before swine," Matthew 7:6. He who affirms that Christ designed to give His saving truth to every one flatly contradicts Christ Himself. To the non-elect, the Bible is a sealed book; and only to the true Christian is it "given" to see and understand these things. So important is this truth that the Holy Spirit has been pleased to repeat six times over in the New Testament this passage from Isaiah (Matthew 13:14, 15; Mark 4:12; Luke 8:10; John 12:40; Acts 28:27; Romans 11:9, 10). Paul tells us that through grace the "election" received salvation, and that the rest were hardened; then he adds, "God gave them a spirit of stupor, eyes that they should not see, and ears that they should not hear." And further, he quotes the words of David to the same effect:

> "Let their table be made a snare and a trap,
> And a stumbling-block, and a recompense unto them;
> Let their eyes be darkened, that they may not see,
> And bow down their backs always," Romans 11:8-10.

The Reformed Doctrine Of Predestination

Hence as regards some, the evangelical proclamations were designed to harden, and not to heal.

This same doctrine finds expression in numerous other parts of Scripture. Moses said to the children of Israel, "But Sihon king of Heshbon would not let you pass by him; for Jehovah thy God hardened his spirit, and made his heart obstinate, that He might deliver him into thy hand, as at this day," Deuteronomy 2:30. In regard to the Canaanitish tribes who came against Joshua it is written, "For it was of Jehovah to harden their hearts, to come against Israel in battle, that He might utterly destroy them, as Jehovah commanded Moses." Joshua 11:20. Hophni and Phinebas, the sons of Eli, when reproved for their wickedness, "hearkened not unto the voice of their father, because Jehovah was minded to slay them," 1 Samuel 2:25. Though Pharaoh acted very arrogantly and wickedly toward the Israelites, Paul assigns no other reason than that he was one of the reprobate whose evil actions were to be overruled for good: "For the Scripture saith unto Pharaoh, For this very purpose did I raise thee up, that I might show in thee my power, and that my name might be published abroad in all the earth," Romans 9:17 (see also Exodus 9:16). In all the reprobate there is a blindness and an obstinate hardness of heart; and when any, like Pharaoh, are said to have been hardened of God we may be sure that they were already in themselves worthy of being delivered over to Satan. The hearts of the wicked are, of course, never hardened by the direct influence of God,--He simply permits some men to follow out the evil impulses which are already in their hearts, so that, as a result of their own choices, they become more and more calloused and obstinate. And while it is said, for instance, that God hardened the heart of Pharaoh, it is also said that Pharaoh hardened his own heart (Exodus 8:15; 8:32; 9:34). One description is given from the divine view-point, the other is given from the human view-point. God is ultimately responsible for the hardening of the heart in that He permits it to occur, and the inspired writer in graphic language simply says that God does it; but never are we to understand that God is the immediate and efficient cause.

Although this doctrine is harsh, it is, nevertheless, Scriptural. And since it is so plainly taught in Scripture, we can assign no reason for the opposition which it has met other than the pure ignorance and unreasoned prejudice with which men's minds have been filled when they come to study it. How applicable here are the words of Rice:--"Happily would it be for the Church of Christ and for the world, if Christian ministers and Christian people could be contented to be disciples,--LEARNERS; if, conscious of their limited faculties, their ignorance of divine things, and their proneness to err through depravity and prejudice, they could be induced to sit at the feet of Jesus and learn of Him. The Church has been corrupted and cursed in almost every age by the undue confidence of men in their reasoning powers. They have undertaken to pronounce upon the reasonableness or unreasonableness of doctrines infinitely above their reason, which are necessarily matters of pure revelation. In their presumption they have sought to comprehend 'the deep things of God,' and have interpreted the Scriptures, not according to their obvious meaning, but according to the decisions of the finite reason." And again he says, "No one ever studied the works of Nature or the Book of Revelation without finding himself encompassed on every side by difficulties he could not solve. The philosopher is obliged to be satisfied with facts; and the theologian must content himself with God's declarations." [56]

Strange to say, many of those who insist that when people come to study the doctrine of the Trinity they should put aside all preconceived notions and should not rely simply upon the unaided human reason to decide what can or cannot be true of God, and who insist that the Scriptures should be accepted here as the unquestioned and authoritative guide, are not willing to follow those rules in the study of the doctrine of Predestination.

The Doctrine of Reprobation is Based on the Doctrine of Original Sin; No Injustice is Done to the Non-elect

It Is obvious that this part of the doctrine of Predestination which affirms that God has, by a sovereign and eternal decree, chosen one portion of mankind to salvation while leaving the other portion to destruction, strikes us at first as being opposed to our common ideas of justice and hence needs a defence. The defence of the doctrine of Reprobation rests upon the preceding doctrine of Original Sin or Total Inability. This decree finds the whole race fallen. None have any claim on God's grace. But instead of leaving all to their just punishment, God gratuitously confers undeserved happiness upon one portion of mankind,--an act of pure mercy and grace to which no one can object,--while the other portion is simply passed by. No undeserved misery is inflicted upon this latter group. Hence no one has any right to object to this part of the decree. If the decree dealt simply with innocent men, it would be unjust to assign one portion to condemnation; but since it deals with men in a particular state, which is a state of guilt and sin, it is not unjust. "The conception of the world as lying in the evil one and therefore judged already (John 8:18), so that upon those who are not removed from the evil of the world the wrath of God is not so much to be poured out but simply abides (John 3:36, cf. 1 John 3:14), is fundamental to this whole presentation. It is therefore, on the one hand, that Jesus represents Himself as having come not to condemn the world, but to save the world (John 8:17; 8:12; 9:5; 12:47; cf. 4:42), and all that He does as having for its end the introduction of life into the world (John 6:33, 51) ; the already condemned world needs no further condemnation, it needs saving." [57]

Guilty man has lost his rights and falls under the will of God. God's absolute sovereignty now comes in and when He shows mercy in some cases we cannot object to His justice in others unless we would call in question His government of the universe. Viewed in this light the decree of Predestination finds mankind one mass of perdition and allows only a portion of it to remain such. When all antecedently deserved punishment it was not unjust for some to be antecedently consigned to it; otherwise the execution of a just sentence would be unjust.

"When the Arminian says that faith and works constitute the ground of election we dissent," says Clark. "But if he says that foreseen unbelief and disobedience constitute the ground of reprobation we assent readily enough. A man is not saved on the ground of his virtues but he is condemned on the ground of his sin. As strict Calvinists we insist that while some men are saved from their unbelief and disobedience, in which all are involved, and others are not, it is still the sinner's sinfulness that constitutes the ground of his reprobation. Election and reprobation proceed on different grounds; one the grace of God, the other the sin of man. It is a travesty on Calvinism to say that because God elects to save a man irrespective of his character or deserts, that therefore He elects to damn a man irrespective of his character or deserts." [58]

This reprobation or passing by of the non-elect is not founded merely upon a foresight of their continuance in sin; for if that had been a proper cause, reprobation would have been the fate of all men, for all were foreseen as sinners. Nor can it be said that those who were passed by were in all cases worse sinners than those who were brought to eternal life. The Scriptures always ascribe faith and repentance to the good pleasure of God and to the special gracious operation of His Spirit. Those who conceive of mankind as innocent and deserving of salvation are naturally scandalized when any portion of the race is antecedently consigned to punishment. But when the doctrine of Original Sin, which is taught so clearly and repeatedly in the Scriptures, is seen in its proper setting, the objections to predestination disappear and the condemnation of the wicked seems only just and natural. Thus salvation is of the Lord alone, and damnation wholly from ourselves. Men perish because they will not come to Christ; yet if they have a will to come, it is God who works the will in them. Grace, electing grace, both draws the will and keeps it steady; and to grace be all the praise.

Furthermore, out of a world of sinful and rebellious subjects, none of whom were in themselves worthy of saving, God has graciously chosen some when he might have passed by all as He did the fallen angels (2 Peter 2:4; Jude 6). He has taken it altogether upon Himself to provide the redemption through which His people are saved. The atonement, therefore, is His own property; and He certainly may, as He most assuredly will, do what He pleases with His own. Grace is given to one and withheld from another as He sees best. It is to be noticed also that the withholding of His grace from the non-elect is but the negative cause of their perishing, just as the absence of a physician from the sick man is the occasion, not the efficient cause, of his death. "In the sight of an infinitely good and merciful God," says Dr. Charles Hodge, "it was necessary that some of the rebellious race of man should suffer the penalty of the law which all have broken. It is God's prerogative to determine who shall be vessels of mercy, and who shall be left to the just recompense of their sins." [59]

Since man has brought himself into this state of sin, his condemnation is just, and every demand of justice would be met in his punishment. Conscience tells us that man perishes justly, since he chooses to follow Satan rather than God. "Ye will not come to me, that ye may have life," said Jesus (John 5:40). And in this connection the words of Prof. F. E. Hamilton are very appropriate: "All God does is to let him (the unregenerate) alone and allow him to go his own way without interference. It is his nature to be evil, and God simply has foreordained to leave that nature unchanged. The picture often painted by opponents of Calvinism, of a cruel God refusing to save those who long to be saved, is a gross caricature. God saves all who want to be saved, but no one whose nature is unchanged wants to be saved." Those who are lost are lost because they deliberately choose to walk in the ways of sin; and this will be the very hell of hells, that men have been self destroyers.

Many people talk as if salvation were a matter of human birthright. And, forgetful of the fact that man had and lost his supremely favorable chance in Adam, they inform us that God would be unjust if He did not give all guilty creatures an opportunity to be saved. In regard to the idea that salvation is given in return for something done by the person, Luther says, "But let us, I pray you, suppose that God ought to be such a one, who should have respect unto merit in those who are damned. Must we not, in like manner, also require and grant that He ought to have respect unto merit in those who are to be saved? For if we are to follow reason, it is equally unjust, that the undeserving should be crowned, as that the deserving should be damned." [60]

No one with proper ideas of God supposes that He suddenly does something which He had not thought of before. Since His is an eternal purpose, what He does in time is what He purposed from eternity to do. Those whom He saves are those whom He purposed from eternity to save, and those whom He leaves to perish are those whom He purposed from eternity to leave. If it is just for God to do a certain thing in time, it is, by parity of argument, just for Him to resolve upon and decree it from

The Reformed Doctrine Of Predestination

eternity, for the principle of the action is the same in either case. And if we are justified in saying that from all eternity God has intended to display His mercy in pardoning a vast multitude of sinners why do some people object so strenuously when we say that from all eternity God has intended to display His justice in punishing other sinners?

Hence if it is just for God to forbear saving some persons after they are born, it was just for Him to form that purpose before they were born, or in eternity. And since the determining will of God is omnipotent, it cannot be obstructed or made void. This being true, it follows that He never did, nor does He now, will that every individual of mankind should be saved. If He willed this, not one single soul could ever be lost, "for who hath resisted His will?" If He willed that none should be lost, He would surely give to all men those effectual means of salvation without which it cannot be had. Now, God could give those means as easily to all mankind as to some only, but experience proves that He does not. Hence it logically follows that it is not His secret purpose or decretive will that all should be saved. In fact, the two truths, that what God does He does from eternity, and that only a portion of the human race is saved, is enough to complete the doctrines of Election and Reprobation.

State of the Heathens

The fact that, in the providential working of God, some men are left without the Gospel and the other means of grace virtually involves the principle set forth in the Calvinistic doctrine of Predestination. We see that in all ages the greater portion of mankind has been left destitute even of the external means of grace. For centuries the Jews, who were very few in number, were the only people to whom God was pleased to make any special revelation of Himself. Jesus confined His public ministry almost exclusively to them and forbade his disciples to go among others until after the day of Pentecost (Matthew 10:5, 6; 28:19; Mark 16:15; Acts 1:4). Multitudes were left with no chance to hear the Gospel, and consequently died in their sins. If God had intended to save them undoubtedly he would have sent them the means of salvation. If he had chosen to Christianize India and China a thousand years ago, He most certainly could have accomplished His purpose. Instead, they were left in gross darkness and unbelief. The past and present state of the world with all its sin, misery, and death, can have no other explanation than that given in Scripture,--namely, that the race fell in Adam and that in mercy God has sovereignly chosen to bring an innumerable multitude to salvation through a redemption which He has Himself provided. It is a perverted and dishonoring view of God to imagine Him struggling along with disobedient men, doing the best He can to convert them, but not able to accomplish His purpose.

If the Arminian theory were true, namely, that Christ died for all men and that the benefits of His death are actually applied to all men we would expect to find that God had made some provision for the Gospel to be communicated to all men. The problem of the heathens, who live and die without the Gospel, has always been a thorny one for the Arminians who insist that all men have sufficient grace if they will but make use of it. Few will deny that salvation is conditioned on the person hearing and accepting the Gospel. The Christian Church has been practically of one mind in declaring that the heathens as a class are lost. That such is the clear teaching of the Bible we can easily show:--

"And in none other is there salvation; for neither is there any other name under heaven, that is given among men, wherein we must be saved," Acts 4:12. "As many as have sinned without the law shall also perish without the law: and as many as have sinned under the law shall be judged by the law," Romans 2:12. "Other foundation can no man lay than that which is laid, which is Jesus Christ," 1 Corinthians 3:11. "I am the vine, ye are the branches; apart from me ye can do nothing," John 15:5. "I am the way, and the truth, and the life: no one cometh unto the Father, but by me," John 14:6. "He that believeth on the Son hath eternal life; but he that obeyeth not the Son shall not see life, but the wrath of God abideth on him," John 3:36. "He that hath the Son hath life; he that hath not the Son of God hath not the life," 1 John 5:12, "And this is eternal life, that they should know thee the only true God, and Him whom thou didst send, even Jesus Christ," John 17:3. "Without faith it is Impossible to be well-pleasing to God," Hebrews 11: 6. "Whosoever shall call upon the name of the Lord shall be saved. How then shall they call on Him in whom they have not believed? and how shall they believe in Him whom they have not heard? and how shall they hear without a preacher?" Romans 10:13, 14 (or, in other words, how can the heathens possibly be saved when they have never even heard of Christ who is the only means of salvation ?). "Jesus therefore said unto them, Verily, verily, I say unto you, except ye eat the flesh of the Son of man and drink His blood, ye have not life in yourselves," John 6:53. When the watchman sees danger coming but does not give the people warning they perish in their iniquity, Ezekiel 33:8,--true, the watchman will be held responsible, yet that does not change the fate of the people. Jesus declared that even the Samaritans who had far higher privileges than the nations outside of Palestine, worshipped they knew not what, and that salvation was of the Jews. See also the first and second chapters of Romans. The Scriptures, then, are plain in declaring that under ordinary conditions those who have not Christ and the Gospel are lost.

And in accordance with this the Westminster Confession, after stating that those who reject Christ cannot be saved, adds: "Much less can men, not professing the Christian religion, be saved in any other way whatsoever, be they never so diligent to frame their lives according to the light of nature, and the law of that religion they do profess . . ." (X:4).

In fact the belief that the heathens without the Gospel are lost has been one of the strongest arguments in favor of foreign missions. If we believe that their own religions contain enough light and truth to save them, the importance of preaching the Gospel to them is greatly lessened. Our attitude toward foreign missions is determined pretty largely by the answer which we give to this question.

We do not deny that God can save some even of the adult heathen people if He chooses to do so, for His Spirit works when and where and how He pleases, with means or without means. If any such are saved, however, it is by a miracle of pure grace. Certainly God's ordinary method is to gather His elect from the evangelized portion of mankind, although we must admit the possibility that by an extraordinary method some few of His elect may be gathered from the unevangelized portion. (The fate of those who die in infancy in heathen lands will be discussed under the subject, "Infant Salvation.")

It is unreasonable to suppose that people can appropriate to themselves something concerning which they know nothing. We readily see that so far as the pleasures and joys and opportunities in this world are concerned the heathens are largely passed by; and on the same principle we would expect them to be passed by in the next world also. Those who are providentially placed in the pagan darkness of western China can no more accept Christ as Savior than they can accept the radio, the airplane, or the Copernican system of astronomy, things concerning which they are totally ignorant. When God places people in such conditions we may be sure that He has no more intention that they shall be saved than He has that the soil of northern Siberia, which is frozen all the year round, shall produce crops of wheat. Had he intended otherwise He would have supplied the means leading to the designed end. There are also multitudes in the nominally Christian lands to whom the Gospel has never been presented in any adequate way, who have not even the outward means of salvation, to say nothing of the helpless state of their heart.

This, of course, does not mean that all of the lost shall suffer the same degree of punishment. We believe that from a common zero point there will be all degrees of reward and all degrees of punishment, and that a person's reward or punishment will, to a certain extent, be based on the opportunity that he has had in this world. Jesus Himself declared that in the day of judgment it would be more tolerable for the heathen city of Sodom than for those cities of Palestine which had heard and rejected His message (Luke 10:12-14); and He closed the parable of the faithful and unfaithful servants with the words: "And that servant, who knew his lord's will, and made not ready, nor did according to his will, shall be beaten with many stripes; but he that knew not, and did things worthy of stripes, shall be beaten with few stripes. And to whomsoever much is given, of him shall much be required; and to whom they commit much, of him will they ask the more," Luke 12:47, 48. So while the heathens are lost, they shall suffer relatively less than those who have heard and rejected the Gospel.

Hence in regard to this problem of the heathen races, Arminians are, at the very outset, involved in difficulties which subvert their whole scheme, difficulties from which they have never been able to extricate themselves. They admit that only in Christ is there salvation; yet they see that multitudes die without ever having heard of Christ or the Gospel. Holding that sufficient grace or opportunity must be given to every man before he can be condemned, many of them have been led to postulate a future probation,--this however is not only without Scripture support, but is contrary to Scripture. As Cunningham says, "Calvinists have always regarded it as a strong argument against the Arminian doctrines of universal grace and universal redemption, and in favor of their own views of the sovereign purposes of God, that, in point of fact, so large a portion of the human race have been always left in entire ignorance of God's mercy, and of the way of salvation revealed in the Gospel; nay, in such circumstances as, to all appearances, throw insuperable obstacles in the way of their attaining to that knowledge of God and of Jesus Christ, which is eternal life." [61]

Only in Calvinism, with its doctrine of the guilt and corruption of all mankind through the fall, and its doctrine of grace through which some are sovereignly rescued and brought to salvation while others are passed by, do we find an adequate explanation of the phenomenon of the heathen world.

Purposes of the Decree of Reprobation

The condemnation of the non-elect is designed primarily to furnish an eternal exhibition, before men and angels, of God's hatred for sin, or, in other words, it is to be an eternal manifestation of the justice of God. (Let it be remembered that God's justice as certainly demands the punishment of sin as it demands the rewarding of righteousness.) This decree displays one of the divine attributes which apart from it could never have been adequately appreciated. The salvation of some through a redeemer is designed to display the attributes of love, mercy, and holiness. The attributes of wisdom, power and sovereignty are displayed in the treatment accorded both groups. Hence the truth of the Scripture statement that, "Jehovah hath made everything for its own end; Yea, even the wicked for the day of evil," Proverbs 16:4; and also the statement of Paul that this arrangement was intended on the one hand,

The Reformed Doctrine Of Predestination

to "make known the riches of His glory upon vessels of mercy, which He afore prepared unto glory," and on the other, "to show His wrath, and to make His power known" upon "vessels of wrath fitted unto destruction," Romans 9:22, 23.

This decree of reprobation also serves subordinate purposes in regard to the elect; for, in beholding the rejection and final state of the wicked, (1) they learn what they too would have suffered had not grace stepped in to their relief, and they appreciate more deeply the riches of divine love which raised them from sin and brought them into eternal life while others no more guilty or unworthy than they were left to eternal destruction. (2) It furnishes a most powerful motive for thankfulness that they have received such high blessings. (3) They are led to a deeper trust of their heavenly Father who supplies all their needs in this life and the next. (4) The sense of what they have received furnishes the strongest possible motive for them to love their heavenly Father, and to live as pure lives as possible. (5) It leads them to a greater abhorrence of sin. (6) It leads them to a closer walk with God and with each other as specially chosen heirs of the kingdom of heaven. (7) In regard to the sovereign rejection of the Jews, Paul destroys at the source any accusation that they were cast off without reason. "Did they stumble that they might fall? God forbid: for by their fall salvation is come to the Gentiles, to provoke them to jealousy," Romans 11:11. Thus we see that God's rejection of the Jews was for a very wise and definite purpose; namely, that salvation might be given to the Gentiles, and that in such a way that it would react for the salvation of the Jews themselves. Historically we see that the Christian Church has been almost exclusively a Gentile Church. But in every age some Jews have been converted to Christianity, and we believe that as time goes on much larger numbers will be "provoked to jealousy" and caused to turn to God. Several verses in the eleventh chapter of Romans indicate that considerable numbers are to be converted and that they will be extremely zealous for righteousness.

Arminians Center Attack on This Doctrine

This doctrine of Reprobation is one upon which the Arminians are very fond of dwelling. They often single it out and emphasize it as though it was the sum and substance of Calvinism, while the other doctrines such as the Sovereignty of God, the purely gracious character of Election, the Perseverance of the saints, etc., which give so much glory to God, are passed by with little or no comment. At the Synod of Dort the Arminians insisted on first discussing the subject of Reprobation, and complained of it as a great hardship when the Synod refused to concede this. To the present day they have generally pursued this same policy. Their object is plain, for they know that it is easy to misrepresent this doctrine and to set it forth in a light that will prejudice men's feelings against it. They often distort the views which are held by Calvinists, then after alleging all that they can against it, they argue that since there can be no such thing as Reprobation, neither can there be any such thing as Election. The unfair over-emphasis on this doctrine indicates anything but an unprejudiced and sincere search for truth. Let them turn rather to the positive side of the system; let them answer and dispose of the large amount of evidence which has been collected in favor of this system.

On the other hand Calvinists usually produce first the evidence in favor of the doctrine of Election and then, having established this, they show that what they hold concerning the doctrine of Reprobation naturally follows. They do not, indeed, regard the latter as wholly dependent on the former for its proof. They believe that it is sustained by independent Scripture proof; yet they do believe that if what they hold concerning the doctrine of Election is proven true, then what they hold concerning the doctrine of Reprobation will follow of logical necessity. Since the Scriptures give us much fuller information about what God does in producing faith and repentance in those who are saved than they give us in regard to His procedure with those who continue in impenitence and unbelief, reason demands that we shall first investigate the doctrine of Election, and then consider the doctrine of Reprobation. This last consideration shows the utter unfairness of Arminians in giving such prominence to the doctrine of Reprobation. As has been said before, this is admittedly an unpleasant doctrine. Calvinists do not shrink from discussing it; yet naturally, because of its awful character, they find no satisfaction in dwelling upon it. They also realize that here men must be particularly careful not to attempt to be wise above what is written, as many are inclined to do when they indulge in presumptuous speculations about matters which are too high for them.

Under No Obligation to Explain All These Things

Let it be remembered that we are under no obligation to explain all the mysteries connected with these doctrines. We are only under obligation to set forth what the Scriptures teach concerning them, and to vindicate this teaching so far as possible from the objections which are alleged against it. The "yea, Father, for so it was well pleasing in thy sight," (Matthew 11:26; Luke 10:21, was, to our Lord, an all-sufficient theodicy in the face of all God's diverse dealings with men. The sufficient and only answer which Paul gives to vain reasoners who would penetrate more deeply into these mysteries is that they are to be resolved into the divine wisdom and sovereignty. The words of Toplady are especially appropriate here: "Say not, therefore, as the opposers of these doctrines did in St. Paul's days: 'Why doth

God find fault with the wicked? for who bath resisted His will? If He, who only can convert them, refrains from doing it, what room is there for blaming them that perish, seeing it is impossible to resist the will of the Almighty?' Be satisfied with St. Paul's answer, 'Nay, but, O man, who art thou that repliest against God?' The apostle hinges the whole matter entirely on God's absolute sovereignty. There he rests it, and there we ought to leave it." [62]

Man cannot measure the justice of God by his own comprehension, and our modesty should be such that when the reason for some of God's works lies hidden we nevertheless believe Him to be just. If any one thinks that this doctrine represents God as unjust, it is only because he does not realize what the Scripture doctrine of Original Sin is, nor to what it commits him. Let him fix his mind upon the existence of real ill-desert antecedent to actual sin, and the condemnation will appear just and natural. The first step mastered, the second presents no real difficulty.

It is hard for us to realize that many of those right around us (in some cases our close friends and relatives) are probably foreordained to eternal punishment; and so far as we do realize it we are inclined to have a certain sympathy for them. Yet when seen in the light of eternity our sympathy for the lost will be found to have been an undeserved and a misplaced sympathy. Those who are finally lost shall then be seen as they really are, enemies of God, enemies of all righteousness, and lovers of sin, with no desire for salvation or the presence of the Lord. We may add further that, since God is perfectly just, none shall be sent to hell except those who deserve to go there; and when we see their real characters we shall be fully satisfied with the disposition that God has made.

As a matter of fact the Arminians do not escape any real difficulty here. For since they admit that God has foreknowledge of all things they must explain why He creates those who He foresees will lead sinful lives, reject the Gospel, die impenitent, and suffer eternally in hell. The Arminians really have a more difficult problem here than do the Calvinists; for the Calvinists maintain that the ones whom God thus creates, knowing that they will be lost, are the non-elect who voluntarily choose sin and in whose merited punishment God designs to manifest His justice, while the Arminians must say that God deliberately creates those who He foresees will be such poor, miserable creatures that without serving any good purpose they will bring destruction upon themselves and will spend eternity in hell in spite of the fact that God Himself earnestly wishes to bring them to heaven, and that God shall be forever grieved in seeing them where He wishes they were not. Does not this represent God as acting most foolishly in bringing upon Himself such dissatisfaction and upon some of His creatures such misery when He could at least have refrained from creating those who, He foresaw, would be lost?

Perhaps there are some who, upon hearing of this doctrine of Predestination, will account themselves reprobate and will be inclined to go into further sin with the excuse that they are to be damned anyway. But to do so is to suck poison out of a sweet flower, to dash one's self against the Rock of Ages. No one has the right to judge himself reprobate in this life, and hence to grow desperate; for final disobedience (the only infallible sign of reprobation) cannot be discovered until death. No unconverted person in this life knows for certain that God will not yet convert him and save him, even though he is aware that no such change has yet taken place. Hence be has no right to number himself definitely among the non-elect. God has not told us who among the unconverted He yet proposes to regenerate and save. If any man feels the pangs of conscience working in him, these may be the very means which God is using to draw him.

We have given considerable space to the discussion of the doctrine of Reprobation because it has been the great stumbling block for most of those who have rejected the Calvinistic system. We believe that if this doctrine can be shown to be Scriptural and reasonable the other parts of the system will be readily accepted.

6. INFRALAPSARIANISM AND SUPRALAPSARIANISM

Among those who call themselves Calvinists there has been some difference of opinion as to the order of events in the Divine plan. The question here is, When the decrees of election and reprobation came into existence were men considered as fallen or as unfallen? Were the objects of these decrees contemplated as members of a sinful, corrupt mass, or were they contemplated merely as men whom God would create? According to the infralapsarian view the order of events was as follows: God proposed (1) to create; (2) to permit the fall; (3) to elect to eternal life and blessedness a great multitude out of this mass of fallen men, and to leave the others, as He left the Devil and the fallen angels, to suffer the just punishment of their sins; (4) to give His Son, Jesus Christ, for the redemption of the elect; and (5) to send the Holy Spirit to apply to the elect the redemption which was purchased by Christ. According to the supralapsarian view the order of events was: (1) to elect some creatable men (that is, men who were to be created) to life and to condemn others to destruction; (2) to create; (3) to permit the fall; (4) to send Christ to redeem the elect; and (5) to send the Holy Spirit to apply this redemption to the elect The question then is as to whether election precedes or follows the fall.

One of the leading motives in the supralapsarian scheme is to emphasize the idea of discrimination and to push this idea into the whole of God's dealings with men. We believe, however, that

The Reformed Doctrine Of Predestination

supralapsarianism over-emphasizes this idea. In the very nature of the case this idea cannot be consistently carried out, e.g., in creation, and especially in the fall. It was not merely some of the members of the human race who were objects of the decree to create, but all mankind, and that with the same nature. And it was not merely some men, but the entire race, which was permitted to fall. Supralapsarianism goes to as great an extreme on the one side as does universalism on the other. Only the infralapsarian scheme is self-consistent or consistent with other facts.

In regard to this difference Dr. Warfield writes: "The mere putting of the question seems to carry its answer with it. For the actual dealing with men which is in question, is, with respect to both classes alike, those who are elected and those who are passed by, conditioned on sin; we cannot speak of salvation any more than of reprobation without positing sin. Sin is necessarily precedent in thought, not indeed to the abstract idea of discrimination, but to the concrete instance of discrimination which is in question, a discrimination with regard to a destiny which involves either salvation or punishment. There must be sin in contemplation to ground a decree of salvation, as truly as a decree of punishment. We cannot speak of a decree discriminating between men with reference to salvation and punishment, therefore, without positing the contemplation of men as sinners as its logical prius." [63]

And to the same effect Dr. Charles Hodge says: "It is a clearly revealed Scriptural principle that where there is no sin there is no condemnation .... He hath mercy upon one and not on another, according to His own good pleasure, because all are equally unworthy and guilty. . . Everywhere, as in Romans 1:24, 26, 28, reprobation is declared to be judicial, founded upon the sinfulness of its object. Otherwise it could not be a manifestation of the justice of God." [64]

It is not in harmony with the Scripture ideas of God that innocent men, men who are not contemplated as sinners, should be foreordained to eternal misery and death. The decrees concerning the saved and the lost should not be looked upon as based merely on abstract sovereignty. God is truly sovereign, but this sovereignty is not exercised in an arbitrary way. Rather it is a sovereignty exercised in harmony with His other attributes, especially His justice, holiness, and wisdom. God cannot commit sin; and in that respect He is limited, although it would be more accurate to speak of His inability to commit sin as a perfection. There is, of course, mystery in connection with either system; but the supralapsarian system seems to pass beyond mystery and into contradiction.

The Scriptures are practically infralapsarian,--Christians are said to have been chosen "out of" the world, John 15:19; the potter has a right over the clay, "from the same lump," to make one part a vessel unto honor, and another unto dishonor, Romans 9:21; and the elect and the non-elect are regarded as being originally in a common state of misery. Suffering and death are uniformly represented as the wages of sin. The infralapsarian scheme naturally commends itself to our ideas of justice and mercy; and it is at least free from the Arminian objection that God simply creates some men in order to damn them. Augustine and the great majority of those who have held the doctrine of Election since that time have been and are infralapsarians,--that is, they believe that it was from the mass of fallen men that some were elected to eternal life while others were sentenced to eternal death for their sins. There is no Reformed confession which teaches the supralapsaian view; but on the other hand a considerable number do explicitly teach the infralapsarian view, which thus emerges as the typical form of Calvinism. At the present day it is probably safe to say that not more than one Calvinist in a hundred holds the supralapsarian view. We are Calvinists strongly enough, but not "high Calvinists." By a "high Calvinist" we mean one who holds the supralapsarian view.

It is of course true that in either system the sovereign choice of God in election is strewed and salvation in its whole course is the work of God. Opponents usually stress the supralapsarian system since it is the one which without explanation is more likely to conflict with man's natural feelings and impressions. It is also true that there are some things here which cannot be put into the time mould,--that these events are not in the Divine mind as they are in ours, by a succession of acts, one after another, but that by one single act God has at once ordained all these things. In the Divine mind the plan is a unit, each part of which is designed with reference to a state of facts which God intended should result from the other parts. All of the decrees are eternal. They have a logical, but not a chronological, relationship. Yet in order for us to reason intelligently about them we must have a certain order of thought. We very naturally think of the gift of Christ in sancification and glorification as following the decrees of the creation and the fall.

In regard to the teaching of the Westminster Confession, Dr. Charles Hodge makes the following comment: "Twiss, the Prolocutor of that venerable body (the Westminster Assembly), was a zealous supralapsarian; the great majority of its members, however, were on the other side. The symbols of that Assembly, while they clearly imply the infralapsarian view, were yet so framed as to avoid offence to those who adopted the supralapsarian theory. In the 'Westminster Confession,' it is said that God appointed the elect unto eternal life, and the rest of mankind, God was pleased, according to the unsearchable counsel of His own will whereby He extendeth or withholdeth mercy as He pleaseth, for the glory of His sovereign power over His creatures, to pass by, and to ordain them to dishonor and wrath for their sin, to the praise of His glorious justice: It is here taught that those whom God passes by are 'the rest of mankind; not the rest of ideal or possible men, but the rest of those human beings who constitute mankind, or the human race. In the second place, the passage quoted teaches that the non-elect are passed by and ordained to wrath 'for their sin.' This implies that they were contemplated as sinful before this foreordination to judgment. The infralapsarian view is still more obviously assumed in the answer to the 19th and 20th questions in the 'Shorter Catechism.' It is there taught that all mankind by the fall lost communion with God, and are under His wrath and curse, and that God out of His mere good pleasure elected some (some of those under His wrath and curse), unto everlasting life. Such has been the doctrine of the great body of Augustinians from the time of Augustine to the present day." [65]

7. MANY ARE CHOSEN

When the doctrine of Election is mentioned many people immediately assume that this means that the great majority of mankind will be lost. But why should any one draw that conclusion? God is free in election to choose as many as I He pleases, and we believe that He who is infinitely merciful and benevolent and holy will elect the great majority to life. There is no good reason why He should be limited to only a few. We are told that Christ is to have the preeminence in all things, and we do not believe that the Devil will be permitted to emerge victor even in numbers.

Our position in this respect has been very ably stated by Dr. W. G. T. Shedd in the following words: "Let it be noticed that the question, how many are elected and how many are reprobated, has nothing to do with the question whether God may either elect or reprobate sinners. If it is intrinsically right for Him either to elect or not to elect, either to save or not to save free moral agents who by their own fault have plunged themselves into sin and ruin, numbers are of no account in establishing the rightness. And if it is intrinsically wrong, numbers are of no account in establishing wrongness. Neither is there any necessity that the number of the elect should be small, and that of the nonelect great; or the converse. The election and the non-election, and also the numbers of the elect and the non-elect, are all alike a matter of sovereignty and optional decision. At the same time it relieves the solemnity and awfulness which overhangs the decree of reprobation, to remember that the Scriptures teach that the number of the elect is much greater than that of the non-elect. The kingdom of the Redeemer in this fallen world is always described as far greater and grander than that of Satan. The operation of grace on earth is uniformly represented as mightier than that of sin. 'Where sin abounded, grace did much more abound.' And the final number of the redeemed is said to be a 'number which no man can number,' but that of the lost is not so magnified and emphasized." [66]

There is, however, a very common practice among Arminian writers to represent Calvinists as tending to consign to everlasting misery a large portion of the human race whom they would admit to the enjoyment of heaven. It is a mere caricature of Calvinism to represent it as based on the principle that the saved will be a mere handful, or only a few brands plucked from the burning. When the Calvinist insists upon the doctrine of Election, his emphasis is upon the fact that God deals personally with each individual soul instead of dealing merely with mankind in the mass; and this is a thing altogether apart from the relative proportion which shall exist between the saved and the lost. In answer to those who are inclined to say, "According to this doctrine God alone can save the soul; there will be few saved," we can reply that they might as well reason, "Since God alone can create stars, there can be but few stars." The objection is not well taken. The doctrine of Election taken in itself tells us nothing about what the ultimate ratio shall be. The only limit set is that not all will be saved.

So far as the principles of sovereignty and personal election are concerned there is no reason why a Calvinist might not hold that all men will finally be saved; and some Calvinists have actually held this view. "Calvinism," wrote W. P. Patterson, of the University of Edinburgh, "is the only system which contains principles--in its doctrines of election and irresistible grace--that could make credible a theory of universal salvation." And Dr. S. G. Craig, Editor of CHRISTIANITY TODAY, and one of the outstanding men in the Presbyterian Church at the present time, says: "No doubt many Calvinists, like many not Calvinists, have, in obedience to the supposed teachings of the Scriptures, held that few will be saved, but there is no good reason why Calvinists may not believe that the saved will ultimately embrace the immensely greater portion of the human race. At any rate, our leading theologians--Charles Hodge, Robert L. Dabney, W. G. T. Shedd, and B. B. Warfield--have so held."

As stated by Patterson, Calvinism, with its emphasis on the intimate personal relation between God and each individual soul, is the only system which would offer a logical basis for universalism if that view were not contradicted by the Scriptures. And in contrast with this, must not the Arminian admit that on his principles only comparatively few actually are saved? He must admit that so far in human history the great proportion of adults, even in nominally Christian lands, exercising their "free will" with a "graciously restored ability" have died without accepting Christ. And unless God is bringing the world to an appointed goal, what grounds are there to suppose that, so long as human nature remains as it is, the situation would be materially different even if the world lasted a billion years?

8. A REDEEMED WORLD OR RACE

Since it was the world, or the race, which fell in Adam, it was the world, or the race, which was redeemed by Christ. This, however, does not mean that every individual will be saved, but that the race as a race will be saved. Jehovah is no mere tribal deity, but is "the God of the whole earth"; and the salvation which He had in view cannot be limited to that of a little select group or favored few. The Gospel was not merely local news for a few villages in Palestine, but was a world message; and the abundant and continuous testimony of Scripture is that the kingdom of God is to fill the earth, "from sea to sea, and from the River unto the ends of the earth." Zechariah 9:10.

Early in the Old Testament we have the promise that "all the earth shall be filled with the glory of Jehovah," Numbers 14:21; and Isaiah repeats the promise that all flesh shall see the glory of Jehovah (40:5). Israel was set as "a light to the Gentiles," and "for salvation unto the uttermost part of the earth," Isaiah 49:6; Acts 13:47. Joel made the clear declaration that in the coming days of blessing, the Spirit hitherto given only to Israel would be poured out upon the whole earth. "And it shall come to pass afterward," said the Lord through His prophet, "that I will pour out my Spirit upon all flesh," 2:28; and Peter applied that prophecy to the outpouring which was begun at Pentecost (Acts 2:16).

Ezekiel gives us the picture of the increasing flow of the healing waters which issue from under the threshold of the temple; waters which were first only to the ankles, then to the knees, then to the loins, then a great river, waters which could not be passed through (47:1-5). Daniel's interpretation of King Nebuchadnezzar's dream taught this same truth. The king saw a great image, with various parts of gold, silver, brass, iron, and clay. Then he saw a stone cut out without hands, which stone smote the image so that the gold, silver, brass, iron, and clay were carried away like the chaff of the summer threshing floor. These various elements represented great world empires which were to be broken in pieces and completely carried away, while the stone cut out without hands represented a spiritual kingdom which God Himself would set up and which would become a great mountain and fill the whole earth. "And in the days of those kings shall the God of heaven set up a kingdom which shall never be destroyed, nor shall the sovereignty thereof he left to another people, but it shall break in pieces and consume all these kingdoms, and it shall stand forever," Daniel 2:44. In the light of the New Testament we see that this kingdom was the one which Christ set up. In the vision which Daniel saw, the beast made war with the saints and prevailed against them for a time,--but, "the time came when the saints possessed the kingdom," 7:22.

Jeremiah gives the promise that the time is coming when it will no longer be necessary for a man to say to his brother or to his neighbors "Know Jehovah"; "for they shall all know Him, from the least to the greatest of them," 31:34. "Ask of me, and I will give thee the nations for thine inheritance, And the uttermost parts of the earth for thy possessions," said the psalmist (2:8). The last book of the Old Testament contains a promise that 'from the rising of the sun unto the going down of the same my name shall be great among the Gentiles, saith Jehovah of hosts," Malachi 1:11.

In the New Testament we find the same teaching. When the Lord does finally shower spiritual blessings on His people, "the residue of men," and "all the Gentiles," are to "seek after the Lord," Acts 15:17. "Christ is the propitiation for our sins; and not for ours only, but also for the whole world," 1 John 2:2. "For God so loved the world, that He gave His only begotten Son, that whosoever believeth on Him should not perish, but have eternal life. For God sent not the Son into the world to judge the world; but that the world should be saved through Him" John 3:16, 17. "The Father hath sent the Son to be the Savior of the world," 1 John 4:14. "Behold the lamb of God, that taketh away the sin of the world!" John 1:29. "We have heard for ourselves, and know that this is indeed the Saviour of the world" John 4:42. "I am the light of the world," John 8:12. "I came not to judge the world, but to save the world," John 12:47. "And I, if I be lifted up from the earth, will draw all men unto me," John 12:32. "God was in Christ reconciling the world unto Himself," 2 Corinthians 5:19. The kingdom of heaven is said to be "like unto leaven which a woman took and hid in three measures of meal till it was all leavened," Matthew 13:33.

In the eleventh chapter of Romans we are told that the acceptance of the Gospel by the Jews shall be as "life from the dead" in its spiritual blessings to the world. By their fall the Gospel was given to the Gentiles--"now if their fall is the riches of the world, and their loss the riches of the Gentiles; how much more their fulness? .... For if the casting away of them is the reconciling of the world, what shall the receiving of them be, but life from the dead?" The universal and complete dominion of Christ is taught again when we are told that He is to sit at the right hand of the Father until all enemies have been placed under His feet.

Thus a strong emphasis is thrown on the universality of Christ's work of redemption, and we are taught that our eyes are yet to behold a Christianized world. And since nothing is told us as to how long the earth shall continue after this goal is reached, possibly we may look forward to a great "golden age" of spiritual prosperity, continuing for centuries, or even millenniums, during which time Christianity shall be triumphant over all the earth, and during which time the great proportion even of adults shall be saved. It seems that the number of the redeemed shall then be swelled until it far surpasses that of the lost.

We cannot, of course, fix even an approximate date for the end of the world. In several places in Scripture we are told that Christ is to return at the end of this present world order; that His coming will be personal, visible, and with great power and glory; that the general resurrection and the general judgment shall then take place; and that heaven and hell shall then be ushered in in their fulness. But it has been expressly revealed that the time of our Lord's coming is "among the secret things that belong unto the Lord our God." "For of that day or that hour knoweth no one, not even the angels in heaven, neither the Son, but the Father only," said Jesus before His crucifixion; and after the resurrection He said, "It is not for you to know the times or the seasons which the Father hath set within His own authority," Acts 1:7. Hence those who presume to tell us when the end of the world is coming are simply speaking without knowledge. In view of the fact that it has now been nearly 2,000 years since Christ came the first time, it may, for all we know, be another 2,000 years before He comes again-- perhaps a much longer, perhaps a much shorter, time.

In this connection Dr. S. G. Craig has well said: "We are told that certain events, such as the preaching of the Gospel among all the nations (Matthew 24:14), the conversion of the Jews (Romans 11:25-27), the overthrow of 'every rulership and every authority and power' opposed to Christ (1 Corinthians 15:24), are to take place before the return of our Lord. It seems clear, therefore, that while the time of our Lord's return is unknown, yet it still lies some distance in the future. Just how far in the future we have no means of knowing. No doubt, if events move as slowly in the future as in the past, the coming of our Lord lies far in the future. In view of the fact, however, that events move so much more swiftly than formerly, so that what formerly was accomplished in centuries is now accomplished in a few years, it is quite possible that the return of Christ lies in the comparatively near future. Whether it comes in the near or remote future as measured in the scale of human lives, we may be certain that it lies in the near future as measured in the scales of God according to whom a thousand years is as one day. In view of present conditions, however, there seems to be little or nothing in the Scriptures to warrant the notion that Jesus will return within the lifetime of the present generation." [67]

The world is perhaps yet young. Certainly God has not yet given any adequate exhibition of what He can do with a world truly converted to righteousness. What we have seen so far appears to be only the preliminary stage, a temporary triumph of the Devil, whose work is to be completely overthrown. God's work spans the centuries. Even the millenniums are insignificant to Him who inhabits eternity. When we associate our theology with our astronomy we find that God works on an unbelievably vast scale. He has spaced millions, perhaps even billions, of fiery suns throughout the universe,--something like ten million have already been catalogued. Astronomers tell us, for instance, that the earth is 92,000,000 miles from the sun and that the light traveling at the rate of 186,000 miles per second requires only eight minutes to traverse that distance. They go on to tell us that the nearest fixed star is so far away that four years are required for its light to reach us; that the light which we now see coming from the North Star has been on its journey for 450 years; and that the light from some of the most distant stars has been on its way for millions of years. In view of what modern science reveals we find that the period during which man has lived on earth has been comparatively insignificant. God may have developments in store for the race which shall be quite startling,--developments of which we have scarcely dreamed.

9. THE VASTNESS OF THE REDEEMED MULTITUDE

The decree of God's electing and predestinating love, though discriminating and particular, is, nevertheless, very extensive. "I saw, and behold, a great multitude, which no man could number, out of every nation and of all tribes and peoples and tongues, standing before the throne and before the Lamb, arrayed in white robes, and palms in their hands; and they cried with a great voice, saying, Salvation unto our God who sitteth on the throne, and unto the Lamb," Revelation 7:9, 10. God the Father has elected untold millions of the human race to everlasting salvation and eternal happiness. Just what proportion of the human family He has included in His purpose of mercy, we have not been informed; but, in view of the future days of prosperity which are promised to the Church, it may be inferred that much the greater part will eventually be found among the number of His elect.

In the nineteenth chapter of John's Revelation a vision is recorded setting forth in figurative terms the struggle between the forces of good and evil in the world. Concerning the description there given Dr. Warfield says: "The section opens with a vision of the victory of the Word of God, the King of Kings and Lord of Lords over all His enemies. We see Him come forth from heaven girt for war, followed by the armies of heaven; the birds of the air are summoned to the feast of corpses that shall be prepared for them; the armies of the enemy-- the beasts and the kings of the earth--are gathered against Him and are totally destroyed; and 'all the birds are filled with their flesh' (19:11-21). It is a vivid picture of a complete victory, an entire conquest, that we have here; and all the imagery of war and battle is employed to give it life. This is the symbol. The thing symbolized is obviously the complete victory of the Son of God over all the hosts of wickedness. Only a single hint of this signification is

The Reformed Doctrine Of Predestination

afforded by the language of the description, but that is enough. On two occasions we are carefully told that the sword by which the victory is won proceeds out of the mouth of the conqueror (verses 15 and 21). We are not to think, as we read, of any literal war or manual fighting, therefore; the conquest is wrought by the spoken word--in short, by the preaching of the Gospel. In fine, we have before us here a picture of the victorious career of the Gospel of Christ in the world. All the imagery of the dread battle and its hideous details are but to give us the impression of the completeness of the victory. Christ's Gospel is to conquer the earth; He is to overcome all His enemies." [68]

To us who live between the first and second coming of Christ it is given to see the conquest taking place. As to how long the conquest continues before it is crowned with victory, or as to how long the converted world is to await her coming Lord, we are not told. Today we are living in a period that is relatively golden as compared with the first century of the Christian era, and this progress is to go on until those on this earth shall see a practical fulfillment of the prayer, "Thy kingdom come, thy will be done in earth as it is in heaven." As we get the broader view of God's gracious dealings with the sinful world, we see that He has not distributed His electing grace with niggard hand, but that His purpose has been the restoration to Himself of the whole world.

The promise was given to Abraham that his posterity should be a vast multitude,--"In blessing I will bless thee, and in multiplying I will multiply thy seed as the stars of the heavens, and as the sand which is upon the sea-shore," Genesis 22:17; "I will make thy seed as the dust of the earth; so that if a man can number the dust of the earth, then may thy seed also be numbered," Genesis 13:16. And in the New Testament we discover that this promise refers not merely to the Jews as a separate people, but that those who are Christians are in the highest sense the true "sons of Abraham." "Know therefore, that they that are of faith, the same are sons of Abraham"; and again, "If ye are Christ's then are ye Abraham's seed, heirs according to promise," Galatians 3:7, 29.

Isaiah declared that the pleasure of Jehovah should prosper in the hands of the Messiah, that He should see of the travail of His soul and be satisfied. And in view of what He suffered on Calvary we know that He will not be easily satisfied.

The idea that the saved shall far outnumber the lost is also carried out in the contrasts drawn in Scripture language. Heaven is uniformly pictured as the next world, as a great kingdom, a country, a city; while on the other hand hell is uniformly represented as a comparatively small place, a prison, a lake (of fire and brimstone), a pit (perhaps deep, but narrow), (Luke 20:35; 1 Timothy 6:17; Revelation 21:1; Matthew 5:3; Hebrews 11:16; 1 Peter 3:19; Revelation 19:20; 20:10, 14, 15; 21:8-27). When the angels and saints are mentioned in Scripture they are said to be hosts, myriads, an innumerable multitude, ten thousand times ten thousand and many more thousands of thousands; but no such language is ever used in regard to the lost, and by contrast their number appears to be relatively insignificant (Luke 2:13; Isaiah 6:3; Revelation 5:11). "The circle of God's election," says Shedd, "is a great circle of the heavens and not that of a treadmill. The kingdom of Satan is insignificant in contrast with the kingdom of Christ. In the immense range of God's dominion, good is the rule, and evil is the exception. Sin is a speck upon the azure of eternity; a spot upon the sun. Hell is only a corner of the universe."

Judging from these considerations it thus appears (if we may hazard a guess) that the number of those who are saved may eventually bear some such proportion to those who are lost as the number of free citizens in our commonwealth today bears to those who are in the prisons and penitentiaries; or that the company of the saved may be likened to the main stalk of the tree which grows and flourishes, while the lost are but as the small limbs and prunings which are cut off and which perish in the fires. Who even among non-Calvinists would not wish that this were true?

But, it may be asked, do not the verses, "Narrow is the gate, and straightened the way, that leadeth unto life, and few are they that find it," and, "Many are called, but few chosen," Matthew 7:14; 22:14, teach that many more are lost than saved? We believe these verses are meant to be understood in a temporal sense, as describing the conditions which Jesus and His disciples saw existing in Palestine in their day. The great majority of the people about them were not walking in the ways of righteousness, and the words are spoken from the standpoint of the moment rather than from the standpoint of the distant Judgment Day. In these words we have presented to us a picture which was true to life as they saw it, and which would, for that matter, describe the world as it has been even up to the present time. But, asks Dr. Warfield, "As the years and centuries and ages flow on, can it never be--is it not to be--that the proportion following 'the two ways' shall be reversed?"

These verses are also designed to teach us that the way of salvation is a way of difficulty and of sacrifice, and that it is our duty to address ourselves to it with diligence and persistence. No one is to assume his salvation as a matter of course. Those who enter into the kingdom of heaven do so through many tribulations; hence the command, "Strive to enter in by the narrow door," Luke 13:24. The choice in life is represented as a choice between two roads, one is broad, smooth, and easy to travel, but leads to destruction. The other is narrow and difficult, and leads to life. "There is no more reason to suppose that this similitude teaches that the saved shall be fewer than the lost than there is to suppose that the parable of the Ten Virgins (Matthew 25:1ff) teaches that they shall be precisely equal in number; and there is far less reason to suppose that this similitude teaches that the saved shall be few comparatively to the lost than there is to suppose that the parable of the Tares in the corn (Matthew 13:24ff) teaches that the lost shall be inconsiderable in number in comparison with the saved--for that, indeed, is an important part of the teaching of that parable." [69] And we may add that there is no more reason to suppose that this reference to the two ways teaches that the number of the saved shall be fewer than the number of the lost than there is to suppose that the parable of the lost sheep teaches that only one out of a hundred goes astray and that even it shall eventually be brought back, which would indeed be absolute restorationism.

10. THE WORLD IS GROWING BETTER

The redemption of the world is a long, slow process, extending through the centuries, yet surely approaching an appointed goal. We live in the day of advancing victory and see the conquest taking place.

There are periods of spiritual prosperity and periods of depression; yet over all there is progress. Looking back across the two thousand years since Christ came, we can see that there has been marvelous progress. This course shall ultimately be completed, and before Christ comes again we shall see a Christianized world. This does not mean that all sin shall ever be eradicated--there shall always be some tares among the wheat until the time of the harvest, and even the righteous, while they remain in this world, sometimes fall victims to sin and temptation. But it does mean that as today we see some Christianized groups and communities, so eventually we shall see a Christianized world.

"The true way of judging the world is to compare its present with its past condition and note in which direction it is moving. Is it going backward, or forward, is it getting worse or better? It may be wrapped in gloomy twilight, but is it the twilight of the evening, or of the morning? Are the shadows deepening into starless night, or are they fleeing before the rising sun? ... One glance at the world as it is today compared with what it was ten or twenty centuries ago shows us that it has swept through a wide arc and is moving toward the morning." [70]

Today there is much more wealth consecrated to the service of the Church than ever before; and, in spite of the sad defection toward Modernism in many places, we believe there is far more really earnest evangelistic and missionary activity than has ever been known before. The number of Bible schools, Christian colleges, and seminaries in which the Bible is systematically studied is growing much more rapidly than the population. Last year over 11,000,000 copies or portions of the Bible in various languages were distributed in the home and foreign lands by the American Bible Society alone--a fact which means that the Bible is being broadcast over the earth as never before.

The Christian Church has made great progress in many parts of the world, and especially during the last two or three centuries it has developed thousands upon thousands of individual churches and has been a powerful influence for good in the lives of millions of people. It has established innumerable schools and hospitals. Under its benign influence ethical culture and social service have greatly advanced in the world, and the moral standards of the nations are much higher today than when the Church was first planted here.

"Already the Church has penetrated every continent and planted itself on every island and flung its outposts around the equator and from pole to pole. It is now the greatest organization on earth, the one world enterprise. And it has results to show that are not unpromising. In our own country Christianity has grown at least five times faster than the population. One hundred years ago there was one professing Christian in every fifteen of the population, and there now is one in every three, and excluding children, one in every two. In the world at large the results are astonishing. In 1500 AD. there were 100,000,000 nominal Christians in the world; in 1800 there were 200,000,000, and the latest statistics show that, out of a total world population of 1,646,491,000 there are now 564,510,000 nominal Christians, or about one-third of the population of the globe. Christianity has grown more in the last one hundred years than in the preceding eighteen hundred." [71]

The statement that Christianity has grown more in the last one hundred years than in the preceding eighteen hundred seems to be approximately correct. According to late statistics, 1950, Christianity has a considerably larger number of nominal adherents than the combined total of any other two world religions. These figures state that there are approximately 640,000,000 Christians, 300,000,000 Confucianists (including Taoists), 230,000,000 Hindus, 220,000,000 Mohammedans, 150,000,000 Buddhists, 125,000,000 Animists, 20,000,000 Shintoists, and 15,000,000 Jews. (And while many of those who are listed as Christians are only "nominally" such, the proportion of true Christians is probably as great or greater than is the proportion in any of the pagan religions). All of these other religions, with the exception of Mohammedanism, are much older than Christianity. Furthermore, Christianity alone is able to grow and flourish under modern civilization, while all of the other religions soon disintegrate when brought under its glaring light.

Only within the last one hundred years have foreign missions really come into their own. As they have recently been developed, with great church organizations behind them, they are in position to carry on a work of evangelism in heathen lands such as the world has never yet seen. It is safe to say that the present generation living in India, China, Korea, and Japan, has seen greater changes in religion, society, and government than occurred in the preceding two thousand years. And when we contrast the rapid spread of Christianity in recent years with the rapid disintegration that is taking place in all of the other world religions, it appears very plain that Christianity is the future world religion. In the light of these facts we face the future confident that the best is yet to be.

11. INFANT SALVATION

Most Calvinistic theologians have held that those who die in infancy are saved. The Scriptures seem to teach plainly enough that the children of believers are saved; but they are silent or practically so in regard to those of the heathens. The Westminster Confession does not pass judgment on the children of heathens who die before coming to years of accountability. Where the Scriptures are silent, the Confession, too, preserves silence. Our outstanding theologians, however, mindful of the fact that God's "tender mercies are over all His works," and depending on His mercy widened as broadly as possible, have entertained a charitable hope that since these infants have never committed any actual sin themselves, their inherited sin would be pardoned and they would be saved on wholly evangelical principles.

Such, for instance, was the position held by Charles Hodge, W. G. T. Shedd, and B. B. Warfield. Concerning those who die in infancy, Dr. Warfield says: "Their destiny is determined irrespective of their choice, by an unconditional decree of God, suspended for its execution on no act of their own; and their salvation is wrought by an unconditional application of the grace of Christ to their souls, through the immediate and irresistible operation of the Holy Spirit prior to and apart from any action of their own proper wills . . . And if death in infancy does depend on God's providence, it is assuredly God in His providence who selects this vast multitude to be made participants of His unconditional salvation . . . This is but to say that they are unconditionally predestinated to salvation from the foundation of the world. If only a single infant dying in irresponsible infancy be saved, the whole Arminian principle is traversed. If all infants dying such are saved, not only the majority of the saved, but doubtless the majority of the human race hitherto, have entered into life by a non-Arminian pathway." [72]

Certainly there is nothing in the Calvinistic system which would prevent us from believing this; and until it is proven that God could not predestinate to eternal life all those whom He is pleased to call in infancy we may be permitted to hold this view.

Calvinists, of course, hold that the doctrine of original sin applies to infants as well as to adults. Like all other sons of Adam, infants are truly culpable because of race sin and might be justly punished for it. Their "salvation" is real. It is possible only through the grace of Christ and is as truly unmerited as is that of adults. Instead of minimizing the demerit and punishment due to them for original sin, Calvinism magnifies the mercy of God in their salvation. Their salvation means something, for it is the deliverance of guilty souls from eternal woe. And it is costly, for it was paid for by the suffering of Christ on the cross. Those who take the other view of original sin, namely, that it is not properly sin and does not deserve eternal punishment, make the evil from which infants are "saved" to be very small and consequently the love and gratitude which they owe to God to be small also.

The doctrine of infant salvation finds a logical place in the Calvinistic system; for the redemption of the soul is thus infallibly determined irrespective of any faith, repentance or good works, whether actual or foreseen. It does not, however, find a logical place in Arminianism or any other system. Furthermore, it would seem that a system such as Arminianism, which suspends salvation on a personal act of rational choice, would logically demand that those dying in infancy must either be given another period of probation after death, in order that their destiny may be fixed, or that they must be annihilated.

In regard to this question Dr. S. G. Craig has written: "We take it that no doctrine of infant salvation is Christian that does not assume that infants are lost members of a lost race for whom there is no salvation apart from Christ. It must be obvious to all, therefore, that the doctrine that all dying in infancy are saved will not fit into the Roman Catholic or Anglo-Catholic system of thought with their teaching of baptismal regeneration; as clearly most of those who have died in infancy have not been baptized. It is obvious also that the Lutheran system of thought provides no place for the notion that all dying in infancy are saved because of the necessity it attaches to the means of grace, especially the Word and the Sacraments. If grace is only in the means of grace--in the case of infants in baptism--it seems clear that most of those who have died in infancy have not been the recipients of grace. Equally clear is it that the Arminian has no right to believe in the salvation of all dying in infancy; in fact, it is not so clear that he has any right to believe in the salvation of any dying in infancy. For according to the Arminians, even the evangelical Arminians, God in His grace has merely provided men with an opportunity for salvation. It does not appear, however, that a mere opportunity for salvation can be of any avail for those dying in infancy." [73]

Though rejecting the doctrine of baptismal regeneration, and turning the baptism of the non-elect into an empty form, Calvinism, on the other hand, extends saving grace far beyond the boundaries of the visible Church. If it is true that all of those who die in infancy, in heathen as well as in Christian lands, are saved, then more than half of the human race even up to the present time has been among the elect. Furthermore, it may be said that since Calvinists bold that saving faith in Christ is the only requirement for salvation on the part of adults, they never make membership in the external Church to be either a requirement or a guarantee of salvation. They believe that many adults who have no connection with the external Church are nevertheless saved. Every consistent Christian will, of course, submit himself for baptism in accordance with the plain Scripture command and will become a member of the external Church; yet many others, either because of weakness of faith or because they lack the opportunity, do not carry out that command.

It has often been charged that the Westminster Confession in stating that "Elect infants, dying in infancy, are regenerated and saved by Christ" (Chap. X. Sec. 3), implies that there are non-elect infants, who, dying in infancy, are lost, and that the Presbyterian Church has taught that some dying in infancy are lost. Concerning this Dr. Craig says: "The history of the phrase 'Elect infants dying in infancy' makes clear that the contrast implied was not between 'elect infants dying in infancy' and 'non-elect infants dying in infancy,' but rather between 'elect infants dying in infancy' and 'elect infants living to grow up.' " However, in order to guard against misunderstanding, furthered by unfriendly controversialists, the Presbyterian Church in the U. S. A. adopted in 1903 a Declaratory Statement which reads as follows: "With reference to Chapter X, Section 3, of the Confession of Faith, that it is not to be regarded as teaching that any who die in infancy are lost. We believe that all dying in infancy are included in the election of grace, and are regenerated and saved by Christ through the Spirit, who works when and where and how He pleases."

Concerning this Declaratory Statement Dr. Craig says: "It is obvious that the Declaratory Statement goes beyond the teaching of Chapter X, Section 3 of the Confession of Faith inasmuch as it states positively that all who die in infancy are saved. Some hold that the Declaratory Statement goes beyond the Scripture in teaching that all those dying in infancy are saved; but, be that as it may, it makes it impossible for any person to even plausibly maintain that Presbyterians teach that there are non-elect infants who die in infancy. No doubt there have been individual Presbyterians who held that some of those who die in infancy have been lost; but such was never the official teaching of the Presbyterian Church and as matters now stand such a position is contradicted by the Church's creed."[74]

It is sometimes charged that Calvin taught the actual damnation of some of those who die in infancy. A careful examination of his writings, however, does not bear out that charge. He explicitly taught that some of the elect die in infancy and that they are saved as infants. He also taught that there were reprobate infants; for he held that reprobation as well as election was eternal, and that the non-elect come into this life reprobate. But nowhere did he teach that the reprobate die and are lost as infants. He of course rejected the Pelagian view which denied original sin and grounded the salvation of those who die in infancy on their supposed innocence and sinlessness. Calvin's views in this respect have been quite thoroughly investigated by Dr. R. A. Webb and his findings are summarized in the following paragraph: "Calvin teaches that all the reprobate 'procure'--(that is his own word)--'procure' their own destruction; and they procure their destruction by their own personal and conscious acts of 'impiety,' 'wickedness,' and 'rebellion.' Now reprobate infants, though guilty of original sin and under condemnation, cannot, while they are infants, thus 'procure' their own destruction by their personal acts of impiety, wickedness, and rebellion. They must, therefore, live to the years of moral responsibility in order to perpetrate the acts of impiety, wickedness and rebellion, which Calvin defines as the mode through which they procure their destruction. While, therefore, Calvin teaches that there are reprobate infants, and that these will be finally lost, he nowhere teaches that they will be lost as infants, and while they are infants; but, on the contrary, he declares that all the reprobate 'procure' their own destruction by personal acts of impiety, wickedness and rebellion. Consequently, his own reasoning compels him to hold (to be consistent with himself), that no reprobate child can die in infancy; but all such must live to the age of moral accountability, and translate original sin into actual sin." [75]

In none of Calvin's writings does he say, either directly or by good and necessary inference, that any dying in infancy are lost. Most of the passages which are brought forth by opponents to prove this point are merely assertions of his well known doctrine of original sin, in which he taught the universal guilt and depravity of the entire race. Most of these are from highly controversial sections where he is discussing other doctrines and where he speaks unguardedly; but when taken in their context the meaning is not often in doubt. Calvin simply says of all infants what David specifically said of himself: "Behold, I was brought forth in iniquity; And in sin did my mother conceive me," Psalm 51:5; or what Paul said, "In Adam all die," 1 Corinthians 15:22; or again, that all are "by nature, the children of wrath," Ephesians 2:3.

We believe that we have now shown that the doctrine of election is in every point Scriptural and a plain dictate of common sense. Those who oppose this doctrine do so because they neither understand nor consider the majesty and holiness of God, nor the corruption and guilt of their own nature. They

The Reformed Doctrine Of Predestination

forget that they stand before their Maker not as those who may justly claim His mercy, but as condemned criminals who deserve only punishment. Furthermore, they want to be independent to work out their own scheme of salvation rather than to accept God's plan which is by grace. This doctrine of election will not harmonize with any covenant of works, nor with a mongrel covenant of works and grace; but it is the only possible outcome of a covenant of pure grace.

12. SUMMARY OF THE REFORMED DOCTRINE OF ELECTION

Election is a sovereign free act of God, through which He determines who shall be made heirs of heaven.

The elective decree was made in eternity.

The elective decree contemplates the race as already fallen.

The elect are brought from a state of sin and into a state of blessedness and happiness.

Election is personal determining what particular individuals shall be saved.

Election includes both means and ends,--election to eternal life includes election to righteous living here in this world.

The elective decree is made effective by the efficient work of the Holy Spirit, who works when, and where, and how He pleases.

God's common grace would incline all men to good if not resisted.

The elective decree leaves others who are not elected--others who suffer the just consequences of their sin.

Some men are permitted to follow the evil which they freely choose, to their own destruction.

God, in His sovereignty, could regenerate all men if He chose to do so.

The Judge of all the earth will do right, and will extend His saving grace to multitudes who are undeserving.

Election is not based on foreseen faith or good works, but only on God's sovereign good pleasure.

Much the larger portion of the human race has been elected to life.

All of those dying in infancy are among the elect.

There has also been an election of individuals and of nations to external and temporal favors and privileges--an election which falls short of salvation.

The doctrine of election is repeatedly taught and emphasized throughout the Scriptures.

Footnotes:

39. Ch. III, sections III-VII.
40. Institutes, Book III, Ch. XXI, sec. I.
41. Pamphlet, Election, p. 10.
42. Warfield, Biblical Doctrines, p. 50.
43. Cunningham, Historical Theology, II, p. 398.
44. Historical Theology, II, p. 467.
45. Theology, p. 230.
46. quoted by Ness, Antidote Against Arminianism, p. 34.
47. Ch. III:2: XVI:2, 3.
48. Warfield, Biblical Doctrins, art. Predestination, p. 63.
49. Ness, Antidote Against Arminianism, p. 31.
50. The Augustinian Doctrine of Predestination, p. 297.
51. Ch. III: Sec. 7
52. Institutes, Book III, Ch. 23.
53. In Praefat, and Epist. ad Rom., quoted by Zanchius, Predestination, p. 92.
54. Biblical Doctrines, art., Predestination, p. 64.
55. Biblical Doctrines, p. 54.
56. Rice, God Sovereign and Man Free, pp. 3, 4.
57. Warfield, Biblical Doctrine, p. 35.
58. A syllabus of Systematic Theology, pp. 219, 220.
59. Systematic Theology, II, p. 652.
60. Bondage of the Will, p. 252.
61. Historical Theology, II, p. 397.
62. Zanchius', Predestination, Introduction, p. 19.
63. The Plan of Salvation, p. 28.
64. Systematic Theology, II, p. 318.
65. Systematic Theology, II, p. 317.
66. Calvinism, Pure and Mixed, p. 84.
67. Jesus as He Was and Is, p. 276.

68. Biblical Doctrines, Art. the Millenium and the Apocalypse, p. 647.
69. Warfield, article, "Are They Few That Be Saved?"
70. The Coming of the Lord, P. 250. For a very excellent discussion of the question, "Is the World Growin. Better?" see Snowden's book, Chap. VIII.
71. Snowden, The Coming of Our Lord, p. 265.
72. Two Studies in the History of Doctrine, p. 230.
73. Christianity Today, Jan. 1931, p. 14.
74. Christianity Today, Jan. 1931. p. 14.
75. Calvin Memorial Addresses, p. 112.

Chapter XII - Atonement

1. Statement of the Doctrine. 2. The Infinite Value of Christ's Atonement. 3. The Atonement is Limited in Purpose and Application. 4. Christ's Work as a Perfect Fulfillment of the Law. 5. A Ransom. 6. The Divine Purpose in Christ's Sacrifice. 7. The Exclusion of the Non-Elect. 8. The Argument from the Foreknowledge of God. 9. Certain Benefits Which Extend to Mankind In General.

1. STATEMENT OF THE DOCTRINE

The question which we are to discuss under the subject of "Limited Atonement" is, Did Christ offer up Himself a sacrifice for the whole human race, for every individual without distinction or exception; or did His death have special reference to the elect? In other words, was the sacrifice of Christ merely intended to make the salvation of all men possible, or was it intended to render certain the salvation of those who had been given to Him by the Father? Arminians hold that Christ died for all men alike, while Calvinists hold that in the intention and secret plan of God Christ died for the elect only, and that His death had only an incidental reference to others in so far as they are partakers of common grace. The meaning might be brought out more clearly if we used the phrase "Limited Redemption" rather than "Limited Atonement." The Atonement is, of course, strictly an infinite transaction; the limitation comes in, theologically, in the application of the benefits of the atonement, that is in redemption. But since the phrase "Limited Atonement" has become well established in theological usage and its meaning is well known we shall continue to use it.

Concerning this doctrine the Westminster Confession says: ". . . Wherefore they who are elected being fallen in Adam, are redeemed in Christ, are effectually called unto faith in Christ by His Spirit working in due season; are justified, adopted, sanctified, and kept by His power through faith unto salvation. Neither are any other redeemed by Christ, effectually called, justified, adopted, sanctified, and saved, but the elect only." [76]

It will be seen at once that this doctrine necessarily follows from the doctrine of election. If from eternity God has planned to save one portion of the human race and not another, it seems to be a contradiction to say that His work has equal reference to both portions, or that He sent His Son to die for those whom He had predetermined not to save, as truly as, and in the same sense that He was sent to die for those whom He had chosen for salvation. These two doctrines must stand or fall together. We cannot logically accept one and reject the other. If God has elected some and not others to eternal life, then plainly the primary purpose of Christ's work was to redeem the elect.

2. THE INFINITE VALUE OF CHRIST'S ATONEMENT

This doctrine does not mean that any limit can be set to the value or power of the atonement which Christ made. The value of the atonement depends upon, and is measured by, the dignity of the person making it; and since Christ suffered as a Divine-human person the value of His suffering was infinite. The Scripture writers tell us plainly that the "Lord of glory" was crucified, 1 Cor. 2:8; that wicked men "killed the Prince of life," Acts 3:15; and that God "purchased" the Church "with His own blood," Acts 20:28. The atonement, therefore, was infinitely meritorious and might have saved every member of the human race had that been God's plan. It was limited only in the sense that it was intended for, and is applied to, particular persons; namely for those who are actually saved.

Some misunderstanding occasionally arises here because of a false assumption that Calvinists teach that Christ suffered so much for one soul, and so much for another, and that He would have suffered more if more were to have been saved. We believe, however, that even if many fewer of the human race were to have been pardoned and saved, an atonement of infinite value would have been necessary in order to have secured for them these blessings; and though many more, or even all men were to have been pardoned and saved, the sacrifice of Christ would have been amply sufficient as the ground or basis of their salvation. Just as it is necessary for the sun to give off as much heat if only one plant is to grow upon the earth as if the earth is to be covered with vegetation, so it was necessary for Christ to suffer as much if only one soul was to be saved as if a large number or even all mankind were to be saved. Since the sinner had offended against a Person of infinite dignity, and had been sentenced to suffer eternally, nothing but a sacrifice of infinite value could atone for him. No one assumes that since the sin of Adam was the ground for the condemnation of the race, he sinned so much for one man and much for another and would have sinned more if there were to have been more sinners. Why then should they make the assumption in regard to the suffering of Christ?

3. THE ATONEMENT IS LIMITED IN PURPOSE AND APPLICATION

While the value of the atonement was sufficient to save all mankind, it was efficient to save only the elect. It is indifferently well adapted to the salvation of one man to that of another, thus making the salvation of every man objectively possible; yet because of subjective difficulties, arising on account of the sinners own inability either to see or appreciate the things of God, only those are saved who are regenerated and sanctified by the Holy Spirit. The reason why God does not apply this grace to all men has not been fully revealed.

When the atonement is made universal its inherent value is destroyed. If it is applied to all men, and if some are lost, the conclusion is that it makes salvation objectively possible for all but that it does not actually save anybody. According to the Arminian theory the atonement has simply made it possible for men to co-operate with divine grace and thus save themselves--if they will. But tell us of one cured of disease and yet dying of cancer, and the story will be equally luminous with that of one eased of sin and yet perishing through unbelief. The nature of the atonement settles its extent. If it merely made salvation possible, it applied to all men. If it effectively secured salvation, it had reference only to the elect. As Dr. Warfield says, "The things we have to choose between are an atonement of high value, or an atonement of wide extension. The two cannot go together." The work of Christ can be universalized only by evaporating its substance.

Let there be no misunderstanding at this point. The Arminian limits the atonement as certainly as does the Calvinist. The Calvinist limits the extent of it in that he says it does not apply to all persons (although as has already been shown, he believes that it is efficacious for the salvation of the large proportion of the human race); while the Arminian limits the power of it, for he says that in itself it does not actually save anybody. The Calvinist limits it quantitatively, but not qualitatively; the Arminian limits it qualitatively, but not quantitatively. For the Calvinist it is like a narrow bridge which goes all the way across the stream; for the Arminian it is like a great wide bridge which goes only half-way across. As a matter of fact, the Arminian places more severe limitations on the work of Christ than does the Calvinist.

4. CHRIST'S WORK AS A PERFECT FULFILLMENT OF THE LAW

If the benefits of the atonement are universal and unlimited, it must have been what the Arminians represent it to have been--merely a sacrifice to blot out the curse which rested upon the race through the fall in Adam, a mere substitute for the execution of the law which God in His sovereignty saw fit to accept in lieu of what the sinner was bound to render, and not a perfect satisfaction which fulfilled the demands of justice. It would mean that God no longer demands perfect obedience as He did of Adam, but that He now offers salvation on lower term. God, then, would remove legal obstacles and would accept such faith and evangelical obedience as the person with a graciously restored ability could render if he chose, the Holy Spirit of course aiding in a general way. Thus grace would be extended in that God offers an easier way of salvation--He accepts fifty cents on the dollar, so to speak, since the crippled sinner can pay no more.

On the other hand Calvinists hold that the law of perfect obedience which was originally given to Adam was "permanent, that God has never done anything which would convey the impression that the law was too rigid in its requirements, or too severe in its penalty, or that it stood in need either of abrogation or of derogation. Divine justice demands that the sinner shall be punished, either in himself or in his substitute. We hold that Christ acted in a strictly substitutionary way for His people, that He made a full satisfaction for their sins, thus blotting out the curse from Adam and all their temporal sins; and that by His sinless life He perfectly kept for them the law which Adam had broken, thus earning for His people the reward of eternal life. We believe that the requirement for salvation now as originally is perfect obedience, that the merits of Christ are imputed to His people as the only basis of their salvation, and that they enter heaven clothed only with the cloak of His perfect righteousness and utterly destitute of any merit properly their own. Thus grace, pure grace, is extended not in lowering the requirements for salvation but in the substitution of Christ for His people. He took their place before the law and did for them what they could not do for themselves. This Calvinistic principle is fitted in every way to impress upon us the absolute perfection and unchangeable obligation of the law which was originally given to Adam. It is not relaxed or set aside, but is fittingly honored so that its excellence is shown. In behalf of those who are saved, for whom Christ acted, and in behalf of those who are subjected to everlasting punishment, the law in its majesty is enforced and executed.

If the Arminian theory were true it would follow that millions of those for whom Christ died are finally lost, and that salvation is thus never applied to many of those for whom it was earned. What benefits, for instance, can we point to in the lives of the heathens and say that they have received them from the atonement? It would also follow that God's plans many times have been thwarted and defeated

The Reformed Doctrine Of Predestination

by His creatures and that while He may do according to His will in the armies of heaven, He does not do so among the inhabitants of the earth.

"The sin of Adam," says Charles Hodge, "did not make the condemnation of all men merely possible; it was the ground of their actual condemnation. So the righteousness of Christ did not make the salvation of men merely possible, it secured the actual salvation of those for whom He wrought."

The great Baptist preacher Charles H. Spurgeon said: "If Christ has died for you, you can never be lost. God will not punish twice for one thing. If God punished Christ for your sins He will not punish you. 'Payment God's justice cannot twice demand; first, at the bleeding Saviour's hand, and then again at mine.' How can God be just if he punished Christ, the substitute, and then man himself afterwards?"

5. A RANSOM

Christ is said to have been a ransom for his people "The Son of man came not to be ministered unto but to minister, and to give His life a ransom for many," Matthew 20:28. Notice, this verse does not say that He gave His life a ransom for all, but for many. The nature of a ransom is such that when paid and accepted it automatically frees the persons for whom it was intended. Otherwise it would not be a true ransom. Justice demands that those for whom it is paid shall be freed from any further obligation. If the suffering and death of Christ was a ransom for all men rather than for the elect only, then the merits of His work must be communicated to all alike and the penalty of eternal punishment cannot be justly inflicted on any. God would be unjust if He demanded this extreme penalty twice over, first from the substitute and then from the persons themselves. The conclusion then is that the atonement of Christ does not extend to all men but that it is limited to those for whom He stood surety; that is, to those who compose His true Church.

6. THE DIVINE PURPOSE IN CHRIST'S SACRIFICE

If Christ's death was intended to save all men, then we must say that God was either unable or unwilling to carry out His plans. But since the work of God is always efficient, those for whom atonement was made and those who are actually saved must be the same people. Arminians suppose that the purposes of God are mutable, and that His purposes may fail. In saying that He sent His Son to redeem all men, but that after seeing that such a plan could not be carried out He "elected" those whom He foresaw would have faith and repent, they represent Him as willing what never takes place,--as suspending His purposes and plans upon the volitions and actions of creatures who are totally dependent on Him. No rational being who has the wisdom and power to carry out his plans intends what he never accomplishes or adopts plans for an end which is never attained. Much less would God, whose--wisdom and power are infinite, work in this manner. We may rest assured that if some men are lost God never purposed their salvation, and never devised and put into operation means designed to accomplish that end.

Jesus Himself limited the purpose of His death when He said, "I lay down my life for the sheep." If, therefore, He laid down His life for the sheep, the atoning character of His work was not universal. On another occasion He said to the Pharisees, "Ye are not my sheep;" and again, "Ye are of your father the Devil." Will anyone maintain that He laid down His life for these, seeing that He so pointedly excludes them? The angel which appeared to Joseph told him that Mary's son was to be called JESUS, because His mission in the world was to save His people from their sins. He then came not merely to make salvation possible but actually to save His people; and what He came to do we may confidently expect Him to have accomplished.

Since the work of God is never in vain, those who are chosen by the Father, those who are redeemed by the Son, and those who are sanctified by the Holy Spirit,--or in other words, election, redemption and sanctification,--must include the same persons. The Arminian doctrine of a universal atonement makes these unequal and thereby destroys the perfect harmony within the Trinity. Universal redemption means universal salvation.

Christ declared that the elect and the redeemed were the same people when in the intercessory prayer He said. "Thine they were, and thou gavest them to me," and "I pray for them: I pray not for the world, but for those whom thou hast given me; for they are thine: and all things that are mine are thine, and thine are mine; and I am glorified in them," John 17:6, 9, 10. And again, "I am the good shepherd; and I know my own, and mine own know me, even as the Father knoweth me, and I know the Father; and I lay down my life for the sheep," John 10:14, 15. The same teaching is found when we are told to "feed the Church of the Lord which He purchased with His own blood," Acts 20:28. We are told that "Christ loved the Church, and gave Himself for it," Ephesians 5:25; and that He laid down His life for His friends, John 15:13. Christ died for such as were Paul and John, not for such as were Pharaoh and Judas, who were" goats and not sheep. We cannot say that His death was intended for all unless we say that Pharaoh, Judas, etc., were of the sheep, friends, and Church of Christ.

Furthermore, when it is said that Christ gave His life for His Church, or for His people, we find it impossible to believe that He gave Himself as much for reprobates as for those whom He intended to save. Mankind is divided into two classes and what is distinctly affirmed of one is impliedly denied of the other. In each case something is said of those who belong to one group which is not true of those who belong to the other. When it is said that a man labors and sacrifices health and strength for his children, it is thereby denied that the motive which controls him is mere philanthropy, or that the design he has in view is the good of society. And when it is said that Christ died for His people it is denied that He died equally for all men.

7. THE EXCLUSION OF THE NON-ELECT

It was not, then, a general and indiscriminate love of which all men were equally the objects, but a peculiar, mysterious, infinite love for His elect, which caused God to send His Son into the world to suffer and die. Any theory which denies this great and precious truth, and which would explain away this love as merely indiscriminate benevolence or philanthropy which had all men for its objects, many of whom are allowed to perish, must be un-Scriptural. Christ died not for an unorderly mass, but for His people, His bride, His Church.

A farmer prizes his field. But no one supposes that he cares equally for every plant that grows there, for the "tares" as well as the "wheat." God's field is the world, Matthew 13:38, and he loves it with an exclusive eye to its "good seed," the children of the kingdom, and not the children of the wicked one. It is not the whole of mankind that is equally loved of God and promiscuously redeemed by Christ. God is not necessarily communicative of His goodness, as the sun of its light, or a tree of its cooling shade, which does not choose its objects, but serves all indifferently without variation or distinction. This would be to make God of no more understanding than the sun, which shines not where it pleases, but where it must. He is an understanding person, and has a sovereign right to choose His own objects.

In Genesis we read that God "put enmity" between the seed of the woman and the seed of the serpent. Now who were meant by the seed of the woman and the seed of the serpent? On first thought we might suppose that the seed of the woman meant the entire human race descended from Eve. But in Galatians 3:16 Paul uses this term "seed," and applies it to Christ as an individual. "He saith not, And to seeds, as of many; but as of one, And to thy seed, which is Christ." On further investigation we also find that the seed of the serpent means not literal descendants of the Devil, but those non-elect members of the human race, who partake of his sinful nature. Jesus said of His enemies, "Ye are of your father, the Devil; and the lusts of your father it is your will to do," John 8:44. Paul denounced Elymas the sorcerer as a son of the Devil and an enemy of all righteousness. Judas is even called a devil, John 6:70. So the seed of the woman and the seed of the serpent are each a part of the human race. In other parts of the Scriptures we find that Christ and His people are "one," that He dwells in them and is united with them as the vine and the branches are united. And since at the very beginning God "put enmity" between these two groups, it is plain that He never loved all alike, nor intended to redeem all alike. Universal redemption and God's sentence on the serpent can never go together.

There is also a parallel to be noticed between the high priest of ancient Israel and Christ who is our high priest; for the former, we are told, was a type of the latter. On the great day of atonement the high priest offered sacrifices for the sins of the twelve tribes of Israel. He interceded for them and for them only. Likewise, Christ prayed not for the world but for His people. The intercession of the high priest secured for the Israelites blessings from which all other peoples were excluded; and the intercession of Christ, which also is limited but of a much higher order, shall certainly be efficacious in the highest sense, for Him the Father heard always. Furthermore, it is not necessary that God's mercy shall extend to all men without exception before it can be truly and properly called infinite; for all men taken together would not constitute a multitude strictly and properly infinite. The Scriptures plainly tell us that the Devil and the fallen angels are left outside of His benevolent purposes. But His mercy is infinite in that it rescues the great multitude of His elect from indescribable and eternal sin and misery to indescribable and eternal blessedness.

While the Arminians hold that Christ died equally for all men and that He obtained sufficient grace to enable all men to repent, believe, and persevere, if they will only co-operate with it, they also hold that those who refuse to co-operate shall on that account and through all eternity be punished far more severely than if Christ had never died for them at all. We see that so far in the history of the human race the large proportion of the adult population have failed to co-operate and have thus been allowed to bring upon themselves greater misery than if Christ had never come. Surely a view which permits God's work of redemption to issue in such failure, and which sheds so little glory on the atonement of Christ, cannot be true. Vastly more of God's love and mercy for His people is seen in the Calvinistic doctrines of unconditional election and limited atonement than is seen in the Arminian doctrine of conditional election and unlimited atonement.

8. THE ARGUMENT FROM THE FOREKNOWLEDGE OF GOD

The argument from the foreknowledge of God is of itself sufficient to prove this doctrine. Is not God's mind infinite? Are not His perceptions perfect? Who can believe that He, like a feeble mortal, would "shoot at the convoy without perceiving the individual birds?" Since He knew beforehand who they were that would be saved--and the more evangelical Arminians admit that God does have exact foreknowledge of all events--He would not have sent Christ intending to save those who he positively foreknew would be lost. For, as Calvin remarks, "Where would have been the consistency of Gods calling to Himself such as He knows will never come?" If a man knows that in an adjoining room there are ten oranges, seven of which are good and three of which are rotten, he does not go into the room expecting to get ten good ones. Or if it is foreknown that out of a group of fifty men to whom invitations to a banquet might be sent a certain ten will not come, the host does not send out invitations expecting those ten as well as the others to accept. They do but deceive themselves who, admitting God's foreknowledge, say that Christ died for all men; for what is that but to attribute folly to Him whose ways are perfect? To represent God as earnestly striving to do what He knows He will not do is to represent Him as acting foolishly.

9. CERTAIN BENEFITS WHICH EXTEND TO MANKIND IN GENERAL

In conclusion let it be said that Calvinists do not deny that mankind in general receive some important benefits from Christ's atonement. Calvinists admit that it arrests the penalty which would have been inflicted upon the whole race because of Adam's sin; that it forms a basis for the preaching of the Gospel and thus introduces many uplifting moral influences into the world and restrains many evil influences. Paul could say to the heathen people of Lystra that God "left not Himself without witness, in that He did good and gave you from heaven rains and fruitful seasons, filling your hearts with food and gladness," Acts 14:17. God makes His sun to shine on the evil and the good, and sends rain on the just and the unjust. Many temporal blessings are thus secured for all men, although these fall short of being sufficient to insure salvation.

Cunningham has stated the belief of Calvinists very clearly in the following paragraph: - "It is not denied by the advocates of particular redemption, or of a limited atonement, that mankind in general, even those who ultimately perish, do derive some advantages or benefits from Christ's death; and no position they hold requires them to deny this. They believe that important benefits have accrued to the whole human race from the death of Christ, and that in these benefits those who are finally impenitent and unbelieving partake. What they deny is, that Christ intended to procure, or did procure, for all men these blessings which are the proper and peculiar fruits of His death, in its specific character as an atonement,--that He procured or purchased redemption--that in, pardon and reconciliation--for all men. Many blessings flow to mankind at large from the death of Christ, collaterally and incidentally, in consequence of the relation in which men, viewed collectively, stand to each other. All these benefits were of course foreseen by God, when He resolved to send His Son into the world; they were contemplated or designed by Him, as what men should receive and enjoy. They are to be regarded and received as bestowed by Him, and as thus unfolding His glory, indicating His character, and actually accomplishing His purposes; and they are to be viewed as coming to men through the channel of Christ's mediation,--of His suffering and death." [77]

There is, then, a certain sense in which Christ died for all men, and we do not reply to the Arminian tenet with an unqualified negative. But what we do maintain is that the death of Christ had special reference to the elect in that it was effectual for their salvation, and that the effects which are produced in others are only incidental to this one great purpose.

Footnotes:

76. Ch. III, Sec. 4.
77. Historical Theology, II, p. 333.

Chapter XIII – Efficacious Grace

1. Teaching of the Westminster Confession. 2. Necessity for the Change. 3. An Inward Change Wrought by Supernatural Power. 4. The Effect Produced in the Soul. 5. The Sufficiency of Christ's Work--Evangelicalism. 6. Arminian View of Universal Grace. 7. No Violation of Man's Free Agency. 8. Common Grace.

1. TEACHING OF THE WESTMINSTER CONFESSION

The Westminster Confession states the doctrine of Efficacious Grace thus:--"All those whom God has predestinated unto life, and those only, He is pleased, in His appointed and accepted time, effectually to call, by His Word and Spirit, out of that state of death, in which they are by nature, to grace and salvation by Jesus Christ; enlightening their minds spiritually and savingly, to understand the things of God; taking away their heart of stone, and giving them a heart of flesh; renewing their wills, and by His almighty power determining them to that which is good; and effectually drawing them to Jesus Christ, yet so as they come most freely, being made willing by His grace.

"This effectual call is of God's free and special grace alone, not from any thing at all foreseen in man, who is altogether passive therein, until, being quickened and renewed by the Holy Spirit, he is thereby enabled to answer this call, and to embrace the grace offered and conveyed by it." [78]

And the Shorter Catechism, in answer to the question "What is effectual calling?" says, "Effectual calling is the Work of God's Spirit, whereby, convincing us of our sin and misery, enlightening our minds in the knowledge of Christ, and renewing our wills, He doth persuade and enable us to embrace Jesus Christ, freely offered to us in the Gospel." [79]

2. NECESSITY FOR THE CHANGE

The merits of Christ's obedience and suffering are sufficient for, adapted to, and freely offered to all men. The question then arises, Why is one saved, and another lost? What causes some men to repent and believe, while others, with the same external privileges, reject the Gospel and continue in impenitence and unbelief? The Calvinist says that it is God who makes this difference, that he efficaciously persuades some to come to Him; but the Arminian ascribes it to the men themselves.

As Calvinists we hold that the condition of men since the fall is such that if left to themselves they would continue in their state of rebellion and refuse all offers of salvation. Christ would then have died in vain. But since it was promised that He should see of the travail of His soul and be satisfied, the effects of that sacrifice have not been left suspended upon the whim of man's changeable and sinful will. Rather, the work of God in redemption has been rendered effective through the mission of the Holy Spirit who so operates on the chosen people that they are brought to repentance and faith, and thus made heirs of eternal life.

The teaching of the Scriptures is such that we must say that man in his natural state is radically corrupt, and that he can never become holy and happy through any power of his own. He is spiritually dead, and must be saved by Christ if at all. Common reason tells us that if a man is so fallen so to be at enmity with God, that enmity must be removed before he can have any desire to do God's will. If a sinner is to desire redemption through Christ, he must receive a new disposition. He must be born again, and from above (John 3:3). It is easy enough for us to see that the Devil and the demons would have to be thus sovereignly changed if they were ever to be saved; yet the innate sinful principles which actuate fallen man are of the same nature, although not yet so intense, as are those which actuate fallen angels. If man is dead in sin, then nothing short of this supernatural life-giving power of the Holy Spirit will ever cause him to do that which is spiritually good. If it were possible for him to enter heaven while still possessed of the old nature, then, for him, heaven would be as bad as hell; for he would be out of harmony with his environment. He would loathe its very atmosphere and would be in misery when in the presence of God. Hence the necessity for the inward work of the Holy Spirit.

In the nature of the case the first movement toward salvation can no more come from man than his body if dead could originate its own life. Regeneration is a sovereign gift of God, graciously bestowed on those whom He has chosen; and for this great re-creative work God alone is competent. It cannot be granted on the foresight of any thing good in the subjects of this saving change, for in their unrenewed nature they are incapable of acts with right motives toward God; hence none could possibly be foreseen.

The Reformed Doctrine Of Predestination

In his unregenerate state man never adequately realizes his utterly helpless condition. He imagines that he is able to reform himself and turn to God if he chooses. He even imagines that he is able to counteract the designs of infinite Wisdom, and to defeat the agency of Omnipotence itself. As Dr. Warfield says, "Sinful man stands in need, not of inducements or assistance to save himself, but precisely of saving; and Jesus Christ has come not to advise, or urge, or woo, or help him to save himself, but to save him."

3. AN INWARD CHANGE WROUGHT BY SUPERNATURAL POWER

In the Scriptures this change is called a regeneration (Titus 3:5), a spiritual resurrection which is wrought by the same mighty power with which God wrought in Christ when He raised Him from the dead (Eph. 1:19, 20), a calling out of darkness into God's marvelous light (1 Peter 2:9), a passing out of death into life (John 5:24), a new birth (John 3:3), a making alive (Col. 2:13), a taking away of the heart of stone and giving of a heart of flesh (Ezek. 11:19), and the subject of the change is said to be a new creature (II Cor. 5:17). Such descriptions completely refute the Arminian notion that regeneration is primarily man's act, induced by moral persuasion or the mere influence of the truth as presented in a general way by the Holy Spirit. And just because this change is produced by power from on high which is the living spring of a new and re-created life, it is irresistible and permanent.

The regeneration of the soul is something which is wrought in us, and not an act performed by us. It is an instantaneous change from spiritual death to spiritual life. It is not even a thing of which we are conscious at the moment it occurs, but rather something which lies lower than consciousness. At the moment of its occurrence the soul is as passive as was Lazarus when he was called back to life by Jesus. Concerning the soul in regeneration Charles Hodge says: "It is the subject, and not the agent of the change. The soul co-operates, or, is active in what precedes and in what follows the change, but the change itself is something experienced, and not something done. The blind and the lame who came to Christ, may have undergone much labor in getting into His presence, and they joyfully exerted the new power imparted to them, but they were entirely passive in the moment of the healing. They in no way co-operated in the production of that effect. The same is true in regeneration." [80] And again he says: "The same doctrine on this subject is taught in other words when regeneration is declared to be a new birth. At birth the child enters upon a new state of existence. Birth is not its own act. It is born. It comes from a state of darkness, in which the objects adapted to its nature cannot act on it or awaken its activities. As soon as it comes into the world all its faculties are awakened; it sees, feels, and hears, and gradually unfolds all its faculties as a rational and moral, as well as a physical being. The scriptures teach that it is thus in regeneration. The soul enters upon a new state. It is introduced into a new world. A whole class of objects before unknown or unappreciated are revealed to it, and exercise upon it their appropriate influence." [81]

Regeneration involves an essential change of character. It is a making the tree good in order that the fruit may be good. As a result of this change, the person passes from a state of unbelief to one of saving faith, not by any process of research or argument, but of inward experience. And as we had nothing to do with our physical birth, but received it as a sovereign gift of God, we likewise have nothing to do with our spiritual birth but receive it also as a sovereign gift. Each occurred without any exercise of our own power, and even without our consent being asked. We no more resist the latter than we resist the former. And as we go ahead and live our own natural lives after being born, so we go ahead and work out our own salvation after being regenerated.

The Scriptures pointedly teach that the pre-requisite for entrance into the Kingdom of God is a radical transformation wrought by the Spirit of God Himself. And since this work on the soul is sovereign and supernatural it may be granted or withheld according to the good pleasure of God. Consequently, salvation, to whomsoever it may be granted, is entirely of grace. The born-again Christian comes to see that God is in reality "the author and perfecter" of his faith (Heb. 12:2), and that in this respect He has done a work for him which He has not done for his unconverted neighbor. In answer to the question, "Who maketh thee to differ? And what hast thou that thou didst not receive?" (I Cor. 4:7), he replies that it is God who has put the difference between men, especially between the redeemed and the lost. If any person believes, it is because God has quickened him; and if any person fails to believe, it is because God has withheld that grace which He was under no oblation to bestow. Strictly speaking there is no such thing as a "self-made" man; the highest type of man is the one who can say with Paul, "By the grace of God I am what I am."

When Jesus said, "Lazarus, come forth," a mighty power went along with the command and gave effect to it. Lazarus, of course, was not conscious of any other than his own power working in him; but when he later understood the situation he undoubtedly saw that he had been called into life wholly by divine power. God's power was primary, his was secondary, and would never have been exerted except in response to the divine. It is in this manner that every redeemed soul is brought from spiritual death to spiritual life. And just as the dead Lazarus was first called back into life and then breathed and ate, so the soul dead in sin is first transferred to spiritual life and then exercises faith and repentance and does good works.

Paul emphasized this very point when he said that although Paul might plant and Apollos might water, it was God who gave the increase. Mere human efforts are unavailing. If a crop of wheat is to be raised, man can do only the most external and mechanical things toward that end. It is God who gives the increase through the sovereign control of forces which are entirely outside the sphere of man's influence. Likewise, in regard to the soul it matters not how eloquent the preacher may be, unless God opens the heart there will be no conversion. Here especially man does only the most external and mechanical things and it is the Holy Spirit who imparts the new principle of spiritual life.

The Scripture doctrine of the fall represents man as morally ruined, unable by nature to do any good thing. The truly converted Christian comes to see his inability and knows that he does not make himself eligible for heaven by his own good works and merits. He realizes that he cannot move spiritually but as he is moved; that like the branches of a tree, he can make no shoot, nor put forth leaves, nor bear fruit, except as he receives sap from the root. Or, as Calvin says, "No man makes himself a sheep, but is created such by divine grace." The elect hear the Gospel and believe--not always at the first hearing, but at the divinely appointed time--the non-elect hear but disbelieve, not because they lack sufficient evidence, but because their inward nature is opposed to holiness. The reason for the two kinds of response is to be traced to an external source. "A new heart also will I give you, and a new spirit will I put within you; and I will make away the stony heart out of your flesh, and I will give you a heart of flesh," Ezek. 36:26. The "heart" in Biblical language includes the whole inner man.

Under the terms of the eternal covenant which was made between the Father and the Son, Christ has been exalted to be the mediatorial Ruler over the whole earth in order that He may direct the developing kingdom. This is one of the rewards of His obedience and suffering. His directing power is exerted through the agency of the Holy Spirit, through whom His purchased redemption is applied to all for whom it was intended and under the precise conditions of time and circumstance predetermined in the covenant. We are told that it is by no ordinary providence of God that a man believes but by the same mighty power that was exerted when Christ was raised from the dead (Eph. 1:19, 20). As certainly as it was effective in the resurrection of Christ it will be effective when put forth in an individual, whether in a physical or a spiritual resurrection.

The physical and the spiritual worlds are each the creation of God. In the physical world the water is sovereignly changed into wine, and the leper is healed by a touch. The Arminian readily admits God's miraculous power in the physical world; why, then, does he deny it in the spiritual world, as if the spirits of men were beyond His control? We believe that God can change a bad man into a good man when He pleases. That is one form of authority which it is the right of the Creator to exercise over the creature. It is one of the means by which the world is governed; and when God sees that it is best for the welfare of the individual and for the development of His kingdom to thus work, it is not only permissible but right that He should do so. The effect follows immediately upon the volition, as when He said, Let there be light. "The Divine saving act," says Mozley, "is the bestowal of this irresistible grace. The subject of the Divine predetermination is rescued by an act of absolute power from the dominion of sin, dragged from it, as it were, by force, converted, filled with the love of God and his neighbor, and qualified infallibly for a state of ultimate reward." [82]

As the physical eye once blinded cannot be restored to sight by any amount or intensity of light falling upon it, so the soul dead in sin cannot acquire spiritual vision by any amount of Gospel truth presented to it. Unless the surgeon's knife or a miracle restore the eye to its normal condition, sight is impossible; and unless the soul be set right through regeneration it will never comprehend and accept the Gospel truth. In regeneration God bids the sinner live; and immediately he is alive, filled with a new spiritual life. Lydia, the seller of purple in the city of Thyatira, gave heed to the things which were spoken by Paul, because the Lord had first opened her heart (Acts 16:14). Christ taught this same truth when in His intercessory prayer He said concerning Himself that God "gave Him authority over all flesh, that to all whom thou hast given Him, He should give eternal life," John 17:2; and again, "For as the Father raiseth the dead and giveth them life, even so the Son also giveth life to whom He will," John 5:21.

Under the covenant made with Adam, man's destiny depended on his own works. We know the results of that trial. Now if man could not work out his salvation when he was upright, what chance has he to do so since he is fallen? Happily for us, God has this time taken the matter into His own hand. And if God again gave man free will by which to work out his own salvation, what would He be doing but again instituting the dispensation which has already been tried and which ended in failure? Suppose a man is carried away by a torrent which he is unable to master, would it be reasonable or wise to take him out only to recruit his strength for a second trial? Would it not be a mockery to save him only to repeat the process? Since God does not repeat His dispensations it follows that the second time He would order salvation on a different plan. If further works are to be wrought, then God, and not man, will be the author; and the new dispensation, like the old, is adjusted to the state in which it finds man.

We are very sure that no property does, or can, attach to the will of man, whether fallen or unfallen, that can take it beyond the reach of God's sovereign control. Saul was called at the height of his persecuting zeal and was transformed into the saintly Paul. The poor dying thief on the cross was called in the last hour of his earthly life. When Paul preached at Antioch "as many as were ordained to eternal life (and only they) believed," Acts 13:48. If God purposed that all men should be saved He most certainly could bring all to salvation. But for reasons which have been only partly revealed, He leaves many impenitent. Through all of His works, however, God does nothing which is inconsistent with man's nature as a rational and responsible being.

One of the great short-comings of Arminianism has been its failure to recognize the necessity for the supernatural work of the Holy Spirit on the heart. Instead, it has resolved regeneration into a more or less gradual change which is carried out by the individual person, a mere change of purpose in the sinner's mind, which is a result of moral persuasion and the general force of truth. It has insisted upon "free will," "the power of contrary choice," etc., and has taught that ultimately the sinner determines his own destiny. In its more consistent forms it makes man a co-savior with Christ, as if the glory in redemption was to be divided between the grace of Christ and the will of man, the latter dividing the spoils with the former.

If, as Arminians say, God is earnestly trying to convert every person, He is making a great failure of His work; for among the adult population of the world up to the present time, where He has succeeded in saving one He has let perhaps twenty-five fall into hell. Such a view sheds little glory on the Divine Majesty. Concerning the Arminian doctrine of resistible grace Toplady says that it is "a doctrine which represents Omnipotence itself as wishing and trying and striving to no purpose. According to this tenet, God, in endeavoring (for it seems that it is only an endeavor) to convert sinners, may, by sinners, be foiled, defeated, and disappointed; He may lay close and long siege to the soul, and that soul can, from the citadel of impregnable free will, hang out a flag of defiance to God Himself, and by a continued obstinacy of defense, and a few vigorous sallies of free will compel Him to raise the siege. In a word, the Holy Spirit, after having for years perhaps, danced attendance on the free will of man, may at length, like a discomfited general, or an unsuccessful politician, be either put to ignominious night, or contemptuously dismissed, re infecta, without accomplishing the end for which He was sent."

It is unreasonable to suppose that the sinner can thus defeat the creative power of Almighty God. "All authority hath been given to me in heaven and on earth," said the risen Lord. No limit is set to that authority. "Is anything too hard for Jehovah?" "He doeth according to His will in the armies of heaven, and among the inhabitants of the earth; and no one can stay His hand, or say unto Him, What doest thou?" In view of these passages and many others to the same effect it ill becomes us to imagine that God is struggling along with man as best He can, persuading, exhorting, pleading, but unable to accomplish His purpose if His creatures will otherwise. If God does not effectually call, we may imagine Him saying, "I will that all men should be saved; nevertheless, it must finally be, not as I will but as they will." He is then put into the same extremity with Darius who would gladly have saved Daniel, but could not (Dan. 6:14). No Christian who is familiar with what the Scriptures teach about the sovereignty of God can believe that He is thus defeated in His creatures. Is it not necessary that a creature must have power to defy and thwart the purposes of Almighty God before his actions can be rewarded or punished. Furthermore, if God actually stood powerless before the majesty of man's lordly will, there would be but little use to pray for Him to convert any one. It would then be more reasonable for us to direct our petitions to the man himself.

4. THE EFFECT PRODUCED IN THE SOUL

The immediate and important effect of this inward, purifying change of nature is that the person loves righteousness and trusts in Christ for salvation. Whereas his natural element was sin, it now becomes holiness; sin becomes repulsive to him, and he loves to do good. This effective and irresistible grace converts the will itself and forms a holy character in the person by a creative act. It removes a man's appetite for sinful things so that he refrains from sin, not as the dyspeptic refuses to eat the dainties for which he longs, lest his indulgence should be punished with the agonies of sickness, but rather because he hates sin for its own sake. The holy and thorough submission to God's will, which the convert before dreaded and resisted, he now loves and approves. Obedience has become not only the obligatory but the preferable good.

But so long as people remain in this world they are subject to temptations and they still have the remnants of the old nature clinging to them. Hence they are often deluded, and commit sin; Yet these sins are only the death struggles and frenzied writhings of the old nature which has already received the death blow. The regenerate also suffer pain, disease, discouragement, and even death itself, although they are steadily advancing toward complete salvation.

At this point many people confuse regeneration and sanctification. Regeneration is exclusively God's work, and it is an act of His free grace in which He implants a new principle of spiritual life in the soul. It is performed by supernatural power and is complete in an instant. On the other hand sanctification is a process through which the remains of sin in the outward life are gradually removed, so that, as the Shorter Catechism says, we are enabled more and more to die unto sin and to live unto righteousness. It is a joint work of God and man. It consists in the gradual triumph of the new nature implanted in regeneration over the evil that still remains after the heart has been renewed. Or, in other words, we may say that complete sanctification lags behind after the life has been in principle won to God. Perfect righteousness is the goal which is set before us all through this life and every Christian should make steady progress toward that goal. Sanctification, however, is not fully completed until death, at which time the Holy Spirit cleanses the soul of every vestige of sin, making it holy and raising it above even the possibility of sinning.

Strictly speaking, we may say that redemption is not fully complete until the saved have received their resurrection bodies. In one sense it was complete when Christ died on Calvary; yet it is applied only gradually by the Holy Spirit. And since the Holy Spirit does thus effectually apply to the elect the merits of Christ's sacrifice, their salvation is most infallibly certain and can by no means be prevented. Hence the certainty that the will of God for the salvation of his people is in no wise disappointed or made void by His creatures.

5. THE SUFFICIENCY OF CHRIST'S WORK--EVANGELICALISM

We now come to discuss the sufficiency of Christ's work in the matter of redemption. We believe that by His vicarious suffering and death He fully paid the debt which His people owed to divine justice, thus releasing them from the consequences of sin, and that by keeping the law of perfect obedience and living a sinless life He vicariously earned for them the reward of eternal life. His work fully provided for their rescue from sin and for their establishment in heaven. These two phases of His work are sometimes referred to as His active and passive obedience. This doctrine of the sufficiency of His work is set forth in the Westminster Confession when we are told that by His perfect obedience and sacrifice of Himself He "fully satisfied the justice of His Father; and purchased not only reconciliation, but an everlasting inheritance in the kingdom of heaven, for all those whom the Father had given Him." [83] Had He only paid the penalty for sin without also earning the reward of eternal life, His people would then only have been raised up to the zero point. They would then have been on the same plane as was Adam before he fell, and would still have been under obligation to earn eternal life for themselves. To Paul's declaration that Christ is all in all in matters of salvation (Col. 3:11), we can add that man is nothing at all as to that work, and has not in himself anything which merits salvation.

Just here we can do no better than to quote the words of Dr. Warfield spoken with special reference to I Tim. 1:15. "Jesus did all that is included in the great word 'save.' He did not come to induce us to save ourselves, or to help us to save ourselves, or to enable us to save ourselves. He came to SAVE us. And it is, therefore, that His name was called Jesus--because He should save His people from their sins. . . . Nothing that we are and nothing that we can do enters in the slightest measure into the ground of our acceptance with God. Jesus did it all. And by doing it all He has become in the fullest and widest and deepest sense the word can bear--our Saviour. For this end did He come into the world--to SAVE sinners; and nothing short of the actual and complete SAVING of sinners will satisfy the account of His work given from His own lips and repeated from them by His apostles. It is in this great fact, indeed, that there lies the whole essence of the gospel. For let us never forget that the gospel is not good advice but good news. It does not come to us to make known to us what we must do to earn salvation, but proclaims to us what Jesus has done to save us. It is salvation, a complete salvation, that is announced to us; and the burden of its message is just the words of our text--that Christ Jesus came into the world to SAVE sinners." [84]

To doubt that any for whom Christ died will be saved, or that righteousness will eventually triumph, is to doubt the sufficiency of Jesus Christ for the work which He undertook in our behalf. On the cross Jesus declared that He had finished the work of redemption which the Father gave Him to do. But as Toplady remarks, "the person with power to accept or reject as he pleases must say: 'No, thou didst not finish the work of redemption which was given thee to do; thou didst indeed a part of it, but I myself must add something to it or the whole of thy performance will stand for naught.'"

Only those views which ascribe to God all the power in the salvation of sinners are consistently evangelical, for the word "evangelical" means that it is God alone who saves. If faith and obedience must be added, depending upon the independent choice of man, we no longer have evangelicalism. Evangelicalism with a universal atonement leads to universal salvation; and in so far as Arminianism holds that Christ died for all men and that the Spirit strives to apply this redemption to all men but that only some are saved, it is not evangelical.

We may further illustrate this principle of evangelicalism by supposing a group of people who are stricken with a fatal disease. Then if a doctor administers to them a medicine which is a certain cure, all who get the medicine will recover. In the same manner, if the work of Christ is effective, and if it is applied to all men by the Spirit, all will be saved. Hence to become evangelical the Arminian must become a universalist. Calvinism alone, which holds to evangelicalism with a limited atonement and asserts that the work of Christ accomplishes what it was intended to accomplish, is consistent with the facts of Scripture and experience.

6. THE ARMINIAN VIEW OF UNIVERSAL GRACE

The universalistic note is always prominent in the Arminian system. A typical example of this is seen in the assertion of Prof. Henry C. Sheldon, who for a number of years was connected with Boston University. Says he: "Our contention is for the universality of the opportunity of salvation, as against an exclusive and unconditional choice of individuals to eternal life." [85] Here we notice not only (1) the characteristic Arminian stress on universalism, but also (2) the recognition that, in the final analysis, all that God does for the salvation of men does not actually save anybody, but that it only opens up a way of salvation so that men can save themselves--and then for all practical purposes we are back on the plane of pure naturalism!

Perhaps the strongest assertion of the Arminian construction is to be found in the creed of the Evangelical Union body, or so-called Morisonians, the very purpose of which was to protest against unconditional election. A summary of its "Three Universalities" is fond in the creed thus: "The love of God the Father, in the gift and sacrifice of Jesus to all men everywhere without distinction, exception, or respect of persons; the love of God the Son, in the gift and sacrifice of Himself as a true propitiation for the sins of the whole world; the love of God the Spirit, in His personal and continuous work applying to the souls of all men the provisions of divine grace" [86]

Certainly, if God loves all men alike, and if Christ died for all men alike, and the Holy Spirit applies the benefits of that redemption to all men alike, one of two conclusions follows. (1) All men alike are saved (which is contradicted by Scripture), or, (2) all that God does for man does not save him, but leaves him to save himself! What then becomes of our evangelicalism, which means that it is God alone who saves sinners? If we assert that after God has done all His work it is still left for man to "accept" or "not resist," we give man veto power over the work of Almighty God and salvation rests ultimately in the hand of man. In this system no matter how great a proportion of the work of salvation God may do, man is ultimately the deciding factor. And the man who does come to salvation has some personal merit of his own; he has some grounds to boast over those who are lost. He can point the finger of scorn and say, "You had as good chance as I had. I accepted and you rejected the offer. Therefore you deserve to suffer." How different is this from Paul's declaration that it is "not of works, that no man should glory," and "He that glorieth, let him glory in the Lord," Eph. 2:9; I Cor. 1: 31.

The tendency in all these universalistic systems in which man proudly seizes the helm and proclaims himself the master of his destiny is to reduce Christianity to a religion of works. Luther had this very point in mind when he satirically remarked concerning the moralists of his day, "Here we are always wanting to urn the tables and do good of ourselves to that poor man, our Lord God, from Whom we are rather to receive it."

Zanchius says that Arminianism gently whispers in the ear of man that even in his fallen state he has "both the will and the power to do what is good and acceptable to God:--that Christ's death is accepted by God as a universal atonement for all men; in order that every one may, if he will, save himself by his own free will and good works:--that in the exercise of our natural powers, we may arrive at perfection, even in the present state of life. "The issue," says Dr. Warfield, "is indeed a fundamental one and it is clearly drawn. Is it God the Lord who saves us, or is it we ourselves? And does God the Lord save us, or does He merely open up the way of salvation, and leave it, according to our choice, to walk in it or not? The parting of the ways is the old parting of the ways between Christianity and autosoterism. Certainly only he can claim to be evangelical who with full consciousness rests entirely and directly on God and on God alone for his salvation." [87]

> "Not the labors of my hands
> Can fulfill Thy law's commands;
> Could my zeal no respite know,
> Could my tears forever flow,
> All for sin could not atone--
> Thou must save, and Thou alone.
> "Nothing in my hands I bring--
> Simply to Thy cross I cling;
> Naked come to Thee for dress--
> Helpless look to Thee for grace;
> Foul, I to thy fountain fly--
> Wash me, Saviour, or I die!"

Loraine Boettner D.D.

7. NO VIOLATION OF MAN'S FREE AGENCY

It is a common thing for opponents to represent this doctrine as implying that men are forced to believe and turn to God against their wills, or, that it reduces men to the level of machines in the matter of salvation. This is a misrepresentation. Calvinists hold no such opinion, and in fact the full statement of the doctrine excludes or contradicts it. The Westminster Confession, after stating that this efficacious grace which results in conversion is an exercise of omnipotence and cannot be defeated, adds, "Yet so as they come most freely, being made willing by His grace." The power by which the work of regeneration is effected is not of an outward and compelling nature. Regeneration does no more violence to the soul than demonstration does to the intellect, or persuasion the heart. Man is not dealt with as if he were a stone or a log. Neither is he treated as a slave, and driven against his own will to seek salvation. Rather the mind is illuminated, and the entire range of conceptions with regard to God, self, and sin, is changed. God sends His Spirit and, in a way which shall forever rebound to the praise of His mercy and grace, sweetly constrains the person to yield. The regenerated man finds himself governed by new motives and desires, and things which were once hated are now loved and sought after. This change is not accomplished through any external compulsion but through a new principle of life which has been created within the soul and which seeks after the food which alone can satisfy it.

The spiritual law, like the civil law, is "not a terror to the good work, but to the evil"; and we find a good analogy for this in human affairs. Compare the law abiding citizen and the criminal. The law-abiding citizen goes about his affairs day after day unconscious of most of the laws of the state and nation in which he lives. He looks to the government officials and to the police as his friends. They represent constituted authority which he respects and in which he delights. He is a free man. For him the law exists only as the protector of his life, his loved ones, and his property. But when we took at the criminal the whole picture is changed. He probably knows more about the statutes than does the law-abiding man. He studies them in order that he may evade them and defeat their purpose. He lives in fear. He defends his secret room with bullet-proof doors, and carries a revolver for fear of what the police or other people may do to him. He is under a constant bondage. His idea of liberty is to eliminate the police, corrupt the courts, and bring into general disrepute the laws and customs of society on which he tries to prey.

All of us have had experiences in our every day lives in which we refuse to do certain things, but upon the introduction of new factors we have changed our minds and have freely and gladly done what we before opposed. Certainly there is nothing in this doctrine to warrant the representation that, upon Calvinistic principles, men are forced to repent and believe whether or not they choose to do so.

But some may ask, Do not the many passages in the Bible such as, "If thou shalt obey," "If thou turn unto Jehovah," "If thou do that which is evil," and so forth, at least imply that man has free will and ability? It does not follow, however, that merely because God commands man is able to obey. Oftentimes parents play with their children in telling them to do this or that when their very purpose is to show them their inability and to induce them to ask for the parents' help. When men of the world hear such language they assume that they have sufficient power in themselves, and, like the self-conceited lawyer to whom Jesus said, "This do, and thou shalt live," they go away believing that they are able to earn salvation by good works. But when the truly spiritual man hears such language he is led to see that he cannot fulfill the commandment, and so cries out to the Father to do the work for him. In these passages man is taught not what he can do, but what he ought to do; and woe to the one who is so blind that he cannot see this truth, for until he does see it he can never adequately appreciate the work of Christ. In answer to the despairing sinner's cry the Scriptures reveal a salvation which is all of grace, the free gift of God's love and mercy in Christ. And the one who sees himself thus saved by grace instinctively cries out with David, "Who am I, O Lord Jehovah, and what is my house, that thou hast brought me thus far?"

The special grace which we refer to as efficacious is sometimes called irresistible grace. This latter term, however, is somewhat misleading since it does suggest that a certain overwhelming power is exerted upon the person, in consequence of which he is compelled to act contrary to his desires, whereas the meaning intended, as we have stated before, is that the elect are so influenced by divine power that their coming is an act of voluntary choice.

8. COMMON GRACE

Apart from this special grace which issues in the salvation of its objects, there is what we may call "common grace," or general influences of the Holy Spirit which to a greater or lesser degree are shared by all men. God causes His sun to rise on the evil and the good, and sends rain upon the just and the unjust. He sends fruitful seasons and gives many things which make for the general happiness of mankind. Among the most common blessings which are to be traced to this source we may name health, material prosperity, general intelligence, talents for art, music, oratory, literature, architecture, commerce, inventions, etc. In many instances the non-elect receive these blessings in greater abundance than do the elect, for we often find that the sons of this world are for their own generation wiser than the sons of light. Common grace is the source of all the order, refinement, culture, common virtue, etc., which we find in the world, and through it the moral power of the truth upon the heart and conscience is increased and the evil passions of men are restrained. It does not lead to salvation, but it keeps this earth from becoming a hell. It arrests the complete effectuation of sin, just as human insight arrests the fury of wild beasts. It prevents sin from being manifested in all its hideousness, and thus hinders the bursting forth of the flames from the smoking fire. Like the pressure of the atmosphere, it is universal and powerful though unfelt.

Common grace, however, does not kill the core of sin, and therefore it is not capable of producing a genuine conversion. Through the light of nature, the workings of conscience, and especially through the external presentation of the Gospel it makes known to man what he should do, but does not give that power which man stands in need of. Furthermore, all of these common influences of the Holy Spirit are capable of being resisted. The Scriptures constantly teach that the Gospel becomes effectual only when it is attended by the special illuminating power of the Spirit, and that without this power it is to the Jews a stumbling block and to the Gentiles foolishness. Hence the unregenerate man can never know God except in an outward way; and for this reason the external righteousness of the scribes and Pharisees is declared to be just no righteousness at all. Jesus said to His disciples that the world could not receive the Spirit of truth, "for it beholdeth Him not, neither knoweth Him;" yet in the same breath He added, "Ye know Him; for He abideth with you, and shall be in you," John 14:17. The Arminian doctrine destroys the distinction between efficacious and common grace, or at best makes efficacious grace to be an assistance without which salvation is impossible, while the Calvinistic makes it to be an assistance by which salvation is made certain.

Concerning the reformations which are produced by common grace Dr. Charles Hodge says:--"It not infrequently happens that men who have been immoral in their lives change their whole course of living. They become outwardly correct in their deportment, temperate, pure, honest, and benevolent. This is a great and praiseworthy change. It is in a high degree beneficial to the subject of it, and to all with whom he is connected. It may be produced by different causes, by the force of conscience, or by a regard for the authority of God and a dread of His disapprobation, or by a regard to the good opinion of men, or by the mere force of an enlightened regard to one's own interest. But whatever may be the proximate cause of such reformation, it falls very far short of sanctification. The two things differ in nature as much as a clean heart from clean clothes. Such external reformation may leave a man's inward character in the sight of God unchanged. He may remain destitute of love to God, of faith in Christ, and of all holy exercises or affections." [88] And says Dr. Hewlitt: "Can the corpse in the graveyard be aroused by the sweetest music that ever has been invented, or by the loudest thunder which seems to shake the poles? Just as soon shall the sinner, dead in trespasses and sins, be moved by the thunder of the law, or by the melody of the Gospel; can the Ethiopian change his skin, or the leopard his spots? Then may ye also do good that are accustomed to do evil (Jer. 13:23)." [89]

The following paragraph by Dr. S. G. Craig very clearly sets forth the limitations of common grace:--"Christianity realizes that education and culture, that leaves Jesus Christ out of consideration, while they may make men clever, polished, brilliant, have no power to change their characters. At the most these things of themselves only cleanse the outside of the cup; they do not affect the nature of its contents. Those who place their confidence in education, culture and such like assume that all that is needed to change the wild olive tree into a good olive tree is pruning, spraying, cultivation and such like, whereas what the tree needs first of all, is that it be grafted with a scion from a good olive tree. And until this is done all labor that is spent on the tree is for the most part wasted. We do not underestimate the value of education and culture, and yet one might as well suppose that he could purify the waters of a river by improving the scenery along the banks as suppose that these things of themselves are capable of transforming the hearts of the children of men. . . . As an old Jewish proverb has it: 'Take the bitter tree and plant it in the garden of Eden and water it with the waters there; and let the angel Gabriel be the gardener and the tree will still bear bitter fruit.'" [90]

Footnotes:

78. Chapter X, Section 1 and 2.
79. Question 31.
80. Systematic Theology, II, p. 688.
81. Systematic Theology, II, p. 35.
82. The Augustinian Doctrine of Predestination, p. 8.
83. Chapter VIII, Sect. 5.
84. The Power of God Unto Salvation, p. 48-50.
85. System of Christian Doctrine, p. 417.
86. The Religious Controversies of Scotland, p. 187.
87. The Plan of Salvation, p. 108.

88. Systematic Theology, III, p. 214.
89. Sound Doctrine, p. 21.
90. Jesus as He Was and Is, p. 191, 199.

Chapter XIV – The Perseverance of the Saints

Statement of the Doctrine. 2. Perseverance Does Not Depend Upon the Person's Good Works But Upon God's Grace. 3. Though Truly Saved the Christian May Temporarily Backslide and Commit Sin. 4. An Outward Profession of Righteousness Not a Guarantee That the Person Is a True Christian. 5. Arminian Sense of Insecurity. 6. Purpose of the Scripture Warnings Against Apostasy. 7. Scripture Proof.

1. STATEMENT OF THE DOCTRINE

The doctrine of the Perseverance of the Saints is stated in the Westminster Confession in the following words: "They whom God hath accepted in His Beloved, effectually called and sanctified by His Spirit, can neither totally nor finally fall away from the state of grace; but shall certainly persevere therein to the end, and be eternally saved." [91]

This doctrine does not stand alone but is a necessary part of the Calvinistic system of theology. The doctrines of Election and Efficacious Grace logically imply the certain salvation of those who receive these blessings. If God has chosen men absolutely and unconditionally to eternal life, and if His Spirit effectively applies to them the benefits of redemption, the inescapable conclusion is that these persons shall be saved. And, historically, this doctrine has been held by all Calvinists, and denied by practically all Arminians.

Those who have fled to Jesus for refuge have a firm foundation upon which to build. Though floods of error deluge the land, though Satan raise all the powers of earth and all the iniquities of their own hearts against them, they shall never fail; but, persevering to the end, they shall inherit those mansions which have been prepared for them from the foundation of the world. The saints in heaven are happier but no more secure than are true believers here in this world. Since faith and repentance are gifts of God, the bestowing of these gifts is a revelation of God's purpose to save those to whom they are given. It is an evidence that God has predestinated the recipients of these gifts to be conformed to the image of His Son, i.e., to be like Him in character, destiny, and glory, and that He will infallibly carry out His purpose. No one can pluck them out of His hands. Those who once become true Christians have within themselves the principle of eternal life, which principle is the Holy Spirit; and since the Holy Spirit dwells within them they are already potentially holy. True, they are still exercised by many trials, and they do not yet see what they shall be, but they should know that that which is begun in them shall be completed to the end, and that the very presence of strife within them is the sign of life and the promise of victory.

Furthermore, let our opponents inform us why it is that in regard to those who become true Christians, but who, as they allege, fall away, God does not take them out of the world while they are in the saved state. Surely no one will have the perversity to say that it was because He could not, or because He did not foresee their future apostasy. Why, then, does He leave these objects of His affection here to fall back into sin and to perish? His gift of continued life to those Christians amounts to an infinite curse placed upon them. Who really believe that the heavenly Father takes no better care of His children than that? This stupid heresy of the Arminians teaches that a person may be a son of God today and a son of the Devil tomorrow, that he may change from one state to another as rapidly as he changes his mind. It teaches that he may be born of the Spirit, justified and sanctified, all but glorified, and yet, that he may become reprobate and perish eternally, his own will and course of conduct being the determining factor. Certainly this is deseperate doctrine. There is scarcely an error more absurd that that which supposes that a sovereign God would permit his children to defeat His love and fall away.

In addition to this, if God knows that a certain Christian is going to rebel and perish, can He love him with any deep affection even before his apostasy? If we knew that some one who is our friend today would be led to become our enemy and betray us tomorrow, we could not receive him with the intimacy and trust which otherwise would be natural. Our knowledge of his future acts would in large measure destroy our present love for him.

No one denies that the redeemed in heaven will be preserved in holiness. Yet if God is able to preserve His saints in heaven without violating their free agency, may He not also preserve His saints on earth without violating their free agency?

The nature of the change which occurs in regeneration is a sufficient guarantee that the life imparted shall be permanent. Regeneration is a radical and supernatural change of the inner nature, through which the soul is made spiritually alive, and the new life which is implanted is immortal. And since it is a change in the inner nature, it is in a sphere in which man does not have control. No creature is at liberty to change the fundamental principles of its nature, for that is the prerogative of God as Creator. Hence nothing short of another supernatural act of God could reverse this change and cause the new life to be lost. The born-again Christian can no more lose his sonship to the heavenly Father than an earthly son can lose his sonship to an earthly father. The idea that a Christian may fall away and perish arises from a wrong conception of the principle of spiritual life which is imparted to the soul in regeneration.

2. OUR PERSEVERANCE NOT DEPENDENT ON OUR OWN GOOD WORKS BUT ON GOD'S GRACE

Paul teaches that believers are not under law, but under grace, and that since they are not under the law they cannot be condemned for having violated the law. "Ye are not under law but under grace," Rom. 6:14. Further sin cannot possibly cause their downfall, for they are under a system of grace and are not treated according to their deserts. "If it is by grace, it is no more of works; otherwise grace is no more grace," Rom. 11:6. "The law worketh wrath; but where there is no law, neither is there transgression," Rom. 4:15. "Apart from the law sin is dead" (that is, where the law is abolished sin can no longer subject the person to punishment), Rom. 7:8. "Ye were made dead to the law through the body of Christ," Rom. 7:4. The one who attempts to earn even the smallest part of his salvation by works becomes "a debtor to do the whole law" (that is, to render perfect obedience in his own strength and thus earn his salvation), Gale 6:3. We are here dealing with two radically different systems of salvation, two systems which, in fact, are diametrically opposed to each other.

The infinite, mysterious, eternal love of God for His people is a guarantee that they can never be lost. This love is not subject to fluctuations but is as unchangeable as His being. It is also gratuitous, and keeps faster hold of us than we of it. It is not founded on the attractiveness of its objects. "Herein is love, not that we loved God, but that He loved us, and sent His Son to be the propitiation for our sins," I John 4:10. "God commendeth His own love toward us, in that while we were yet sinners, Christ died for us. Much more then, being now justified by His blood, shall we be saved from the wrath of God through Him. For if, while we were enemies, we were reconciled to God through the death of His Son, much more, being reconciled, shall we be saved by His life," Rom. 5:8-10. Here the very point stressed in that our standing with God is not based on our deserts. It was "while we were enemies" that we were brought into spiritual life through sovereign grace; and if He has done the greater, will He not do the lesser? The writer of the book of Hebrews also teaches that it is impossible for one of God's chosen to be lost when he says that Christ is both "the Author and Perfecter of our faith." We are there taught that the whole course of our salvation is divinely, planned and divinely guided. Neither the grace of God nor its continuance is given according to our merits. Hence if any Christian fell away, it would be because God had withdrawn His grace and changed His method of procedure--or, in other words, because He had put the person back under a system of law.

Robert L. Dabney has expressed this truth very ably In the following paragraph: "The sovereign and unmerited love is the cause of the believer's effectual calling. Jer. 33:3; Rom. 8:30. Now, as the cause is unchangeable, the effect is unchangeable. That effect is, the constant communication of grace to the believer in whom God hath begun a good work. God was not induced to bestow His renewing grace in the first instance, by anything which He saw, meritorious or attractive, in the repenting sinner; and therefore the subsequent absence of everything good in him would be no new motive to God for withdrawing His grace. When He first bestowed that grace, He knew that the sinner on whom He bestowed it was totally depraved, and wholly and only hateful in himself to the divine holiness; and therefore no new instance of ingratitude or unfaithfulness, of which the sinner may become guilty after his conversion, can be any provocation to God, to change His mind, and wholly withdraw His sustaining grace. God knew all this ingratitude before. He will chastise it, by temporarily withdrawing His Holy Spirit, or His providential mercies; but if He had not intended from the first to bear with it, and to forgive it in Christ, He would not have called the sinner by His grace at first. In a word, the causes for which God determined to bestow His electing love on the sinner are wholly in God, and not at all in the believer; and hence, nothing in the believer's heart or conduct can finally change that purpose of love. Is. 54:10; Rom. 11:29. Compare carefully Rom. 5:8-10; 8:32, with the whole scope of Rom. 8:28-end. This illustrious passage is but an argument for our proposition; 'What shall separate us from the love of Christ?'" [92]

"God's love in this respect," says Dr. Charles Hodge "is compared to parental love. A mother does not love her child because it is lovely. Her love leads her to do all she can to render it attractive and to

The Reformed Doctrine Of Predestination

keep it so. So the love of God, being in like manner mysterious, unaccountable by anything in its objects, secures His adorning His children with the graces of His Spirit, and arraying them in all the beauty of holiness. It is only the lamentable mistake that God loves us for our goodness, that can lead any one to suppose that His love is dependent on our self-sustained attractiveness." [93]

Concerning the salvation of the elect, Luther says, "God's decree of predestination is firm and certain; and the necessity resulting from it is, in like manner, immovable, and cannot but take place. For we ourselves are so feeble, that if the matter were left in our hands, very few, or rather none, would be saved; but Satan would overcome us all."

The more we think of these matters, the more thankful we are that our perseverance in holiness and assurance of salvation is not dependent on our own weak nature, but upon God's constant sustaining power. We can say with Isaiah, "Except Jehovah of hosts had left us a very small remnant, we should have become as Sodom, we should have been like unto Gomorrah." Arminianism denies this doctrine of Perseverance, because it is a system, not of pure grace, but of grace and works; and in any such system the person must prove himself at least partially worthy.

3. THOUGH TRULY SAVED THE CHRISTIAN MAY TEMPORARILY BACKSLIDE AND COMMIT SIN

This doctrine of Perseverance does not mean that Christians do not temporarily fall the victims of sin, for alas, this is all too common. Even the best of men backslide temporarily. But they are never completely defeated; for God, by the exercise of His grace on their hearts infallibly prevents even the weakest saint from final apostasy. As yet we have this treasure in earthen vessels, that the exceeding greatness of the power (or the glory) may be of God, and not from ourselves (II Cor. 4:7).

Concerning his own personal experience even the great apostle Paul could write: "The good which I would I do not; but the evil which I would not, that I practice. But if what I would not, that I do, it is no more I that do it, but sin that dwelleth in me. . . . I find then the law, that, to me who would do good, evil is present. For I delight in the law of God after the inward man; but I see a different law in my members, warring against the law of my mind, and bringing me into captivity under the law of sin which is in my members. Wretched man that I am I who shall deliver me out of the body of this death? I thank God through Jesus Christ our Lord. So then I of myself with the mind, indeed, serve the law of God; but with the flesh the law of sin." Rom. 7:19-25. In these lines every true Christian reads his own experience.

It is, of course, inconsistent for the Christian to commit sin, and the writer of the book of Hebrews says that those who do sin "crucify to themselves the Son of God afresh and put Him to an open shame" (6:6). After David had committed sin and had repented he was told by the prophet Nathan that his sin would be forgiven, but that nevertheless through it he had "given great occasion to the enemies of Israel to blaspheme," II Sam. 12:14. David and Peter fell away temporarily, but the basic principles of their natures called them back. Judas fell away permanently because he lacked those basic principles.

As long as the believer remains in this world his state is one of warfare. He suffers temporary reverses and may for a time appear to have lost all faith; yet if he has been once truly saved, he cannot fall away completely from grace. If once he has experienced the inner change which comes through regeneration he will sooner or later return to the fold and be saved. When he comes to himself he confesses his sins and asks forgiveness, never doubting that he is saved. His lapse into sin may have injured him severely and may have brought destruction to others; but so far as he is personally concerned it is only temporary. Paul taught that the life work of many people should be burned since it is constructed of wrong materials, though they themselves shall be saved "so as by fire," I Cor. 3:12-15; and it was this teaching which Jesus brought out in the parable of the lost sheep which the shepherd sought and brought back to the fold.

If true believers fell away, then their bodies, which are called "temples of the Holy Spirit," would become the habitations of the Devil, which of course would make the Devil rejoice and insult over God (I Cor. 6:19). "The Christian is like a man making his way up hill, who occasionally slips back, yet always has his face set toward the summit. The unregenerate man has his face turned downwards, and he is slipping all the way,"--A. H. Strong. "The believer, like a man on shipboard, may fall again and again on the deck, but he will never fall overboard."--C. H. Spurgeon.

Each one of the elect is like the prodigal son, in that for a time he is deluded by the world and is led astray by his own carnal appetite. He tries to feed on the husks, but they do not satisfy. And sooner or later he is obliged to say, "I will arise and go to my father, and will say unto him, Father, I have sinned against heaven, and in thy sight." And he meets with the same reception, tokens of unchanging love; and a father's welcome voice echoes through the soul, and melts the heart of the poor returning backslider,--"This my son was dead, and is alive again; and was lost, and is found." Let it be noticed that this is a thoroughly Calvinistic parable in that the prodigal was a son, and could not lose that relationship. Those who are not sons never have the desire to arise and go to the Father.

Our judgments may at times be wrong, as was that of the bewitched Galatians (3:1); and our affections may cool, as in the Ephesian Church (Rev. 2:4). The Church may become drowsy, yet her heart awakes (Song 5:3). Grace may at times seem to be lost to a child of God when it is indeed not so. The sun is eclipsed, but regains its former splendor. The trees lose all their leaves and fruit in winter, but has fresh buddings with the spring. Israel flees once, or even twice, before her enemies, and yet they conquer the land of promise. The Christian, too, falls many times, but is finally saved. It is unthinkable that God's elect should fail of salvation. "There is no possibility of their escaping the omnipotent power of God. so that, like Jonah, who fled from the will of God, which was to carry the message to Nineveh, yet was pursued even into the belly of the fish by the power of God until he willingly obeyed God's command, so they will eventually return to the Saviour, and after confession receive pardon for their sins and be saved." [94]

4. AN OUTWARD PROFESSION OF RIGHTEOUSNESS NOT ALWAYS A PROOF THAT THE PERSON IS A TRUE CHRISTIAN

We have no great difficulty in disposing of those cases where apparently true believers have gone into final apostasy. Both Scripture and experience teach us that we are often mistaken in our judgment of our fellow men, that sometimes it is practically impossible for us to know for certain that they are true Christians. The tares were never wheat, and the bad fish were never good, in spite of the fact that their true nature was not at first recognized. Since Satan can so alter his appearance that he is mistaken for an angel of light (II Cor. 11:14), it is no marvel that sometimes his ministers also fashion themselves as doers of righteousness, with the most deceptive appearances of holiness, devotion, piety and zeal. Certainly an outward profession is not always a guarantee that the soul is saved. Like the Pharisees of old, they may only desire to "make a fair show in the flesh," and deceive many. Jesus warned His disciples, "there shall arise false Christs, and false prophets, and shall show great signs and wonders; so as to lead astray, if possible, even the elect," Matt. 24:24; and He quoted the prophet Isaiah to the effect that, "This people honoreth me with their lips; but their heart is far from me. But in vain do they worship me, Teaching as their doctrines the precepts of men," Mark 7:6, 7. Paul warned against those who were "false apostles, deceitful workers, fashioning themselves into apostles of Christ," II Cor. 11:13. And to the Romans he wrote, "They are not all Israel, that are of Israel: neither, because they are Abraham's seed are they all children," Rom. 9:6, 7. John mentions those who "call themselves apostles, and they are not," Rev. 2:2; and a little later he adds, "I know thy works, that thou hast a name that thou livest, and thou art dead," Rev. 3:1.

But however effectively these may deceive men, God all the time knows "the blasphemy of them that say they are Jews, and they are not, but are a synagogue of Satan," Rev. 2:9. We live in a day when multitudes claim the name of "Christian," who are destitute of Christian knowledge, experience, and character,--in a day when, in many quarters, the distinction between the Church and the world has been wiped out. Like Samuel, we are often deceived by the outward appearance, and say, "Surely the Lord's anointed is before us," when if we really knew the motives behind their works we would conclude otherwise. We are often mistaken in our judgment of others, in spite of the best precautions that we can take. John gave the true solution for these cases when he wrote: "They went out from us, but they were not of us; for if they had been of us, they would have continued with us: but they went out, that they might be made manifest that they all are not of us," I John 2:19. All of those who fall away permanently come under this class.

Some persons make a great profession of religion although they know nothing of the Lord Jesus in sincerity and in truth. These persons may outstrip many a humble follower in head-knowledge, and for a season they may quite deceive the very elect; yet all the time their hearts have never been touched. In the judgment day many of those who at some time in their lives have been externally associated with the Church will say, "Lord, Lord, did we not prophesy by thy name, and by thy name cast out demons, and by thy name do many mighty works?" And then He will reply to them, "I never knew you: depart from me, ye that work iniquity," Matt. 7:22, 23; which, of course, would not be true if at some time He had known them as real Christians. When every man shall appear in his own colors, when the secrets of all hearts shall be manifest, many who at times appeared to be true Christians will be seen never to have been among God's people. Some fall away from a profession of faith, but none fall away from the saving grace of God. Those who do fall have never known the latter. They are the stony-ground hearers, who have no root in themselves, but who endure for a while; and when tribulation or persecution arises, straightway they stumble. They are then said to have given up or to have made shipwreck of that faith which they never possessed except in appearance. Some of these become sufficiently enlightened in the scheme of the doctrines of the Gospel that they are able to preach or to teach them to others, and yet are themselves entirely destitute of real saving grace. When such fall away they are no proofs nor instances of the final apostasy of real saints.

Mere church membership, of course, is no guarantee that the persons are real Christians. Not every member of the Church militant will be a member of the Church triumphant. To answer certain purposes, they make an outward profession of the Gospel, which obliges them for a time to be outwardly moral and to associate themselves with the people of God. They appear to have true faith and continue thus for a while. Then either their sheep's clothing is stripped off, or they throw it off themselves, and return again to the world. If we could see the real motives of their hearts, we would discover that at no time were they ever actuated by a true love of God. They were all this while goats, and not sheep, ravening wolves, and not gentle lambs. Hence Peter says of them, "It has happened unto them according to the true proverb, The dog turning to his own vomit again, and the sow that had been washed to wallowing in the mire," II Peter 2:22. They thereby show that they never belonged to the number of the elect.

Many of the unconverted listen to the preaching of the Gospel as Herod listened to John the Baptist. We are told that "Herod feared John, knowing that he was a righteous and holy man, and kept him safe. And when he heard him he was much perplexed; and he heard him gladly," Mark 6:20. Yet no one who knows of Herod's decree to put John the Baptist to death, and of his life in general, will say that he was ever a Christian.

In addition to what has been said it is to be admitted that often times the common operations of the Spirit on the enlightened conscience lead to reformation and to an externally religious life. Those so influenced are often very strict in their conduct and diligent in their religious duties. To the awakened sinner the promises of the Gospel and the exhibition of the plan of salvation contained in the Scriptures appear not only as true but as suited to his condition. He receives them with joy, and believes with a faith founded on the moral force of truth. This faith continues as long as the state of mind by which it is produced continues. When that changes, he relapses into his usual state of insensibility, and his faith disappears. It is to this class of persons that Christ referred when He spoke of those who receive the Word in stony places or among thorns. Numerous examples of this temporary faith are found in the Scriptures and are often seen in every day life. These experiences often precede or accompany genuine conversion; but in many cases they are not followed by a real change of heart. They may occur repeatedly, and yet those who experience them return to their normal state of unconcern and worldliness. Often times it is impossible for an observer or even the person himself to distinguish these experiences from those of the truly regenerated. "By their fruits ye shall know them," is the test given by our Lord. Only when these experiences issue in a consistently holy life can their distinctive character be known.

5. ARMINIAN SENSE OF INSECURITY

A consistent Arminian, with his doctrines of free will and of falling from grace, can never in this life be certain of his eternal salvation. He may, indeed, have the assurance of his present salvation, but he can have only a hope of his final salvation. He may regard his final salvation as highly probable, but he cannot know it as a certainty. He has seen many of his fellow Christians backslide and perish after making a good start. Why may not he do the same thing? So long as men remain in this world they have the remnants of the old sinful nature clinging to them; they are surrounded by the most alluring and deceptive pleasures of the world and the most subtle temptations of the Devil. In many of the supposedly Christian churches they hear the false teaching of modernistic, and therefore unchristian, ministers. If Arminianism were true, Christians would still be in very dangerous positions, with their eternal destiny suspended upon the probability that their weak, creaturely wills would continue to choose right. Furthermore, Arminianism would logically hold that no confirmation in holiness is possible, not even in heaven; for even there the person would still retain his free will and might commit sin any time he chose.

By comparison the Arminian is like the person who has inherited a fortune of, say, $100,000. He knows that many others who have inherited such fortunes have lost them through poor judgment, fraud, calamity, etc., but he has enough confidence in his own ability to handle money wisely that he does not doubt but that he will keep his. His assurance is based largely on self-confidence. Others have failed, but he is confident that he will not fail. But what a delusion is this when applied to the spiritual realm! What a pity that any one who is at all acquainted with his own tendency to sin should base his assurance of salvation upon such grounds! His system places the cause of his perseverance, not in the hands of an all-powerful, never-changing God, but in the hands of weak sinful man.

And does not the logic of the Arminian system tell us that the wise thing for the Christian to do is to die as soon as possible and thus confirm the inheritance which to him is of infinite value? In view of the fact that so many have fallen away, is it worth while for him to remain here and risk his eternal salvation for the sake of a little more life in this world? What would be thought of a business man who, in order to gain a few more dollars, would risk his entire fortune in some admittedly questionable venture? In fact, does it not at least suggest that the Lord has made many mistakes in not removing these people while they were true Christians? The writer, at least, is convinced that if he held the Arminian view and knew himself to be a saved Christian he would want to die as soon as possible and thus place his salvation beyond all possible doubt.

In regard to spiritual matters, a state of doubt is a state of misery. The assurance that Christians can never be separated from the love of God is one of the greatest comforts of the Christian life. To deny this doctrine is to destroy the grounds for any rejoicing among the saints on earth; for what kind of rejoicing can those have who believe that they may at any time be deceived and led astray? If our sense of security is based only on our changeable and wavering natures, we can never know the inward calm and peace which, should characterize the Christian. Says McFetridge, in his very illuminating little book, Calvinism In History, "I can well conceive of the terror to a sensitive soul of dark uncertainty as to salvation, and of that ever-abiding consciousness of the awful possibility of falling away from grace after a long and painful Christian life, which is taught by Arminianism. To me such a doctrine has terrors which would cause me to shrink away from it for ever, and which would fill me with constant and unspeakable perplexities. To feel that I were crossing the troubled and dangerous sea of life dependent for my final security upon the actings of my own treacherous nature were enough to fill me with a perpetual alarm. If it is possible, I want to know that the vessel to which I commit my life is seaworthy, and that, having once embarked, I shall arrive in safety at my destination." (P. 112.)

It is not until we duly appreciate this wonderful truth, that our salvation is not suspended on our weak and wavering love to God, but rather upon His eternal and unchangeable love to us, that we can have peace and certainty in the Christian life. And only the Calvinist, who knows himself to be absolutely safe in the hands of God, can have that inward sense of peace and security, knowing that in the eternal counsels of God he has been chosen to be cleansed and glorified and that nothing can thwart that purpose. He knows himself to be held to righteousness by a spiritual power which is as exhaustless and unvarying as the force of gravitation, and as necessary to the development of the spirit as sunshine and vitamins are to the body.

6. PURPOSE OF THE SCRIPTURE WARNINGS AGAINST APOSTASY

Arminians sometimes bring forth from the Scriptures the warnings against apostasy or falling away, which are addressed to believers, and which, it is argued, imply a possibility of their failing away. There is, of course, a sense in which it is possible for believers to fail away,---when they are viewed simply in themselves, with reference to their own powers and capacities, and apart from God's purpose or design with respect to them. And it is admitted by all that believers can fall into sin temporarily. The primary purpose of these passages, however, is to induce men to co-operate willingly with God for the accomplishment of His purposes. They are inducements which produce constant humility, watchfulness, and diligence. In the same way a parent, in order to get the willing co-operation of a child, may tell it to stay out of the way of an approaching automobile, when all the time the parent has no intention of ever letting the child get into a position where it would be injured. When God plies a soul with fears of falling it is by no means a proof that God in His secret purpose intends to permit him to fall. These fears may be the very means which God has designed to keep him from falling. Secondly, God's exhortations to duty are perfectly consistent with His purpose to give sufficient grace for the performance of these duties. In one place we are commanded to love the Lord our God with all our heart; in another, God says, "I will put my Spirit within you, and cause you to walk in my statutes." Now either these must be consistent with each other, or the Holy Spirit must contradict Himself. Plainly it is not the latter. Thirdly, these warnings are, even for believers, incitements to greater faith and prayer. Fourthly, they are designed to show man his duty rather than his ability, and his weakness rather than his strength. Fifthly, they convince men of their want of holiness and of their dependence upon God. And, sixthly, they serve as restraints on unbelievers, and leave them without excuse.

Nor is any more proven by the passages, "Destroy not with thy meat him for whom Christ died," Rom. 14:15; and, "For through thy knowledge he that is weak perisheth, the brother for whose sake Christ died," I Cor. 8:11. In the same manner the influence of a particular person, when looked at merely in itself, might be said to be destroying our American civilization; yet America goes ahead and prospers, because other influences more than offset that one. In these passages the principle asserted is simply this: Whatever their divine security, the responsibility of the one who casts a stumbling block in the path of his brother is not decreased; and that anyone who does cast a stumbling block in the way of his brother is doing all he can towards his brother' destruction.

7. SCRIPTURE PROOF

The Scripture proof for this doctrine is abundant and clear. We shall now consider some of these passages.

"Who shall separate us from the love of Christ? Shall tribulation, or anguish, or persecution, or famine, or nakedness or peril, or sword? Nay, In all these things we are more than conquerors through Him that loved us. For I am persuaded that neither death, nor life, nor angels, nor principalities, nor things present, nor things to come, nor powers, nor height, nor depth, nor any other creature, shall be able to separate us from the love of God, which is in Christ Jesus our Lord," Rom. 8:35-39.

"Sin shall not have dominion over you: for ye are not under law, but under grace," Rom. 6:14. "He that believeth hath eternal life," John 6:47. "He that heareth my word, and believeth Him that sent me, hath eternal life, and cometh not into judgment, but hath passed out of death into life," John 5:24. The

The Reformed Doctrine Of Predestination

moment one believes, eternal life becomes a reality, a present possession, and not merely a conditional gift of the future. "I am the living bread which came down out of heaven: if any man eat of this bread, he shall live forever," John 6:51. He does not say that we have to eat many times, but that if we eat at all, we shall live for ever. "Whosoever drinketh of the water that I shall give him shall never thirst; but the water that I shall give him shall become in him a well of water springing up unto eternal life," John 4:14.

"Being confident of this very thing, that He who began a good work in you will perfect it until the day of Jesus Christ," Phil. 1:6. "Jehovah will perfect that which concerneth me," Ps. 138:8. "The gifts and calling of God are not repented of:" Rom. 11:29. "The witness is this, that God gave unto us eternal life," I John 5:11. "These things have I written unto you that ye may know that ye have eternal life," I John 5:13. "For by one offering He bath perfected for ever them that are sanctified," Heb. 10:14. "The Lord will deliver me from every evil work, and will save me unto His heavenly kingdom," II Tim. 4:18. "For whom He foreknew, He also foreordained. . . . and whom He foreordained, them He also called; and whom He called, them He also justified; and whom He justified, them He also glorified," Rom. 8:29. "Having foreordained us unto adoption as sons through Jesus Christ unto Himself, according to the good pleasure of His will," Eph. 1:5.

Jesus declared, "I give unto them (the true followers, or 'sheep') eternal life; and they shall never perish, and no one shall snatch them out of my hand. My Father, who hath given them unto me, is greater than all; and no one is able to snatch them out of the Father's hand," John 10:28. Here we find that our security and God's omnipotence are equal; for the former is founded on the latter. God is mightier than the whole world, and neither men nor Devil can rob Him of one of His precious jewels. It would be as easy to pluck a star out of the heavens as to pluck a saint out of the Father's hand. Their salvation stands in His invincible might and they are placed beyond the peril of destruction. We have Christ's promise that the gates of hell shall not prevail against His Church; yet if the Devil could snatch one here and another there and large numbers in some congregations, the gates of hell would to a great extent prevail against it. In principle, if one could be lost, all might be lost, and thus Christ's assurance would be reduced to idle words.

When we are told that "There shall arise false Christs, and false prophets, who shall show great signs and wonders; so as to lead astray, IF POSSIBLE, even the elect," Matt. 24:24, the unprejudiced believing mind readily understands that it is IMPOSSIBLE to lead astray the elect.

The mystic union which exists between Christ and believers is a guarantee that they shall continue steadfast. "Because I live, ye shall live also," John 14:19. The effect of this union is that believers participate in His life. Christ is in us, Rom. 8:10. It is not we that live, but Christ that liveth in us, Gal. 2:20. Christ and the believers have a common life such as that which exists in the vine and the branches. The Holy Spirit so dwells in the redeemed that every Christian is supplied with an inexhaustible reservoir of strength.

Paul warned the Ephesians, "Grieve not the Holy Spirit of God, in whom ye were sealed unto the day of redemption," Eph. 4:30. He had no fear of apostasy for he could confidently say, "Thanks be to God who always leadeth us in triumph in Christ," II Cor. 2:14. The Lord, speaking through the prophet Jeremiah said, "I have loved you with an everlasting love," 31:3,--one of the best proofs that God's love shall have no end is that it has no beginning, but is eternal. In the parable of the two houses, the very point stressed was that the house which was founded on the rock (Christ) did not fall when the storms of life came. Arminianism sets up another system in which some of those who are founded on the rock do fall. In the twenty-third Psalm we read, "And I shall dwell in the house of the Lord forever." The true Christian is no temporary visitor, but a permanent dweller in the house of the Lord. How those rob this psalm of its deeper and richer meaning who teach that the grace of God is a temporary thing!

Christ makes intercession for His people (Rom. 8:34; Heb. 7:25), and we are told that the Father hears Him always (John 11:42). Hence the Arminian, holding that Christians may fall away, must deny either the passages which declare that Christ does make intercession for His people, or he must deny those which declare that His prayers are always heard. Let us consider here how well protected we are: Christ is at the right hand of God pleading for us, and in addition to that, the Holy Spirit makes intercession for us with groanings which cannot be uttered, Rom. 8:26.

In the wonderful promise of Jer. 32:40, God has promised to preserve believers from their own backslidings: "And I will make an everlasting covenant with them, and I will not turn away from following them, to do them good; and I will put my fear in their hearts, that they may not depart from me." And in Ezek. 11:19, 20, He promises to take from them the "stony heart," and to give them a "heart of flesh," so that they shall walk in his statutes and keep his ordinances, and so that they shall be His people and He their God. Peter tells us that Christians cannot fall away, for they "by the power of God are guarded through faith unto a salvation ready to be revealed at the last time," I Peter 1:5. Paul says, "God is able to make all grace to abound unto you; that ye, having always all sufficiency in everything, may abound unto every good work," II Cor. 9:8. He declares that the Lord's servant "shall be made to stand; for the Lord hath power to make him stand," Rom. 14:4.

And Christians have the further promise, "There hath no temptation taken you but such as man can bear: but God is faithful, and will not suffer you to be tempted above that ye are able; but will with the temptation make also the way of escape, that ye may be able to endure it," I Cor. 10:13. Their removal from certain temptations which would be too strong for them is an absolute and free gift from God, since it is entirely an arrangement of His providence as to what temptations they encounter in the course of their lives, and what ones they escape. "The Lord is faithful and will establish you and guard you from the evil one," II Thess. 3:3. And again, "The angel of the Lord encampeth round about them that fear Him and delivereth them," Ps. 34:7. Amid all his trials and hardships Paul could say, "We are pressed on every side, yet not straightened; perplexed, yet not unto despair; pursued, yet not forsaken; smitten down, yet not destroyed; .... knowing that He that raised up the Lord Jesus Christ shall raise us also with Jesus," II Cor. 4:8, 9, 14.

The saints, even in this world, are compared to a tree that does not wither, Ps. 1:3; to the cedars which flourish on Mount Lebanon, Ps. 92:12; to Mount Zion which cannot be moved, but which abideth forever, Ps. 125:1; and to a house built on a rock, Matt. 7:24. The Lord is with them in their old age, Is. 46: 4, and is their guide even unto death, Ps. 48:14, so that they cannot be totally and finally lost.

Another strong argument is to be noticed concerning the Lamb's book of life. The disciples were told to rejoice, not so much over the fact that the demons were subject to them, but that their names were written in the Lamb's book of life. This book is a catalogue of the elect, determined by the unalterable counsel of God, and can neither be increased nor diminished. The names of the righteous are found there; but the names of those who perish have never been written there from the foundation of the world. God does not make the mistake of writing in the book of life a name which He will later have to blot out. Hence none of the Lord's own ever perish. Jesus told His disciples to find their chief joy in the fact that their names were written in heaven, Luke 10:20; yet there would have been small grounds for joy in this respect if their names written in heaven one day could have been blotted out the next. Paul wrote to the Philippians, "Our citizenship is in heaven," 3:20; and to Timothy he wrote, "The Lord knoweth them that are His," II Tim. 2:19. For the Scripture teaching concerning the book of life, see Luke 10:20; Phil. 4:3; Rev. 3:5; 13:8; 17:8; 20:12-15; 21:27.

Here, then, are very simple and plain statements that the Christian shall continue in grace, the reason being that the Lord takes it upon Himself to preserve him in that state. In these promises the elect are secured on both sides. Not only will God not depart from them, but He will so put His fear into their hearts that they shall not depart from him. Surely no Spirit-taught Christian can doubt that this doctrine is taught in the Bible. It seems that man, poor, wretched and impotent as he is, would welcome a doctrine which secures for him the possessions of eternal happiness despite all attacks from without and all evil tendencies from within. But it is not so. He refuses it, and argues against it. And the causes are not far to seek. In the first place he has more confidence in himself than be has any right to have. Secondly, the scheme is so contrary to what he is used to in the natural world that he persuades himself that it cannot be true. Thirdly, he perceives that if this doctrine be admitted, the other doctrines of free grace will logically follow. Hence he twists and explains away the Scripture passages which teach it, and clings to some which appear on the surface to favor his preconceived views. In fact, a system of salvation by grace is so utterly at variance with his every-day experience, in which be sees every thing and person treated according to works and merits, that he has great difficulty in bringing himself to believe that it can be true. He wishes to earn his own salvation, though certainly he expects very high wages for very sorry work.

Footnotes:

91. Chapter XVII, Section 1.
92. Theology, p. 690.
93. Systematic Theology, III, p. 112.
94. F. E. Hamilton, Article, The Reformed Faith and the Presbyterian Church.

Section III

Chapter XV

1. It Is Fatalism

Much misunderstanding arises through confusing the Christian Doctrine of Predestination with the heathen doctrine of Fatalism. There is, in reality, only one point of agreement between the two, which is, that both assume the absolute certainty of all future events. The essential difference between them is that Fatalism has no place for a personal God. Predestination holds that events come to pass because an infinitely wise, powerful, and holy God has so appointed them. Fatalism holds that all events come to pass through the working of a blind, unintelligent, impersonal, non-moral force which cannot be distinguished from physical necessity, and which carries us helplessly within its grasp as mighty river carries a piece of wood.

Predestination teaches that from eternity God has had one unified plan or purpose which He is bringing to perfection through this world order of events. It holds that all of His decrees are rational determinations founded on sufficient reason, and that He has fixed one great goal "toward which the whole creation moves." Predestination holds that the ends designed in this plan are first, the glory of God; and second, the good of His people. On the other hand Fatalism excludes the idea of final causes. It snatches the reins of universal empire from the hands of infinite wisdom and love, and gives them into the hands of a blind necessity. It attributes the course of nature and the experiences of mankind to an unknown, irresistible force, against which it is vain to struggle and childish to repine.

According to the doctrine of Predestination the freedom and responsibility of man are fully preserved. In the midst of certainty God has ordained human liberty. But Fatalism allows no power of choice, no self-determination. It makes the acts of man to be as utterly beyond his control as are the laws of nature. Fatalism, with its idea of irresistable, impersonal, abstract power, has no room for moral ideas, while Predestination makes these the rule of action for God and man. Fatalism has no place for and offers no incentives to religion, love, mercy, holiness, justice, or wisdom, while Predestination gives these the strongest conceivable basis. And lastly, Fatalism leads to skepticism and despair, while Predestination sets forth the glories of God and of His kingdom in all their splendor and gives an assurance which nothing can shake.

Predestination therefore differs from Fatalism as much as the acts of a man differ from those of a machine, or as much as the unfailing love of the heavenly Father differs from the force of gravitation. "It reveals to us," says Smith, "the glorious truth that our lives and our sensitive hearts are held, not in the iron cog-wheels of a vast and pitiless Fate, nor in the whirling loom of a crazy Chance, but in the almighty hands of an infinitely good and wise God." [95]

Calvin emphatically repudiated the charge that his doctrine was Fatalism. "Fate," says he, "is a term given by the Stoics to their doctrine of necessity, which they had formed out of a labyrinth of contradictory reasonings; a doctrine calculated to call God Himself to order, and to set Him laws whereby to work. Predestination I define to be, according to the Holy Scriptures, that free and unfettered counsel of God by which He rules all mankind, and all men and things, and also all parts and particles of the world by His infinite wisdom and incomprehensible justice." And again, ". . . had you but been willing to look into my books, you would have been convinced at once how offensive to me is the profane term fate: nay, you would have learned that this same abhorrent term was cast in the teeth of Augustine by his opponents." [96]

Luther says that the doctrine of Fatalism among the heathen is a proof that "the knowledge of Predestination and of the prescience of God, was no less left in the world than the notion of divinity itself." [97] In the history of philosophy Materialism has proven itself essentially fatalistic. Pantheism also has been strongly tinged with it.

No man can be a consistent fatalist. For to be consistent he would have to reason something like this: "If I am to die today, it will do me no good to eat, for I shall die anyway. Nor do I need to eat if I am to live many years yet, for I shall live anyway. Therefore I will not eat." Needless to say, if God has foreordained that a man shall live, He has also foreordained that he shall be kept from the suicidal folly of refusing to eat.

"This doctrine," says Hamilton, "is only superficially like the pagan 'fate.' The Christian is in the hands not of a cold, immutable determinism, but of a warm, loving heavenly Father, who loved us and gave His Son to die for us on Calvary! The Christian knows that 'all things work together for good to them that love God, even to them that are called according to His purpose.' The Christian can trust God because he knows He is all-wise, loving, just and holy. He sees the end from the beginning, so that there is no reason to become panicky when things seem to be going against us."

Hence, only a person who has not examined this doctrine of Predestination, or one who is maliciously inclined, will rashly charge that it is Fatalism. There is no excuse for anyone making this mistake who knows what Predestination is and what Fatalism is.

Since the universe is one systematized unit we must choose between Fatalism, which ultimately does away with mind and purpose, and this biblical doctrine of Predestination, which holds that God created all things, that His providence extends to all His works, and that while free Himself He has also provided that we shall be free within the limits of our natures. Instead of our doctrine of Predestination being the same with the heathen doctrine of Fatalism, it is its absolute opposite and only alternative.

Footnotes:

95. The Creed of Presbyterians, p. 167.
96. The Secret Providence of God, reprinted in Calvin's Calvinism, pp. 261, 262.
97. Bondage of the Will, p. 31.

Chapter XVI

2. It Is Inconsistent with the Free Agency and Moral Responsibility of Man

1. The Problem of Man's Free Agency. 2. This Objection Bears Equally Against Foreknowledge. 3. Certainty is Consistent with Free Agency. 4. Man's Natural Will is Enslaved to Evil. 5. God Controls the Minds of Men and Gives His People the Will to come. 6. The Way in Which the Will is Determined. 7. Scripture Proof.

1. THE PROBLEM OF MAN'S FREE AGENCY

The problem which we face here is, How can a person be a free and responsible agent if his actions have been foreordained from eternity? By a free and responsible agent we mean an intelligent person who acts with rational self-determination; and by foreordination we mean that from eternity God has made certain the actual course of events which takes place in the life of every person and in the realm of nature. It is, of course, admitted by all that a person's acts must be without compulsion and in accordance with his own desires and inclinations, or he cannot be held responsible for them. If the acts of a free agent are in their very nature contingent and uncertain, then it is plain that foreordination and free agency are inconsistent.

The philosopher who is convinced of the existence of a vast Power by whom all things exist and are controlled, is forced to inquire where the finite will can find expression under the reign of the Infinite. The true solution of this difficult question respecting the sovereignty of God and the freedom of man, is not to be found in the denial of either, but rather in such a reconciliation as gives full weight to each, yet which assigns a preeminence to the divine sovereignty corresponding to the infinite exaltation of the Creator above the sinful creature. The same God who has ordained all events has ordained human liberty in the midst of these events, and this liberty is as surely fixed as is anything else. Man is no mere automaton or machine. In the Divine plan, which is infinite in variety and complexity which reaches from everlasting to everlasting, and which includes millions of free agents who act and inter-act upon each other, God has ordained that human beings shall keep their liberty under His sovereignty. He has made no attempt to give us a formal explanation of these things, and our limited human knowledge is not able fully to solve the problem. Since the Scripture writers did not hesitate to affirm the absolute sway of God over the thoughts and intents of the heart, they felt no embarrassment in including the acts of free agents within His all-embracing plan. That the makers of the Westminster Confession recognized the freedom of man is plain; for immediately after declaring that "God has freely and unchangeably ordained whatsoever comes to pass," they added, "Yet so as thereby neither is God the author of sin, nor is violence offered to the will of the creatures, nor is the liberty or contingency of second causes taken away, but rather established."

While the act remains that of the individual, it is nevertheless due more or less to the predisposing agency and efficacy of divine power exerted in lawful ways. This may be illustrated to a certain extent in the case of a man who wishes to construct a building. He decides on his plan. Then he hires the carpenters, masons, plumbers, etc., to do the work. These men are not forced to do the work. No compulsion of any kind is used. The owner simply offers the necessary inducements by way of wages, working conditions, and so on, so that the men work freely and gladly. They do in detail just what he plans for them to do. His is the primary and theirs is the secondary will or cause for the construction of the building. We often direct the actions of our fellow men without infringing on their freedom or responsibility. In a similar way and to an infinitely greater degree God can direct our actions. His will for the course of events is the primary cause and man's will is the secondary cause; and the two work together in perfect harmony.

In one sense we can say that the kingdom of heaven is a democratic kingdom, paradoxical as that may sound. The essential principle of a democracy is that it rests on "the consent of the governed." Heaven will be truly a kingdom, with God as the supreme Ruler; yet it will rest on the consent of the governed. It is not forced on believers against their consent. They are so influenced that they become willing, and accept the Gospel, and find it the delight of their lives to do their Sovereign's will.

Loraine Boettner D.D.

2. THIS OBJECTION BEARS EQUALLY AGAINST FOREKNOWLEDGE

Let it be noticed that the objection that foreordination is inconsistent with free agency bears equally against the doctrine of the foreknowledge of God. If God foreknows an event as future, it must be as inevitably certain as if fore-ordained; and if one is inconsistent with free agency, the other is also. This is often frankly admitted; and the Unitarians, while not evangelical, are at this point more consistent than the Arminians. They say that God knows all that is knowable, but that free acts are uncertain and that it is doing no dishonor to God to say that He does not know them.

We find, however, that the Scriptures contain predictions of many events, great and small, which were perfectly fulfilled through the actions of free agents. Usually these agents were not even conscious that they were fulfilling divine prophecy. They acted freely, yet exactly as foretold. A few examples are: the rejection of Jesus by the Jews, the parting of Jesus' garments and the casting lots by the Roman soldiers, Peter's denials of Jesus; the crowing of the cock, the spear thrust, the capture of Jerusalem and the carrying away of the Jews into captivity, the destruction of Babylon, etc. It is plain that the writers of Scripture believed these free acts to be fully foreknown by the divine mind and therefore absolutely certain to be accomplished. The foreknowledge of God did not destroy the freedom of Judas and Peter-- at least they themselves did not think so, for Judas later came back and said, "I have sinned in that I have betrayed innocent blood;" and when Peter heard the cock crow and remembered the words of Jesus, he went out and wept bitterly.

In regard to the events which were connected with Jesus' triumphant entry into Jerusalem it is written: "These things understood not His disciples at the first: but when Jesus was glorified, then remembered they that these things were written of Him, and that they had done these things unto Him," John 12:16. Because we know beforehand that an upright judge will refuse a bribe, and a miser will clutch a nugget of gold, does this alter the nature or prejudice the freedom of their acts? And if we, with our very limited knowledge of other men's natures and of the influences which will play upon them, are able to predict their actions with reasonable accuracy, shall not God, who understands perfectly their natures and these influences, know exactly what their actions will be?

Hence the certainty of an action is consistent with the liberty of the agent in executing it; otherwise God could not foreknow such actions as certain. Foreknowledge does not make future acts certain but only assumes them to be so; and it is a contradiction of terms to say that God foreknows as certain an event which in its very nature is uncertain. We must either say that future events are certain and that God knows the future, or that they are uncertain and that He does not know the future. The doctrines of God's foreknowledge and foreordination stand or fall together.

3. CERTAINTY IS CONSISTENT WITH FREE AGENCY

Nor does it follow from the absolute certainty of a person's acts that he could not have acted otherwise. He could have acted otherwise if he had chosen to have done so. Oftentimes a man has power and opportunity to do that which it is absolutely certain he will not do, and to refrain from doing that which it is absolutely certain he will do. That is, no external influence determines his actions. Our acts are in accordance with the decrees, but not necessarily so we can do otherwise and often should. Judas and his accomplices were left to fulfill their purpose, and they did as their wicked inclinations prompted them. Hence Peter charged them with the crime, but he at the same time declared that they had acted according to the purpose of God,--"Him being: delivered up by the determinate counsel and foreknowledge of God, ye by the hands of lawless men did crucify and slay," Acts 2:23.

On other grounds also it may be shown that certainty is consistent with free agency. We are often absolutely certain how we will act under given conditions so far as we are free to act at all. A parent may be certain that he will rescue a child in distress, and that in doing so he will act freely. God is a free agent, yet it is certain that He will always do right. The holy angels and redeemed saints are free agents, yet it is certain that they will never sin; other- wise there would be no assurance of their remaining in heaven. On the other hand, it is certain that the Devil, the demons and fallen men will commit sin, although they are free agents. A father often knows how his son will act under given circumstances and by controlling these he determines beforehand the course of action which the son follows, yet the son acts freely. If he plans that the son shall be doctor, he gives him encouragement along that line, persuades him to read certain books, to attend certain schools, and so presents the outside inducements that his plan works out. In the same manner and to an infinitely greater extent God controls our actions so that they are certain although we act freely. His decree does not produce the event, but only renders its occurrence certain; and the same decree which determines the certainty of the action at the same time determines the freedom of the agent in the act.

4. MAN'S NATURAL WILL IS ENSLAVED TO EVIL

Strictly speaking we may say man has free will only in the sense that he is not under any outside compulsion which interferes with his freedom of choice or his just accountability. In his fallen state he only has what we may call "the freedom of slavery." He is in bondage to sin and spontaneously follows Satan. He does not have the ability or incentive to follow God. Now, we ask, is this a thing worthy the name "free"? and the answer is, No. Not freewill but self-will would more appropriately describe man's condition since the fall. It is to be remembered that man was not created a captive to sin but that he has come into that condition by his own fault; and a loss which he has brought upon himself does not free him from responsibility. After man's redemption is complete he will spontaneously follow God, as do the holy angels; but never will he become entirely his own master.

That this was Luther's doctrine cannot be denied. In his book, "The Bondage of the Will," the main purpose of which was to prove that the will of man is by nature enslaved to evil only, and that because it is fond of that slavery it is said to be free, he declared: "Whatever man does, he does necessarily, though not with any sensible compulsion, and he can only do what God from eternity willed and foreknew he should, which will of God must be effectual and His foresight must be certain . . . Neither the Divine nor human will does anything by constraint, and whatever man does, be it good or bad, he does with as much appetite and willingness as if his will was really free. But, after all, the will of God is certain and unalterable, and it is the governess of ours." [98] In another place he says, "When it is granted and established, that Free-will, having once lost its liberty, is compulsively bound to the service of sin, and cannot will anything good; I from these words, can understand nothing else than that Free-will is an empty term, whose reality is lost. And a lost liberty, according to my grammar, is no liberty at all." [99] He refers to Free-will as "a mere lie," [100] and later adds, "This, therefore, is also essentially necessary and wholesome for Christians to know: that God foreknows nothing by contingency, but that He foresees, purposes and does all things according to his immutable, eternal, and infallible will. By this thunderbolt, Free-will is thrown prostrate, utterly dashed to pieces .... It follows unalterably, that all things which we do, although they may appear to us to be done mutably and contingently, and even may be done thus contingently by us, are yet, in reality, done necessarily and immutably, with respect to the will of God. For the will of God is effective and cannot be hindered; because the very power of God is natural to Him, and His wisdom is such that He cannot be deceived." [101]

It is some times objected that unless man's will is completely free, God commands him to do what he cannot do. In numerous places in Scripture, however, men are commended to do things which in their own strength they are utterly unable to do. The man with the withered hand was commanded to stretch it forth. The paralytic was commanded to arise and walk; the sick man to arise, take up his bed and walk. The dead Lazarus was commanded to come forth. Men are commanded to believe; yet faith is said to be the "gift of God." "Awake, thou that sleepest, and arise from the dead, and Christ shall shine upon thee," Eph. 6:14. "Ye therefore shall be perfect, as your heavenly Father is perfect," Matt. 5:48. Man's self-imposed inability in the moral sphere does not free him from obligation.

5. GOD CONTROLS THE MINDS OF MEN AND GIVES HIS PEOPLE THE WILL TO COME

God so governs the inward feelings, external environment, habits, desires, motives, etc., of men that they freely do what He purposes. This operation its inscrutable, but none the less real; and the mere fact that in our present state of knowledge we are not able fully to explain how this influence is exerted without destroying the free agency of man, certainly does not prove that it cannot be so exerted.

We do have enough knowledge, however, to know that God's sovereignty and man's freedom are realities, and that they work together in perfect harmony. Paul plants, and Apollos, waters, but God gives the increase. Paul commanded the Philippians, "Work out your own salvation with fear and trembling;" and in the immediately following verse the reason which he assigns for this is, "For it is God who worketh in you both to will and to work, for His good pleasure" (2:15, 13). And the psalmist declared, "They people offer themselves willingly in the day of thy power" (110:3).

The actions of a creature are to a great extent predetermined when God stamps upon it a particular "nature" at its creation. If it is given human nature, its actions will be those common to men; if horse nature, those common to horses; or if vegetable nature, those common to the vegetable world. Plain it is that those given human nature were foreordained not to walk on four feet, nor to neigh like a horse. An act is not free if determined from without; but it is free if rationally determined from within, and this is precisely what God's foreordination effects. The comprehensive decree provides that each man shall be a free agent, possessing a certain character, surrounded by a certain environment, subject to certain external influences, internally moved by certain affections, desires, habits, etc., and that in view of all these he shall freely and rationally make a choice. That the choice will be one thing and not another, is certain; and God, who knows and controls the exact causes of each influence, knows what that choice will be, and in a real sense determines it. Zanchius expressed this idea very clearly when he declared that man was a free agent, and then added, "Yet he acts, from the first to the last moment of his life, in absolute subserviency (though, perhaps he does not know it, nor design it) to the purposes and decrees of God concerning him; notwithstanding which, he is sensible of no compulsion, but acts freely and voluntarily, as if he were subject to no control, and absolutely lord of himself." And Luther says, "Both good and evil men, though by their actions they fulfill the decrees and appointments of God, yet are not forcibly constrained to do anything, but act willingly."

In accordance with this we believe that, without destroying or impairing the free agency of men, God can exercise over them a particular providence and work in them through His Holy Spirit so that they will come to Christ and persevere in His service. We believe further that none have this will and desire except those whom God has previously made willing and desirous; and that He gives this will and desire to none but His own elect. But while thus induced, the elect remain as free as the man that you persuade to take a walk or to invest in government securities.

An illustration which well shows God's relation with both the saved end the lost is given by H. Johnson,--"Here are two hundred men in prison for violation of law. I make Provision for their pardon, so that justice is satisfied and the law vindicated, while yet the prisoners may go free. The prison doors are unbarred, the bolts thrown back, and promise of absolute pardon is made and assurance is given every prisoner that he can now step out a free man. But not a man moves. Suppose now I determine that my provision for their pardon shall not be in vain. So I personally go to one hundred and fifty of these condemned and guilty men, and by a kind of loving violence persuade them to come out. That's election. But have I kept the other fifty in? The provision for pardon is still sufficient, the prison doors are still unbarred, the gates of their cells are still unlocked and open, and freedom is promised to everyone who will step out and take it; and every man in that prison knows he can be a free man if he will. Have I kept the other fifty in?" [102]

The old Pelagian tenet, which has sometimes been adopted by Arminians, that virtue and vice derive their praiseworthiness or blameworthiness from the power of the individual beforehand to choose the one or the other, logically leads one to deny goodness to the angels in heaven, or to the saints in glory, or even to God Himself, since it is impossible for the angels, saints, or for God to sin. Virtue, then, in the heavenly state would cease to be meritorious, because it required no effort of choice. The idea that the power of choice between good and evil is that which ennobles and dignifies the will is a misconception. It does, indeed, raise man above the brute creation; but it is not the perfection of his will. Says Mozley: "The highest and the perfect state of the will is a state of necessity; and the power of choice, so far from being essential to a true and genuine will, is its weakness and defect. That can be a greater sign of an imperfect and immature state of the will than that, with good and evil before it, it should be in suspense which to do?" [103] In this life that grace from which good actions necessarily follow is not given with uniformity, and consequently even the regenerate occasionally commit sin; but in the next life it will be either constantly given or taken away entirely, and then the determination of the will will be constant either for good or for evil.

Perhaps some idea of the manner in which the Divine and human agencies harmonize to produce one work may be gained from a consideration of the way in which the Scriptures were written. These are, in the highest sense, and at the same time, the words of God and also the words of men. It is not merely certain parts or elements which are to be assigned to God or to men; but rather the whole of Scripture in all of its parts, in form of expression as well as in substance of teaching, is from God, and also from men. Although the writers were so influenced by the Holy Spirit that they wrote what God wanted written, and were fully preserved from error, they retained their free agency, and we should recognize both the divine and the human side of Scripture.

Undoubtedly there is a contradiction in supposing that "chance happenings," or those events produced by free will agents, can be the objects of definite foreknowledge or the subjects of previous arrangement. In the very nature of the case they must be both radically and eventually uncertain, "so that," as Toplady says, "any assertor of self-determination is in fact, whether he means it or no, a worshiper of the heathen lady named Fortune, and an ideal deposer of providence from its throne."

Unless God could thus govern the minds of men He would be constantly engaged in devising new expedients to offset the effects of the influences introduced by the millions of His creatures. If men actually had free will, then in attempting to govern or convert a person, God would have to approach him as a man approaches his fellowmen, with several plans in mind so that if the first proves unsuccessful he can try the second, and if that does not work, then the third, and so on. If the acts of free agents are uncertain, God is ignorant of the future except in a most general way. He is then surprised times without number and daily receives great accretions of knowledge. But such a view is dishonoring to God, and is both unreasonable and unscriptural. Unless God's omniscience is denied we must hold that He knows all truth, past, present, and future; and that while events may appear uncertain from our human view-point, from His view-point they are fixed and certain. This argument is so conclusive that its force is generally admitted. The weaker objection. which is sometimes urged that God voluntarily wills not to know some of the future acts of men in order to leave them free has no support either in Scripture or in reason. Furthermore, it represents God as acting like the father of a lot of bad boys who goes and hides because he is afraid he will see them do something of which he would not approve. If

The Reformed Doctrine Of Predestination

God is limited either by an outside force or by His own acts, we have only a finite God.

The Arminian theory that God is anxiously trying to convert sinners but not able to exert more than persuasive power without doing violence to their natures, is really much the same in this respect as the old Persian view that there were two eternal principles of good and evil at war with each other, neither of which was able to overcome the other. Free-will tears the reins of government out of the hands of God, and robs Him of His power. It places the creatures beyond His absolute control and in some respects gives them veto power over His eternal will and purpose. It even makes it possible that angels and saints in heaven might sin, that there might again be a general rebellion in heaven such as is supposed to have occurred when Satan and the fallen angels were cast out, and that evil might become dominant or universal.

6. THE WAY IN WHICH THE WILL IS DETERMINED

Since man is a rational agent there must always be a sufficient cause for his acting in a particular way. For the will to decide in favor of the weaker motive and against the stronger, or without motives at all, is to have an effect without a sufficient cause. Conscience teaches us that we always have reasons for the things we do, and that after acting we are conscious that we might have acted differently had other views or feelings been present. The reason for a particular act may not be strong and it may even be based on a false judgment, but in each particular instance it is strong enough to control. Scales will swing in the opposite direction only when there is a cause adequate to the effect. A person may choose that which in some respects is disagreeable; but in each case some other motive is present which influences the person to a choice which otherwise would not have been made. For instance, a person may willingly have a tooth pulled out; but he will not do so unless some inducement is present which for the time being at least makes this the stronger inclination. As it has been expressed, "a man cannot prefer against his preference or choose against his choice." A person who prefers to live in California cannot, by a mere act of will, prefer to live in New York.

Man's volitions are, in fact, governed by his own nature, and are in accordance with the desires, dispositions, inclinations, knowledge, and character of the person. Man is not independent of God, nor of mental and physical laws, and all of these exert their particular influences in his choices. He always acts in the way in which the strongest inclinations or motives lead; and conscience tells us that the things which appeal to us most powerfully at the time are the things which determine our volitions. Says Dr. Hodge, "The will is not determined by any law of necessity; it is not independent, indifferent, or self-determined, but is always determined by the preceding state of mind; so that a man is free so long as his volitions are the conscious expression of his mind; or so long as his activity is determined and controlled by his reason and feelings." [104]

Unless a person's volitions were based on and determined by his character they would not really be his, and he could not be held responsible for them. In our relations with our fellow men we instinctively assume that their good or bad volitions are determined by good or bad character, and we judge them accordingly. "By their fruits ye shall know them. Do men gather grapes of thorns, or figs of thistles? Even so every good tree bringeth forth good fruit; but the corrupt tree bringeth forth evil fruit. A good tree cannot bring forth evil fruit, neither can a corrupt tree bring forth good fruit . . . Therefore by their fruits ye shall know them," Matt. 7:16-20. And again, "Out of the abundance of the heart the mouth speaketh." The tree is not free to produce good or bad fruit at random, but is governed by its nature. It is not the goodness of the fruit which causes the goodness of the tree, but the reverse. And according to the parable of Jesus, the same is true of man. And unless conduct does reveal character, how are we to know that the man who does good acts is really a good man, or that the man who does evil acts is really an evil man? While some for the sake of argument may insist that the will is free, in every day life all men assume that the will is both a product and a revelation of the person's nature. When a man exerts a volition which results in robbery or murder, we instinctively conclude that this is a true indicator of character and deal with him accordingly.

The very essence of rationality is that the volitions must be based on the understanding, principles, feelings, etc., and the person whose volitions are not so based is considered foolish. If after every decision the will reverted to a state of indecision and oscillation equipoised between good and evil, the basis for confidence in our fellow men would be gone. In fact a person whose will was really "free" would be a dangerous associate; his acts would be irrational and we would have no way of knowing what he might do under any conditions.

It is this fact (that volitions are a true expression of the person's nature) which guarantees the permanence of the states of the saved and of the lost in the next world. If mere free agency necessarily exposed a person to sin there would be no certainty that even the redeemed in heaven would not sin and be cast down to hell as were the fallen angels. The saints, however, possess a necessity on the side of goodness, and are therefore free in the highest sense. There is an absence of strife, and their wills, confirmed in holiness, go on producing good acts and motions with the ease and uniformity of physical law. On the other hand the state of the wicked is also permanent. After the restraining influences of the

Holy Spirit are withdrawn, they become bold, defiant, blasphemous, and sin with an irremediable obstinacy. They have passed into a permanent disposition of malice and wickedness and hate. They are no longer guests and strangers, but citizens and dwellers, in the land of sin. Further, if the theory of free-will were true, it would give the possibility of repentance after death; for is it not reasonable to believe that at least some of the lost, after they began to suffer the torments of hell, would see their mistake and return to God? In this world mild punishments are often effective in turning; men from sin; why should not severer punishments in the next world be more effective? Only the Calvinistic principle that the will is determined by the nature of the person and the inducements presented, reaches a conclusion in harmony with that of Scripture which affirms that "there is a great gulf fixed," so that none can pass over,--that the states of the saved and the lost alike are permanent.

The person who has not given the matter any special thought assumes that he has great freedom. But when he comes to examine this boasted freedom a little more closely he finds that he is much more limited than at first appeared. He is limited by the laws of the physical world, by his particular environment, habits, past training, social customs, fear of punishment or disapproval, his present desires, ambitions, etc., so that he is far from being the absolute master of his actions. At any moment he is pretty much what his past has made him. But so long as he acts under the control of his own nature and determines his actions from within, he has all the liberty of which a creature is capable. Any other kind of liberty is anarchy.

A man may carry a bowl of gold-fish wherever he pleases; yet the fish feel themselves free, and move unrestrainedly within the bowl. The science of Physics tells us of molecular motion amid molar calm,--when we look at the piece of stone, or wood, or metal, it appears to the naked eye to be perfectly quiet; yet if we had a magnifying glass powerful enough to see the individual molecules and atoms and electrons, we should find them whirling in their orbits at incredible speeds.

Predestination and free agency are the twin pillars of a great temple, and they meet above the clouds where the human gaze cannot penetrate. Or again, we may say that Predestination and free agency are parallel lines; and while the Calvinist may not be able to make them unite, the Arminian cannot make them cross each other. Furthermore, if we admit free will in the sense that the absolute determination of events is placed in the hands of man, we might as well spell it with a capital F and a capital W; for then man has become like God,--a first cause, an original spring of action,--and we have as many semi-Gods as we have free wills. Unless the sovereignty of God be given up, we cannot allow this independence to man. It is very noticeable--and in a sense it is reassuring to observe the fact--that the materialistic and metaphysical philosophers deny as completely as do Calvinists this thing that is called free will. They reason that every effect must have a sufficient cause; and for every action of the will they seek to find a motive which for the moment at least is strong enough to control.

7. SCRIPTURE PROOF

The Scriptures teach that Divine sovereignty and human freedom co-operate in perfect harmony; that while God is the sovereign Ruler and primary cause, man is free within the limits of his nature and is the secondary cause; and that God so controls the thoughts and wills of men that they freely and willingly do what He has planned for them to do.

A classic example of the co-operation of Divine sovereignty and human freedom is found in the story of Joseph. Joseph was sold into Egypt where he rose in authority and rendered a great service by supplying food in time of famine. It was, of course, a very sinful act for those sons of Jacob to sell their younger brother into slavery in a heathen country. They knew that they acted freely, and years later they admitted their full guilt (Gen. 42:21; 45:3). Yet Joseph could say to them, "Be not grieved, nor angry with yourselves, that ye sold me hither; for God did send me before you to preserve life. . . . So now it was not you that sent me hither, but God;" and again, "As for you, ye meant evil against me; but God meant it for good, to bring to pass, as it is this day, to save much people alive," Gen. 45:5, 8; 50:20. Joseph's brothers simply followed the evil inclinations of their natures; yet their act was a link in the chain of events through which God fulfilled His purpose; and their guilt was not the least diminished by the fact that their intended evil was overruled for good.

Pharaoh acted very unjustly toward his subject people, the Children of Israel; yet he simply fulfilled the purpose of God, for Paul writes, "The scripture saith unto Pharaoh, For this very purpose did I raise thee up, that I might show in thee my power, and that my name might be published abroad in all the earth," Rom. 9:17; Ex. 9:16; 10:1, 2. Some of God's plans are carried out by restraining the sinful acts of men. When the Israelites went up to Jerusalem three times a year for the set feasts, God restrained the greed of the neighboring tribes so that the land was not molested, Ex. 34:24. He put it into the heart of Cyrus, the heathen king of Persia, to rebuild the temple at Jerusalem, Ezra 1:1-3. We are told, "The king's heart is in the hand of Jehovah, as the watercourses; He turneth it whithersoever He will," Prov. 21:1. And if He turns the king's heart so easily surely he can turn the hearts of common men also.

In Isaiah 10:5-15 we have a very remarkable illustration of the way in which divine sovereignty

The Reformed Doctrine Of Predestination

and human freedom work together in perfect harmony: "Ho, Assyrian, the rod of mine anger, the staff in whose hand is mine indignation! I will send him against a profane nation, and against the people of my wrath will I give him a charge, to take the spoil, and to take the prey, and to tread them down like the mire of the streets. Howbeit he meaneth not so, neither doth his heart think so; but it is in his heart to destroy, and to cut off nations not a few. For he saith, Are not my princes all of them kings? Is not Calno as Carchemish? Is not Hamath as Arpad? Is not Samaria as Damascus? As my hand hath found the kingdoms of the idols, whose graven images did excel them of Jerusalem and Samaria; shall I not, as I have done unto Samaria and her idols, so do to Jerusalem and her idols?

"Wherefore it shall come to pass, that, when the Lord hath performed His whole work upon mount Zion and on Jerusalem, I will punish the fruit of the stout heart of the king of Assyria, and the glory of his high looks. For he hath said, by the strength of my hand I have done it, and by my wisdom; for I have understanding; and I have removed the bounds of the peoples, and have robbed their treasures, and like a valiant man I have brought down them that sit on thrones; and my hand hath found as a nest the riches of the peoples; and as one gathereth eggs that are forsaken, have I gathered all the earth; and there was none that moved the wing, or opened the mouth, or chirped.

"Shall the axe boast itself against him that heweth therewith? Shall the saw magnify itself against him that wieldeth it? As if a rod should wield them that lift it up, or as if a staff should lift up him that is not wood."

Concerning this passage Rice says: "What is the obvious meaning of this passage? It does most unequivocally teach, in the first place, that the king of Assyria, though a proud and ungodly man, was but an instrument in the hands of God, just as the axe, the saw, or the rod in the hands of a man, to execute His purposes upon the Jews; and that God had perfect control of him. It teaches, in the second place that the free agency of the king was not destroyed or impaired by this control, but that he was perfectly free to form his own plans and to be governed by his own desires. For it is declared that he did not design to execute God's purposes, but to promote his own ambitious projects. 'Howbeit he meaneth not so, neither doth his heart think so; but it is in his heart to destroy and to cut off nations not a few.' It consequently teaches, thirdly, that the king was justly held responsible for his pride, and wickedness, although God so overruled him that he fulfilled His wise purposes. God decreed to chastise the Jews for their sin. He chose to employ the king of Assyria to execute His purpose, and therefore sent him against them. He would afterward punish the king for his wicked plans. Is it not evident, then, beyond all cavil, that the Scriptures teach that God can and does, so control men, even wicked men, as to bring to pass His wise purposes without interfering with their free agency?" [105]

For any one who accepts the Bible as the word of God it is absolutely certain that the crucifixion of Christ--the most sinful event in all history--was foreordained: "For of a truth in this city against thy holy servant Jesus, whom thou didst anoint, both Herod and Pontius Pilate, with the Gentiles and the peoples of Israel, were gathered together, to do whatsoever thy hand and thy counsel foreordained to come to pass," Acts 4:27, 28; "Him being delivered up by the determinate counsel and foreknowledge of God, ye by the hands of lawless men did crucify and slay," Acts 2:23; and "The things which God foreshowed by the mouth of all the prophets, that His Christ should suffer, He thus fulfilled," Acts 3:18. "For they that dwell in Jerusalem, and their rulers because they knew Him not, nor the voice of the prophets which are read every Sabbath, fulfilled them in condemning Him. And though they found no cause of death in Him, yet they asked Pilate that He should be slain. And when they had fulfilled all things that were written of Him, they took Him down from the tree, and laid Him in a tomb," Acts 13:27-29.

And not only the crucifixion itself was foreordained, but many of the attending event, such as: the parting of Christ's garments and the casting of lots for His vesture (Ps. 22:18; John 19:24); the giving of gall and vinegar to drink (Ps. 69:21; Matt. 27:34; John 19:29); the mockery on the part of the people (Ps. 22:6-8; Matt. 27:39); the fact that they associated Him with thieves (Is. 53:12; Matt. 27:38); that none of His bones were to be broken (Ps. 34:20; John 19:36); the spear thrust (Zech. 12:10; John 19:34-37); and several other recorded events. Listen to the babble of hell around the cross, and tell us if those men were not free! Yet read all the forecast and prophecy and record of the tragedy and tell us if every incident of it was not ordained of God! Furthermore, these events could not have been predicted in detail by the Old Testament prophets centuries before they came to pass unless they had been absolutely certain in the foreordained plan of God. Yet while foreordained, they were carried out by agents who were ignorant of who Christ really was, and who were also ignorant of the fact that they were fulfilling the divine decrees, Acts 13:27, 29; 3:17. Hence if we swallow the camel in believing that the most sinful event in all history was in the foreordained plan of God, and that it was overruled for the redemption of the world, shall we strain at the gnat in refusing to believe that the smaller events of our daily lives are also in that plan, and that they are designed for good purposes?

FURTHER SCRIPTURE PROOF

Prov. 16:9: A man's heart deviseth his way; But Jehovah directeth his steps.

Jer. 10:23: O Jehovah, I know that the way of man is not in himself; it is not in man that walketh to direct his steps.

Ex. 12:36: And Jehovah gave the people favor in the sight of the Egyptians, so that they let them have what they asked.

Ezra 6:22: For Jehovah had made them joyful, and had turned the heart of the king of Assyria unto them, to strengthen their hands in the work of the house of God (rebuilding the temple).

Ezra 7:6: And the king (Artaxerxes) granted him (Ezra) all his request, according to the hand of Jehovah his God upon him.

Is. 44:28: (Jehovah) that saith of Cyrus (the heathen king of Persia), He is my shepherd, and shall perform all my pleasure, even saying of Jerusalem, She shall be built; and of the temple, Thy foundation shall be laid.

Rev. 17:17: (Concerning the wicked it is said) God did put in their hearts to do His mind, and to come to one mind, and to give their kingdom unto the beast, until the words of God should be accomplished.

I Sam. 2:25: They (Eli's sons) harkened not unto the voice of their father, because Jehovah was minded to slay them.

I Kings 12:11, 15: And now whereas my father (Solomon) did lade you with a heavy yoke, I (Rehoboam) will add to your yoke; my father chastised you with whips, but I will chastise you with scorpions. . . . So the king harkened not unto the people; for it was a thing brought about of Jehovah.

II Sam. 17:14: And Absalom and all the men of Israel said, The Counsel of Hushai is better than the counsel of Ahithophel. For Jehovah had ordained to defeat the counsel of Ahithophel, to the intent that Jehovah might bring evil upon Absalom .

Footnotes:

98. Quoted by Zanchius, p. 56.
99. Bondage of the Will, p. 125.
100. id. p. 5.
101. id. pp. 26, 27.
102. Pamphlet,--The Love of God for Every Man.
103. The Augustinian Doctrine of Predestination, p. 73.
104. Systematic Theology, II., p. 288.
105. God Sovereign and Man Free, p. 70, 71.

Chapter XVII

3. It Makes God the Author of Sin

1. The Problem of Evil. 2. Instances in Which Sin Has Been Overruled for Good. 3. The Fall of Adam Was Included in the Divine Plan. 4. The Result of Adam's Fall. 5. The Forces of Evil Are Under God's Perfect Control. 6. Sinful Acts Occur Only by Divine Permission. 7. Scripture Proof. 8. Comments by Smith and Hodge. 9. God's Grace is More Deeply Appreciated After the Person Has Been the Victim of Sin. 10. Calvinism Offers a More Satisfactory Solution of the Problem of Evil Than Does Any Other System.

1. THE PROBLEM OF EVIL

The objection may be raised that if God has foreordained the entire course of events in this world He must be the Author of Sin. To begin with, we readily admit that the existence of sin in a universe which is under the control of a God who is infinite in His wisdom, power, holiness, and justice, is an inscrutable mystery which we in our present state of knowledge cannot fully explain. As yet we only see through a glass darkly. Sin can never be explained on the grounds of logic or reason, for it is essentially illogical and unreasonable. The mere fact that sin exists has often been urged by atheists and skeptics as an argument not merely against Calvinism but against theism in general.

The Westminster Standards, in treating of the dread mystery of evil, are very careful to guard the character of God from even the suggestion of evil. Sin is referred to the freedom which is given to the agent, and of all sinful acts whatever they emphatically affirm that "the sinfulness thereof proceedeth only from the creature and not from God, who, being most holy and righteous, neither is, nor can be the author or approver of sin." (V; 4.)

And while it is not ours to explain how God in His secret counsel rules and overrules the sinful acts of men, it is ours to know that whatever God does He never deviates from His own perfect justice. In all the manifestations of His character He shows Himself pre-eminently the Holy One. These deep workings of God are mysteries which are to be adored, but not to be inquired into; and were it not for the fact that some persons persist in declaring that the doctrine of Predestination makes God the author of sin, we could let the matter rest here.

A partial explanation of sin is found in the fact that while man is constantly commanded in Scripture not to commit it, he is, nevertheless, permitted to commit it if he chooses to do so. No compulsion is laid on the person; he is simply left to the free exercise of his own nature, and he alone is responsible. This, however, is never a bare permission, for with full knowledge of the nature of the person and of his tendency to sin, God allows him or allows him to be in a certain environment, knowing perfectly well that the particular sin will be committed. But while God permits sin, His connection with it is purely negative and it is the abominable thing which he hates with perfect hatred. The motive which God has in permitting it and the motive which man has in committing it are radically different. Many persons are deceived in these matters because they fail to consider that God wills righteously those things which men do wickedly. Furthermore, every person's conscience after he has committed a sin tells him that he alone is responsible and that he need not have committed it if he had not voluntarily chosen to do so.

The Reformers recognized the fact that sin, both in its entrance into the world and in all its subsequent appearances, was involved in the divine plan; that the explanation of its existence, so far as any explanation could be given, was to be found in the fact that sin was completely under the control of God; and that it would be overruled for a higher manifestation of His glory. We may rest assured that God would never have permitted sin to have entered at all unless, through His secret and overruling providence, He was able to exert a directing influence on the minds of wicked men so that good is made to result from their intended evil. He works not only all the good and holy affections which are found in the hearts of His people, but He also perfectly controls all the depraved and impious affections of the wicked, and turns them as He pleases, so that they have a desire to accomplish that which He has planned to accomplish by their means. The wicked so often glory in themselves at some accomplishment of their purposes; but as Calvin says, "the event at length proves that they were only fulfilling all the while that which had been ordained of God, and that too, against their own will, while they knew nothing of it." But while God does overrule the depraved affections of men for the accomplishment of His own purposes, He nevertheless punishes them for their sin and makes them to stand condemned in their own consciences.

"A ruler may forbid treason; but his command does not oblige him to do all in his power to prevent disobedience to it. It may promote the good of his kingdom to suffer the treason to be committed, and the traitor to be punished according to law. That in view of this resulting good he chooses not to prevent the treason, does not imply any contradiction or opposition of it in the monarch." [106]

In regard to the problem of evil, Dr. A. H. Strong advances the following considerations: "(1) That freedom of will is necessary to virtue; (2) that God suffers from sin more than does the sinner; (3) that, with the permission of sin, God has provided a redemption; and, (4) that God will eventually overrule all evil for good." And then he adds, "It is possible that the elect angels belong to a moral system in which sin is prevented by constraining motives. We cannot deny that God could prevent sin in a moral system. But it is very doubtful whether God could prevent sin in the best moral system. The most perfect freedom is indispensable to the attainment of the highest virtue." [107] Fairbairn has given us some good thought in the following paragraph: "But why did God create a being capable of sinning? Only so could He create a being capable of obeying. The ability to do good implies the capability of doing evil. The engine can neither obey nor disobey, and the creature who was without this double capacity might be a machine, but could be no child. Moral perfection can be attained, but cannot be created; God can make a being capable of moral action, but not a being with all the fruits of moral action garnered within him."

2. INSTANCES IN WHICH SIN HAS BEEN OVERRULED FOR GOOD

Throughout the Scriptures we find numerous instances In which sinful acts were permitted and then overruled for good. We shall first notice some Old Testament examples. Jacob's deception of his old, blind father, though a sinful act in itself, was permitted and used as a link in the chain of events through which the already revealed plan of God that the elder should serve the younger was carried out. Pharaoh and the Egyptians were permitted to wrong the Israelites, that by their deliverance God's wonders might be multiplied in the land of Egypt (Ex. 11:9), that these things might be told to future generations (Ex. 10:1, 2), and that His glory might be declared throughout all the earth (Ex. 9:16). The curse Balaam tried to pronounce upon the Israelites was turned into a blessing (Nu. 24:10; Neh. 13:2). The proud, heathen king of Assyria unconsciously became the servant of Jehovah in executing vengeance upon an apostate people: "Howbeit he meaneth not so, neither doth his heart think so," Is. 10:5-15. The calamities which befell Job, as seen from the human viewpoint appear to be mere misfortunes, accidents, chance happenings. But with further knowledge we see God behind it all, exercising complete control, giving the Devil permission to afflict so far but no farther, designing the events for the development of Job's patience and character, and using even the seemingly meaningless waste of the storm to fulfill His high and loving purposes.

In the New Testament we find the same teaching. The death of Lazarus, as seen from the human viewpoint of Mary and Martha and those who came to mourn for him, was a very great misfortune; but when seen from the divine viewpoint it was "not unto death, but for the glory of God, that the Son of God might be glorified thereby," John 11: 4. The manner of Peter's death (which apparently was by crucifixion) was to glorify God (John 21:19). When Jesus crossed the sea of Galilee with His disciples He could have prevented the storm and have ordered them a pleasant passage, but that would not have been so much for His glory and the confirmation of their faith as was their deliverance. Paul, by his stern rebukes, made the Corinthians "sorry unto repentance," "after a godly sort ;" "for godly sorrow worketh repentance unto salvation, a repentance which bringeth no regret; but the sorrow of the world worketh death," II Cor. 7:9, 10. The Lord often temporarily delivers a person over to Satan, that his bodily and mental sufferings may react for his salvation, (I Cor. 5:5). Paul, in speaking of the adversities which he had suffered, said, "Now I would have you know, brethren, that the things which happened unto me have fallen out rather unto the progress of the gospel," Phil. 1:12. When he saw that his "thorn in the flesh" was something which had been divinely sent upon him, "a messenger of Satan to buffet him," so that he "should not be exalted over much," he accepted it with the words, 'Most gladly therefore will I rather glory in my weakness, that the power of Christ may rest upon me," II Cor. 12:7-10. In that instance God made the poison of the cruelest and most sinful monster of all time to be an antidote to cure the apostle's pride.

To a certain extent we can say that the reason for the permission of sin is that, "Where sin abounded, grace did much more abound." Such deep, unfathomable grace could not have been shown if sin had been excluded.

As a matter of fact we gain more through salvation in Christ than we lost by the fall in Adam. When Christ became incarnate, human nature was, as it were, taken into the very bosom of Deity, and the redeemed reach a far more exalted position through union with Christ than Adam could have attained had he not fallen but persevered and been admitted into heaven.

The Reformed Doctrine Of Predestination

This general truth was expressed by Calvin in the following words: "But, God, who once commanded light to shine out of darkness, can marvelously bring, if He pleases, salvation out of hell itself, and thus turn darkness itself to light. But what worketh Satan? In a certain sense, the work of God! That is, God, by holding Satan fast bound in obedience to His Providence, turns him whithersoever He will, and thus applies the great enemy's devices and attempts to the accomplishment of His own eternal principles. [108]

Even the persecutions which are permitted to come upon the righteous are designed for good purposes. Paul declares that "our light affliction, which is for the moment, worketh for us more and more exceedingly an eternal weight of glory," II Cor. 4:17. To suffer with Christ is to be more closely united to Him, and great reward in heaven is promised to those who suffer in His behalf (Matt. 5:10-12). To the Philippians it was written, "To you it hath been granted in the behalf of Christ not only to believe on Him but else to suffer in His behalf," Phil. 1:29; and we read that after the apostles had been publicly abused, "They departed from the presence of the council, rejoicing that they were accounted worthy to suffer dishonor for the Name," Acts 5:41. The writer of the book of Hebrews stated this same truth when he wrote, "All chastening seemeth for the present to be not joyous but grievous; yet afterward it yieldeth peaceable fruit to them that have been exercised thereby, even the fruit of righteousness," Heb. 12:11.

"The acts of the wicked in persecuting the early Church," says Dr. Charles Hodge, "were ordained of God as the means for the wider and more speedy proclamation of the Gospel. The sufferings of the martyrs were the means not only of extending but of purifying the Church. The apostasy of the man of sin being predicted, was predetermined. The destruction of the Huguenots in France, the persecution of the Puritans in England, laid the foundation for the planting of North America with a race of godly energetic men, who were to make this land the land of refuge for the nations, the home of liberty, civil and religious. It would destroy the confidence of God's people could they be persuaded that God does not foreordain whatever comes to pass. It is because the Lord reigns, and doeth His pleasure in heaven and on earth, that they repose in perfect security under His guidance and protection." [109]

Many of the divine attributes were displayed through the creation and government of the world, but the attribute of justice could be shown only to creatures deserving punishment, and the attribute of mercy or grace could be shown only to creatures in misery. Until man's fall into sin, and redemption from it, these attributes, so far as we can learn, had been unexercised and undisplayed, and consequently were unknown to any but God Himself from all eternity. Had not sin been admitted to the creation these attributes would have remained buried in an eternal night. And the universe, without the knowledge of these attributes, would be like the earth without the light of the sun. Sin, then, is permitted in order that the mercy of God may be shown in its forgiveness, and that His justice may be shown in its punishment. Its entrance is the result of a settled design which God formed in eternity, and through which He purposed to reveal Himself to His rational creatures as complete and full-orbed in all conceivable perfections.

3. THE FALL OF ADAM WAS INCLUDED IN THE DIVINE PLAN

Even the fall of Adam, and through him the fall of the race, was not by chance or accident, but was so ordained in the secret counsels of God. We are told that Christ was "foreknown indeed (as a sacrifice for sin) before the foundation of the world," I Peter 1:20. Paul speaks of "the eternal purpose" which was purposed in Jesus Christ our Lord, Eph. 3:11. The writer of Hebrews refers to "the blood of an eternal covenant," 13:20. And since the plan of redemption is thus traced back into eternity, the plan to permit man to fall into the sin from which he was thus to be redeemed must also extend back into eternity; otherwise there would have been no occasion for redemption. In fact the plan for the whole course of the world's events, including the fall, redemption, and all other events, was before God in its completeness before He ever brought the creation into existence; and He deliberately ordered it that this series of events, and not some other series, should become actual.

And unless the fall was in the plan of God, what becomes of our redemption through Christ? Was that only a makeshift arrangement which God resorted to in order to offset the rebellion of man? To ask such a question is to answer it. Throughout the Scriptures redemption is represented as the free, gracious purpose of God from eternity. In the very hour of man's first sin, God sovereignly intervened with a gratuitous promise of deliverance. While the glory of God is displayed in the whole realm of creation, it was to be especially displayed in the work of redemption. The fall of man, therefore, was only one part and a necessary part in the plan; and even Watson, though a decided Arminian, says, "The redemption of man by Christ was certainly not an afterthought brought in upon man's apostasy; it was a provision, and when man fell he found justice hand in hand with mercy." [110]

Consistent Arminianism, however, pictures God as an idle, inactive spectator sitting in doubt while Adam fell, and as quite surprised and thwarted by the creature of His hands. In contrast with this, we hold that God fore-planned and fore-saw the fall; that it in no sense came as a surprise to Him; and that after it had occurred He did not feel that He had made a mistake in creating man. Had He wished

Loraine Boettner D.D.

He could have prevented Satan's entrance into the garden and could have preserved Adam in a state of holiness as He did the holy angels. The mere fact that God fore-saw the fall is sufficient proof that He did not expect man to glorify Him by continuing in a state of holiness.

Yet God in no way compelled man to fall. He simply withheld that undeserved constraining grace with which Adam would infallibly not have fallen, which grace He was under no obligation to bestow. In respect to himself, Adam might have stood had he so chosen; but in respect to God it was certain that he would fall. He acted as freely as if there had been no decree, and yet as infallibly as if there had been no liberty. The Jews, so far as their own free agency was concerned, might have broken Christ's bones; yet in reality it was not possible for them to have done so, for it was written, "A bone of Him shall not be broken," Ps. 34:20; John 19:36. God's decree does not take away man's liberty; and in the fall Adam freely exercised the natural emotions of his will.

The reason for the fall is assigned in that "God hath shut up all unto disobedience, that He might have mercy on all," Rom. 11:32; and again, "We ourselves have had the sentence of death within ourselves, that we should not trust in ourselves, but in God who raiseth the dead," II Cor. 1:9; and it would be difficult to find language which would assert the Divine control and Divine initiative more explicitly than this. For wise reasons, God was pleased to permit our first parents to be tempted and to fall, and then to overrule their sin for His own glory. Yet this permission and overruling of sin does not make Him the author of it. It seems that He has permitted the fall in order to show what free will would do; and then, by overruling it, He has shown what the blessings of His grace and the judgments of His justice can do.

It may be well just at this point, to say something more about the nature of the fall. Adam was given a most favorable opportunity to secure eternal life and blessedness for himself and his posterity. He was created holy and was placed in a world free from sin. He was surrounded by all the beauty of paradise and was graciously given permission to eat of all the fruits with the exception of one, which was certainly no irksome restraint. God Himself came down into the Garden and was Adam's companion. In unmistakably clear language Adam was warned that if he did eat of the fruit he would certainly die. He was thus placed under a pure test of obedience, since the eating would not in itself have been either morally right or wrong. Obedience is here set up as the virtue which, in the rational creature, is, as it were, the mother and guardian of all the others.

4. THE RESULT OF ADAM'S FALL

But, in spite of all his advantages, Adam deliberately disobeyed, and the threatened sentence of death was executed. This plainly includes more than the dissolution of the body. The word "death" as used in the Scriptures in reference to the effects of sin includes any and every form of evil which is inflicted in punishment of sin. It means primarily spiritual death, or separation from God, which is both temporal and eternal--a loss of His favor in all ways. It meant the opposite of the reward promised, which was blessed and eternal life in Heaven. It meant, therefore, the eternal miseries of hell, together with the fore-tastes of those miseries which are felt in this life. Its nature can be partly seen in the effects of sin which have actually fallen upon the human race. And finally, the nature of the death which fell upon Adam and his descendants can be seen by contrast with the life which the redeemed have with Christ. It was a death which caused sin instead of holiness to become man's natural element, so that now in his unregenerate nature the gospel and all holy things are repulsive to him. He is as utterly unable to appreciate redemption through faith in Christ, as a dead man is to hear the sounds of this world. That the death threatened was not primarily physical death is shown by the fact that Adam lived many years after the fall, while spiritually he was immediately alienated from God and was cast out of Paradise. In his fallen state man is terrified by any appearance of the supernatural. And even in regard to physical death, that was also in a sense immediately executed; for though our first parents lived many years, they immediately began to grow old. Since the fall, life has become an unceasing march toward the grave. Says Charles Hodge, "In the day in which Adam ate the forbidden fruit he did die. The penalty threatened was not a momentary infliction but permanent subjection to all the evils which flow from the righteous displeasure of God." [111]

Furthermore, the whole Christian world has believed that in the fall, Adam, as the natural and federal head of the race, injured not only himself but all of his posterity, so that, as Dr. Hodge says, "in virtue of the union, federal and natural, between Adam and his posterity, his sin, although not their act, is so imputed to them that it is the judicial ground of the penalty threatened against him coming also on them . . . To impute sin, in Scriptural and theological language, is to impute the guilt of sin. And by guilt is meant not criminality, or moral ill-desert, or demerit, much less moral pollution, but the judicial obligation to satisfy justice," [112] His sin is laid to their account. Even infants, who have no personal sin of their own, suffer pain and death. Now the Scriptures uniformly represent suffering and death as the wages of sin. It would be unjust for God to execute the penalty on those who are not guilty. Since the penalty falls on infants, they must be guilty; and since they have not personally committed sin, they must be guilty of Adam's sin. All those who have inherited human nature from Adam were in him as the fruit in the germ, and have, as it were, grown up one person with him. By the fall Adam was entirely and absolutely ruined. The state of original righteousness or holiness in which he was created was lost and its place was taken by an overwhelming state of sin, which was brought about as effectively as one puncture of the eye involves the person in perpetual darkness. The wrath and curse of God rested upon him and he was possessed with a sense of guilt, shame, pollution, degradation, a dread of punishment, and a desire to escape from the presence of God.

In fact, there is a strict parallel between the way in which the guilt of Adam is imputed to us and that in which the righteousness of Christ is imputed to us, so that the one illustrates the other, We were cursed through Adam and were redeemed through Christ, although we were of course no more personally guilty of Adam's sin than we are personally meritorious because of Christ's righteousness. It is utterly absurd to hold to salvation through Christ unless we also hold to damnation through Adam, for Christianity is based on this representative principle. Unless the race had been cursed through Adam, there would have been no occasion for Christ to have redeemed it. The history of the fall, recorded in a manner at once profound and childlike in the third chapter of Genesis, has, therefore, universal significance. And Calvinism alone does justice to the idea of the organic unity of the human race, and to the profound parallel which Paul draws between the first and the second Adam.

5. THE FORCES OF EVIL ARE UNDER GOD'S PERFECT CONTROL

We believe that God actually rules in the affairs of men, that His decrees are absolute, and that they include all events. Consequently we believe that nations and individuals are predestined to all of every kind of good and evil which befalls them. When we get the larger view we see that even the sinful acts of men have their place in the divine plan, and that it is only because of our finite and imperfect nature, which does not comprehend all the relations and connections, that these acts appear to be contrary to that plan. To illustrate this, when we see the sheet music running through the player piano we readily understand how it is used; but if we were to find the same paper apart from the piano and had never seen it used, we might readily conclude that it was only wrapping paper, and poor wrapping paper at that, for it would be full of holes. Yet when it is put in its proper place it produces the most beautiful music. Unless we do believe that God has ordained the whole course of events, and that the courses he has outlined for our individual lives are good ones, we are certain to become discouraged in times of adversity. Like Jacob of old who in the face of the apparent misfortunes immediately before meeting his favorite son, Joseph, concluded, "All these things are against me," we may become discouraged when perhaps at that very time the Lord is preparing great things for us.

The Scripture doctrine, as stated before, is that God restrains sin within certain limits, that He brings good out of intended evil, and overrules the evil for His own glory. Since God is infinite in power and wisdom, sin could have no existence except by His permission. God was free to create, or not to create; to create this particular world-order, or one entirely different. All evil forces are under His absolute control and could be blotted out of existence in an instant if He so willed. The murderer is kept in life and is indebted to God for the strength to kill his victim, and also for the opportunity. When Jesus said, "Get thee hence, Satan," Satan immediately went; and when Jesus commanded the evil spirits to hold their peace and come out of the possessed persons, they immediately obeyed. The psalmist expressed his confidence in God's power to overrule sinners when contemplating their works, he wrote, "He that sitteth in the heavens will laugh; the Lord 'will have them in derision," 2: 4. Job said, "The deceived and the deceiver are His," 12:16; by which he meant that both good and evil men are under God's providential control.

Unless sin occurs according to the divine purpose and permission of God, it occurs by chance. Evil then becomes an independent and uncontrollable principle and the pagan idea of dualism is introduced into the theory of the universe. The doctrine that there are powers of sin, rebellion, and darkness in the very nature of free agency, which may prove an over-match for divine omnipotence, imperils even the eternal safety and happiness of the saints in glory.

Luther expressed his belief concerning this question in the following words: "What I assert and contend for is this:--that God, where He operates without the grace of His Spirit, works all in all, even in the ungodly; and He alone moves, acts on, and carries along by the motion of His omnipotence, all those things 'which He alone has created, which motion those things can neither avoid nor change, but of necessity follow and obey, each one according to the measure of power given of God:--thus all things, even the ungodly co-operate with God." [113] And Zanchius wrote, "We should, therefore, be careful not to give up the omnipotence of God under a pretense of exalting His holiness; He is infinite in both, and therefore neither should be set aside or obscured. To say that God absolutely nills the being and commission of sin, while experience convinces us that sin is acted every day, is to represent the Deity as a weak, impotent being who would fain have things go otherwise than they do, but cannot accomplish His desire." [114]

One of the best of more recent comments is that of E. W. Smith in his admirable little book, "The Creed of Presbyterians." "Did we believe that so potent and fearful a thing as sin had broken into the original holy order of the universe in defiance of God's purpose, and is rioting in defiance of His power, we might well surrender ourselves to terror and despair. Unspeakably comforting and strengthening is the Scriptural assurance of our Standards (V:4) that beneath all this wild tossing and lashing of evil purposes and agencies there lies, in mighty and controlling embrace, a Divine purpose that governs them all. Over sin as over all else, God reigns supreme. His sovereign Providence 'extendeth to the first fall and all other sins of angels and men,' so that these are as truly parts and developments of His Providence as are the movements of the stars or the activities of unfallen spirits in heaven itself. Having chosen, for reasons most wise and holy though unrevealed to us, to admit sin, He hath joined to this bare permission a 'most wise and powerful bounding' of all sin, so that it can never overleap the lines which He has prescribed for its imprisonment, and such an 'ordering and governing' of it, as will secure 'His own holy ends,' and manifest in the final consummation not only His 'almighty Power,' but His 'unsearchable Wisdom" and His 'infinite Goodness'" (p. 177).

And Floyd E. Hamilton has written: "God created the human being with the possibility of sinning, and He has the power to interfere at any time to prevent the evil act. Even though He has no purpose to work out in the permission of the act the very permission of the act when He has the power to interfere, places the ultimate responsibility for the act squarely upon God. Moreover, if He has no purpose to work out, then He is certainly reprehensible in not preventing the act! It is attempted to avoid this conclusion by saying that God does not interfere because to do so would be to take away manes freedom. In that case man's freedom is regarded as of more value than his eternal salvation! But even that does not remove the ultimate responsibility for the permission of the evil act from God; God has the power to prevent the evil act, has no purpose to work out in permitting it, but nevertheless, in order to protect man's freedom, allows man to bring eternal punishment upon himself! Assuredly that would be a poor kind of a god!" [115]

Hence God Himself is ultimately responsible for sin in that He has power to prevent it but does not do so, although the immediate responsibility rests on man alone God is, of course, never the efficient cause in the production of sin. Augustine, Luther and Calvin often stressed this truth of God's full and sovereign control when proving that the present course of the world is the one which from eternity God planned that it should follow.

6. SINFUL ACTS OCCUR ONLY BY DIVINE PERMISSION

The good acts of men then are rendered certain by the positive decree of God, and the sinful acts occur only by His permission. Yet it is more than a bare permission by which the sinful acts occur, for that would leave it uncertain whether or not they would be done. Concerning this subject David S. Clark says: "The most reasonable explanation is that the sinful nature will go to the boundary set by the permission of God; hence God's bounding of sin renders certain what and how much will come to pass. Satan could go no farther with Job than God permitted; but it is certain that he would go as far as God allowed." [116] And in accordance with this is the statement of W. D. Smith: "When it is known, certainly, that it will be done unless prevented, and there is a determination not to prevent it, it is rendered as certain as if it were decreed to be done by positive agency. In the one case, the event is rendered certain by agency put forth; and, in the other case, it is rendered equally certain by agency withheld. It is an unchangeable decree in both cases. The sins of Judas, and the crucifixion of the Saviour, were as unchangeably decreed, permissively, as the coming of the Saviour into the world was decreed positively. From this you can perceive the consistency of the Confession of Faith with common sense, when it says, that 'God from all eternity did, by the most wise and holy counsel of His own will, freely and unchangeably foreordain whatsoever comes to pass,' etc. You perceive, also, that this is clearly reconcilable with the following sentiment, 'He is not the author of sin,' etc." [117]

Augustine expressed a similar thought when he said: "Wherefore those mighty works of God, exquisitely perfect. according to every bent of His will, are such that, in a wonderful and ineffable way, that is not done without the will of God which is even done contrary to His will, because it could not be done at all, unless He permitted it to be done; and yet, He does not permit unwillingly, but willingly. Nor, as the God of goodness, would He permit a thing to be done evilly, unless, as the God of omnipotence, He could work good even out of the evil done." [118]

Even the works of Satan are so controlled and limited that they serve God's purposes. While Satan eagerly desires the destruction of the wicked and diligently works to bring it about, yet the destruction proceeds from God. It is, in the first place, God who decrees that the wicked shall suffer, and Satan is merely permitted to lay the punishment upon them. The motives which underlie God's purposes and those which underlie Satan's are, of course, infinitely different. God willed the destruction of Jerusalem; Satan also desired the same, yet for different reasons. As Augustine tells us, God wills with a good will that which Satan wills with an evil will,--as was the case in the crucifixion of Christ, which was over-ruled for the redemption of the world. Sometimes God uses the wicked wills and passions of men, rather than the good wills of His own servants, to accomplish His purposes. This truth has been very clearly expressed by Dr. Warfield in the following words: "All things find their unity in His eternal plan; and

The Reformed Doctrine Of Predestination

not their unity merely, but their justification as well; even the evil, though retaining its quality as evil and hateful to the holy God, and certain to be dealt with as hateful, yet does not occur apart from His provision or against His will, but appears in the world which He has made only as the instrument by means of which He works the higher good." [119]

7. SCRIPTURE PROOF

That this is the doctrine of the Scriptures is abundantly plain. The sale of Joseph into Egypt by his brothers was a very wicked act; yet we see that it was overruled not only for Joseph's good but also for the good of the brothers themselves. When it is traced to its source we see that God was the author. it had its exact place in the divine plan. Joseph later said to his brothers, "And now be not grieved nor angry with yourselves, that ye sold me hither; for God did send me before you to preserve life. . . . So now it was not you that sent me hither but God. . . . And as for you, ye meant evil against me, but God meant it for good," Gen. 45:5, 8; 50:20. It is said that God hardened the heart of Pharaoh, Ex. 4:21; 9:12; and the very words which God addressed to Pharaoh were, "But in every deed for this cause have I made thee to stand, to show thee my power, and that my name might be declared throughout all the earth," Ex. 9:16. And to Moses God said, "And I, behold I will harden the hearts of the Egyptians and they shall go (into the Red Sea) after them; and I will get me honor upon Pharaoh and upon all his host, and upon his chariots, and upon his horsemen," Ex. 14:17.

Shimei cursed David, because Jehovah had said, "Curse David"; and when David knew this, he said, "Let him alone, and let him curse; for Jehovah hath bidden him," II Sam. 16:10, 11. And after David had suffered the unjust violence of his enemies he recognized that "God hath done all this." Of the Canaanites it was said, "And it was of Jehovah to harden their hearts, to come against Israel in battle, that He might utterly destroy them, that they might have no favor, and that He might destroy them, as Jehovah commanded Moses," Josh. 11:20. Hophni and Phinehas, the two evil sons of Eli, "hearkened not unto the voice of their father, because Jehovah was minded to slay them," I Sam. 2:25.

Even Satan and the evil spirits are made to carry out the divine purpose. As an instrument of divine vengeance in the punishment of the wicked an evil spirit was openly given the command to go and deceive the prophets of King Ahab: "And Jehovah said, Who shall entice Ahab, that he may go up and fall at Ramoth-gilead? And one said on this manner; and another on that manner. And there came forth a spirit, and stood before Jehovah, and said, I will entice him. And Jehovah said unto him, Wherewith? And he said, I will go forth, and will be a lying spirit in the mouth of his prophets. And He said, Thou shalt entice him, and shalt prevail; Go forth and do so. Now therefore (said Micaiah), behold, Jehovah hath put a lying spirit in the mouth of all these thy prophets; and Jehovah hath spoken evil concerning thee," I Kings 22:20-23. Concerning Saul it is written, "an evil spirit from Jehovah troubled him," I Sam. 16:14. "And God sent an evil spirit between Abimelech and the men of Shechem; and the men of Shechem dealt treacherously with Abimelech," Judges 9:23. Hence it is from Jehovah that evil spirits proceed to trouble sinners. And it is from him that the evil impulses which arise in the hearts of sinners take this or that specific form, II Sam. 24:1.

In one place we are told that God, in order to punish a rebellious people, moved the heart of David to number them (II Sam. 24:1, 10); but in another place where this same act is referred to, we are told that it was Satan who instigated David's pride and caused him to number them (I Chr. 21:1). In this we see that Satan was made the rod of God's wrath, and that God impels even the hearts of sinful men and demons whithersoever He will. While all adulterous and incestuous intercourse is abominable to God, He sometimes uses even such sins as these to punish other sins, as was the case when He used such acts in Absalom to punish the adultery of David. Before Absalom had committed his sin it was announced to David that this was the form which his punishment was to take: "Thus saith Jehovah, Behold I will raise up evil against thee out of thine own house; and I will take thy wives before thine eyes, and give them unto thy neighbor, and he shall lie with thy wives in the sight of the sun," II Sam. 12:11. Hence these acts were not in every way contrary to the will of God.

In I Chr. 10: 4 we read that "Saul took a sword and fell upon it." This was his own deliberate, sinful act. Yet it executed Divine justice and fulfilled a divine purpose which was revealed years before concerning David; for a little later we read, "So Saul died for his transgressions which he committed against Jehovah. . . . He inquired not of Jehovah; therefore He slew him and turned the kingdom unto David the son of Jesse," I Chr. 10:14. There is a sense in which God is said to do what he permits or impels His creatures to do.

The evil which was threatened against Jerusalem for her apostasy is described as directly sent of God, II Kings 22:20. The psalmist recognized that even the hate of their enemies was stirred up by Jehovah to punish a rebellious people, Ps. 105:25. Isaiah recognized that even the apostasy and disobedience of Israel was in the divine plan: "O Jehovah, why dost thou make us to err from thy ways, and hardenest our hearts from thy fear?" Is. 63:17. In I Chr. 5:22 we read, "There fell many slain, because the war was of Jehovah." Rehoboam's foolish course which caused the disruption of the kingdom was "a thing brought about by Jehovah," I Kings 12:15. All of these things are summed up in that passage of Isaiah, "I form the light, and create darkness; I make peace, and create evil: I am Jehovah that doeth all these things," 45:7 and again in Amos, "Shall evil befall a city and Jehovah hath not done it?" Amos 3:6.

When we come to the New Testament we find the same doctrine set forth. We have already shown that the crucifixion of Christ was a part of the divine plan. Though slain by the hands of lawless men who did not understand the importance of the event which they were carrying out, "The things which God foreshowed by the mouth of all the prophets, that His Christ should suffer, He thus fulfilled," Acts 3:18. The crucifixion was the cup which the Father had given Him to drink, John 18:11. It was written, "I will smite the shepherd, and the sheep of the flock shall be scattered abroad," Matt. 26:31. When Moses and Elijah appeared to Jesus on the Mount of Transfiguration, they spoke of "His decease which He was about to accomplish at Jerusalem," Luke 9:31. Concerning His own death Jesus said, "The son of man indeed goeth, as it hath been determined; but woe unto that man through whom He is betrayed," Luke 22:22; again, "Did ye never read in the Scriptures, The stone which the builders rejected, The same was made the head of the corner; This was from the Lord, And it is marvelous in your eyes?" Matt. 21:42; and never did He teach more plainly that the cross was in the divine plan than when in the garden of Gethsemane He said, "Not as I will, but as thou wilt," Matt. 26:39. Jesus deliberately surrendered Himself to be crucified when He might have called to his defence "more than twelve legions of angels," had He chosen to have done so, Matt. 26:53. Pilate thought that he had power to crucify Jesus or to release Him as he pleased; but Jesus told him he could have no power against Him at all except it were given him from above, John 19:10, 11.

It was in the plan of God that Christ should come into the world, that He should suffer, that He should die a violent death, and thus make atonement for His people. Hence God simply permitted sinful men to sinfully lay that burden upon Him, and overruled their acts for His own glory in the redemption of the world. Those who crucified Christ acted in perfect harmony with the freedom of their own sinful natures, and were alone responsible for their sin. On this occasion, as on many others, God has made the wrath of man to praise Him. It would be hard to frame language which would more explicitly set forth the idea that God's plan extends to all things than is here used by the Scripture writers. Hence the crucifixion on Calvary was not a defeat, but a victory; and the cry, "It is finished," announced the successful achievement of the work of redemption which had been committed to the Son. That which "stands written of Jesus in the Old Testament Scriptures has its certain fulfillment in Him; and that enough stands written of Him there to assure His followers that in the course of His life, and in its, to them, strange and unexpected ending, He was not the prey of chance or the victim of the hatred of men, to the marring of His work or perhaps even the defeat of His mission, but was following step by step, straight to its goal, the predestined pathway marked out for Him in the counsels of eternity, and sufficiently revealed from of old in the Scriptures to enable all who were not 'foolish and slow of heart to believe in all that the prophets have spoken,' to perceive that the Christ must needs have lived just this life and fulfilled just this destiny." [120]

Other events recorded in the New Testament also teach the same lesson. When God cast off the Jews as a people it was not a purposeless destruction, nor in order merely that "they might fall"; "but that by their fall salvation might come to the Gentiles, to provoke them to jealousy," so that they in turn shall also embrace Christianity, Rom. 11:11. The blindness of one man is said to have been, not because of his own or his parent's sin, but in order to give Jesus a chance to display His power and glory in restoring the sight, or, as the writer puts it, "that the works of God should be made manifest in him," John 9:3. The Old Testament statement that the very purpose which God had in raising up Pharaoh was to show His power and to publish abroad his name is repeated in Rom. 9:17. This general teaching is climaxed with Paul's declaration that "To them that love God all things work together for good, even to them that are called according to His purpose." Rom. 8:28.

No one can rationally deny that God foreordained sin if, as the Scriptures assert, He foreordained the crucifixion of Christ, and these other events to which we have referred. That sinful acts do have their place in the divine plan is repeatedly taught. And if any persons are inclined to take offence at this, let them consider how many times the Scriptures declare the judgments of God to be a "great deep." Hence those who hastily charge that our doctrine makes God the author of sin, bring that charge not only against us, but against God Himself; for our doctrine is the clearly revealed doctrine of the Scriptures.

8. COMMENTS BY SMITH AND HODGE

God's relation to sin is admirably illustrated in the following paragraph which we shall take the liberty of quoting from W. D. Smith's little book, What Is Calvinism? "Suppose to yourself a neighbor who keeps a distillery or dram shop, which is a nuisance to all around--neighbors collecting, drinking, and fighting on the Sabbath, with consequent misery and distress in families, etc. Suppose, further, that I am endowed with a certain foreknowledge, and can see, with absolute certainty, a chain of events, in connection with a plan of operations which I have in view, for the good of that neighborhood. I see that by preaching there, I will be made the instrument of the conversion, and consequent reformation, of the owner of the distillery, and I therefore determine to go. Now, in so doing, I positively decree the reformation of the man; that is I determine to do what renders his reformation certain and I fulfill my decree by positive agency. But, in looking a little further in the chain of events, I discover, with the same absolute certainty, that his drunken customers will be filled with wrath, and much sin will be committed, in venting their malice upon him and me. They will not only curse and blaspheme God and religion, but they will even burn his house, and attempt to burn mine. Now, you perceive that this evil, which enters into my plan, is not chargeable upon me at all, though I am the author of the plan which, in its operations, I know will produce it. Hence, it is plain, that any intelligent being may set on foot a plan, and carry it out, in which he knows, with absolute certainty, that evil will enter, and yet he is not the author of the evil, or chargeable with it in any way. . . . In looking a little further in the chain of events, I discover, that if they be permitted they will take his life; and, I see, moreover, that if his life be spared, he will now be as notorious for good as he was for evil, and will prove a rich blessing to the neighborhood and to society. . . . Therefore, upon the whole plan, I determine to act; and, in so doing, I positively decree the reformation of that man, and the consequent good; and I permissively decree the wicked actions of the others; yet, it is very plain, that I am not in any way, chargeable for their sins. Now, in one or the other of these ways, God 'has foreordained whatsoever comes to pass'" (P. 33-35).

And Charles Hodge says in this connection: "A righteous judge, in pronouncing sentence on a criminal, may be sure that he will cause wicked and bitter feelings in the criminal's mind, or in the hearts of his friends, and yet the judge be guiltless. A father, in excluding a reprobate son from his family, may see that the inevitable consequences of such exclusion will be his greater wickedness, and yet the father may do right. It is the certain consequence of God's leaving the fallen angels and the finally impenitent to themselves, that they will continue in sin, and yet the holiness of God remain untarnished. The Bible clearly teaches that God judicially abandons men to their sins, giving them up to a reprobate mind, and He therein is most just and holy. It is not true, therefore, that an agent is responsible for all the certain consequences of his acts. It may be, and doubtless is, infinitely wise and just in God to permit the occurrence of sin, and to adopt a plan of which sin is a certain consequence or element; yet, as He neither causes sin, nor tempts men to its commission, He is neither its author nor approver." [121]

9. GOD'S GRACE IS MORE DEEPLY APPRECIATED AFTER THE PERSON HAS BEEN THE VICTIM OF SIN

We are often permitted to fall into sin, that, after being delivered from it, we shall appreciate our salvation all the more. In the parable of the two debtors the one owed five hundred shillings and the other fifty. When they had nothing with which to pay the lender forgave them both. Which of them, therefore, would love him most? Naturally the one to whom he forgave most. As Jesus spoke this parable they were seated at meat and the application was made to Simon the Pharisee and to the penitent woman who had anointed His feet. The latter had been forgiven much and was profoundly grateful, but the former had received no such favor and felt no gratitude. "To whom little is forgiven, the same loveth little," Luke 7:41-50.

Sometimes the person, like the prodigal son, will not appreciate the Father's home nor respect His authority until he has experienced the ravaging effects of sin and the pangs of hunger, sorrow and disgrace. It seems that man with his freedom must, to a certain extent, learn by experience before he is fully able to appreciate the ways of righteousness and to render unquestioned obedience and honor to God. We have quoted Paul's statement to the effect that "God hath shut up all unto disobedience, that He might have mercy on all," Rom. 11:32, and that the sentence of death was passed within us that we should not trust in ourselves but only in God, II Cor. 1: 9. The creature cannot adequately appreciate God's mercy until he has been rescued from a state of misery. After the lame beggar had been healed by Peter and John at the door of the temple, he appreciated his health as never before, and "entered with them into the temple, walking, and leaping, and praising God." And after being delivered from the power and guilt of sin, we appreciate God's grace as we never could have otherwise. We read that even our Lord Jesus Christ in His human nature was made "perfect through sufferings," although He was, of course, totally separate from all sin.

10. CALVINISM OFFERS A MORE SATISFACTORY SOLUTION OF THE PROBLEM OF EVIL THAN DOES ANY OTHER SYSTEM

The real difficulty which we face here, is to explain why a God of infinite holiness, power, and wisdom, would have brought into existence a creation in which moral evil was to prevail so extensively; and especially to explain why it should have been permitted to issue in the everlasting misery of so many of His creatures. This difficulty, however, bears not only against Calvinism, but against theism in general; and while other systems are found to be wholly inadequate in their explanation of sin, Calvinism can give a fairly adequate explanation in that it recognizes that God is ultimately responsible since He could have prevented it; and Calvinism further asserts that God has a definite purpose in the permission of every individual sin having ordained it "for His own glory." As Hamilton says, "If we are to accept theism at all, the only respectable kind is Calvinism." "Calvinism teaches that God not only knew what He was doing when He created man, but that He had a purpose even in permitting sin." And what better explanation than this can be advanced by any one else who believes that God is the Creator and Ruler of this universe?

In regard to the first fall of man, we assert that the proximate cause was the instigation of the Devil and the impulse of his own heart; and when we have established this, we, have removed all blame from God. Paul tells us that God "dwelleth in the light which no man can approach unto." Our mental vision can no more comprehend His deep mysteries than our unaided physical eyes can endure the light of the sun. When the Apostle contemplated these things he broke forth, 'O the depth of the riches both of the wisdom and knowledge of God! how unsearchable are His judgments and His ways past tracing out!" And since our human intellects cannot soar to such stupendous heights, it is ours to adore with reverence, fear, and trembling, but not to explain, that mystery which is too high and too deep for even the angels themselves to penetrate. Let us remember also that along with this sin, God has provided a redemption graciously wrought out by Himself; and no doubt it is due to our limitations that we do not see this to be the all-sufficient explanation. The decree of redemption is as old as the decree of apostasy; and He who ordained sin has also ordained a way of escape from it.

Since the Scriptures tell us that God is perfectly righteous, and since in all of His acts upon which we are capable of passing judgment we find that He is perfectly righteous, we trust Him in those realms which have not yet been revealed to us, believing that He has solutions for those problems which we are not able to solve. We can rest assured that the Judge of all the earth will do right, and as His plan is more fully revealed to us we learn to thank Him for that which is past and to trust him for that which is future.

It avails nothing, of course, to say that God foresaw the evil but did not include it in His plan,--for if He foresaw it and in spite of it brought the world into existence, the evil acts were certainly a part of the plan, although an undesirable part. To deny this foresight makes God blind; and He would then be conceived of as working something like the school boy who mixes chemicals in the laboratory not knowing what may happen. In fact, we could not even respect a God who worked in that manner. And furthermore, that view still leaves the ultimate responsibility for sin resting upon God, for at least he could have refrained from creating.

That the sinful acts of men have their place and a necessary place in the plan is plainly seen in the course of history. For instance, the assassination of President McKinley was a sinful act,--yet upon that act depended the role which Theodore Roosevelt was to play as President of the United States; and if that one link in the chain of events had been otherwise, the entire course of history from that time to the end of the world would have been radically different. The same is true in the case of Lincoln. If God intended that the world should reach this state in which we find ourselves today, those events were indispensable. A moment's consideration will convince us that all of even the apparently insignificant events have their exact place, that they start rapidly growing influences which soon extend to the ends of the earth, and that if one of them had been omitted, say fifty years ago, the world today would have been far different.

A further important proof that Paul taught the doctrine which Calvinists have understood him to teach is found in the objections which he put in the mouths of his opponents,--that it represented God as unrighteous: "Is there unrighteousness with God?" Rom. 9:14; and, that it destroyed man's responsibility: "Thou wilt then say unto me, Why doth He still find fault? For who withstandeth His will?" Rom. 9:19. These are the very objections which today, on first thought, spring into men's minds, in opposition to the Calvinistic doctrine of Predestination; but they have not even the least plausibility when directed against the Arminian doctrine. A doctrine which does not afford the least grounds for these objections cannot have been the one that the Apostle taught.

Footnotes:

106. Tyler, Memoir and Lectures, p. 250-252.
107. Strong, Systematic Theology, p. 357.
108. The Secret Providence of God; reprinted it Calvin's Calvinism, p. 240.
109. Systematic Theology, I., p. 545.
110. Theological Institutes, II., ch. 18.
111. Systematic Theology, II., p. 120.
112. id. P. 193.
113. Bondage of the Will, p. 301.
114. Predestination, p. 55.
115. Article II, The Reformed Faith and the Presbyterian Church.
116. A Syllabus of Systematic Theology, p. 103.

117. What Is Calvinism, p. 32.
118. Quoted in Calvin's Calvinism, p. 290.
119. Biblical Doctrines, article, Predestination, p. 21.
120. Warfield, Biblical Doctrines, article, The Foresight of Jesus, p. 73.
121. Systematic Theology, I., p. 547.

Chapter XVIII

4. It Discourages All Motives to Exertion
   1. The Means as well as the Ends are Foreordained. 2. Practical Results.

1. THE MEANS AS WELL AS THE ENDS ARE FOREORDAINED

    The objection that the doctrine of Predestination discourages all motives to exertion, is based on the fallacy that the ends are determined without reference to the means. It is not merely a few isolated events here and there that have been foreordained, but the whole chain of events, with all of their inter-relations and connections. All of parts form a unit in the Divine plan. If the means should fail, so would the ends. If God has purposed that a man shall reap, He has also purposed that he shall sow. If God has ordained a man to be saved, He has also ordained that he shall hear the Gospel, and that he shall believe and repent. As well might the farmer refuse to till the soil according to the laws disclosed by the light of nature and experience until he had first learned what was the secret purpose of God to be executed in His providence in regard to the fruitfulness of the coming season, as for any one to refuse to work in the moral and spiritual realms because he does not know what fruitage God may bring from his labor. We find, however, that the fruitage is commonly bestowed where the preliminary work has been faithfully performed. If we engage in the Lord's service and make diligent use of the means which He has prescribed, we have the great encouragement of knowing that it is by these very means that He has determined to accomplish His great work.

    Even those who accept the Scripture statements that God "worketh all things after the counsel of His will," and similar declarations to the effect that God's providence control extends to all the events of their lives. know that this does not interfere in the slightest with their freedom. Do those who make this objection allow their belief in the Divine sovereignty to determine their conduct in temporal affairs? Do they decline food when hungry, or medicine when sick, because God has appointed the time and manner of their death? Do they neglect the recognized means of acquiring wealth or distinction because God gives riches and honor to whom He pleases? When in matters outside of religion one recognizes God's sovereignty, yet works in the exercise of conscious freedom, is it not sinful and foolish to offer as an excuse for neglecting his spiritual and eternal welfare the contention that he is not free and responsible? Does not his conscience testify that the only reason why he is not a follower of Jesus Christ is that he has never been willing to follow Him? Suppose that when the palsied man was brought to Jesus and heard the words, "Rise up and walk," he had merely replied, "I cannot; I am palsied!" Had he done so he would have died a paralytic. But, realizing his own helplessness and trusting the One who gave the command, he obeyed and was made whole. It is the same almighty Saviour who calls on sinners dead in sin to come to Him, and we may be sure that the one who comes will not find his efforts vain. The fact is, that unless we regard God as the sovereign Disposer of all events, who in the midst of certainty has ordained human liberty, we have but little encouragement to work. If we believed that our success and our destiny was primarily dependent on the pleasure of weak and sinful creatures, we would have but little incentive to exertion.

    "On his knees, the Arminian forgets those logical puzzles which have distorted Predestination to his mind and at once thankfully acknowledges his conversion to be due to that prevenient grace of God, without which no mere will or works of his own would ever have made him a new creature. He prays for that outpouring of God's Spirit to restrain, convince, renew, and sanctify men; for that divine direction of human events, and overturning of the counsels and frustrating of the plans of wicked men; he gives to the Lord glory and honor for what is actually done in this regard, which implies that God reigns, that He is the sovereign disposer of all events, and that all good, and all thwarting of evil are due to Him, while all evil is itself due to the creature. He recognizes the completeness of the divine foreknowledge as bound up inseparably with the wisdom of His eternal purpose. His prayers for assurance of hope, or his present fruition of it, presuppose the faith that God can and will keep his feet from falling, and heaven from revolt, and that His purpose forms such an infallible nexus between present grace and eternal glory, that nothing shall be able to separate him from the love of God, which is in Christ Jesus our Lord." [122]

    Since the future events are hidden and unknown to us we should be as industrious in our work and as earnest in the performance of our duty as if nothing had been decreed concerning it. It has often been said that we should pray as though everything depended on God, and work as though everything depended on ourselves. Luther's observation here was: "We are commanded to work the more for this very reason, because all things future are to us uncertain; as saith Ecclesiastes, 'In the morning sow thy seed, and in the evening withhold not thine hand; for thou knowest not which shall prosper, whether this or that, or weather they both shall be alike good,' Eccl. 11: 6. All things future, I say are to us uncertain in knowledge, but necessary in event. The necessity strikes into us fear of God that we presume not, or become secure, while the uncertainty works in us a trusting that we sink not into despair." [123]

"The farmer who, after hearing a sermon on God's decrees, took the break-neck road instead of the safe one to his home and broke his wagon in consequence, concluded before the end of the journey that he at any rate had been predestinated to be a fool, and that he had made his calling and election sure." [124]

Some may be inclined to say, If nothing but the creative power of God can enable us to repent and believe, then all we can do is to wait passively until that power is exerted. Or it may be asked, If we cannot effect our salvation, why work for it? In every line of human endeavor, however, we find that the result is dependent on the co-operation of causes over which we have no control. We are simply to make use of the appropriate means and trust to the co-operation of the other agencies. We do have the express promise of God that those who seek shall find, that those who ask shall receive, and that to those who knock it shall be opened. This is more than is given to the men of the world to stimulate them in their search for wealth, knowledge, or position; and more than this cannot rationally be demanded. He who reads and meditates upon the word of God is ordinarily regenerated by the Holy Spirit, perhaps in the very act of reading. "While Peter yet spake these words, the Holy Spirit fell on all them that heard the word," Acts 10:44. Shakespeare makes one of his characters say: "The fault, dear Brutus, is not in our stars, but in ourselves, that we are underlings," (Julius Caesar, 1:2).

The sinner's inability to save himself, therefore, should not make him less diligent in seeking his salvation in the way which God has appointed. Some leper when Christ was on earth might have reasoned that since he could not cure himself, he must simply wait for Christ to come and heal him. The natural effect, however, of a conviction of utter helplessness is to impel the person to make diligent application at the source from whence alone help can come. Man is a fallen, ruined, and helpless creature, and until he knows it he is living without hope and without God in the world.

2. PRACTICAL RESULTS

The genuine tendency of these truths is not to make men indolent and careless, but to energize and stimulate them to redoubled efforts. Heroes and conquerors, such as Cæsar and Napoleon, have often been possessed with a sense of destiny which they were to fulfill. This sense steels the nerve, redoubles the courage, and fixes in of an indomitable purpose to carry his work through to a successful finish. Large and difficult objects can only be achieved by men who have confidence in themselves, and who will not allow obstacles to discourage them. "This idea of destiny once embraced," says Mozley, "as it is the natural effect of the sense of power, so in its turn adds greatly to it. The person as soon as he regards himself as predestined to achieve some great object, acts with so much greater force and constancy for the attainment it; he is not divided by doubts, or weakened by scruples or fears; he believes fully that he shall succeed, and that belief is the greatest assistance to success. The idea of a destiny in a considerable degree fulfills itself . . . . It must be observed that this is true of the moral and spiritual, as well as of the natural man, and applies to religious aims and purposes, as well as to those connected with human glory." [125]

E. W. Smith, in his valuable little book, "The Creed of Presbyterians," writes as follows: "The most comforting and ennobling is also the most energizing of faiths. That its grim caricature, fatalism, has developed in human hearts an energy at once sublime and appalling is one of the common-places of history. The early and overwhelming onrush of Mohammedanism, which swept the East and all but overthrew the West, was due to its devotees' conviction that in their conquests they were but executing the decrees of Allah. Attila the Hun was upborne in his terrible and destructive course by his belief that he was the appointed 'Scourge of God.' The energy and audacity which enabled Napoleon to attempt and achieve apparent impossibilities was nourished by the secret conviction that he was 'the man of destiny.' Fatalism has begotten a race of Titans. Their energy has been superhuman, because they believed themselves the instruments of a super-human power.

"If the grim caricature of this doctrine has breathed such energy, the doctrine itself must inspire a yet loftier, for all that is energizing in it remains with added force when for a blind fate, or a fatalistic deity, we substitute a wise, decreeing God. Let me but feel that in every commanded duty, in every needed reform, I am but working out an eternal purpose of Jehovah; let me but hear behind me, in every battle for the right, the tramp of the Infinite Reserves; and I am lifted above the fear of man or the possibility of final failure." (pp. 180, 181).

In an English newspaper, "The Daily Express," of April 18, 1929, we read the following concerning Earl Haig, who was Commander-in-Chief of the British armies in the First World War, and who was a Scotsman and a Calvinistic Presbyterian: "Most remarkable as regards Haig's own personality is the disclosure that this reserved, cold, formal man had a profound faith, and in the greatest crises of the war believed implicitly that help would come from above, and that he regarded himself as the chosen of the Lord, the Cromwell who alone could smite the foe. He was genuinely convinced that the position to which he had now been called was one which he and he alone in the British Army could fill. It was not conceit. There was no man who was less inclined to over-estimate his own value or capacity; it was opinion based upon the discernment of all the factors. HE CAME TO REGARD HIMSELF WITH ALMOST CALVINISTIC FAITH AS THE PREDESTINATED INSTRUMENT OF PROVIDENCE FOR THE ACHIEVEMENT OF VICTORY FOR THE BRITISH ARMIES. HIS ABUNDANT SELF-RELIANCE WAS REINFORCED BY THIS CONCEPTION OF HIMSELF AS THE CHILD OF DESTINY."

The genuine tendency of these truths, then, as stated before, is not to make men indolent and careless, nor to lull them to sleep on the lap of presumption and carnal security, but to energize and to inspire confidence. Both reason and experience teach us that the greater one's hope of success, the stronger becomes the motive to exertion. The person who is sure of success in the use of appropriate means has the strongest of incentives to work, while on the other hand, where there is but little hope there will be but little disposition for one to exert himself; and where there is no hope, there will be no exertion. The Christian, then, who has before him the definite commands of God, and the promise that the work of those who obediently and reverently avail themselves of the appointed means shall be blessed, has the highest possible motives for exertion. Furthermore, he is elevated and inspired by the firm conviction that he himself is marked out for a heavenly crown.

Who ever stated the doctrine of election more plainly or in more forcible language than did the Apostle Paul? And yet who was ever more zealous and more untiring in his labors than Paul? His theory made him a missionary and impelled him to set forth Christianity as final and triumphant. How cheering it must have been for him in Corinth to hear the words, "Be not afraid, but speak and hold not thy peace; for I am with thee, and no man shall set on thee to harm thee; for I have much people in this city," Acts 18:10. What greater incentive to action could have been given him than this, that his preaching was the divinely appointed means for the conversion of many of those people? Notice, God did not tell him how many people He had in that city, nor who the individuals were. The minister of the Gospel can go forward confident of success, knowing that through this appointed means God has determined to save a vast number of the human family in every age. In fact, one of the strongest pleas for missions is that evangelism is the will of God for the whole world; and only when one acknowledges the sovereignty of God in every realm of life can he have the deepest passion for the Divine glory.

The experience of the Church in all ages has been that this doctrine has led men, not to neglect, nor to stolid unconcern, nor to rebellious opposition to God, but to submission and to a sure trust in Divine power. The promise given to Jacob that his posterity was to be a great people did not in the least prevent him from using every available means for protection when it looked as though Esau might kill him and his family. When Daniel understood from the prophecies of Jeremiah that the time for the restoration of Israel was at hand, he set himself earnestly to pray for it (Dan. 9:2, 3). Immediately after it had been revealed to David that God would establish his house, he prayed earnestly for that very thing (II Sam. 7:27-29). Although Christ knew what had been appointed for His people, He prayed earnestly for their preservation (John, Ch. 17). And although Paul had been told that he was to go to Rome and bear witness there, it did not in the least cause him to be careless of his life. He took every precaution to protect himself against an unfair trial by the Jerusalem mob, and against an unwise voyage (Acts 23:11; 25:10, 11; 27:9, 10). The decree of God was that all those on board the ship should be saved, but that decree took in the free and courageous and skillful activity of the seamen. Their freedom and responsibility were not in the least diminished. The practical effect of this doctrine, then, has been to lead men to frequent and fervent prayer, knowing that their times are in God's hands and that every event of their lives is of His disposing.

Furthermore, it may be said that so long as the sinner remains ignorant of his lost and helpless condition, he remains negligent. Probably there is not a careless sinner in the world who does not believe in his perfect ability to turn to God at any time he pleases; and because of this belief he puts off repentance, fully intending to come at some more convenient time. Just in proportion as his belief in his own ability increases, his carelessness increases, and he is lulled to sleep on the awful brink of eternal ruin. Only when he is brought to feel his entire helplessness and dependence upon sovereign grace does he seek help where alone it is to be found.

Footnotes:

122. Atwater, article, Calvinism in Doctrine and Life; The Presbyterian Quarterly and Princeton Review, Jan. 1875, p. 84.
123. Bondage of the Will, p. 287.
124. Strong, Systematic Theology, p. 361.
125. The Augustinian Doctrine of Predestination, p. 41.

Loraine Boettner D.D.

Chapter XIX

1. Difficulties Faced By All Systems. 2. God Is No Respecter of Persons. 3. God Plainly Does Not Treat All People Alike; He Gives to Some What He Withholds From Others. 4. God's Partiality Is Partly Explained By the Fact that He Is Sovereign and that His Gifts Are of Grace.

1. DIFFICULTIES FACED BY ALL SYSTEMS

If all men are dead in sin, and destitute of the power to restore themselves to spiritual life, why, it is asked, does God exercise His almighty power to regenerate some, while He leaves others to perish? Justice, it is said, demands that all should have an equal opportunity; that all should have, either by nature or by grace, power to secure their own salvation. It is to be remembered, however, that objections such as these do not bear exclusively against the Calvinistic system. They are urged by atheists against Theism. It is argued, If God is infinite in power and holiness, why does He allow so much sin and misery to exist in the world? And why are the wicked often allowed to prosper through long periods of time, while the righteous often must endure poverty and suffering?

It is plain enough that the anti-Calvinistic systems can offer no real solutions for these difficulties. Admitting that regeneration is the sinner's own act, and that every man has sufficient ability and knowledge to secure his own salvation, it remains true that in the present state of the world only comparatively few are saved, and that God does not interpose to prevent the majority of adult men from perishing in their sins. Calvinists do not deny that these difficulties exist; they only maintain that such problems are not peculiar to their system, and they rest content with the partial solution of them which is given in the Scriptures. The Bible teaches that man was created holy; that he deliberately disobeyed the divine law and fell into sin; that as a result of that fall Adam's posterity come into the world in a state of spiritual death; that God never pushes them into further sin, but that on the contrary He exerts influences which should induce rational creatures to repent and seek His sanctifying grace; that all who sincerely repent and seek this grace are saved; and that by the exercise of His mighty power, vast multitudes which otherwise would have continued in their sin are brought to salvation.

2. GOD IS NO RESPECTER OF PERSONS

A "respecter of Persons" is one who, acting as judge, does not treat those who come before him according to their character, but who withholds from some what is justly theirs and gives to others what is not justly theirs--one who is governed by prejudice and sinister motives, rather than by justice and law. The Scriptures deny that God is a respecter of persons in this sense; and if the doctrine of Predestination represented God as doing these things, we admit that it would charge Him with injustice and that the objection would be fatal.

In the Scriptures God is said to be no respecter of persons, for He does not choose one and reject another because of outward circumstances such as race, nationality, wealth, power, nobility, etc. Peter says that God is no respecter of persons because He makes no distinction between Jews and Gentiles. His conclusion after being divinely sent to preach to the Roman centurion, Cornelius, was, "Of a truth, I perceive that God is no respecter of persons; but in every nation he that feareth Him and worketh righteousness is acceptable to Him," Acts 10:35. Throughout their entire past history the Jews had believed that they as a people were the exclusive objects of God's favor. A careful reading of Acts 10:1 to 11:18 will show what a revolutionary idea it was that the Gospel should be preached to the Gentiles also.

Paul likewise says, "Glory and honor and peace to every man that worketh good, to the Jew first, and also to the Greek; for there is no respect of persons with God," Rom. 2:10, 11. And again, "There can be neither Jew nor Greek, there can be neither bond nor free, there can be no male and female; for they all are one man in Christ Jesus." Then he adds that it is not those who are Jews externally, but those who are Christ's that are in the highest sense "Abraham's seed," and "heirs according to the promise," Gal. 3:28, 29. In Eph. 6:5-9 the slaves and the masters are commanded to treat each other justly; for God, who is the Master of both, is no respecter of persons; and likewise in Col. 3:25 the relations between fathers and children and between wives and husbands are included. James says that God is no respecter of persons because He makes no distinction between the rich and poor, nor between those who wear fine clothing and those who are plainly dressed (2:1-9). The term "person" in these verses signifies, not the inner man, or the soul, but the outward appearance, which often carries so much influence with us. Hence when the Scriptures say that God is no respecter of persons they do not mean that He treats all people alike, but that the reason for His saving one and rejecting another is not that one is a Jew and the other a Gentile, or that the one is rich and the other poor, etc.

3. GOD PLAINLY DOES NOT TREAT ALL PEOPLE ALIKE; HE GIVES TO SOME WHAT HE WITHHOLDS FROM OTHERS

It is a fact that in His providential government of the world God does not confer the same or equal favors upon all people. The inequality is too glaring to be denied. The Scriptures tell us, and the experiences of every day life show us, that there is the greatest variety in the distribution of these,--and justly so, for all of these are of grace, and not of debt. The Calvinist here falls back upon the experienced reality of facts. It is true, and no argument can disprove it, that men in this world find themselves unequally favored, both in inward disposition and outward circumstances. One child is born to health, honor, wealth, of eminently good and wise parents who train him up from infancy in the nurture and admonition of the Lord, and who afford him every opportunity of being taught the truth as it is in the Scriptures. Another is born to disease, shame, poverty, of dissipated and depraved parents who reject and ridicule anddespise Christianity, and who take care to prevent their child from coming under the influence of the Gospel. Some are born with susceptible hearts and consciences, which make lives of innocence and purity natural for them; others are born with violent passions, or even with distinct tendencies to evil, which seemingly are inherited and unconquerable. Some are happy, others are miserable. Some are born in Christian and civilized lands where they are carefully educated and watched over; others are born in complete heathen darkness. As a general rule the child that is surrounded with the proper Christian influences becomes a devout Christian and lives a life of great service, while the other whose character is formed under the influence of corrupt teaching and example lives in wickedness and dies impenitent. The one is saved and the other is lost. And will any one deny that the influences favorable to salvation which are brought to bear upon some individuals are far more favorable than those brought to bear upon others? Will it not be admitted by every candid individual that if the persons had changed places, they probably would have changed characters also?--that if the son of the godly parents had been the son of infidels, and had lived under the same corrupting influences, he would, in all probability, have died in his sins? In His mysterious providence God has placed persons under widely different influences, and the results are widely different. He of course foresaw these different results before the persons were born. These are facts which no one can deny or explain away. And if we are to believe that the world is governed by a personal and intelligent Being, we must also believe that these inequalities have not risen by chance or accident, but through purpose and design, and that the lot of every individual has been determined by the sovereign good pleasure of God. "Even Arminians," says N. L. Rice, "are obliged to acknowledge that God does make great differences in the treatment of the human family, not only in the distribution of temporal blessings, but of spiritual gifts also,--a difference which compels them, if they would be consistent, to hold the doctrine of election. . . . If the sending of the Gospel to a people, with the divine influence accompanying it, does not amount to a personal election, most assuredly the withholding of it from a people amounts generally to reprobation." [126]

Calvinists merely assume that in the dispensation of His grace God acts precisely as He does in giving other favors. If it were unjust in principle for God to be partial in the distribution of spiritual goods, it would be no less unjust for Him to be partial in His distribution of temporal goods. But as a matter of fact we find that in the exercise of His absolute sovereignty He makes the greatest possible distinctions among men from birth, and that He does so irrespective of any personal merits both in the allotments of temporal goods and of the essential means to salvation. Hence the statement that the Holy Spirit "divideth to each one severally as He will," I Cor. 12:11; and nowhere in Scripture is it said that God is impartial in the communication of His grace. In regard to His dealings with nations we find that God has favored some much more highly than others,--namely, Israel in ancient times, and Europe and America in modern times, while Africa and the Orient have lain in darkness and under the curse of false religions,--and this is a fact which all must admit.

Although the Jews were a small and disobedient people, God conferred favors on them which He did not give to the other nations of the world. "You only have I known of all the families of the earth," Amos 3:2. "He hath not dealt so with any nation; And as for His ordinances, they have not known them," Ps. 147:20. And again, "What advantage then hath the Jew? Or what is the advantage of circumcision? Much every way: first of all, that they were entrusted with the oracles of God," Rom. 3:1, 2. These favors did not come because of any merits in the Jews themselves, for they were repeatedly reproached for being "a stiff-necked and rebellious people." In Matt. 11:25 we read of a prayer in which Jesus said, "I thank thee, O Father, Lord of heaven and earth, that thou didst hide these things from the wise and understanding, and didst reveal them unto babes; yea, Father, for so it was well-pleasing in thy sight." In those words He thanked the Father for doing that very thing which Arminians exclaim against

Loraine Boettner D.D.

as unjust and censure as partial.

If it be asked, Why does God not bestow the same or equal blessings upon all people? we can only answer, that has not been fully revealed. We see that in actual life He does not treat all alike. For wise reasons known to Himself, He has given to some blessings to which they had no claim thus making them great debtors to His grace--and has withheld from others gifts which He was under no obligation to bestow.

There is, in fact, no single member of this fallen race who is not treated by his Maker better than he deserves. And since grace is favor shown to the undeserving, God has the sovereign right to bestow more grace upon one subject than upon another. "The bestowment of common grace upon the non-elect," says W. G. T. Shedd, "shows that non-election does not exclude from the kingdom of heaven by Divine efficiency, because common grace is not only an invitation to believe and repent, but an actual help toward it; and a help that is nullified solely by the resistance of the non-elect, and not by anything in the nature of common grace, or by any preventive outward action of God. The fault or the failure of common grace to save the sinner, is chargeable to the sinner alone; and he has no right to plead a fault of his own as the reason why he is entitled to special grace." [127]

If it be objected that God must give every man an opportunity to be saved, we reply that the outward call does give every man who hears it an opportunity to be saved. The message is: "Believe on the Lord Jesus Christ and thou shalt be saved." This is an opportunity to be saved; and nothing outside the man's own nature prevents his believing. Shedd has expressed this idea very well in the following words: "A beggar who contemptuously rejects the five dollars offered by a benevolent man, cannot charge stinginess upon him because after this rejection of the five dollars he does not give him ten. Any sinner who complains of God's passing him by' in the bestowment of regenerating grace after his abuse of common grace, virtually says to the High and Holy one who inhabits eternity, 'Thou hast tried once to convert me from sin; now try again, and try harder.'" [128]

A strong argument against the Arminian objection that this doctrine makes God unjustly partial, is found in the fact that while God has extended His saving grace toward fallen men, He has made no provision for the redemption of the Devil and the fallen angels. If it was consistent with God's infinite goodness and justice to pass by the whole body of fallen angels and to leave them to suffer the consequences of their sin, then certainly it is consistent with His goodness and justice to pass by some of the fallen race of men and to leave them in their sin. When the Arminian admits that Christ died not for the fallen angels or demons, but only for fallen men, he admits limited atonement and in principle makes the same kind of a distinction as does the Calvinist who says that Christ died for the elect only.

Men, with their limited and often mistaken knowledge, have no right to censure God's distribution of His grace. It would be as unreasonable to charge Him with injustice for not having made all of His creatures angels, and for not having preserved them in holiness as He did the angels in heaven and as He had power to do, as to charge Him with injustice for not having redeemed all mankind. It is as hard for us to understand why He allows any to perish eternally, as for us to understand why He saves some and not others. He plainly does not prevent the perdition of those whom, beyond doubt, He has the power to save. And if those who admit God's providence say that He has wise reasons for permitting so many of our race to perish, those who advocate His sovereignty can say that He has wise reasons for saving some and not others. It might as reasonably be argued that since God punishes some, He should punish all; but no one goes to that extreme.

It may be admitted that from our human view-point it would seem more plausible and more consistent with the character of God that sin and misery should never have been allowed to enter the universe; or if, when they had entered, provision had been made for their ultimate elimination from the system, so that all rational creatures should be perfectly holy and happy for eternity. There would be no end to such plans if every person were at liberty to construct a plan of divine operations in accordance with his oven views as to what would be wisest and best. We are, however, shut up to the facts as they are found in the Bible, in the providential workings about us, and in our own religious experiences; and we find that only the Calvinistic system is satisfied by these.

4. GOD'S PARTIALITY IS PARTLY EXPLAINED BY THE FACT THAT HE IS SOVEREIGN AND THAT HIS GIFTS ARE OF GRACE

It cannot be said that God acts unjustly toward those who are not included in this plan of salvation. People who make this objection neglect to take into consideration the fact that God is dealing not merely with creatures but with sinful creatures who have forfeited every claim upon His mercy. Augustine well said: "Damnation is rendered to the wicked as a matter of debt, justice and desert, whereas the grace given to those who are delivered is free and unmerited, so that the condemned sinner cannot allege that he is unworthy of his punishment, nor the saint vaunt or boast as if he were worthy of his reward. Thus, in the whole course of this procedure, there is no respect of persons. They who are condemned and they who are set at liberty constituted originally one and the same lump, equally infected with sin and liable to vengeance. Hence the justified may learn from the condemnation of the

The Reformed Doctrine Of Predestination

rest that that would have been their own punishment had not God's grace stepped in to their rescue." And to the same effect Calvin says, "The Lord, therefore, may give grace to whom He will, because He is merciful, and yet not give it to all because He is a just Judge; may manifest His free grace by giving to some what they never deserve, while by not giving to all He declares the demerit of all."

"Partiality," in the sense that objectors commonly use the word, is impossible in the sphere of grace. It can exist only in the sphere of justice, where the persons concerned have certain claims and rights. We may give to one beggar and not to another for we do not owe anything to either. The parable of the talents was spoken by our Lord to illustrate the doctrine of the Divine sovereignty in the bestowment of unmerited gifts; and the regeneration of the soul is one of the greatest of these gifts.

The central teaching in the parable of the laborers in the vineyard is that God is sovereign in the dispensation of His gifts. To the saved and the unsaved alike He can say, "Friend, I do thee no wrong; . . . Is it not lawful for me to do what I will with mine own? Or is thine eye evil, because I am good?" Matt. 20:13-15. It was said to Moses, "I will have mercy on whom I will have mercy, and I will have compassion on whom I will have compassion"; and Paul adds, "So then it is not of him that willeth, nor of him that runneth, but of God that hath mercy. . . . . So then He hath mercy on whom He will and whom He will He hardeneth," Rom. 9:15-18. He will extend mercy to some, and inflict justice on others, and will be glorified by all. Just as a man may give alms to some and not to others, so God may give His grace, which is heavenly alms, to whom He pleases. Grace, from its own nature, must be free; and the very inequality of its distribution demonstrates that it is truly gratuitous. If any one could justly demand it, it would cease to be grace and would become of debt. If God is robbed of His sovereignty in this respect, salvation then becomes a matter of debt to every person.

If ten men each owe a certain creditor one thousand dollars and he for reasons of his own forgives the debts of seven but collects from the other three, the latter have no grounds for complaint. If three criminals are sentenced to be hanged for having committed murder and then two of them are pardoned-- perhaps it is found that they have rendered distinguished service to their country in time of war--does that render the execution of the third unjust? Plainly, No; for in his case there is no intervening cause as to why he should not suffer for his crime. And if an earthly prince may justly do this, shall not the sovereign Lord of all be allowed to act in the same manner toward His rebellious subjects? When all mankind might have been punished, how can God be charged with injustice if He punishes only a part of them?--and that no doubt a comparatively small part.

Warburton gives a very fitting illustration here. He supposes a case in which a lady goes to an orphans' home and from the hundreds of children there, chooses one, adopts it as her own child and leaves the rest. "She might have chosen others; she had the means to keep others; but she chose one. Will you tell me that woman is unjust? Will you tell me that she is unfair, or unrighteous, because in the exercise of her undisputed right and privilege she chose out that one child to enjoy the comforts of her home, and become the heir of her possessions, and left all the others, possibly to perish in want, or sink into the wretched condition of gutter-children? . . . Have you ever heard any lay the charge of injustice, or of unrighteousness against the one who has done such an action? Do men not rather hold such an action up to praise? Do they not speak in the highest terms of the love, the pity, and the compassion of such a person? Now why do they do this? Why do they not condemn the taking of the one, and the leaving of the rest? Why do they not complain that it was unjust for this particular one to be chosen, and not another, or not all? . . . The reason is this--because men know--as we also know--that all those children were in exactly the same plight and that not one of them had a single claim, or the least vestige of a claim, upon the person whose will and pleasure it was to adopt one as her own . . . Do you, or can you, see anything different in this act of God's from that of my neighbor's? The children in that foundling home had no claim upon my neighbor. Neither had fallen man any claim upon God; and God's choice, therefore, just as it was free and unmerited, so was it also righteous and just. And this free and unmerited fore-choice of God in view of man's self-procured ruin, is all that is meant by the Calvinistic doctrine of Predestination."

Since the merits of Christ's sacrifice were of infinite value, the plan which usually first suggests itself to our hearts is that God should have saved all. But He chose to make an eternal exhibition of His justice as well as His mercy. If every person had been saved, it would not have been seen what sin deserved; if no person had been saved, it would not have been seen what grace could bestow. Furthermore, the fact that salvation was provided, not for all, but only for some, makes it all the more appreciated by those to whom it is given. All in all, it was best for the universe at large that some should be permitted to have their own way and thus show what a dreadful thing is opposition to God.

But some one may ask, What about this unregenerate man, this one of the non-elect who is left in sin, subject to eternal punishment, unable even to see the kingdom of God? We reply, Go back to the doctrine of original sin,--in Adam, who was appointed the federal head and representative of all his descendants, the race had a most fair and favorable opportunity to gain salvation, but lost it. The justification for the election of some and the passing by of others is that "all have sinned and come short of the glory of God." Doubtless there are the best of reasons for the choosing of some and the passing by of others, but these have not been made known to us. We do know, however, that none of the lost suffer any unmerited punishment. In this world they enjoy the good things of providence in common with the children of God, and very often in a much higher degree. Conscience and experience testify that we are members of an apostate race, and every man who comes short of eternal life knows that the responsibility rests primarily upon himself. Furthermore, if all men are in their present lost and ruined condition by the operation of just principles on the part of God (and who will say that they are not?), they may justly be left to deserved punishment. It is absurd to say that they are justly exposed to eternal misery, and yet that it would be unjust for them to suffer; for that is the same as saying that the execution of a just penalty is unjust. It may also be added that man in his fallen state has no desire for salvation, and that from this corrupt mass God "hath mercy on whom He will and whom He will He hardeneth." This is the uniform teaching of Scripture. He who denies this denies Christianity and calls in question God's government of the world.

As a matter of fact all of us are partial. We treat the members of our own family or our friends with great partiality, although at the time we may know that they are no more deserving, or perhaps even less deserving than are many others with whom we are associated. It does not follow that if we grant favors to some, we must grant the same or equal favors to all. Yet the Arminian absolutely prescribes it as a rule to the Most High, that He ought to extend His bounty to all equally as from a public treasury. "Should an earthly friend," says Toplady, "make me a present of ten thousand pounds, would it not be unreasonable, ungrateful and presumptuous in me, to refuse the gift, and revile the giver, only because it might not be his pleasure to confer the same favor on my next door neighbor?"

Hence, then, to the objection that the doctrine of Predestination represents God as "partial," we answer, It certainly does. But we insist that it does not represent Him as unjustly partial

Footnotes:

126. God Sovereign and Man Free, pp. 136, 139.
127. Calvinism, Pure and Mixed, p. 59.
128. Calvinism, Pure and Mixed, p. 51.

Chapter XX

1. The Means as Well as the Ends are Foreordained. 2. Love and Gratitude to God for What He Has Done for Us is the Strongest Possible and Only Permanent Basis for Morality. 3. The Practical Fruits of Calvinism in History are its Best Vindication.

1. THE MEANS AS WELL AS THE ENDS ARE FOREORDAINED

The objection is sometimes made that this system encourages men to be careless and indifferent about their moral conduct and their growth in grace, on the ground that their eternal welfare has already been secured. This objection is primarily directed against the doctrines of Election, and the Perseverance of the Saints.

This objection, however, like the one to the effect that this system discourages all motives to exertion, is completely answered by the great principle which we hold and teach, namely, that the means as well as the ends are foreordained. God's decree that the earth should be fruitful did not exclude, but included, the sunlight, the showers, the tillage of the husbandman, etc. If God has foreordained a man to have a crop of corn, He has also foreordained him to plow and plant and cultivate and to do all other necessary things to secure the crop. Just as a purpose to build includes the hewing of stone, the squaring of timbers, and the preparation of all other materials which enter into the structure; and as a declaration of war implies arms, ammunition, ships, and all other necessary equipment; so the election of some to the eternal enjoyment of heaven includes their election to holiness here. It is not the individual as such, but the individual as holy and virtuous, that is predestinated to eternal life.

In the plainest of language Paul taught that the very purpose of election is, "That we should be holy and without blemish before Him in love," Eph. 1:4; that we are "foreordained to be conformed to the image of His Son," Rom. 8:29; and that "God chose you from the beginning unto salvation in sanctification of the Spirit and belief of the truth," II Thess. 2:13. "As many as were ordained to eternal life believed," Acts 13:48. The predestinated, called, justified, glorified ones are the same, Row. 8:29, 30. Therefore the purpose of God according to election must stand, Rom. 9:11.

The belief of Calvinists concerning this subject is well expressed in the Westminster Confession, where we read: "As God hath appointed the elect unto glory, so hath He, by the eternal and most free purpose of His will, foreordained all the means thereunto. Wherefore they who are elected being fallen in Adam, are redeemed by Christ, are effectually called unto faith in Christ by His Spirit working in due season; are justified, adopted, sanctified, and kept by His power through faith unto salvation." (III: 6).

"God decreed that fifteen years should be added to Hezekiah's life; this made him neither careless of his health, nor negligent of his food; he said not, 'Though I run into the fire, or into the water, or drink poison, I shall nevertheless live so long'; but natural providence, in the due use of means co-wrought so as to bring him on to that period of time pre-ordained by him." [129] Since all events are more or less intimately connected, and since God works by means, if He did not determine the means as well as the events, the certainty as to the events themselves would be destroyed. In the redemption of man He determined not only the work of Christ and of the Holy Spirit, but also the faith, repentance and perseverance of all His people.

When this same doctrine was preached by Paul on another occasion and this same objection was brought against it--namely, that he "made the law of none effect through faith," or in other words, that since we are saved through faith we do not need to keep the moral law--his emphatic reply was, "God forbid; nay, we establish the law," Rom. 3 :31. There is, then, an invariable connection established between eternal salvation as an end, and faith and holiness as a means leading to that end.

The ideal Christian, of course, would commit no sin at all. Though certainly saved, he is saved for good works, and is commanded to "give no occasion of stumbling in anything, that our ministration be not blamed," II Cor. 6:3. The Scriptures know of no perseverance which is not a perseverance in holiness, and they give no encouragement to any sense of security which is not connected with a present and ever increasing holiness. Virtue and piety, therefore, are the effect and not the cause of election, for which no cause is to be assigned except God's sovereign good pleasure. It is true that some become much more advanced in holiness here and continue in that state over a much longer period of time than do others; yet it is vain for any who do not partake in some degree of holiness in this world to hope to enjoy happiness in the next. All those whom God has designed to render perfectly happy in eternity, He has designed to make in part happy in this world; and as holiness is essential to the happiness of an intelligent creature, so there is begun in them in this world that holiness without which no one shall see the Lord.

2. LOVE AND GRATITUDE TO GOD FOR WHAT HE HAS DONE FOR US IS THE STRONGEST POSSIBLE AND ONLY PERMANENT BASIS FOR MORALITY

Those who make the objection that we are now considering assume that believers--those who through the almighty power of God have been brought from death to life, from sin to holiness; who have partially beheld the love and glory of God as it is revealed in Christ--are still incapable of being influenced by any motives except those which arise from a selfish and exclusive regard to their own safety and happiness. And, as Cunningham says, they do virtually make a confession, "first, that any outward decency which their conduct may at present exhibit, is to be traced solely to the fear of punishment; and, secondly, that if they were only secured against punishment, they would find much greater satisfaction in serving the Devil than in serving God; and that they would never think of showing any gratitude to Him who had conferred the safety and deliverance on which they place so much reliance." [130]

The contrast between the Calvinistic and the Arminian basis for morality is clearly stated in the following section from McFetridge: "The two great springs by which men are moved are, on the one hand, conviction and idea, on the other, emotion and sentiment; as these control, so the moral character will be shaped. The man who is ruled by convictions and ideas is the man of stability; he cannot be changed until his conscience is changed; the man who is ruled by emotion and sentiment is the man of instability. Now, the appeal of Arminianism is chiefly to the sentiments. Regarding man as having the absolute free moral control of himself, and as able at any moment to determine his own eternal state, it naturally applies itself to the arousing of his emotions. Whatever can lawfully awaken the feelings it considers expedient. Accordingly, the senses, above all things, must be addressed and affected. Hence the Arminian is, religiously, a man of feeling, of sentiment, and consequently disposed to all those things which interest the eye and please the ear. His morality, therefore, as depending chiefly upon the emotions, is, in the nature of the case, liable to frequent fluctuation, rising or falling with the wave of sensation upon which it rides. Calvinism, on the other hand, is a system which appeals to idea rather than sentiment, to conscience rather than emotion. In its views all things are under a great and perfect system of divine laws, which operate in defiance of feeling, and which must be obeyed at the peril of the soul. . . . Its thought is not sentiment, but conviction. . . . It makes the voice of God, speaking in the soul, a guide in all conduct. It seeks rather to convince men than to fill them with a transient sensation. Thus a deep sense of duty is the greatest thing in the moral life of the Calvinist. His first and last question is, Is it right? Of that he must first be convinced. Hence with him conscience has the first place in all practical questions. . . . In the Calvinistic conception God has marked out the way in which man is to walk--a way which He will not change; and man is required to walk in it, joyously or sorrowfully, with as much or as little sentiment as he pleases. Hence the Calvinist is not, religiously, a man of demonstrations, but rather a man of thoughtfulness; so that his morality, whatever it may be otherwise, is characterized by stability and strength, which may sometimes lapse into stubbornness and harshness." [131]

Our love to God would at best be only lukewarm if we believed that His love and favor toward us depended only on our good behavior. His love toward us is as an immense sun, which shone without beginning and which will shine without end, while ours toward Him is, at its best, as only a little flame. Hence the assurance that the objects of God's love shall never be permitted to fall away. Love which is founded on self-interest is commonly recognized as not being moral in the highest sense; yet Calvinism is the only system of faith which presents a purely unselfish motive, namely the consciousness that it is alone the free grace and unmerited love of God, to the exclusion of all human merit, that saves men. When the Christian remembers that he was saved only through the suffering and death of Christ his substitute, love and gratitude overflow his heart; and, like Paul, he feels that the least he can offer Christ in return is his whole life in loving service. Seeing himself saved by grace alone, he learns to love God for His own sake and finds it the joy of his life to serve Him with the whole heart. Obedience becomes not only the obligatory but the preferable good.

The motive which actuates the saints on earth is the same in principle, though not so intense, as that which actuates the saints in glory, whose constant delight is to perform the noblest actions and service, namely, that of praising God, and punctually performing His will without interruptions or defeats. "As they have always a ravishing sense of His goodness to them, so they exercise their perfectly pure minds in ascriptions of praise and glory to him for delivering them from deserved ruin, and placing them in the blissful mansions where they find themselves possessed of ease, delight, complacency, and glory wholly unmerited." [132]

Pure love and gratitude to God, and not selfish fear, is the very fuel of acceptable obedience, and these are the elements from which alone anything like high and pure morality will ever proceed. Jesus

The Reformed Doctrine Of Predestination

had no fear that a sense of eternal security would lead to licentiousness in His disciples, for He said to them, "Rejoice that your names are written in heaven." The elect, therefore, have the utmost reason to love and glorify God which any beings can have, and it is a sheer calumny to represent the doctrine of Predestination as tending to licentiousness and as unfavorable to good morality.

3. THE PRACTICAL FRUITS OF CALVINISM IN HISTORY ARE ITS BEST VINDICATION

Calvinism answers the charge that it is unfavorable to good morality, not merely by opposing reason against reason, but by putting facts of world-wide reputation over against these fictitious claims. It simply asks, What rival fruits can other systems oppose if we point to the achievements of the Protestant leaders of the Reformation period, and to the high moral earnestness of the Puritans? Luther, Calvin, Zwingli, and their immediate helpers were all thorough-going "Calvinists," and the greatest spiritual revival of all time was brought about under their influence. Those in England who held this system of faith were so very strict regarding purity of doctrine, purity of worship, and purity of daily life, that by their very enemies, who thus were their best witnesses, they were called "Puritans." The Puritans in England, the Covenanters in Scotland, and the Huguenots in France, were men of the same religious faith and of like moral qualities. That the system of Calvin should have developed precisely the same kind of men in each of these different countries is a proof of its power in the formation of character.

Concerning the Puritans in this country McFetridge says: "Amongst all the people in the American colonies, they (the Puritans, Calvinists of New England) stood morally without peers. They were the men and the women of conscience, of sterling convictions. They were not, indeed, greatly given to sentimentalism. With mere spectacular observances in religion they had no sympathy. Life to them was an experience too noble and earnest and solemn to be frittered away in pious ejaculations and emotional rhapsodies. They believed with all their soul in a just God, a heaven and a hell. They felt, in the innermost core of their hearts, that life was short and its responsibilities great. Hence their religion was their life. All their thoughts and relations were imbued with it. Not only men, but beasts also, were made to feel its favorable influences. Cruelty to animals was a civil offense. In this respect they were two centuries in advance of the bulk of mankind. They were industrious, frugal and enterprising, and consequently affluence followed in their path and descended to their children and children's children. Drunkenness, profanity and beggary were things little known to them. They needed neither lock nor burglar-proof to secure their honestly-gotten possessions. The simple wooden bolt was enough to protect them and their wealth where honesty was the rule of life. As the result of such a life they were healthy and vigorous. They lived long and happily, reared large and devoted families, and descended to the grave 'like as a shock of corn cometh in his season,' in peace with God and their fellow-men, rejoicing in the hope of a blessed resurrection." [133]

It is further to be remembered as a diadem upon the brow of Calvinistic morality, that in all the history of the Puritans there is said to have been not one case of divorce. What a crying need there is for some such influence today! Lawlessness in general was scarcely, if ever, more unknown than among the Puritans. If, then, Calvinism was actually unfavorable to morality, as charged, it would indeed be a strange coincidence that where there has been the most of Calvinism there has been the least of crime. "This is the problem," says Froude, "Grapes do not grow on bramble bushes. Illustrious natures do not form themselves upon narrow and cruel theories. Spiritual life is full of apparent paradoxes. . . . The practical effect of a belief is the real test of its soundness. Where we find heroic life appearing as the uniform fruit of a particular opinion, it is childish to argue in the face of fact that the result ought to have been different." [134]

"There is no system," says Henry Ward Beecher, "which equals Calvinism in intensifying, to the last degree, ideas of moral excellence and purity of character. There never was a system since the world stood which puts upon man such motives to holiness, or which builds batteries which sweep the whole ground of sin with such horrible artillery. They tell us that Calvinism plies men with hammer and with chisel. It does; and the result is monumental marble. Other systems leave men soft and dirty; Calvinism makes them of white marble, to endure forever." [135]

Instead of being a system which leads to immorality and despair, it has worked out exactly the opposite way in every-day life. No other system has so fired people with ideals of religious and civil freedom, nor led to such high ideals of morality and endeavor in all phases of human life. Wherever the Reformed Faith has gone it has made the country to blossom like the rose, even though it was a poor country like Holland, or Scotland, or New England. This has been admitted by Macaulay and many others, and is a very comforting thought.

Footnotes:

129. Ness, Antidote Against Arminianism, p. 41.
130. Historical Theology, II., p. 279.
131. Calvinism in History, pp. 107, 108.
132. Walmsley, S. G. U. pamphlet No. 173, p. 67.
133. Calvinism in History, p. 128.
134. Calvinism, p. 8.
135. Quoted by McFetridge, Calvinism in History, p. 121.

Chapter XXI

7. It Precludes a Sincere Offer of the Gospel to the Non-Elect
    1. The Same Objection Applies Against God's Foreknowledge. 2. The Offer Is Sincerely Made.

1. THE SAME OBJECTION APPLIES AGAINST GOD'S FOREKNOWLEDGE

    Although the Gospel is offered to many who will not, and who for subjective reasons cannot, accept, it is, nevertheless, sincerely offered to all. The objection so strenuously urged on some occasions by Arminians, to the effect that if the doctrine of Predestination is true the Gospel cannot be sincerely offered to the non-elect, should be sufficiently answered by the fact that it bears with equal force against the doctrine of God's Foreknowledge. We might ask, How can the offer of salvation be sincerely made to those who God foreknows will despise and reject it, especially when their guilt and condemnation will only be increased by their refusal? Arminians admit that God knows beforehand who will accept and who will reject the message; yet they know themselves to be under a divine command to preach to all men, and they do not feel that they act insincerely in doing so.

    The difficulty, however, in both cases is purely subjective, and is due to our limited knowledge and to our inability to comprehend the ways of God, which are past finding out. We do know that the Judge of all the earth will do right, and we trust Him even though our feeble reason cannot always follow His ways. We know definitely that abundant provision has been made for all who will come, and that every one who sincerely accepts will be saved. From Christ's own lips we have a parable which illustrates the love of God for His children. The father saw the returning prodigal when he was still a great way off, and ran and fell on his neck and kissed him. And the welcome given to this prodigal God is willing to give to any prodigal.

2. THE OFFER IS SINCERELY MADE

    God commanded Moses to gather together the elders of Israel, to go to Pharaoh and demand that they be allowed to go three days' journey into the wilderness to hold a feast and offer sacrifices. Yet in the very next verse God Himself says, "I know that the king of Egypt will not give you leave to go, no, not by a mighty hand," Ex. 3:18,19. If it is not inconsistent with God's sincerity for Him to command all men to love Him, or to be perfect (Luke 10:27; Matt. 5:48), it is not inconsistent with His sincerity for Him to command them to repent and believe the Gospel. A man may be altogether sincere in giving an invitation which he knows will be refused. A father who knows that his boys are going to do wrong feels constrained to tell them what is right. His warnings and pleadings are sincere; the trouble is in the boys.

    Will any one contend that God cannot sincerely offer salvation to a free moral agent unless in addition to the invitation He exerts a special influence which will induce the person to accept it? After a civil war in a country it often happens that the victorious general offers free pardon to all those In the opposing army, provided they will lay down their arms, go home, and live peaceable lives, although he knows that through pride or malice many will refuse. He makes the offer in good faith even though for wise reasons he determines not to constrain their assent, supposing him possessed of such power.

    We may imagine the case of a ship with many passengers on board sinking some distance out from shore. A man hires a boat from a near-by port and goes to rescue his family. Incidentally it happens that the boat which he takes is large enough to carry all the passengers, so he invites all those on the sinking vessel to come on board, although he knows that many of them, either through lack of appreciation of their danger, or because of personal spite toward him, or for other reasons, will not accept. Yet does that make his offer any the less sincere? "If a man's family were with others held in captivity, and from love of them and with the purpose of their redemption, a ransom should be offered sufficient for the delivery of the whole body of captives, it is plain that the offer of deliverance might be extended to all on the ground of that ransom, although specially intended only for a part of their number. Or, a man may make a feast for his own friends and the provisions be so abundant that he may throw open his doors to all who are willing to come. This is precisely what God, according to the Calvinistic doctrine, has actually done. Out of special love to His people, and with the design of securing their salvation He has sent His Son to do what justifies the offer of salvation to all who choose to accept it." [136]

Loraine Boettner D.D.

When the Gospel is presented to mankind in general nothing but a sinful unwillingness on the part of some prevents their accepting and enjoying it. No stumbling block is put in their way. All that the call contains is true; it is adapted to the conditions of all men and freely offered if they will repent and believe. No outside influence constrains them to reject it. The elect accept; the non-elect may accept if they will, and nothing but their own nature determines them to do otherwise. "According to the Calvinistic scheme," says Dr. Hodge, "the non-elect have all the advantages and opportunities of securing their salvation, that, according to any other scheme, are granted to mankind indiscriminately. Calvinism teaches that a plan of salvation adapted to all men and adequate for the salvation of all, is freely offered to the acceptance of all, although in the secret purpose of God He intended that it should have precisely the effect which in experience it is found to have. He designed in its adoption to save His own people, but consistently offers its benefits to all who are willing to receive them. More than this no anti-Calvinist can demand." [137]

Arminians object that God could not offer the Gospel to those who in His secret counsel were not designed to accept it; yet we find the Scriptures declaring that He does this very thing. His commands to Pharaoh have already been referred to. Isaiah was commissioned to preach to the Jews, and in 1:18, 19, we find that he extended a gracious offer of pardon and cleansing. But in 6:9-13, immediately following his glorious vision and official appointment, he is informed that this preaching is destined to harden his countrymen to their almost universal destruction. Ezekiel was sent to speak to the house of Israel, but was told beforehand that they would not hear, Ezek. 3:4-11. Matt. 23:33-37 presents the same teaching. In these passages God declares that He does the very thing which Arminians say He must not do. Hence the objection now under consideration has arisen not because of any Calvinistic misstatement of the divine plan, but through erroneous assumptions made by Arminians themselves.

The decree of election is a secret decree. And since no revelation has been given to the preacher as to which ones among his hearers are elect and which are non-elect, it is not possible for him to present the Gospel to the elect only. It is his duty to look with hope on all those to whom he is preaching, and to pray for them that they may each be among the elect. In order to offer the message to the elect, he must offer it to all; and the Scripture command is plain to the effect that it should be offered to all. Even the elect must hear before they can believe and accept, Romans 10:13-17. The attentive reader, however, will perceive that the invitations are not, in the strict sense, general, but that they are addressed to the "weary," the "thirsty," the "hungry," the "willing," those who "labor and are heavy laden," and not to those who are unconscious of any need and unwilling to be reformed. While the message is preached to all, it is God who chooses among the hearers those to whom He is speaking, and He makes this selection known to them through the inward testimony of the Holy Spirit. The elect thus receive the message as the promise of salvation, but to the non-elect it appears only as foolishness, or if their conscience is aroused, as a judgment to condemnation. As a rule, the non-elect are not concerned about salvation, do not envy the elect their hope of salvation, but rather laugh and scorn at them. And since the secret as to which ones in the audience belong to the elect is hidden from the preacher, usually he does not know who got the message to salvation and who got it to judgment. Among the elect themselves there are so many weaknesses, and on the other hand the evil one is so able to appear as an angel of light and to make such an outward show of good deeds and words, that the preacher usually cannot be sure of the outcome. The effect of the preaching is not in the preacher's hands, but in God's hands; and it often happens that the sermons which seemed unsuccessful were strengthened and made effective by the Holy Spirit.

Yet while it is certain that the non-elect will not turn to God, repent of their sins, and live good moral lives, it is, nevertheless, their duty to do so. Though members of a fallen race, they are still free moral agents, responsible for their character and conduct. God is, therefore, perfectly consistent in commanding them to repent. For Him not to do so would be for Him to give up the claims of His law. We commonly hear the idea expressed that man is under no obligation to do anything for which he has not full and perfect ability in himself. The reasoning, however, is fallacious; for man labors under a self-acquired inability. He was created upright and voluntarily sank himself into sin. He is, therefore, as responsible as is the person who in order to escape military service deliberately mutilates a hand or an eye. If inability canceled obligation, then Satan with his inherent depravity would be under no obligation to do right, and his fiendish enmity toward God and men would be no sin. Sinners in general would then be lifted above the moral law.

In conclusion it may be further said that even in regard to the non-elect the preaching is not altogether vain; for they are thus made the objects of general restraining and directing influences which prevent them from sinning as much as they otherwise would.

Footnotes:

136. Hodge, Systematic Theology, II., p. 556.
137. Systematic Theology, II., p. 644.

Chapter XXII

8. It Contradicts the Universalistic Scripture Passages
1. The Terms "Will" and "All." 2. The Gospel is for Jews and Gentiles Alike. 3. The Term "World" is Used in Various Senses. 4. General Considerations.

1. THE TERMS "WISH," "WILL," AND "ALL"

It may be asked, Is not the doctrine of Predestination flatly contradicted by the Scriptures which declare that Christ died for "all men," or for "the whole world," and that God wills the salvation of all men? In 1 Tim. 2:3, 4 Paul refers to "God our Saviour, who would have all men to be saved, and to come to the knowledge of the truth." (And the word "all," we are dogmatically informed by our opponents, must mean every human being.) In Ezek. 33:11 we read, "As I live, saith the Lord Jehovah, I have no pleasure in the death of the wicked; but that the wicked turn from his way and live"; and in II Peter 3:9 we read that God is "not wishing that any should perish, but that all should come to repentance." The King James Version reads, "Not willing that any should perish..."

These verses simply teach that God is benevolent, and that He does not delight in the sufferings of His creatures any more than a human father delights in the punishment which he must sometimes inflict upon his son. God does not decretively will the salvation of all men, no matter how much He may desire it; and if any verses taught that He decretively willed or intended the salvation of all men, they would contradict those other parts of the Scripture which teach that God sovereignly rules and that it is His purpose to leave some to be punished.

The word "will" is used in different senses in Scripture and in our every day conversation. It is sometimes used in the sense of "decree," or "purpose," and sometimes in the sense of "desire," or "wish." A righteous judge does not will (desire) that anyone should be hanged or sentenced to prison, yet at the same time he wills (pronounced sentence, or decrees) that the guilty person shall be thus punished. In the same sense and foe sufficient reasons a man may will or decide to have a limb removed, or an eye taken out, even though he certainly does not desire it. The Greek words thelo and boulomai, which are sometimes translated "will," are also used in the sense of "desire," or "wish;" e.g., Jesus said to the mother of James and John, "What wouldest thou?" Matt. 20:21; of the scribes it was said they "desire to walk in long robes," Luke 20:46; certain of the Scribes and Pharisees said to Jesus, "Teacher, we would see a sign from thee," Matt. 12:38; Paul said, "I had rather speak five words with my understanding, that I might instruct others also, than ten thousand words in a tongue," I Cor. 14:19.

In like manner the word "all" is unmistakably used in different senses in Scripture. In some cases it certainly does not mean every individual; e.g., of John the Baptist it was said, "And there went out unto him all the country of Judea, and all they of Jerusalem; and they were baptized of him in the river Jordan, confessing their sins," Mark 1:5. After Peter and John had healed the lame man at the door of the temple, we read that "all men glorified God for that which was done," Acts 4:21. Jesus told his disciples that they would be "hated of all men" for His name's sake, Luke 21:17. Paul was accused of "teaching all men everywhere against the people, and the law, and this place" (the temple), Acts 21:28. When Jesus said, "And I, if I be lifted up from the earth, will draw all men unto myself," John 12:32, He plainly meant not every individual of mankind, for history shows that not every individual has been drawn to Him. He certainly does not draw the many millions of heathens who die in utter ignorance of the true God. What He meant was, that a large multitude from all nations and classes would be saved; and this is what we see coming to pass. In Heb. 2:9, we read that Jesus tasted death "for every man." The original Greek, however, does not use the word "man" here at all, but simply says, "for every." So in principle, if the meaning is not to be limited to those who are actually saved, why limit it to men? Why not include the fallen angels, even the Devil himself, and the irrational animals?

When it is said, "For as in Adam all die, so also in Christ shall all be made alive," I Cor. 15:22, it must mean not absolutely all, but the all in Adam and the all in Christ. Otherwise the verse would teach absolute restorationism; for through all the writings of Paul, to be "in Christ" means to be a Christian, to be saved; and plainly not all men reach that state. The context also shows this, for there is no reference to unbelievers in the whole chapter. If it were understood to mean that Christ's work was co-extensive with that of Adam, then one of two results would be inevitable; viz: either that all men are saved, or that all men are put in the same position which Adam occupied before the fall; but each of these conclusions contradicts Scripture and experience. The only possible conclusion is that Christ's work was not co-extensive with that of Adam; that Adam represented the entire human race, but that Christ represented only those who are given Him by the Father. The statement in II Cor. 5:15, that Christ "died for all," is perhaps to be explained by the fact that the epistle is written to "the Church of God which is at Corinth, with all the saints that are in the whole of Achaia," and the "all" which Paul has in mind are those saved Christians.

It was not the whole of mankind which was equally loved of God and promiscuously redeemed by Christ. John's hymn of praise, "Unto Him that loves us, and loosed us from our sins by His blood; and made us to be a kingdom, to be priests unto His God and Father," evidently proceeds on the hypothesis of a definite election and a limited atonement since God's love was the cause and the blood of Christ the efficacious means of their redemption. The declaration that Christ died for "all" is made clearer by the song which the redeemed now sing before the throne of the Lamb: "Thou wast slain, and didst purchase unto God with thy blood men of every tribe, and tongue, and people, and nation," Rev. 5:9; 1:5. The word all must be understood to mean all the elect, all His Church, all those whom the Father has given to the Son, etc., not all men universally and every man individually. The redeemed host will be made up of men from all classes and conditions of life, of princes and peasants, of rich and poor, of bond and free, of male and female, of young and old, of Jews and Gentiles, men of all nations, and races, from north to south, and from east to west.

2. THE GOSPEL IS FOR JEWS AND GENTILES ALIKE

In some instances the word "all" is used in order to teach that the gospel is for the Gentiles as well as for the Jews. Through the many centuries of their past history the Jews had, with few exceptions, been the exclusive recipients of God's saving grace. They had greatly abused their privileges as the chosen people. They supposed that this same distinction would be kept up in the Messianic era, and they were always inclined to appropriate the Messiah exclusively to themselves. So rigid was the Pharisaic exclusivism that the Gentiles were called strangers, dogs, common, unclean; and it was not lawful for a Jew to keep company with or have any dealings with a Gentile (John 4:9; Acts 10:28; 11:3).

The salvation of the Gentiles was a mystery which had not been made known in other ages (Eph. 3:4-6; Col. 1:27). It was for that reason that Peter was taken to task: by the Church at Jerusalem after he had preached the Gospel to Cornelius, and we can almost hear the gasp of wonder in the exclamation of the leaders when after Peter's defense they said, "Then to the Gentiles also hath God granted repentance unto life," Acts 11:18. To understand what a revolutionary idea this was, read Acts 10:1-11:18. Consequently this was a truth which it was then peculiarly necessary to enforce, and it was brought out in the fullest and strongest terms. Paul was to be a witness "unto all men," that is, to Jews and Gentiles alike, of what he had seen and heard, Acts 22:15. As used in this sense the word "all" has no reference to individuals, but means mankind in general.

3. THE TERM "WORLD" IS USED IN VARIOUS SENSES

When it is said that Christ died "not for our sins only but for the sins of the whole world," I John 2:2, or that He came to "save the world," John 12:47, the meaning is that not merely Jews but Gentiles also are included in His saving work; the world as a world or the race as a race is to be redeemed. When John the Baptist said, "Behold the Lamb of God that taketh away the sin of the world!" he was not giving a theological discourse to saints, but preaching to sinners; and the unnatural thing then would have been for him to have discussed Limited Atonement or any other doctrine which could have been understood only by saints. We are told that John the Baptist "came for a witness, that he might bear witness of the light, that all might believe through him," John 1:7. But to say that John's ministry afforded an opportunity for every human being to have faith in Christ would be unreasonable. John never preached to the Gentiles. His mission was to make Christ "manifest to Israel," John 1:31; and in the nature of the case only a limited number of the Jews could be brought to hear him.

Sometimes the term "world" is used when only a large part of the world is meant, as when it is said that the Devil is "the deceiver of the whole world," or that "the whole earth" wonders after the beast, Revelation 13:3. If in I John 5:19, "We know that we are of God, and the whole world lieth in the evil one," the author meant every individual of mankind, then he and those to whom he wrote were also in the evil one, and he contradicted himself in saying that they were of God. Sometimes this term means only a relatively small part of the world, as when Paul wrote to the new Christian Church at Rome that their faith was "proclaimed throughout the whole world," Rom. 1:8. None but believers would praise those Romans for their faith in Christ, and in fact the world at large did not even know that such a Church existed at Rome. Hence Paul meant only the believing world or the Christian Church, which was a comparatively insignificant part of the real world. Shortly before Jesus was born, "There went out a decree from Caesar Augustus that all the world should be enrolled," . . . "and all went to enroll themselves," Luke 2:1, 3; yet we know that the writer had in mind only that comparatively small part of the world which was controlled by Rome. When it was said that on the day of Pentecost, "there were

The Reformed Doctrine Of Predestination

dwelling at Jerusalem Jews, devout men, from every nation under heaven," Acts 2:5, only those nations which were immediately known to the Jews were intended, for verses 9-11 list those which were represented. Paul says that the Gospel was "preached in all creation under heaven." Col. 1:23. The goddess Diana of the Ephesians was said to have been worshipped by "all Asia and the world," Acts 19:27. We are told that the famine which came over Egypt in Joseph's time extended to "all the earth," and that "all countries came into Egypt to Joseph to buy grain," Gen. 41:57.

In ordinary conversation we often speak of the business world, the educational world, the political world, etc., but we do not mean that every person in the world is a business man, or educated, or a politician. When we say that a certain automobile manufacturer sells automobiles to everybody, we do not mean that he actually sells to every individual, but that he sells to every one who is willing to pay his price. We may say of one lone teacher of literature in a city that he teaches everybody,--not that everybody studies under him, but that all of those who study at all study under him. The Bible is written in the plain language of the people and must be understood in that way.

Verses like John 3:16, "For God so loved the world, that He gave his only begotten Son, that whosoever believeth on Him should not perish, but have eternal life," give abundant proof that the redemption which the Jews thought to monopolize is universal as to space. God so loved the world, not a little portion of it, but the world as a whole, that He gave His only begotten Son for its redemption. And not only the extensity, but the intensity of God's love is made plain by the little adverb "so,"--God so loved the world, in spite of its wickedness, that He gave His only begotten Son to die for it. But where is the oft-boasted proof of its universality as to individuals? This verse is sometimes pressed to such an extreme that God is represented as too loving to punish anybody, and so full of mercy that He will not deal with men according to any rigid standard of justice regardless of their deserts. The attentive reader, by comparing this verse with other Scripture, will see that some restriction is to be placed on the word "world." One writer has asked, "Did God love Pharaoh? (Rom. 9:17). Did He love the Amalekites? (Ex. 17:14). Did He love the Canaanites, whom He commanded to be exterminated without mercy? (Deut. 20:16). Did He love the Ammonites and Moabites whom He commanded not to be received into the congregation forever? (Deut. 23:3). Does He love the workers of iniquity? (Ps. 5:5). Does He love the vessels of wrath fitted for destruction, which He endures with much long-suffering? (Rom. 9:22). Did He love Esau? (Rom. 9:13)."

4. GENERAL CONSIDERATIONS

Nor does the prophetic invitation, "Ho, every one that thirsteth, come ye to the waters," Is. 55:1, and other references to the same effect, contradict this view; for the majority of mankind are not thirsty but dead, dead in sin, hopeless and willing servants of Satan, and in no state to hunger and thirst after righteousness. The gracious invitation to come to Christ is rejected, not because there is anything outside their own person which prevents their coming, but because until they are graciously given a new birth through the agency of the Holy Spirit they have neither the will nor the desire to accept. It is God who gives this will and excites this desire in those who are predestined to life, Rom. 11:7, 8; 9:18. He that will, may come; but a person who is completely immersed in heathenism, for instance, has no chance to hear the Gospel offer and so cannot possibly come. "Faith cometh by hearing;" and where there is no faith there can be no salvation. Neither can that person come who has heard the Gospel but who is still governed by principles and desires which cause him to hate it. He is a bondservant to sin and acts accordingly. He that will may escape from a burning building while the stairway is safe; hut he that is asleep, or he that does not think the fire serious enough to flee from, hasn't the will, and perishes in the flames. Says Clark, "Arminians are fond of quoting: 'whosoever will let him come,' or 'Whosoever believeth,' implying that belief and decision are wholly the acts of man, and that this is an offset to sovereign election. True as these statements are they do not touch the point at issue. Miles deeper down than this lies the vital point; viz., how does a man become willing? If a man is willing he can certainly choose; but the sinful nature averse to God must be made willing, by God's word, by God's grace, by God's Spirit, or by sovereign intervention." [138] Strictly speaking, these are not divine offers indiscriminately made to all mankind, but are addressed to a chosen people and are incidentally heard by others.

If the words of 1 Tim. 2:4, that God "would have all men to be saved, and come to the knowledge of the truth," be taken in the Arminian sense it follows either that God is disappointed in His wishes, or that all men without exception are saved. Furthermore, the doctrine which imputes disappointment to Deity contradicts that class of Scripture passages which teach the sovereignty of God. His will in this respect has been the same through the centuries. And if He had willed that the Gentiles should be saved, why was it that He confined the knowledge of the way of salvation to the narrow limits of Judea? Surely no one will deny that He might as easily have made known His Gospel to the Gentiles as to the Jews. Where He has not provided the means we may be sure that He has not designed the ends. The reply of Augustine to those who advanced this objection in his day is worth quoting: "when our Lord complains that though he wished to gather the children of Jerusalem as a hen gathereth her chickens under her wings, but she would not, are we to consider that the will of God was overpowered by a number of weak men, so that He who was Almighty God could not do what He wished or willed to do? If so, what is to become of that omnipotence by which He did whatsoever pleased Him in Heaven and in? Moreover, who will be found so unreasonable as to say that God cannot convert the evil wills of men, which He pleases, when He pleases, and as He pleases, to good? Now, when He does this, He does it in mercy; and when He doeth it not, in judgment He doeth it not." Verses such as 1 Tim. 2:4 it seems best understood not to refer to men individually but as teaching the general truth that God is benevolent and that He does not delight in the sufferings and death of His creatures. It may be further remarked that if the universalistic passages are taken in an evangelical sense and applied as widely as the Arminians wish to apply them, they will prove universal salvation,--a result which is contradicted by Scripture, and which in fact is not held by Arminians themselves.

As was stated in the chapter on Limited Atonement there is a sense in which Christ did die for mankind in general. No distinction is made as to age or country, character or condition. The race fell in Adam and the race taken in the collective sense is redeemed in Christ. The work of Christ arrested the immediate execution of the penalty of sin as it related to the whole race. His work also brings many temporal and physical blessings to mankind in general, and lays the foundation for the offer of the Gospel to all who hear it. These are admitted to be the results of His work and to apply to all mankind. Yet this does not mean that He died equally and with the same design for all.

It is true that some verses taken in themselves do seem to imply the Arminian position. This, however, would reduce the Bible to a mass of contradictions; for there are other verses which teach Predestination, Inability, Election, Perseverance, etc., and which cannot by any legitimate means be interpreted in harmony with Arminianism. Hence in these cases the meaning of the sacred writer can be determined only by the analogy of Scripture. Since the Bible is the word of God it is self-consistent. Consequently if we find a passage which in itself is capable of two interpretations, one of which harmonizes with the rest of the Scriptures while the other does not, we are duty bound to accept the former. It is a recognized principle of interpretation that the more obscure passages are to be interpreted in the light of clearer passages, and not vice versa. We have shown that the evidence which is brought forward in defense of Arminianism, and which at first sight appears to possess considerable plausibility, can legitimately be given an interpretation which harmonizes with Calvinism. In view of the many Calvinistic passages, and the absence of any genuine Arminian passages, we unhesitatingly assert that the Calvinistic system is the true system.

This is the true universalism of the Scriptures--the universal Christianization of the world and the complete defeat of the forces of spiritual wickedness. 'This, of course, does not mean that every individual will be saved, for many are unquestionably lost. Just as in the salvation of the individual much possible service to Christ is lost and many sins are committed through the period of incomplete salvation, so it is in the salvation of the world. A considerable number are lost; yet the process of salvation is to end in a great triumph, and our eyes are yet to behold "the glorious spectacle of a saved world." The words of Dr. Warfield are very appropriate here: "The human race attains the goal for which it was created, and sin does not snatch it out of God's hands; the primal purpose of God with it is fulfilled; and through Christ, the race of man, though fallen into sin, is recovered to God and fulfills its original destiny." [139]

So while Arminianism offers us a spurious universalism, which is at best a universalism of opportunity, Calvinism offers us the true universalism in the salvation of the race. And only the Calvinist, with his emphasis on the doctrines of sovereign Election and Efficacious Grace, can look to the future confidently expecting to see a redeemed world.

Footnotes:

138. Syllabus of Systematic Theology, p. 208.
139. The Plan of Salvation, p. 131.

Section IV

Chapter XXIII – Salvation by Grace

1. Man's Ill-desert. 2. God May Give or Withhold Grace as He Pleases. 3. Salvation not to be Earned by Man. 4. Scripture Proof. 5. Further Remarks.

The Bible declares that the salvation of sinful men is a matter of grace. From Eph. 1:7-10 we learn that the primary purpose of God in the work of redemption was to display the glory of this divine attribute so that through succeeding ages the intelligent universe might admire it as it is made known through His unmerited love and boundless goodness to guilty, vile, helpless creatures. Accordingly all men are represented as sunk in a state of sin and misery, from which they are utterly unable to deliver themselves. When they deserved only God's wrath and curse, He determined that He would graciously provide redemption for them by sending His own eternal Son to assume their nature and guilt and to obey and suffer in their stead, and His Holy Spirit to apply the redemption purchased by the Son. On the same representative principle by which Adam's sin is imputed to us, that is, set to our account in such a way that we are held fully responsible for it and suffer the consequences of it, our sin in its turn is imputed to Christ and His righteousness is imputed to us. This is briefly, yet clearly expressed in the Shorter Catechism, which says, "Justification is an act of God's free grace, wherein He pardoneth all our sins, and accepteth us as righteous in His sight, only for the righteousness of Christ imputed to us, and received by faith alone." Ans. to Q. 88.

We should keep clearly in mind the distinction between the two covenants: that of works, under which Adam was placed and which resulted in the fall of the race into sin; and that of grace, under which Christ was sent as a Redeemer. As stated in another connection, the Arminian system makes no essential distinction in principle between the covenant of works and the covenant of grace, unless it be that God now offers salvation on lower terms and instead of demanding perfect obedience He accepts only such faith and evangelical obedience as the crippled sinner is able to render. In that system the burden of obedience is still thrown upon man himself and his salvation in the first place depends upon his own works.

The word "grace" in its proper sense means the free and undeserved love or favor of God exercised toward the undeserving, toward sinners. It is something which is given irrespective of any worthiness in man; and to introduce works or merit into any part of this scheme vitiates its nature and frustrates its design. Just because it is grace, it is not given on the basis of preceding merits. As the very name imports, it is necessarily gratuitous; and since man is enslaved to sin until it is given, all the merits that he can have prior to it are bad merits and deserve only punishment, not gifts, or favor. Whatever of good men have, that God has given; and what they have not, why, of course, God has not given it. And since grace is given irrespective of preceding merits, it is therefore sovereign and is bestowed only on those whom God has selected for its reception. It is this sovereignty of grace, and not its foresight or the preparation for it, which places men in God's hands and suspends salvation absolutely on His unlimited mercy. In this we find the basis for His election or rejection of particular persons.

Because of His absolute moral perfection God requires spotless purity and perfect obedience in his intelligent creatures. This perfection is provided in Christ's spotless righteousness being imputed to them; and when God looks upon the redeemed He sees them clothed with the spotless robe of Christ's righteousness not with anything of their own. We are distinctly told that Christ suffered as a substitute, "the just for the unjust"; and when man is encouraged to think that he owes to some power or art of his own that salvation which in reality is all of grace, God is robbed of part of His glory. By no stretch of the imagination can a man's good works in this life be considered a just equivalent for the blessings of eternal life. Benjamin Franklin, though by no means a Calvinist, expressed this idea well when he wrote: "He that for giving a drink of water to a thirsty person, should expect to be paid with a good plantation, would be modest in his demands, compared with those who think they deserve heaven for the little good they do on earth." We are, in fact, nothing but receivers; we never bring any adequate reward to God, we are always receiving from Him, and shall be unto all eternity.

Loraine Boettner D.D.

2. GOD MAY GIVE OR WITHHOLD GRACE AS HE PLEASES

Since God has provided this redemption or atonement at His own cost, it is His property and He is absolutely sovereign in choosing who shall be saved through it. There is nothing more steadily emphasized in the Scripture doctrine of redemption than its absolutely gracious character. Hence, by their separation from the original mass, not through any works of their own but only through the free grace of God, the vessels of mercy see how great a gift has been bestowed upon them. It will be found that many who inherit heaven were much worse sinners in this world than were many others who are lost.

The doctrine of Predestination cuts down every self-righteous imagination which would detract from the glory of God. It convinces the one who is saved that he can only be eternally thankful that God saved him. Hence in the Calvinistic system all boasting is excluded and that honor and glory which belong to God alone is fully preserved. "The greatest saint," says Zanchius, "cannot triumph over the most abandoned sinner, but is led to refer the entire praise of his salvation, both from sin and hell, to the mere good-will and sovereign purpose of God, who hath graciously made him to differ from that world which lieth in wickedness." [140]

3. SALVATION NOT TO BE EARNED BY MAN

All men naturally feel that they should earn their salvation, and a system which makes some provision in that regard readily appeals to them. But Paul lays the axe to such reasoning when he says, "If there had been a law given which could make alive, verily righteousness would have been of the law," Gal. 3:21; and Jesus said to His disciples, "when ye shall have done all the things that are commanded of you, say, We are unprofitable servants; we have done that which it was our duty to do," Luke 17:10.

Our own righteousness, says Isaiah, is but as a polluted garment--or, as the King James Version puts it, as filthy rags--in the sight of God (64:6). And when Isaiah wrote, "Ho, every one that thirsteth, come ye to the waters, and he that hath no money; come ye, buy and eat; yea, come, buy wine and milk without money and without price," 55:1, he invited the penniless, the hungry, the thirsty, to come and take possession of, and enjoy the provision, free of all cost, as if by right of payment. And to buy without money must mean that it has already been produced and provided at the cost of another. The further we advance in the Christian life, the less we are inclined to attribute any merit to ourselves, and the more to thank God for all. The believer not only looks forward to everlasting life, but also looks backward into the antemundane eternity and finds in the eternal purpose of divine love the beginning and the firm anchorage of his salvation.

If salvation is of grace, as the Scriptures so clearly teach, it cannot he of works, whether actual or foreseen. There is no merit in believing, for faith itself is a gift of God. God gives His people an inward working of the Spirit in order that they may believe, and faith is only the act of receiving the proffered gift. It is, then, only the instrumental cause, and not the meritorious cause, of salvation. What God loves in us is not our own merits, but His own gift; for His unmerited grace precedes our meritorious works. Grace is not merely bestowed when we pray for it, but grace itself causes us to pray for its continuance and increase.

In the book of The Acts we find that the very inception of faith itself is assigned to grace (18:27); only those who were ordained to eternal life believed (13:48); and it is God's prerogative to open the heart so that it gives heed to the gospel (16:14). Faith is thus referred to the counsels of eternity, the events in time being only the outworking. Paul attributes it to the grace of God that we are "His workmanship, created in Christ Jesus for good works, which God afore prepared that we should walk in them," Eph. 2:10. Good works, then, are in no sense the meritorious ground but rather the fruits and proof of salvation.

Luther taught this same doctrine when he said of some that "They attribute to Free-will a very little indeed, yet they teach us that by that very little we can attain unto righteousness and grace. Nor do they solve that question, Why does God justify one and leave another? in any other way than by asserting the freedom of the will, and saying, Because the one endeavors and the other does not; and God regards the one for endeavoring, and despises the other for his not endeavoring; lest, if he did otherwise, he should appear to be unjust." [141]

It is said that Jeremy Taylor and a companion were once walking down a street in London when they came to a drunk man lying in the gutter. The other man made some disparaging remark about the drunk man. But Jeremy Taylor, pausing and looking at him, said, "But for the grace of God, there lies Jeremy Taylor!" The spirit which was in Jeremy Taylor is the spirit which should be in every sin-rescued Christian. It was repeatedly taught that Israel owed her separation from the other peoples of the world not to anything good or desirable in herself, but only to God's gracious love faithfully persisted in despite apostasy, sin, and rebellion.

Paul says concerning some who would base salvation on their own merits, that, "going about to establish their own righteousness, they did not submit themselves to the righteousness of God," and

The Reformed Doctrine Of Predestination

were, therefore, not in the Church of Christ. He makes it plain that "the righteousness of God" is given to us through faith, and that we enter heaven pleading only the merits of Christ.

The reason for this system of grace is that those who glory should glory in the Lord, and that no person should ever have occasion to boast over another. The redemption was purchased at an infinite cost to God Himself, and therefore it may be dispensed as He pleases in a purely gracious manner. As the poet has said:

> *"None of the ransomed ever knew,*
> *How deep were the waters crossed,*
> *Nor how dark was the night that the Lord passed through,*
> *To find the sheep that was lost."*

4. SCRIPTURE TEACHING

Let us now notice some of those scriptures which teach that our sins were imputed to Christ; and then notice some which teach that His righteousness is imputed to us.

"Surely He hath borne our griefs, and carried our sorrows; yet we did esteem Him stricken, smitten of God and afflicted. But He was wounded for our transgressions; He was bruised for our iniquities; the chastisement of our peace was upon Him; and with His stripes we are healed. All we like sheep have gone astray; we have turned every one to his own way; and Jehovah hath laid on Him the iniquity of us all," Is. 53: 4, 5. "By the knowledge of Himself shall my righteous servant justify many, and He shall bear their iniquities. . . . He bare the sin of many," Is. 53:11, 12. "Him who knew no sin He made to be sin on our behalf; that we might become the righteousness of God in Him," II Cor. 5:21. Here both truths are plainly stated,--our sins are set to His account, and His righteousness to ours. There is no other conceivable sense in which He could be "made sin," or we "made the righteousness of God." It was Christ "who His own self bare our sins in His body upon the tree, that we, having died unto sins, might live unto righteousness; by whose stripes we are healed," I Peter 2:24. Here, again, both truths are thrown together. "Because Christ also suffered for sins once, the righteous for the unrighteous, that He might bring us to God," I Peter 3:18. These, and many other such verses, prove the doctrine of His substitution in our stead, as plainly as language can put it. If they do not prove that the death of Christ was a true and proper sacrifice for sin in our stead, human language cannot express it.

That His righteousness is imputed to us is taught in language equally plain. "By the works of the law shall no flesh be justified in His sight. . . . But now apart from the law a righteousness of God hath been manifested . . . even the righteousness of God through faith in Jesus Christ unto all them that believe . . . being justified freely by His grace through the redemption that is in Christ Jesus, whom God set forth to be a propitiation, through faith, in His blood, to show His righteousness because of the passing over of the sins done aforetime, in the forbearance of God; for the showing, I say, of His righteousness at this present season; that He might himself be just, and the justifier of him that hath faith in Jesus. Where then is the glorying? It is excluded. By what manner of law? of works? Nay, hut by the law of faith. We reckon therefore that a man is justified by faith apart from the works of the law," Rom. 3:20-28. "So then as through one trespass the judgment came unto all men to condemnation; even so through one act of righteousness the free gift came unto all men to justification of life. For as through the one man's disobedience the many were made sinners, even so through the obedience of the one shall the many be made righteous," Rom. 5:18, 19. Paul's testimony in regard to himself was: "I have suffered the loss of all things, and do count them but refuse, that I may gain Christ, and be found in Him, not having a righteousness of my own, even that which is of the law, but that which is through faith in Christ, the righteousness which is from God by faith," Phil. 3:8, 9. Now, is it not strange that any one who pretends to be guided by the Bible, could, in the face of all this plain and unequivocal language, uphold salvation by works, in any degree whatever?

Paul wrote to the Romans, "Sin shall not have dominion over you; for ye are not under law, but under grace." 6:14. That is, God had taken them out from under a system of law and had placed them under a system of grace; and as their Sovereign, it was not His purpose to let them again fall under the dominion of sin. In fact, if they were to fall, it could only be because God had taken them out from under grace and again placed them under law, so that their own works determined their destiny. In the very nature of the case as long as the person is under grace he is entirely free from any claim that the law may have on him through sin. For one to be saved through grace means that God is no longer treating him as he deserves but that He has sovereignly set the law aside and that He saves him in spite of his ill-desert--cleansing him from his sin, of course, before he is fit to enter the divine presence.

Paul goes to great pains to make it clear that the grace of God is not earned by us, is not secured by us in any way, but is just given to us. If it be earned, it ceases by that very fact to be grace, Rom. 11:6.

5. FURTHER REMARKS

In the present state of the race all men stand before God, not as citizens of a state, all of whom must be treated alike and given the same "chance" for salvation, but rather as guilty and condemned criminals before a righteous judge. None have any claim to salvation. The marvel is, not that God doesn't save all, but that when all are guilty He pardons so many; and the answer to the question, Why does He not save all? is to be found, not in the Arminian denial of the omnipotence of His grace, but in the fact that, as Dr. Warfield says, "God in His love saves as many of the guilty race of man as He can get the consent of His whole nature to save." [142] For reasons known to Himself He sees that it is not best to pardon all, but that some should be permitted to have their own way and be left to eternal punishment in order that it may be shown what an awful thing is sin and rebellion against God.

Time and again the Scriptures repeat the assertion that salvation is of grace, as if anticipating the difficulty which men would have in coming to the conclusion that they could not earn salvation by their own works. Thus also they destroy the widespread notion that God owes salvation to any. "By grace have ye been saved through faith; and that not of yourselves; it is the gift of God; not of works, that no man should glory," Eph. 2:8, 9. "But if it is of grace, it is no more of works; otherwise grace is no more grace," Rom. 11:6. "By the works of the law shall no flesh be justified," Rom. 3:20. "Now to him that worketh, the reward is not reckoned as of grace, but as of debt," Rom. 4:4. "Who maketh thee to differ? and what hast thou that thou didst not receive?" I Cor. 4:7. "By the grace of God I am what I am," I Cor. 15:10. "Who hath first given to Him, and it shall he recompensed unto him again?" Rom. 11:35. "The free gift of God is eternal life in Christ Jesus our Lord," Rom. 6:23.

Grace and works are mutually exclusive; and as well might we try to bring the two poles together as to effect a coalition of grace and works in salvation. As well might we talk of a "purchased gift," as to talk of "conditional grace," for when grace ceases to be absolute it ceases to be grace. Therefore when the Scriptures say that salvation is of grace we are to understand that it is through its whole process the work of God and that any truly meritorious works done by man are the result of the change which has already been wrought.

Arminianism destroys this purely gracious character of salvation and substitutes a system of grace plus works. No matter how small a part these works may play they are necessary and are the basis of the distinction between the saved and the lost and would then afford occasion for the saved to boast over the lost since each had equal opportunity. But Paul says that all boasting is excluded, and that he who glories should glory in the Lord (Rom. 3:27; I Cor. 1:31). But if saved by grace, the redeemed remembers the mire from which he was lifted, and his attitude toward the lost is one of sympathy and pity. He knows that but for the grace of God he too would have been in the same state as those who perish, and his song is, "Not unto us, O Lord, not unto us, but unto thy name give glory, for thy mercy and for thy truth's sake."

Footnotes:

140. Predestination, p. 140.
141. Bondage of the Will, p. 338.
142. The Plan of Salvation, p. 93.

Chapter XXIV – Personal Assurance That One Is Among the Elect

1. Basis For Assurance. 2. Scripture Teaching. 3. Conclusion.

1. BASIS FOR ASSURANCE

All true Christians may and should know that they are among those who have been predestinated to eternal life. Since faith in Christ, which is a gift from God, is the means of salvation, and since this is not given to any but the elect only, the person who knows that he has this faith can be assured that he is among the elect. The mere presence of faith, no matter how weak it may be, provided it is real faith, is a proof of salvation. "As many as were ordained to eternal life (and they only) believed," Acts 13:48. Faith is a miracle of grace within those who have already been saved--a spiritual token that their salvation was "finished" on the cross, and certified on the resurrection morn. The truly saved know that the love of God has been shed abroad in their hearts and that their sins have been forgiven. In Pilgrim's Progress we read that when Christian's sins were forgiven a heavy burden rolled from his shoulders and that he experienced a great relief. Every converted man should know that he is among the elect, for the Holy Spirit renews only those who are chosen by the Father and redeemed by the Son. "It is folly to fancy that a sincere lover of Jesus Christ who trusts in Him as his Saviour and lovingly obeys Him as his Lord, can possibly lack the election of God. It is only because he is one of God's elect that he can believe in Christ for the salvation of his soul, and follow after Christ in the conduct of his life. . . . It is impossible, that a believer in Christ should not be elected of God, because it is only by the election of God that one becomes a believer in Christ. . . . We need not, we must not, seek elsewhere for the proof of our election. If we believe Christ and obey Him, we are His elect children." [143]

Every person who loves God and has a true desire for salvation in Christ is among the elect, for the non-elect never have this love or this desire. Instead, they love evil and hate righteousness in accordance with their sinful natures. "Does a man do his duty to God and his neighbor? Is he honest, just, charitable, pure? If he is, and if he is conscious of the power to continue so, so far as he can depend on this consciousness, so far he may reasonably believe himself to be predestinated to future happiness." [144]

"We know that we have passed out of death into life, because we love the brethren. He that loveth not abideth in death," I John 3:14. "He that is begotten of God doeth no sin, because his seed abideth in him; and he cannot sin, because he is begotten of God," I John 3:9. That is, it is against his inner principles to commit sin. When he thinks deeply and soberly about it, sin is repulsive to him and he hates it. Just as a good American citizen does nothing which will be detrimental to his country, so the true believer does nothing which injures the kingdom of God. As a matter of practice, no one in this world lives a perfectly sinless life; yet this is the ideal standard which he seeks to reach.

Says Dr. Warfield, "Peter exhorts us, II Peter 1:10, to make our 'calling and election sure' precisely by diligence in good works. He does not mean that by good works we may secure from God a decree of election in our behalf. He means that by expanding the germ of spiritual life which we have received from God into its full efflorescence, by 'working out' our salvation, of course not without Christ but in Christ, we can make ourselves sure that we have really received the election to which we make claim. . . . Good works become thus the mark and test of election, and when taken in the comprehensive sense in which Peter is here thinking of them, they are the only marks and tests of election. We can never know that we are elected of God to eternal life except by manifesting in our lives the fruits of election--faith and virtue, knowledge and temperance, patience and godliness, love of brethren. . . . It is idle to seek assurance of election outside of holiness of life. Precisely what God chose His people to before the foundation of the world was that they should be holy. Holiness, because it is the necessary product, is therefore the sure sign of election." [145]

As Toplady says, "A person who is at all conversant with the spiritual life knows as certainly whether he indeed enjoys the light of God's countenance, or whether he walks in darkness, as a traveler knows whether he travels in sunshine or in rain."

How may I know that I am among the elect? One may as well ask, How do I know that I am a loyal American citizen, or how shall I distinguish between white and black, or between sweet and bitter? Every one knows instinctively what his attitude is toward his country, and the Scriptures and conscience give as clear evidence of whether or not we are among God's people as white and black do of their color, or sweet and bitter do of their taste. Every person who is already a child of God should be fully conscious of the fact. Paul exhorted the Corinthians, "Try your own selves, whether ye are of the faith; prove your own selves. Or know ye not as to your own selves, that Jesus Christ is in you? Unless indeed ye be reprobate," II Cor. 13:5.

2. SCRIPTURE TEACHING

We have the assurance that "The Spirit Himself beareth witness with our spirit, that we are children of God," Rom. 8:16. "He that believeth on the Son of God hath the witness in him," I John 5:10. "And the witness is this, that God gave unto us eternal life, and this life is in His Son. He that hath the Son hath the life; he that hath not the Son of God hath not the life. These things have I written unto you, that ye may know that ye have eternal life, even unto you that believe on the name of the Son of God," I John 5:11-13. The born-again Christian welcomes the Gospel in his heart, but the unregenerate push it off: "We are of God: He that knoweth God heareth us; he that is not of God heareth us not. By this we know the spirit of truth, and the spirit of error," I John 4:6. "And hereby we know that He abideth in us, by the Spirit which He gave us," I John 3:24. "Because ye are sons, God sent forth the Spirit of His Son into our hearts, crying, 'Abba, Father,'" Gal. 4:6. The regenerated person instinctively recognizes God as his Father. "We know that we have passed out of death into life, because we love the brethren," I John 3:14. "Whosoever believeth that Jesus is the Christ is born of God," I John 5:1,--this means all who confess Him as Lord--what blessed assurance! "Ye know that everyone that doeth righteousness is born of Him," I John 2:29. Those who hear and welcome the Gospel are actuated by this inner saving principle.

"He that believeth on the Son hath eternal life; but he that obeyeth not the Son hath not life, but the wrath of God abideth on him," John 3:36. "No man speaking in the Spirit of God saith, Jesus is anathema; and no man can say, Jesus is Lord, but in the Holy Spirit," I Cor. 12:3. By this we are taught that a truly saved person cannot cast Jesus off and revile Him, and that anyone who looks to Jesus as the Lord and his Lord, has been regenerated and is among the elect. This, then, is a proof of his salvation. Each person knows what his attitude toward Jesus is; and knowing this, he is able to judge whether or not he is saved. Let each one ask himself this question, What is my attitude toward Christ? Would I be glad for Him to appear and talk personally to me this moment? Would I welcome Him as my Friend, or would I shrink from meeting Him? Those who look forward with joy to the coming of Christ may know that they are saved.

Since these certain marks of salvation are laid down in Scripture, a person, by honestly examining himself, may know whether or not he is among God's people. And by the same rule he may with caution judge of others; for if we see the external fruits of election in them and are convinced of their sincerity, we may reasonably conclude that they are elect. Paul had assurance concerning the Christians at Thessalonica, for he wrote, "Knowing, brethren, beloved of God, your election, how that our Gospel came not to you in words only, but also in power, and in the Holy Spirit, and in much assurance," I Thess. 1:4, 5. He also knew that God had chosen the Ephesians in Christ, for he wrote to them: "He chose us in Him before the foundation of the world, that we should be holy and without blemish before Him in love; having foreordained us unto adoption as sons through Jesus Christ unto Himself, according to the good pleasure of His will," Ephesians 1:4, 5.

3. CONCLUSION

But on the other hand we should not pronounce any living person to be non-elect, no matter how sinful he may be at present; for even the vilest person may, so far as we know, yet be brought to faith and repentance by the Holy Spirit. The conversion of many of the elect is still future. Hence no one has a right to declare positively that he or any other person is among the non-elect, for he does not know what God may have in store for him or them. We can, however, say that those who die impenitent are certainly lost, for the Scriptures are explicit on that.

We cannot say that every true Christian has this assurance; for it can only properly arise from a knowledge of one's own moral resources and strength, and the one who underestimates himself may innocently be without it. The Christian may at times become very discouraged because of weak faith, but this does not prove him to be among the non-elect. When faith is strengthened and erroneous views of salvation are cleared up, it is the privilege and duty of every Christian to know himself saved, and to escape that fear of apostasy which must constantly haunt every consistent Arminian so long as he continues in this life. Hence, while assurance is desirable and easily obtainable for any one who has made some progress in the Christian way, it cannot always be made the test of a true Christian.

Through the Scriptures God repeatedly gives us the promises that those who come to Him in Christ shall in no wise be cast out, that whosoever will may take of the water of life without money and without price, and that he who asks shall receive. The grounds for our assurance, then, are both within us and without us. If, therefore, any true believer lacks the assurance that he is forever safe among God's people, the fault is in himself and not in the plan of salvation, or in the Scriptures.

Footnotes:

143. Warfield, pamphlet, Election, p. 18.
144. Mozley, The Augustinian Doctrine of Predestination, p. 45.
145. Pamphlet, Election, pp. 17, 18.

Loraine Boettner D.D.

Chapter XXV – Predestination in the Physical World

1. The Uniformity of Natural Law. 2. Comments by Noted Scientists and Theologians. 3. The Calvinistic System Alone Harmonizes With Modern Science and Philosophy.

1. THE UNIFORMITY OF NATURAL LAW

As far as the material universe apart from mind is concerned we have no trouble at all to believe in absolute Predestination. The course of events which would follow was, in a very strict sense, immutably predetermined when God created the world and implanted the natural laws of gravity, light, magnetism, chemical affinity, electrical phenomena, etc. Apart from the interference of mind or miracle, the course of nature is uniform and predictable. This has not only been admitted but dogmatically held and asserted by many of the greatest scientists. The atoms follow their exactly prescribed courses. The material objects we handle are governed by fixed laws. If we have accurate knowledge of all the factors involved, we can determine exactly what will be the effect of a falling stone, an explosion, or an earthquake. The telescope reveals to us millions of distant fiery suns, each of which follows an exact, predetermined course, and their positions can be predicted for thousands of years to come.

Within the solar system the planets and satellites swing perfectly in their orbits, and eclipses can be predicted with exactness. Before the eclipse of the sun in 1924 the astronomers announced the course which the shadow of the moon would take across the earth and calculated the time for certain cities down to the seconds, which calculation was later shown by the eclipse to be in error only four seconds!

Astronomers tell us that the same principles which govern in our solar system are also found in the millions of stars which are trillions of miles away. Physicists analyze the light which comes from the sun and from the stars and tell us that not only are the same elements, such as iron, carbon, oxygen, etc., which are found on the earth also found on them, but that these elements are found in practically the same proportion there as here.

From the law of gravitation we learn that every material object in the universe attracts every other material object with a force which is directly proportional to their masses and inversely proportional to the square of the distance between their centers. Hence every grain of sand in the desert or on the seashore is linked up with every sun in the universe. The sluggish earth mounts upward to meet the falling snowflake. The microscope reveals marvels just as wonderful as those revealed by the telescope. God's providence extends to the atoms as well as to the stars and each one exerts its particular influence, small but exact. Everywhere there is perfect order and God has slighted His work nowhere.

2. COMMENTS BY NOTED SCIENTISTS AND THEOLOGIANS

Huxley once said that if man had possessed exact knowledge of natural laws before the rise of plants and animals on the earth, he could have predicted not only the geographical contour and climate of a given region, but also the exact flora and fauna which would have been found there,--arising, as he supposed, through the spontaneous generation of life from non-living matter,--and while we do not accept his extreme statement about the origin of life, this, nevertheless, gives us some idea of the uniformity that a great scientist expects to find in the laws of nature.

The writer was once in a discussion group conducted by Dr. H. N. Russell, head of the Department of Astronomy in Princeton University, and one of the outstanding astronomers of our time, in which Dr. Russell declared that apart from the influence of mind in the world he believed in an absolute predestination made effective through the fixed laws of nature.

"The uniformity of the laws of nature," says Dr. Charles Hodge, "is a constant revelation of the immutability of God. They are now what they were at the beginning of time, and they are the same in every part of the universe. No less stable are the laws which regulate the operations of the reason and conscience." And again he says: "As in all these lower departments of His work, God acts according to a preconceived plan. It is not to be supposed that in the higher sphere of His operations, which concern the destiny of men, everything would be left to chance and allowed to take its undetermined course to an undetermined end. We accordingly find that the Scriptures distinctly assert in reference to the dispensations of grace not only that God sees the end from the beginning, but that He works all things

The Reformed Doctrine Of Predestination

according to the counsel of His will, or, according to His eternal purpose." [146]

Dr. Abraham Kuyper, who was admittedly one of the outstanding theologians of the last century, tells us: "It is a fact that the more thorough development of science in our age has almost unanimously decided in favor of Calvinism with regard to the antithesis between the unity and stability of God's decree, which Calvinism professes, and the superficiality and looseness, which the Arminians preferred. The systems of the great philosophers are, almost to one, in favor of unity and stability." He goes on to say that these systems "clearly demonstrate that the development of science in our age presupposes a cosmos which does not fall a prey to the freaks of chance, but exists and develops from one principle, according to a firm order, aiming at one fixed plan. This is a claim which is, as it clearly appears, diametrically opposed to Arminianism, and in complete harmony with Calvinistic belief, that there is one supreme will in God, the cause of all existing things, subjecting them to ordinances and directing them towards a pre-established plan." And again, he asks, What does the doctrine of foreordination mean except that "the entire cosmos, instead of being a plaything of caprice and chance, obeys law and order, and that there exists a firm will which carries out its design both in nature and in history?" [147]

3. THE CALVINISTIC SYSTEM ALONE HARMONIZES WITH MODERN SCIENCE AND PHILOSOPHY

The Calvinistic world- and life-view, which so emphasizes the fixity and certainty of the course of events, is thus in striking harmony with modern Science and Philosophy. How preposterous is that claim which is sometimes made, that no matter how clearly this doctrine of Predestination is taught in the Scriptures, it is disproved by established truth from other sources! That claim is made by many who wish to establish a different system of theology. But any one who is at all familiar with modern Science and Philosophy (with physiological psychology, for example), with their emphasis on universally fixed laws, knows that just the opposite is true. Witness the present day emphasis on behaviourism, determinism, and heredity. And what is Mendel's law but Predestination in the realm of Genetics? The tendency is strongly against the free and the contingent. The Universe is conceived of as one systematic whole, interrelated in all of its parts, and following a very definite, prearranged course. With a different nomenclature and a different idea of the supernatural, the foremost modern scientists and philosophers hold the Calvinistic view in regard to the world as a unit. They may deny God's freedom, or even His personality, and their necessitarian metaphysics may be radically at variance with the true doctrine of His providence and grace; they may attempt to explain the thought processes of the brain, and even life itself, by physical and chemical laws; yet their impression of the co-ordinated facts of life and nature is thoroughly Calvinistic.

Without faith in the unity, stability, and order of things such as that to which Predestination leads us, it is impossible for Science to go beyond mere conjectures. Science is based on faith in the organic inter-connection or unity of the universe, a firm conviction that our entire lives must be under the sway of laws or principles established by some extra-mundane Power or Creator. The more we learn about Science the more clearly do we see the unity which underlies it all.

And when we come to study History we find that it is a "chain of events." Just as every grain of sand is related to every sun in the universe, so every event has its exact and necessary place in the unfolding of History. All of us remember comparatively insignificant events which have changed the courses of our lives; and had one of these links been omitted the result would have been radically different. Often times a very small thing sets off a course of events which convulses the world, as was the case in 1914 when a Serbian conspirator fired a shot at the Archduke of Austria, and the World War followed. Quite naturally many people have drawn back from attributing all the free acts of men and angels, and especially their sinful acts, to the foreordination of God. Nevertheless, if God is to rule the world at all His plan and providential control must extend to all events, not only in the natural world, but also in the realm of human affairs; and the Scriptures plainly teach that the free acts of men and angels are as certainly foreordained of God as are the events in the material world.

This four-fold argument of Science, Philosophy, History, and sacred Scriptures is not to be taken lightly. In Science, Philosophy, and History the doctrine is reduced to the cold severity of impersonal force. But when the radiant light of the glorious Gospel is thrown upon this, showing that the racial choices, the personal elections, the divine calls, are made by sovereign grace and not simply by sovereign will, we see that God's eternal purposes are in favor of man and not against him; and the heart finds rest and comfort in the fact that God's love and mercy are as tender as His purposes are strong.

Footnotes:

146. Systematic Theology, I., p. 539; II., p. 314.
147. Lectures on Calvinism, pp. 149, 150.

Loraine Boettner D.D.

Chapter XXVI – A Comparison with the Mohammedan Doctrine of Predestination

1. Elements Which the Two Doctrines Have in Common. 2. Mohammedan Tendency Toward Fatalism. 3. Christian Doctrine Not Derived From Mohammedanism. 4. The Two Doctrines Contrasted.

1. ELEMENTS WHICH THE TWO DOCTRINES HAVE IN COMMON

While Mohammedanism is a false religion and utterly destitute of power to save the soul from sin, there are certain elements of truth in the system, and we are under obligation to honor truth regardless of the source from which it comes. "The strength of Mohammedanism," says Froude, "was that it taught the omnipotence and omnipresence of one eternal Spirit, the Maker and Ruler of all things, by whose everlasting purpose all things were, and whose will all things must obey." [148] The striking similarity between the Biblical and the Koranic doctrines of Predestination has been noticed by many writers. Dr. Samuel M. Zwemer, who in a very real sense can be referred to as "the apostle to the Mohammedan world," calls attention to the strange parallel between the Reformation in Europe under Calvin and that in Arabia under Mohammed. Says he: "Islam is indeed in many respects the Calvinism of the Orient. It, too, was a call to acknowledge the sovereignty of God's will. 'There is no god but God.' It, too, saw in nature and sought in revelation the majesty of God's presence and power, and manifestations of His glory, transcendent and omnipotent. 'God,' says Mohammed, 'there is no god but He, the living, the self-subsistent, slumber seizeth Him not, nor sleep--His throne embraceth the heavens and the earth and none can intercede with Him save by His permission. He alone is exalted and great' . . . . It is this vital theistic principle that explains the victory of Islam over the weak divided and idolatrous Christendom of the Orient in the sixth century. . . . The Message of Mohammed, when he first unfurled the green banner, 'There is no god but God; God is king, and you must and shall obey His will,' was one of the simplest accounts ever offered of the nature of God and His relation to man. . . . This was Islam, as it was offered at the sword's point to people who had lost the power of understanding any other argument." [149]

In addition to the Koran there are a number of orthodox traditions which claim to give Mohammed's teachings on the subject. Some of these tell in almost identical language how before the person is born an angel descends and writes his destiny. It is said that the angel inquires, "O my Lord, miserable or blessed? whereupon one or the other is written down; and: O my Lord, a male or a female? whereupon one or the other is written down. He also writes down the moral conduct of the new being, its career, its term of life, and its allotment of good. Then (it is said to him): Roll up the leaves, for no addition shall be made thereto, nor anything taken therefrom." In another tradition we read of a messenger of God speaking thus: "There is no one of you--there is no soul born whose place, whether Paradise or Hell, has not been predetermined by God, and which has not been registered beforehand as either miserable or blessed." [150]

But while the Koran and the traditions teach a strict foreordination of moral conduct and future destiny, they also present a doctrine of human freedom which makes it necessary for us to qualify the sharper assertions of divine Predestination in harmony with it. And here, too, as in the Scriptures, no attempt is made to explain how the apparently opposite truths of Divine sovereignty and human freedom are to be reconciled.

2. MOHAMMEDAN TENDENCY TOWARD FATALISM

As a matter of fact, however, Mohammedanism places such an emphasis on God as the sole cause of all events that second causes are practically excluded. The idea that man is in any way the cause of his own acts has nearly ceased to exist, and Fatalism, the normal belief of the Arabs in their state of semi-civilization before Mohammed, is the controlling force in the speculations and practices of the Moslem world. "According to these traditions," says Dr. Zwemer, "and the interpretation of them for more than ten centuries in the life of Moslems, this kind of Predestination should be called Fatalism and nothing else. For Fatalism is the doctrine of an inevitable necessity and implies an omnipotent and arbitrary sovereign power." [151]

Practically, Mohammedanism holds to a predestination of ends regardless of means. The contrast

The Reformed Doctrine Of Predestination

with the Christian system is seen in the following story. A ship crowded with Englishmen and Mohammedans was ploughing through the waves. Accidentally one of the passengers fell overboard. The Mohammedans looked after him with indifference, saying, "If it is written in the book of destiny that he shall be saved, he shall be saved without us; and if it is written that he shall perish, we can do nothing"; and with that they left him. But the Englishmen said, "Perhaps it is written that we should save him." They threw him a rope and he was saved.

3. CHRISTIAN DOCTRINE NOT DERIVED FROM MOHAMMEDANISM

But whatever may be said about the doctrine of Predestination, no reasonable person will charge that the Christian doctrine is borrowed from the Mohammedan. Augustine, who is admitted by Protestants and Catholics alike to have been the outstanding man in the Christian Church at his time, and whom Protestants rate as the greatest between Paul and Luther, had taught this doctrine with great conviction more than two centuries before Mohammedanism arose; and it was aggressively taught by Christ and the apostles at the beginning of the Christian era, to say nothing of the place which it occupied in the Old Testament.

A study of the history and teachings of Mohammedanism reveals that it is made up of three parts, one of which was borrowed from the Jews, another from the Christians, and the third from the heathen Arabs. Hence a part of the system is nothing more nor less than Christianity at second hand. But would any reasonable Christian give up certain articles of his creed only because Mohammed adopted them in his? What great gaps such conduct would make in our creed can be seen when we learn that Mohammed believed in only one true God, that he utterly abolished all idol worship, that he believed in angels, a general resurrection and judgment, a heaven and hell, that he allowed both the Old and New Testaments, and recognized both Moses and Christ as prophets of God. It is small wonder, then, that elements of the Christian doctrine of Predestination were incorporated into the Mohammedan system and united with the heathen doctrine of Fatalism.

Furthermore, an historical study of this subject shows us that the Mohammedans have had their sort of Arminians as truly as we, and that the questions of Predestination and Free Will have been agitated among the Mohammedan doctors with as much heat and vehemence as ever they were in Christendom. The Turks of the sect of Omar hold the doctrine of absolute Predestination, while the Persians of the sect of Ali deny Predestination and assert Free Will with as much fervor as any Arminian.

4. THE TWO DOCTRINES CONTRASTED

Although the terms used in describing the Reformed and the Mohammedan doctrines of Predestination have much similarity the results of their reasoning are as far apart as the East is from the West. In fact, the further investigation proceeds the more superficial does the resemblance become. Their greatest resemblance seems to be in the teachings of each that everything which occurs happens according to the will of God. Yet very different ideas are meant by the "will of God." Islam reduces God to a category of the will and makes Him a despot, an oriental despot, who stands at abysmal heights above humanity. He cares nothing for character, but only for submission. The only affair of men is to obey His decrees, so that, as Zanchius says, Predestination becomes "a sort of blind, rapid, overbearing impetus, which, right or wrong, with means or without, carries all things violently before it, with little or no attention to the peculiar and respective nature of second causes." And concerning human freedom Dr. Zwemer says that in the doctrine of Islam, "God's omnipotence is so absolute that it excludes all self-activity on the part of the creature. . . . Whatever freedom is permitted is only under the term Kasb; that is, the appropriation of an act as his own which, after all, he is compelled to execute as a part of God's will."

The Koran and orthodox traditions have practically nothing to say about the concepts of sin and moral responsibility, and the morality of the Mohammedan system is notoriously defective. In Islam it is difficult to avoid the conclusion that God is the author of sin. The origin of sin and its character are wholly different concepts in Islam and in Christianity.

In Islam there is no doctrine of the Fatherhood of God and no purpose of redemption to soften the doctrine of the decrees. God is represented as having arbitrarily created one group of people for paradise and another group for hell, and the events of every person's life are so ordered that little place is left for moral responsibility and guilt. They deny that there has been any election in Christ to grace and glory, and that Christ died a sacrificial death for his people. They have nothing to say about the efficacy of saving grace or about perseverance, and even in regard to the predestination of temporal events the ideas are often gross and confused. The attribute of love is absent from Allah. The ideas that God should love us or that we should love God are strange ideas to Islam, and the Koran hardly hints at this subject of which the Bible is so full.

In conclusion it may be said that the Arminian creed has little appeal for the Mohammedan. So far as mission work is concerned, the Calvinistic churches entered the world of Islam earlier and more vigorously than any other group of churches, and for more than one hundred years they and they alone have challenged Islam in the land of its birth. They have occupied the strategic centers and today are carrying on far the larger part of the mission work in the Moslem world. With God's sovereignty as basis, God's glory as goal, and God's will as motive, the Presbyterian and Reformed churches are peculiarly fitted to win Moslem hearts to the allegiance of Christ, and are facing, with bright hopes of success, that most difficult of all missionary tasks, the evangelization of the Moslem world.

Footnotes:

148. Calvinism, p. 38.
149. Article, Calvinism and the World of Islam.
150. Salisbury, article, Mohammedan Doctrine of Predestination and Free Will.
151. Moslem Doctrine of God, p. 97.

Section V

1. Influence of the Doctrine in Daily Living. 2. A Source of Security and Courage. 3. Calvinistic Emphasis on the Divine Agency in Man's Salvation. 4. Only Calvinism Will Stand All Tests. 5. These Doctrines Not Unreasonable When Understood. 6. The Westminster Assembly and the Westminster Confession. 7. These Doctrines Should be Publicly Taught and Preached. 8. Ordination Vows and the Minister's Obligation. 9. The Presbyterian Church is Truly Broad and Tolerant. 10. Reason for the Depressed Fortunes of Calvinism Today.

1. INFLUENCE OF THE DOCTRINE IN DAILY LIVING

This is not a cold, barren, speculative theory, not an unnatural system of strange doctrines such as many people are inclined to believe, but a most warm and living, a most vital and important account of God's relations with men. It is a system of great practical truths which are designed and adapted, under the influence of the Holy Spirit, to mould the affections of the heart and to give right direction to the conduct. Calvin's own testimony in this respect is: "I would, in the first place, entreat my readers carefully to bear in memory the admonition which I offer; that this great subject is not, as many imagine, a mere thorny and noisy disputation, nor a speculation which wearies the minds of men without any profit; but a solid discussion eminently adapted to the service of the godly, because it builds us up soundly in the faith, trains us to humility, and lifts us up into an admiration of the unbounded goodness of God toward us, while it elevates us to praise this goodness in our highest strains. For there is not a more effectual means of building up faith than the giving our open ears to the election of God, which the Holy Spirit seals upon our heart while we hear, showing us that it stands in the eternal and immutable goodwill of God towards us; and that, therefore, it cannot be moved or altered by any storms of the world, by any assaults of Satan, by any changes, by any fluctuations or weaknesses of the flesh. For our salvation is then sure to us, when we find the cause of it in the breast of God." [152] These, we think, are true words and much needed today.

The Christian who has this doctrine in his heart knows that he is following a heaven-directed course; that his course has been foreordained for him personally; and that it is a good course. He does not yet understand all of the details, but even amid adversities he can look forward confident of the future, knowing that his eternal destiny is fixed and forever blessed, and that nothing can possibly rob him of this priceless treasure. He realizes that after he has finished the course here he shall look back over it and see that every single event in it was designed of God for a particular purpose, and that he will be thankful for having been led through those particular experiences. Once convinced of these truths, he knows that the day is surely coming when to all those who grieve or persecute him he shall be able to say, as did Joseph to his brothers, "As for you, ye meant evil against me, but God meant it for good." This exalted conception of God as high and lifted up yet personally concerned with even the smallest events leaves no place for what men commonly call chance, or luck, or fortune. When a person sees himself as one of the Lord's chosen and knows that every one of his acts has an eternal significance, he realizes more clearly how serious life is, and he is fired with a new determination to make his life count for great things.

2. A SOURCE OF SECURITY AND COURAGE

"It is the doctrine of a particular providence," says Rice, "that gives to the righteous a feeling of security in the midst of danger; that gives them assurance that the path of duty is the path of safety and of prosperity; and that encourages them to the practice of virtue, even when it exposes them to the greatest reproach and persecution. How often, when clouds and darkness seem to gather over them, do they rejoice in the assurance given by their Saviour, 'I will never leave thee, nor forsake thee.'" [153] The sense of security which this doctrine gives to the struggling saint results from the assurance that he is not committed to his own power, or rather weakness, but into the sure hands of the Almighty Father,-- that over him is the banner of love and underneath are the everlasting arms. He realizes that even the Devil and wicked men, regardless of whatever tumults they may cause, are not only restrained of God but are compelled to do His pleasure. Elisha, lonely and forgotten, counted those who were with him more than those who were against him, because he saw the chariots and horsemen of the Lord moving in the clouds. The disciples, knowing that their names were written in heaven, were prepared to endure persecutions, and on one occasion we read that after being beaten and reviled "they departed from the presence of the council rejoicing that they were accounted worthy to suffer dishonor for the Name," Acts 5:41.

"The godly consideration of predestination, and our election in Christ," says the seventeenth article in the creed of the Church of England, "is full of sweet, pleasant, and unspeakable comfort to godly persons." Paul's injunction was, "In nothing be anxious." And it is only when we know that God actually rules from the throne of the universe, and that He has ordained us to be his loved ones, that we can have that inward peace in our hearts.

Dr. Clarence E. Macartney, in a sermon on Predestination, said: "The misfortunes and adversities of life, so called, assume a different color when we look at them through this glass. It is sad to hear people trying to live over their lives again and saying to themselves: 'If I had chosen a different profession,' 'If I had taken a different turning of the road,' 'If I had married another person.' All this is weak and unChristian. The web of destiny we have woven, in a sense, with our own hands, and yet God had His part in it. It is God's part in it, and not our part, that gives us faith and hope." And Blaise Pascal, in a wonderful letter written to a bereaved friend, instead of repeating the ordinary platitudes of consolation comforted him with the doctrine of Predestination, saying: "If we regard this event, not as an effect of chance, not as a fatal necessity of nature, but as a result inevitable, just, holy, of a decree of His Providence, conceived from all eternity, to be executed in such a year, day, hour, and such a place and manner, we shall adore in humble silence the impenetrable loftiness of His secrets; we shall venerate the sanctity of His decrees; we shall bless the acts of His providence; and uniting our will with that of God Himself, we shall wish with Him, in Him and for Him, the thing that He has willed in us and for us for all eternity."

Since the true Calvinist sees God's hand and wise purpose in everything, he knows that even his sufferings, sorrows, persecutions, defeats, etc., are not the results of chance or accident, but that they have been foreseen and foreappointed, and that they are chastisements or disciplines designed for his own good. He realizes that God will not needlessly afflict His people; that in the divine plan these are all ordered in number, weight and measure; and that they shall not continue a moment longer than God sees necessary. In sorrow his heart instinctively clings to this faith, feeling that for reasons wise and gracious though unknown, the affliction was sent. However keenly afflictions may at first wound, a little reasoned thought quickly brings him to himself again, and the sorrows and tribulations, in great measure, become pointless.

And in accordance with this the Scriptures say: "To them that love God all things work together for good," Rom. 8:28; "My son, regard not lightly the chastening of the Lord, Nor faint when thou art reproved of Him; For whom the Lord loveth He chasteneth, And scourgeth every son whom he receiveth," Heb. 12:5, 6. "It is Jehovah: let Him do what seemeth Him good," I Sam. 3:18. "For I reckon that the sufferings of this present time are not worthy to be compared with the glory which shall be revealed to us-ward," Rom. 8:18. "Blessed are ye when men shall reproach you, and persecute you, and say all manner of evil against you falsely, for my sake. Rejoice, and be exceeding glad; for great is your reward in heaven; for so persecuted they the prophets that were before you," Matt. 5:11, 12. "If we endure (suffer with Him) we shall also reign with Him," II Tim. 2:12. "Jehovah gave, and Jehovah hath taken away; Blessed be the name of Jehovah," Job 1:21. When someone slanders us we shall at least not be so angry if we remember with David that "the Lord hath bidden him curse," II Sam. 16:11.

Our predestination is our one sure guarantee of salvation. Other things may give us comfort, but only this can give us certainty. It makes the Gospel to be what the word really means, "Good News." Any other system which holds that Christ's sacrifice did not actually save anyone but that it merely made salvation possible for all if they would comply with certain terms, reduces it to good advice; and any system which carries with it only a "chance" for salvation, also carries with it, of logical necessity, a "chance" to be lost. And what a difference it makes to fallen man as to whether the Gospel is good news or good advice! The world is full of good advice; even the books of heathen philosophers contained much of it; but the Gospel alone contains for man the good news that God has redeemed him.

This system, logical and severe though it may be, does not make one sad and silent, but courageous and active. Knowing himself to be immortal until his work is done, courage is a natural result. Smith's estimate of the Calvinist is expressed in the following words: "His feet plucked from the horrible pit and planted on the Eternal Rock, his heart thrilled with an adoring gratitude, his soul conscious of a Divine love that will never forsake him and a Divine energy that in him and through him is working out eternal purposes of good, he is girded with invincible strength. In a nobler sense than Napoleon ever dreamed, he knows himself to be a 'man of destiny.'" And again he says, "Calvinism is at once the most satisfying and the most stimulating of creeds." [154]

Yet along with these motives for courage are to be found others which keep the person properly humble and grateful. In the present stage of the world he sees himself as a brand plucked from the burning. Knowing himself to have been saved not by any merit or wisdom of his own, but only by God's grace and mercy, he is deeply conscious of his dependence on God, and has the greatest incentive to right living. All in all no surer way will be found to fill the mind at one time with reverence, humility, patience, and gratitude than to have it thoroughly saturated with this doctrine of Predestination.

3. CALVINISTIC EMPHASIS ON THE DIVINE AGENCY IN MAN'S SALVATION

He will be only a very imperfect Christian who does not know these deeper truths which are brought to light by the doctrine of Predestination. He can have no adequate appreciation of the glory of God, nor of the riches of grace which are given him through redemption in Christ; for nowhere else as brightly as in the predestination of the elect to life does the glory of God shine out in its full-orbed splendor, undimmed and unsullied by human works of any kind. It shows us that all that we are and all that we have that is desirable we owe to His grace. It rebukes human pride and exalts Divine mercy. It makes man to be nothing and God to be everything, and thus preserves the proper relation between the creature and the infinitely exalted Creator. It exalts one absolute Sovereign, who is the universal Ruler, and humbles all other sovereigns before Him, thus showing that all men in themselves and apart from God's special favor are on the same level. It has championed the rights of mankind wherever it has gone, in the State as well as in the Church.

The doctrine of Predestination emphasizes the Divine side of salvation while its rival system emphasizes the human side. It impresses upon us the fact that our salvation is purely of grace, and that we were no better than those who are left to suffer for their sins. It thus leads us to be more charitable and tolerant toward the unsaved and to be eternally thankful that God has saved us. It shows us that in our fallen state our wisdom is folly, our strength weakness, and our righteousness of no account. It teaches us that our hope is in God, and that from Him must come all our help. It teaches us that lesson of which so many are fatally ignorant, the blessed lesson of self-despair. Luther tells us that he "used frequently to be much offended at this doctrine," because it drove him to self-despair; but that he afterward found this kind of despair was profitable and near of kin to divine grace. In fact we may say that it solves more questions, it involves fewer difficulties, it gives more solid ground for faith and hope, and it more exalts and glorifies God than does any doctrine which contradicts it. We do not go too far in saying that it is fundamental to the religious conceptions of the Biblical writers, and that to eradicate it from either the Old or the New Testament would transform the entire Scriptural representation. The matter was well put by Dr. J. Gresham Machen when he said, "A Calvinist is constrained to regard the Arminian theology as a serious impoverishment of the Scripture doctrine of divine grace; and equally serious is the view which the Arminian must hold as to the doctrines of the Reformed Churches." [155]

It must be evident that there are just two theories which can be maintained by evangelical Christians upon this important subject; that all men who have made any study of it, and who have reached any settled conclusions regarding it, must be either Calvinists or Arminians. There is no other position which a "Christian" can take. Those who deny the sacrificial nature of Christ's death turn to a system of self salvation or naturalism, and cannot be called "Christians" in the historical and only proper sense of the term.

By way of comparison we may say that the Lutheran Church emphasizes the fact that salvation is by faith alone; the Baptist Church emphasizes the importance of the sacraments, particularly baptism, and the right of individuals and of congregations to exercise private judgment in religious affairs; the Methodist Church emphasises the love of God to men, and man's responsibility to God; the Congregational Church emphasizes the right of private judgment and of local congregations to manage their own affairs; the Roman Catholic Church emphasizes the unity of the Church, and the importance of a connection with the Apostolic church. But all of these, while good in themselves, are paled by the great doctrine of the sovereignty and majesty of God which is emphasized by the Presbyterian and Reformed Churches. While the others are more or less anthropological principles, this is a theological principle, and it presents to us a GREAT GOD who is high and lifted up, who is seated upon the throne of universal dominion.

Dr. Warfield has given us a good analysis of the formative principles which underlie the Lutheran and the Reformed Churches. After saying that the distinction is not that the Lutherans deny the sovereignty of God, nor that the Reformed deny that salvation is by faith alone he adds: "Lutheranism, springing from the throes of a guilt-burdened soul seeking peace with God, finds this peace in faith, and stops right there . . . It will know nothing beyond the peace of the justified soul. Calvinism asks with the same eagerness as Lutheranism the great question: 'What shall I do to be saved?' and answers it precisely as Lutheranism answers it. But it cannot stop there. The deeper question presses upon it, 'Whence this faith by which I am justified?' . . . It has zeal, no doubt, for salvation, but its highest zeal is for the honor of God, and it is this question which quickens its emotions and vitalizes its efforts. It begins, it centers, and it ends with the vision of God in His glory; and it sets itself before all things to render to God His rights in every sphere of life activity." [156] And again he says: "It is the vision of God in His majesty, in a word, which lies at the foundation of Calvinistic thinking," and after a man has seen this vision he "is filled on the one hand with a sense of his own unworthiness to stand in God's sight, as a creature, and much more as a sinner, and on the other with adoring wonder that nevertheless this God is a God who receives sinners." All dependence on self is gone, and he casts himself on the grace of God alone. In nature, in history, in grace, everywhere, from eternity to eternity, he sees the all-pervading activity of God.

If God has a definite plan for the redemption of man it is very important that we shall know what that plan is. The person who looks at a complicated machine but who is ignorant of the purpose it was designed to accomplish and ignorant of the relation of its several parts, must be unable to understand or usefully to apply it. Likewise, if we are ignorant of the plan of salvation, the great end aimed at, or the relation of the several parts, or if we misunderstand these, our views will be confused and erroneous; we shall be unable properly to apply it to ourselves or to exhibit it to others. Since the doctrine of Predestination reveals to us so much concerning the way of salvation, and since it gives so great comfort and assurance to the Christian, it is a great and blessed truth.

We have no hesitation in affirming that this system of belief and doctrine, as given by inspiration of the Holy Spirit, is the true and final system of Philosophy. Furthermore, Theology studies God Himself, while the physical sciences and liberal arts study only His garments. In the very nature of the case, therefore Theology must be the "Queen of the Sciences." Philosophy, as it has usually been studied by the different schools of thought, is indeed the ground and mistress of the merely human sciences, but is itself only an auxiliary science in the study of Theology.

Calvinistic Theology is the greatest subject that has ever exercised the mind of man. Its very starting point is a profound apprehension of the exaltation and perfection of God. With its sublime doctrines of God's sovereign grace, power, and glory, it rises to far greater heights than does any other system. In fact, the one to whom it is presented is moved to cry with the psalmist, "Such knowledge is too wonderful for me; It is high, I cannot attain unto it"; or to exclaim with the apostle Paul, "O the depth of the riches both of the wisdom and the knowledge of God! how unsearchable are His judgments, and His ways past finding out!" (Ps. 139:6; Rom. 11:33). It is a subject which has challenged the intellects of all great thinkers in earnest times, and there is little wonder that we are told that these are things which angels desire to look into. To pass from other systems to this one is like passing from the mouth of a river and launching out on the mighty ocean. We leave the shallows behind and feel ourselves out on the great broad deep.

4. ONLY CALVINISM WILL STAND ALL TESTS

The harmony which exists between all the branches of Scriptural doctrine is such that truth or error in regard to any of them almost inevitably produces truth or error, in a greater or less degree, in regard to all the others,--which means that only Calvinists hold views which are, in all respects, Scriptural in regard to any of the leading doctrines of Christianity. This does not mean that the main substance of the most important doctrines, such as the Divinity of Christ, His sacrificial death, His resurrection, the work of the Holy Spirit, etc., are not held by others; but that the general tendency of mistaken views in regard to these distinctively Calvinistic tenets is to lead to greater departures from sound doctrines on other subjects. As a general rule anti-Calvinists so seriously impoverish doctrines such as the atonement, the agency of the Holy Spirit, the guilt and inability of man, regeneration, etc., that these are often little more than empty words; and along with this impoverishment goes the tendency to neglect them entirely. Anti-Calvinists commonly make little distinction between the objective work of Christ for us, and the subjective work in us; and for all practical purposes the atonement is reduced to little or nothing else than an exhibition and proof of God's indiscriminate love to men, through which it is shown that God is ready and willing to forgive. The tendency of other systems is to the "moral persuasion" theory of the atonement, while Calvinism holds that the suffering of Christ was a full satisfaction made to the justice of God,--that his sufferings were a full equivalent of those which were due to His people for their sin.

We are living in a day in which we see practically all of the historic Protestant churches attacked by unbelief from within. Many of them have already succumbed; and the line of descent has invariably been from Calvinism to Arminianism, and from Arminianism to Modernism or Unitarianism; and this latter state has proved to be self-destructive. We firmly believe that the fortunes of Christianity are bound up with the fortunes of Calvinism. Certainly the history of Modernism and Unitarianism in this country has proved that they are too weak to maintain themselves. Where the principles of Calvinism are abandoned, there is a powerful tendency leading downward into the depths of Naturalism. Some have declared--and rightly we believe--that there is no consistent middle ground between Calvinism and Atheism.

These distinctions which we have set forth between Calvinism and Arminianism are broad and important; and until one has made a special study of these truths he does not realize what a large amount of heresy has been incorporated into the Arminian system. If one system is true, the other is radically false. As strict Calvinists we believe these doctrines to embody final truth and to be eternally right. We believe this to be the only system of Christian truth which is taught in the Bible and the only one that can be logically and respectably defended before the world. And certainly it is much easier to defend a

The Reformed Doctrine Of Predestination

type of Christianity which is in harmony with both Scripture and reason than to defend any other type. We believe that Calvinism and consistent theism do not merely have points of contact but that they are identical, and that to fall away from Calvinism is to fall away by just so much from a truly theistic conception of the universe. Dr. Warfield has said that Calvinism is "Theism come to its rights," that it is "Evangelicalism in its pure and only stable expression," that it is "religion at the height of its conception." We believe that the future of Christianity--as its past has done--lies in its hands, and that as Christianity progresses in the world this system of doctrine will gradually come to the front.

Because of the inconsistent position of Arminianism as a half-way measure between a religion of grace and a religion of works, it has been able to offer but little resistance to the naturalistic tendencies of the last few years. Practically all of the professedly Arminian churches have been swallowed up by the present day Liberalism.

"If we are not only to defend Christianity against modern attacks," says Dr. S. G. Craig, "but to commend it with any hope of success to the modern world, we must undertake the task armed with a consistent and scientifically conceived life and world view that rests on Christian facts and principles. . . . I hold with those who believe that such a consistent Christian life and world view is given us only in Calvinism, and hence that a renaissance of Calvinism is an outstanding need of the times if we are successfully to defend even what we call common Christianity in the forum of the world's thought." The late Henry B. Smith was right at least in principle when he wrote, "One thing is certain--that infidel science will rout everything excepting thorough-going Christian orthodoxy. All the flabby theories, and the molluscous formations, and the immediate purgatories of speculation will go by the board. The fight will be between a stiff thorough-going othodoxy and a stiff thorough-going infidelity. It will be, e.g., Augustine or Comte, Athanasius or Hegel, Luther or Schopenhauer, J. S. Mill or John Calvin." The fight is between the naturalism of science and the supernaturalism of Christianity; all compromising schemes are doomed to failure. (Let it be understood at this point that we have no quarrel with true science as such. We recognize the great value of Biology, Chemistry, Physics, Astronomy, etc., and realize that much of our twentieth century progress has been possible only through the contributions which these sciences have made. We welcome truth from whatever source it comes, and believe that in the end it will be seen to substantiate Christianity. The psalmist declared, "The heavens declare the glory of God; And the firmament showeth His handiwork," Ps. 19:1; and again, "O Jehovah, our Lord, how excellent is thy name in all the earth," Ps. 8:1; and certainly the more we know about these things the better we shall understand God. Our quarrel rather is with certain unbelieving scientists who attempt to bring their anti-Christian or even atheistic theories over into the spheres of religion and philosophy, and who profess to speak with authority on subjects concerning which they are ignorant.)

It is very interesting to notice how, in the history of the Church, other systems of theology have risen and fallen while this system has steadily endured. Arminianism, in its present form at least, is of comparatively recent date. From the time of the Reformation until late in the eighteenth century it was consistently outlawed by Protestant church counsels and creeds. Nor has it fared much better in the Catholic Church. In the fourth century Augustine succeeded in making his doctrine of Predestination the recognized doctrine of Christendom and at no time has the Catholic Church consistently and officially adopted the tenets of Arminianism. Likewise Neatorianism, Arianism, Pelagianism, Semi-Pelagianism, Socinianism, etc., have risen, have had their day, and passed out; while this system, known in different ages as Augustinianism or Calvinism, has remained fundamentally the same in its basic principles. Is not this in itself a strong proof that it is the true system? In regard to the Calvinism of the Westminster Confession, Dr. C. W. Hodge has said: "The newer modifications of Calvinism have passed away, and this pure consistent form of supernaturalism and evangelicalism stands as an impregnable barrier against the floods of naturalism which threaten to overwhelm all the churches in Christendom."

In Calvinism alone does the logical and consistent mind find rest. That it is a logical system is admitted even by its opponents. A man who is acquainted with Calvinism will either love or hate it, but even if he hates it, he cannot but speak respectfully of it. The criticism is sometimes made that it places too much stress on logic and too little on emotion. It is true that this anthracite Calvinism does not blaze up like straw; but it is also true that once afire it produces an intense and steady heat. "Calvinism," says Prof. H. H. Meeter, "bears the distinction among religious groups of being highly intellectual. Calvinism is known for its dialectics. The Calvinists are recognized as the logicians par excellence among theologians. Oliver Wendell Holmes even went so far as to satirize this aspect of Calvinism in his burlesque: 'The Deacon's Masterpiece.' The old one-hoss shay, which was so well constructed that every nut and bolt and bar and spoke was of equal strength and collapsed all at once before the meeting house, was to him the story of Calvinism. As a masterpiece of logic it had continued for ages, but was supposed to have collapsed completely when transcendentalism gained the ascendancy in New England." [157]

The objection, however, that it over-emphasizes logic, has no adequate basis, as anyone who approaches the system from a sympathetic standpoint can readily see. Yet if we are to err on either side it is probably better to err on the side of the intellect than on the side of the emotions. But who ever heard of a system being thrown out because it was too logical? Instead we glory in its logical consistency.

5. THESE DOCTRINES NOT UNREASONABLE WHEN UNDERSTOOD

Perhaps no other system of thought has been so grossly and grievously and at times so deliberately misrepresented as has Calvinism. Many of those who have criticized Calvinism have done so without making any adequate study of the system, and it may truly be said that our opponents in general know little of our opinions except what they have picked up by hearsay in which there is neither connection nor consistency. The doctrine of Predestination especially makes the wisdom of the world a laughing stock, and in turn the wisdom of the world scoffs at Predestination. If any doctrine is to the Jews a stumbling block and to the Gentiles foolishness, certainly this one is. Nakedly stated, the doctrine of Predestination seems paradoxical; and those who are acquainted with no more than the mere statement of it are likely to feel surprised that it could have been maintained by the pious and thoughtful minds that have maintained it. But in this case, as in many others, when we carefully examine its ground and construction, its paradoxical character is at least diminished, if it does not disappear altogether.

Hence we ask that this system shall be examined without passion and that it shall be studied in its relations and logical consistency. We have already seen that it is abundantly established on Scripture authority; and when we add to this the evidence which comes from the laws of Nature and the facts of human life, it becomes altogether possible, probable, just, and righteous. Viewed in this light it ceases to be the arbitrary illogical, immoral doctrine that its opponents delight to picture, and becomes a doctrine which sheds glory on the divine Majesty. These, of course, are not the doctrines which the natural man expects to find. Salvation by works is the system which most naturally appeals to unenlightened reason; and if we had been left to develop a system ourselves, there is hardly one chance in a thousand that we would have developed a system in which a redeemer acting in his representative capacity would have earned these blessings and graciously given them to his people. Says Zanchius, "The judgment of the flesh, or of mere unregenerates reason, usually starts back from this truth with horror; but, on the contrary, the judgment of a spiritual man will embrace it with affection," (p. 152). "If Arminianism most commends itself to our feelings," says Froude, "Calvinism is nearer to the facts, however harsh and forbidding those facts may seem." It is plain that Calvinism makes its appeal to Divine revelation rather than to man's reason; to facts rather than sentiment; to knowledge rather than supposition; to conscience rather than to emotion.

As stated before, many people see nothing in this system but a strange sort of foolishness. But when studied with a little care these doctrines are found to be neither so uncertain nor so difficult as men would lead us to believe; and the uncertainty and difficulty which does attach to them is due largely to our pride, love of sin, and ignorance of the real state of our heart. Those who have come to accept this system almost feel that they are living in a different world, so different is their outlook upon life. "Wherever the sons of God turn their eyes," says Calvin, "they behold such wonderful instances of blindness, ignorance and insensibility, as fills them with horror; while they, in the midst of such darkness, have received Divine illumination, and know it, and feel it, to be so." [158]

If we may paraphrase the words of Pope we can most fittingly say of this subject: "A little Predestination is a dangerous thing; Then drink deep, or else touch not the sacred spring." Here, as in some other instances, first draughts confuse and unsettle the mind, but deeper draughts overcome the intoxicating effects and bring us back to our right senses.

This sublime philosophy of God's sovereignty and man's freedom is found in all parts of the Bible. No attempt, however, is made to explain to us how these two factors are related. The unvarying assumption is that God is the Sovereign Ruler who governs even the intimate thoughts and feelings and impulses of men; yet on the other hand man is never represented as anything else than an intelligent, free, moral agent who is responsible for his actions. The doctrines of foreordination, sovereignty, and effectual providential control, go hand in hand with those of the liberty and responsibility of rational creatures. It is not claimed that the doctrine of Predestination is free from all difficulties, but it is claimed that its denial is attended with more and greater difficulties. That a Being of infinite wisdom, power and goodness would create a universe and then turn it adrift like some huge vessel without a pilot, is a supposition which subverts our basic ideas of God, which contradicts the repeated testimony of the Scriptures, and which is contrary to our daily experience and common sense. Charles Hodge prefaces his discussion of "The Decrees of God," with the following statement: "It must be remembered that Theology is not Philosophy. It does not assume to discover truth, or to reconcile what it teaches as true with all other truths. Its province is simply to state what God has revealed in His word, and to vindicate those statements as far as possible from misconceptions and objections. This limited and humble office of Theology it is especially necessary to bear in mind, when we come to speak of the acts and purposes of God. 'The things of God knoweth no man; but the Spirit of God' (1 Cor. 2:11). In treating, therefore, of the decrees of God, all that is proposed is simply to state what the Spirit has seen fit to reveal on that subject." [159]

6. THE WESTMINSTER ASSEMBLY AND THE WESTMINSTER CONFESSION

This system of Theology, which is usually referred to as Calvinism or the Reformed Faith, finds its most perfect expression in the Westminster Confession. The Westminster Assembly was called together by the English Parliament. Its work extended over a period of five and one half years, and was finished in 1648. It was a representative body, made up of one hundred and twenty-one ministers or theologians, eleven lords, twenty commoners, from all the counties of England and the Universities of Oxford and Cambridge, with seven commissioners from Scotland. And whether judged by the extent and ability of its labors, or by its influence upon later generations, it stands first among Protestant councils. The most important production of the Assembly was its Confession of Faith, a matchless compendium of Biblical truth which was the noblest achievement of the best period of British Protestantism. It has rightly been called the theological masterpiece of the last four centuries. Dr. Warfield said of the Westminster Confession that it was "The most complete, the most fully elaborated and carefully guarded, the most perfect, and the most vital expression that has ever been framed by the hand of man, of all that enters into what we call evangelical religion, and of all that must be safeguarded if evangelical religion is to persist in the world."

Dr. F. W. Loetscher, in an address before the General Assembly of the Presbyterian Church, U. S. A., 1929, referred to the Westminster Standards as, "these incomparable works of religious and theological genius;" "those noblest products of the great religious revival that we call the Reformation; those matchless formularies which at least English-speaking Christendom has come to regard as the most comprehensive, precise, and adequate embodiment of the pure Gospel of the grace of God." And in the same address he also said, "I realize that such a characterization of these venerable documents will appear to many, even among those whom I have the honor of addressing on this occasion, as an unwarranted exaggeration, if not a sheer anachronism. For the fashion of the day minimizes the value of creeds, and our Confession, like many others, must often undergo the sorrowful experience of being damned with faint praise even in the home of its reputed adherents."

Dr. Curry, who for a time was Editor of the "Methodist Advocate" of New York, in an editorial on Creeds, called the Westminster Confession "the ablest, clearest, and most comprehensive system of Christian doctrine ever framed--a wonderful monument to the intellectual greatness of its framers."

In these standards we have the grandest conception of theological truth that has ever entered the mind of man. As a system it exhibits far more depth of theological insight than does any other, and it is worthy the admiration of the ages. It is a system which produces men of strong doctrinal convictions. The person who holds it has a definite basis for belief and is not "tossed to and fro and carried about with every wind of doctrine, by the sleight of men, in craftiness, after the wiles of error."

But while the Westminster Confession is so logically wrought out, so clear and comprehensive in its statements, how sadly it is neglected today by the members and even by the ministers of the Presbyterian and Reformed Churches! "The Confession of Faith," says Dr. Frank H. Stevenson, the first president of the Board of Trustees of Westminster Theological Seminary, "remains in the Constitution of the Presbyterian Church, neglected, well-nigh forgotten, but unamended, untinkered with in twenty-five years of doctrinal confusion. It is the creed of the church, and every line sustains a courageous stand. Not for its own sake alone, but because it gives full honor to Christ it is a worthy standard beneath which to carry on what Paul prophetically called 'the good fight of faith.'" [160] With those words we fully agree.

7. THESE DOCTRINES SHOULD BE PUBLICLY TAUGHT AND PREACHED

The doctrine of sovereign Predestination, as well as the other distinctive doctrines of the Calvinistic system, should be publicly taught and preached in order that true believers may know themselves to be special objects of God's love and mercy, and that they may be confirmed and strengthened in the assurance of their salvation. What a misfortune it is for the truth which reflects so much glory upon its Author and which is the very foundation of happiness in man to be suppressed or to be confined merely to those who are specializing in Theology! For the Christian this should be one of the most comforting doctrines in all the Scriptures. Furthermore, there is scarcely a distinctive Christian doctrine that can be preached in its purity and fullness without a reference to Predestination. These doctrines are so reciprocally related and interwoven that any one has a bearing on others; and this doctrine of Predestination is the one which unites and organizes all the others. Apart from it the others cannot be seen in their true light nor their relative importance properly estimated. Concerning the place of the doctrine of Predestination in the Christian system, Zanchius writes as follows: "The whole circle of arts have a kind of mutual bond and connection, and by a sort of reciprocal relationship are held together and interwoven with each other. Much the same may be said of this important doctrine; it is the bond which connects and keeps together the whole Christian system, which, without this, is like a system of sand, ever ready to fall to pieces. It is the cement which holds the fabric together; nay, it is the very soul that animates the whole frame. It is so blended and interwoven with the entire scheme of

Gospel doctrine that when the former is excluded, the latter bleeds to death." [161]

We are commanded to go and "preach the gospel"; but in so far as any part of it is mutilated or passed over in silence we are unfaithful to that command. Certainly no Christian minister is at liberty to take his scissors and cut out of his Bible all of those passages which are not to his liking. Yet for all practical purposes is not that the effect when important doctrines are deliberately passed over in silence? Paul could say to his Christian converts, "I shrank not from declaring unto you anything that was profitable"; and again, "I testify unto you this day, that I am pure from the blood of all men. For I shrank not from declaring unto you the whole counsel of God," Acts 20:20, 26, 27. If the Christian minister today would be able to say this, let him beware of withholding such important truth. Paul repeatedly referred to these doctrines. His letter to the Romans (chs. 8 to 11) and to the Ephesians (chs. 1 and 2) are the most prominent in this respect. In writing to the Romans he was in effect bringing these things before the whole world and stamping a universal imprimatur upon them; and if he considered them so important that they should be written to the primitive Christians in the young church at Rome which he had not visited, we may be sure that they are important for Christians today. Christ and the apostles preached these things, and that not merely to a few people but to the multitudes. There is hardly a chapter in the Gospel of John which does not either mention or imply election or reprobation. When a plain, straight-forward, common-sense man asks, "Is the doctrine of Predestination taught in the Bible?" the answer certainly should be in the affirmative,--that it is constantly taught in both the Old and the New Testaments. Furthermore, the Westminster Confession states it very explicitly. Hence we are to teach it and to explain it in so far as that is possible. Paul urges us to "put on the whole armor of God"; yet what a large part of that armor a person lacks if he is ignorant of this great doctrine of Predestination!

Augustine rebuked those in his day who were passing over the doctrine of Predestination in silence, and when he was sometimes charged with preaching it too freely he refuted the charge by saying that where Scripture leads we may follow. Luther, and especially Calvin, strongly emphasized these truths, and Calvin developed them so clearly and forcefully that the system has ever since been called "Calvinism." Not only in the countries where the Reformation was at its best, but later in Holland, Scotland, England at the time of the Westminster Assembly, and America during the earlier periods of her history, these doctrines were commonly preached and were the means of developing deep religious convictions in all classes of people.

It was Calvin's conviction that the doctrine of Election should be made the very center of the Church's confession, and that if it were not thus emphasized the Church should be prepared to see this wonderful doctrine buried and forgotten. The correctness of his views is shown by the fact that those groups which did not emphasize it, whether in England, Scotland, Holland, the United States, or Canada, have, for all practical purposes, lost it completely.

The one who is entrusted with a message from the King must give it as he has received it; and surely the greatest of all messages, that of predestination unto life, should not be passed over in silence. "An ambassador," says Zanchius, "is to deliver the whole message with which he is charged. He is to omit no part of it, but must declare the mind of the sovereign he represents, fully and without reserve. He is to say neither more nor less than the instructions of his court require, else he comes under displeasure, perhaps loses his head. Let the minister of Christ weigh this well." [162] These are doctrines which have been expressly given by divine revelation. They make wholly for the divine glory, bringing comfort and courage to the elect, and leaving sinners without excuse. True, man does not like to be told that he is a sinner and unable to help himself. Such doctrine is too humiliating. But if he is lost without Christ, the sooner he knows it the better. For us to refuse to preach it is to be false to our Lord and negligent in our duty to our fellow men. To ignore it is to act like a doctor who refuses to operate to save the life of a patient because he knows the operation will cause the patient pain. If these truths were fearlessly and courageously preached Modernism and unbelief would not creep into our churches as they are doing. The group of professing Christians would perhaps be smaller but more loyal and effective in Christian works.

The preaching of these doctrines will, of course, stir up some controversy. But controversy is not to he looked upon as an unmixed evil. As long as error exists there must be controversy. The attacks which were made upon the doctrines of the Church by the pagans and heretics during the early Christian centuries and in the Middle Ages forced the Church to reexamine her doctrines, to work them out, to explain, purify and fortify them. They compelled a closer study of the Bible. A number of brilliant churchmen arose who wrote books and articles on the Christian Faith, and as a result the Church was greatly enriched by the intellectual and spiritual fruits thus produced.

It is a mistake to say that people will no longer listen to doctrinal preaching. Let the minister believe his doctrines; let him present them with conviction and as living issues, and he will find sympathetic audiences. Today we see thousands of people turning away from pulpit discussions of current events, social topics, political issues, and merely ethical questions, and trying to fill themselves with the husks of occult and puerile philosophies. In many ways we are spiritually poorer than we

The Reformed Doctrine Of Predestination

should be, because in our theological confusion and bewilderment we have failed to do justice to these great doctrinal principles. If rightly preached these doctrines are most interesting and profitable. The author's experience as a Bible teacher has shown him that no other subjects so electrify and hold the attention of students as do these. Furthermore, we may ask, What excuse has the Presbyterian Church for its continued existence as a separate denomination if Calvinism is to be discarded as a non-essential? Much of our present-day weakness is due to the fact that our people have had but little instruction concerning these distinctive doctrines of the Presbyterian system, and this lack of instruction has led directly into the ecumenical movement in which attempts are being made to unite churches of very different types with only a minimum of doctrine.

The doctrine of Predestination is a doctrine for genuine Christians. Considerable caution should be exercised in preaching it to the unconverted. It is almost impossible to convince a non-Christian of its truthfulness, and in fact the heart of the unregenerate man usually revolts against it. If it is stressed before the simpler truths of the Christian system are mastered, it will likely be misunderstood and in that case it may only drive the person into deeper despair. In preaching to the unconverted or to those who are just beginning the Christian life, our part consists mainly in presenting and stressing man's part in the work of salvation,--faith, repentance, moral reform, etc. These are the elementary steps so far as man's consciousness extends. At that early stage little need be said about the deeper truths which relate to God's part. As in the study of Mathematics we do not begin with algebra and calculus but with the simple problems of arithmetic, so here the better way is to first present the more elementary truths. Then after the Person is saved and has traveled some distance in the Christian way he comes to see that in his salvation God's work was primary and his was only secondary, that he was saved through grace and not by his own works. As Calvin himself put it, the doctrine of Predestination is "not a matter for children to think much about"; and Strong says, "This doctrine is one of those advanced teachings of Scripture which requires for its understanding a mature mind and a deep experience. The beginner in the Christian life may not see its value or even its truth, but with increasing years it will become a staff to lean upon."[163] But while it is true that this doctrine cannot be adequately appreciated by the unconverted nor by those who are just beginning the Christian life, it should be the common property of all those who have traveled some distance in that way.

It is worthy of notice that in developing his "Institutes" Calvin did not treat the doctrine of Predestination in the early chapters. He first developed the other doctrines of the Christian system and deliberately passed over this even in several cases where we might naturally have expected to find it. Then in the last part of his theological discussion it is developed fully and is made the crown and glory of the entire system.

It may be further said that in preaching this doctrine care should be taken not to exaggerate any statements, and also to show that it is founded not upon arbitrary will but upon infinite wisdom and love.

8. ORDINATION VOWS AND THE MINISTER'S OBLIGATION

Every minister and elder who is ordained in the Presbyterian and Reformed churches solemnly vows before God and men that he sincerely receives and adopts the Confession of Faith of his church as containing the system of doctrine taught in the Holy Scriptures, (Pres. Ch. U. S. A., see Form of Government, XIII:IV; XV:XII).Since these confessions are thoroughly Calvinistic, this means that none but Calvinists can honestly and intelligently accept this ordination. An Arminian has not the slightest right to be a minister in a Calvinistic church, and any Arminian who does become a minister in a Calvinistic church lacks good morality as well as good theology. To declare one thing and believe the contrary is hardly consistent with the character of an honest man. And yet while our ordination vows are so thoroughly Calvinistic, how few ministers there are who proclaim these doctrines! One could scarcely tell from the pulpit utterances of the nominally Calvinistic churches today what the essentials of the Reformed Faith really are. Our pulpits as well as our church publications, our schools and seminaries, ring with the Arminian doctrines of merit and free-will. The present day Presbyterian and Reformed Churches seem to have no adequate conception of the fundamental importance of their great doctrinal heritage. The writings of Calvin and Luther, of the great Puritan divines, and of the great theologians since that time should be better known to our young theologians than merely by their titles. The scholastic form and cumbersome style of these works has perhaps deterred many from making a thorough study of them, but we should remember that the study of Theology is not indulged in merely for the pleasure it affords. We do not expect to find novels when we take up the folios of the old masters in Theology.

Many young men enter the ministry without any real acquaintance with the doctrine of the Church in which they intend to serve, and when they hear of any who preach agreeably to the Westminster Standards they consider them as "setters forth of strange doctrines." The great need of the Church today is for men of firm convictions and settled minds rather than the latitudinarian type of Modernists or Liberals who wander to and fro rejoicing that they have no dogmatic opinions and no theological preferences. It seems that the majority of our ministers no longer believe these Calvinistic doctrines, and that many of them, contrary to their solemn ordination vows, are putting forth by crafty and unfair methods their strongest efforts to destroy the faith that they have solemnly sworn they have been moved by the Holy Spirit to defend. If these doctrines are true they should be clearly and aggressively taught and defended in our churches, seminaries, and colleges. If they are not true they should be stricken from the Confession of Faith. Honesty is as important in theology as in trade or commerce, as important in a religious denomination as in a political party. A Presbyterian minister is not a free lance, but is a presbyter who has pledged himself to this system of doctrine. Those who deny these doctrines in Presbyterian pulpits are being false to their ordination vows, and should withdraw to denominations holding their views. Certainly no church officer has a right to accept the honors and remunerations which come from the outward acceptance of a creed which he does not believe or teach.

"The creed of a Church," says Shedd, "is a solemn contract between church-members: even more so than the platform of a political party is between politicians. The immorality of violating a contract, some people do not seem to perceive when a religious denomination is concerned; but when a political party is the body to be affected by the breach of the pledge none are sharper to see and none are more vehement to denounce the double-dealing. Should a faction arise within the Republican party, for example, and endeavor to alter the platform while still retaining the offices and salaries which they had secured by professing entire allegiance to the party, and promising to adopt the fundamental principles upon which it was founded and by which it is distinguished from the Democratic and other political parties, the charge of political dishonesty would ring through the whole rank and file of Republicanism. And when in the exercise of party discipline such factionists are turned out of office, and perhaps expelled from the political organization, if the cry of political heresy-hunting and persecution should be raised, the only answer vouchsafed by the Republican press would be that of scorn. When political dishonesty would claim toleration under cover of more 'liberal' policies than the party is favoring, and would keep hold on party emoluments while advocating different sentiments from those of the mass of the party, it is curtly told that no one is compelled to join the Republican party or to remain in it, but that if a person does join it or remains in it, he must strictly adopt the party creed and make no attempts, secret or open, to alter it. That a Republican creed is for Republicans and no others, seems to be agreed on all sides; but that a Calvinistic creed is for Calvinists and no others, seems to be doubted by some. . .

"If in the heart of the Democratic party a school should arise which would claim the right, while remaining in the party, to convert the body to Republican principles and measures, it would be told that the proper place for such a project is outside of Democracy, not within it. The right of the school to its own opinions would not be disputed, but the right to maintain and spread them with the funds and influences of the Democratic party would be denied. . . . They would say to the malcontents 'We cannot prevent you from having your own peculiar views and do not desire to, but you have no right to ventilate them in our organization.'" [164]

Calvinistic churches are sometimes accused of intolerance or persecution when departures from the church creed are made the subject of judicial inquiry. We submit, however, that this charge is unjust and that such a church is entirely within her rights when she requires her ministers and teachers to conform their preaching and teaching to the denominational standards.

From these considerations it will be clear why many of us have so little enthusiasm for church union movements which would unite groups holding widely different systems of doctrine. We believe the Calvinistic system to be the only one set forth in the Scriptures and vindicated by reason, and therefore the most stable and influential in the production of righteousness. Yet to all who differ from us we cordially allow the right of private judgment, and sincerely rejoice in the good which they are able to accomplish. We rejoice that other systems of theology approximate ours; yet we cannot consent to impoverish our message by setting forth less than what we find the Scriptures to teach. If a union could be consummated in which Calvinism would be accepted as the system of truth taught in the Bible, we should be delighted to enter into it; but we believe that for us to accept anything short of that would be to surrender vital truth, and that anything vague enough to embrace Calvinism and other systems of doctrine would not be worth propagating. We believe that the superficial advantage of numbers which would result from such a union would amount to but little when balanced against the spiritual discord which would inevitably follow. Hence, we wish to remain Presbyterian until the doctrines of the Reformed Faith, which are simply the doctrines of the Word of God, become the doctrines of the Church universal.

These doctrines, now so disregarded or unknown if not openly opposed, were universally believed and maintained by the reformers, and following the Reformation were written into the creeds, catechisms, or articles of every one of the Protestant churches. Any one who will compare the printed pulpit utterances of our own day with those of the Reformers will have no difficulty in perceiving how contradictory and irreconcilably hostile they are to each other.

The Reformed Doctrine Of Predestination

9. THE PRESBYTERIAN CHURCH IS TRULY BROAD AND TOLERANT

While the Presbyterian Church is pre-eminently a doctrinal Church, she never demands the full acceptance of her standards by any applicant for admission to her fold. A credible profession of faith in Christ is her only condition of Church membership. She does demand that her ministers and elders shall be Calvinists; yet this is never demanded of lay members. As Calvinists we gladly recognize as our fellow Christians any who trust Christ for their salvation, regardless of how inconsistent their other beliefs may be. We do believe, however, that Calvinism is the only system which is wholly true. And while one can be a Christian without believing the whole Bible, his Christianity will be imperfect in proportion as he departs from the Biblical system of doctrine. In this connection Prof. F. E. Hamilton has well said: "A blind, deaf and dumb man can, it is true, know something of the world about him through the senses remaining, but his knowledge will be very imperfect and probably inaccurate. In a similar way, a Christian who never knows or never accepts the deeper teachings of the Bible which Calvinism embodies, may be a Christian, but he will be a very imperfect Christian, and it should be the duty of those who know the whole truth to attempt to lead him into the only storehouse which contains the full riches of true Christianity." "The Calvinist," says Dr. Craig, "does not differ from other Christians in kind, but only in degree, as more or less good specimens of a thing differ from more or less bad specimens of a thing." We are not all Calvinists as we travel the road to heaven, but we shall all be Calvinists when we get there. It is our firm conviction that every redeemed soul in heaven will be a thorough-going Calvinist. Christians in general must admit that when we all "attain unto the unity of the faith" (Eph. 4:13), and know the full truth, we shall be either all Calvinists or all Arminians.

It must always be kept in mind that Calvinism includes much more than those peculiar features which distinguish it from Arminianism. It holds firmly to the great doctrines of the Trinity, the Divinity of Christ, the Miracles, the Atonement, the Resurrection, the Inspiration of the Scriptures, etc., which form the common faith of evangelical Christendom.

In regard to the truly broad and tolerant nature of the Presbyterian Church we shall now take the privilege of quoting rather extensively from Dr. E. W. Smith's admirable little book, "The Creed of Presbyterians,"--more than sixty-five thousand copies of which have already been distributed.

"The catholicity of Presbyterianism, its liberality of thought and feeling, its freedom from sectarian narrowness and bigotry, is one of its crowning characteristics . . . The catholicity of Presbyterianism is no mere sentiment. It is not a thing of individual profession or platform declamation. It is rooted in our creed. It is proclaimed in our Standards. It is embodied in our doctrine of the Church. 'The visible Church,' says our Confession, 'consists of all those throughout the world who profess the true religion together with their children.' (Conf. of F., XXV:2). Thus, formally and publicly do we repudiate the name of 'the' church and claim only to be a church of Jesus Christ. Not only do our Standards contain no denunciation of the antagonistic views of sister Evangelical churches, they are said to be the only church Standards in existence which make explicit and authoritative recognition of other evangelical churches as 'true branches of the Church of Jesus Christ.' (Book of Church Order, Chap. II, sec. II, par. II). To the 'Communion of Saints,' our Confession devotes an entire chapter. We are there taught that our 'holy fellowship and communion,' in each other's gifts and graces, in worship and mutual service of love, 'is to be extended unto all who in every place call upon the name of the Lord Jesus.' (XXVI:2).

"The catholicity of our standards finds beautiful expression in the Presbyterian attitude toward all sister evangelical churches. While a branch of evangelical Christendom unchurches all sister denominations, such action is abhorrent to Presbyterian feeling and unknown to Presbyterian practice. Members and ministers of other evangelical churches we treat as in all respects true members and ministers equally with ourselves of the Church of Christ.

"While several of these churches decline giving letters of dismission from their own to other communions, we make no distinctions. We dismiss members to Baptist, Episcopal or other Christian congregations, in precisely the same form, and with the same affectionate confidence, as though we were transferring them to churches of our own name.

"Some evangelical denominations deny the validity of ordinances performed by sister churches, and when a minister or a member would come to them from a sister denomination, the one must be re-ordained, the other re-baptized. Such denial is utterly contrary to the Presbyterian spirit and usage. We never repeat the rite. The ordinance of a sister church we accept as no less valid than if performed by ourselves.

"While from many evangelical pulpits the ministers of sister churches are shut out, or from co-officiation in sacred ceremonies, such exclusion is never practiced by us. It is alien to the Presbyterian heart and habit. We are as free and cordial in asking Episcopal, Baptist, or other evangelical ministers, to occupy our pulpits, or assist us officially in administering the Lord's Supper, as in asking our own pastors.

"We unchurch no true Christian. We reject no ministerial ordination. We repudiate no administered scriptural sacrament of a sister church. Returning good for evil, we recognize our high-church fellow clergyman as a true minister of Christ, and our immersionist brother as having been validly baptized. We respond with all our hearts to the 'Amen' of the Methodists; we join with our brethren in any psalmody that puts the crown upon the brow of Jesus; and most lovingly do we invite our fellow Christians of every name and denomination to partake with us of the emblems of His broken body and His shed blood. We have no prejudice, no peculiarity, no crotchet of any kind, to restrict our Christian sympathies and dig a chasm between us and other servants of our Master. Our catholicity is wide as evangelical Christendom," (pp. 189-193).

And again he says: "The catholicity of the Presbyterian Church appears in her one condition of church membership. She demands nothing whatever for admission to her fold except a confession, uncontradicted by the life, of faith in the Lord Jesus Christ. The applicant is not asked to subscribe to our Standards or assent to our theology. He is not required to be a Calvinist, but only to be a Christian. He is not examined as to his orthodoxy, but only as to his 'faith in and obedience unto Christ.' (Conf. of Faith, 28:4). He may have imperfect notions about the Trinity and the Atonement; he may question infant baptism, election, and final perseverance; but if he trusts and obeys Christ as his personal Saviour and Lord, the door of the Presbyterian Church is open to him, and all the privileges of her communion are his.

"When churches prescribe conditions of membership other than the simple conditions of salvation, they are guilty of making it harder to get into the Church than into heaven. To such ecclesiastical tyranny and exclusiveness the Presbyterian Church stands in utter contrast. Her Standards declare that as simple faith in Christ makes us members of God's family, so 'those who have made a profession of faith in Christ are entitled to all the rights and privileges of the Church.' (Bk. Ch. Order, III, 3.) Thus with a broad and beautiful catholicity the gates of our Presbyterian Zion are flung wide as the gates of Heaven for all the children of God," (pp. 199, 200).

After declaring that the Presbyterian and Reformed constitute the largest Protestant family in the world, Dr. Smith, in eloquent language, gives the following grand summary of her missionary achievement: "More catholic and imposing even than the Presbyterian numbers is the worldwide range of the Presbyterian empire. While the adherents of other Protestant communions are more or less massed in single countries, the Lutherans in Germany, the Episcopalians in England, the Methodists and Baptists in the United States, the line of the Presbyterian Church is gone out through all the earth. She thrives this hour in more continents, among a greater number of nations and peoples and languages than any other evangelical church in the world. As her witness in Continental Europe, she has the historic Presbyterian Reformed Churches of Austria. Bohemia, Galicia, Moravia, Hungary, Belgium, France, Germany, Italy, Greece, the Netherlands, of Russia, and Switzerland and Spain. She is rooted and fruitful in Africa, in Australia, in Asia, in Great Britain, in North America, in South America, in the West Indies, in New Zealand, in Melanesia,--the people of this faith and order gird the earth. Presbyterianism possesses a power of adaptation unparalleled by any other system. It has furnished an unduly large proportion of the outstanding preachers, evangelists, editors, authors, educators, statesmen, and civic leaders; and from its abundant spiritual life are going forth the mighty forces of Christian missions into all the heathen world," (p. 211).

10. REASONS FOR THE DEPRESSED FORTUNES OF CALVINISM TODAY

What reasons are we to assign for the present day defection from Calvinism? That the celebrated five points of the Calvinistic star are not shining so brightly today will hardly be disputed by any one. When we consider the trend of present day thought we readily conclude that the fortunes of Calvinism (if we may change the figure) are not at their flood. In many places where it once flourished it has now almost disappeared. There are practically no "Calvinists without reserve" left among the acknowledged leaders of religious thought in France, Switzerland, or Germany where Calvinism was once able to give such a good account of itself. In England Calvinism has practically disappeared. In America there is no longer any large church in its corporate capacity aggressively maintaining the Calvinistic heritage. In Scotland, however, we are glad to say that the heroic Free Church still raises its voice amid the sad defection of the larger bodies. And in the great free church of Holland, the "Gereformeerde kerken," we have a truly Calvinistic church in the modern world,--one in which the Christian religion is aggressively set forth on the basis of Holy Scripture in the Reformed Faith.

History shows us quite plainly, however, that periods of spiritual prosperity alternate with periods of spiritual depression. But above all, we believe in the invincibility of truth. "Truth crushed to earth shall rise again; The unending years of God are hers."

That Calvinism has many adversaries is not to be wondered at. As long as the fact remains that, "The natural man receiveth not the things of the Spirit of God; for they are foolishness unto him; and he cannot know them, because they are spiritually judged" (I Cor. 2:14), so long will this be a strange, foolish system to the natural man. As long as fallen human nature remains as it is, and as long as the decree stands that Christ Himself is to be "a stone of stumbling and a rock of offence" to the natural man (I Peter 2:8), these things will be an offense to many. Nor was it to be marveled at that the

The Reformed Doctrine Of Predestination

immortal Swiss reformer who was called to such a prominent place in the development and defence of these doctrines has been on the one hand the most passionately loved and admired, and on the other the most bitterly hated and abused, among all the outstanding leaders in the Church.

Since faith and repentance are special gifts from God, we should not be astonished at the unbelief of the world; for even the wisest and acutest of men cannot believe unless they receive these gifts. It is very appropriately written, "I will destroy the wisdom of the wise, and the discernment of the discerning will I bring to naught" (I Cor. 2:19); and again, "The wisdom of this world is foolishness with God. For it is written, He taketh the wise in their craftiness; and again, The Lord knoweth the reasonings of the wise, that they are vain. Wherefore let no one glory in men," (I Cor. 3:19-21). The cause of any person believing is the will of God; and the outward sound of the Gospel strikes the ear but in vain until God is pleased to touch the heart within.

This is a system which has always been strongly opposed by the world, and it is as strongly opposed now as ever. Indeed, how could it be otherwise when man by nature is at enmity and war with Him from whose mind it has emanated? It is not to be expected that God in His wisdom and man in his folly would agree. God is an all-wise and all-holy sovereign; man unchanged is a sin-blinded rebel, who wants no ruler and most certainly not an absolute ruler. Since the enmity of man's heart toward the distinctive doctrines of the Cross is as great and as intense as ever, a system such as Pelagianism or Naturalism, which teaches salvation by our own good works, or such as Arminianism, which teaches salvation partly by works and partly by grace, strikes a quicker response in the unregenerate heart. When the Gospel becomes palatable to the natural man it ceases to be the Gospel that Paul preached. And it is worth remembering here that in nearly every town in which Paul preached his Gospel did cause either a riot or a revival and not infrequently both. "Calvinism may be unpopular in some quarters," says McFetridge. "But what of that? It cannot be more unpopular than the doctrines of sin and grace as revealed in the New Testament"

Another reason for the depressed fortunes of Calvinism today is its tremendous emphasis upon the supernatural. In all events and in all things, from eternity to eternity, Calvinism sees God. His hand is visible in all the phenomena of nature and in all the events of history. Through all occurrences His one increasing purpose runs. We live in an age which is anti-supernaturalistic; hence it is distinctively hostile to Calvinism. The emphasis today is upon the physical sciences, upon rationalism in thought and sentiment. Even in present day Christianity the tendency is to take the Bible merely as a human production and to look upon Christ merely as the outstanding man. Present day Modernism, which in its consistent form is pure naturalism and autosoteric, is the very antithesis of Calvinism. All of this has produced a naturalistic religion which says, "Hands off," to God; and it is not strange that Calvinism, with its great emphasis on the supernatural, is not popular in our day. We need not be surprised, then, when the adherents to these doctrines are found to be in the minority. The truth or falsity of Scripture doctrines cannot be left to the outcome of a popular vote.

In the following words Dr. B. B. Warfield, that giant of thought and action, has given us a good analysis of the attitude which the world has taken toward Calvinism in recent years. After saying that Calvinism is "Theism come to its rights," that it is "religion at the height of its conception," and that it is "Evangelicalism in its pure and only stable expression," he adds: "Consider the pride of man, his assertion of freedom, the boast of power, his refusal to acknowledge the sway of another's will. Consider the ingrained confidence of the sinner in his own fundamentally good nature and his full ability to perform all that can be justly demanded of him.

"Is it strange that in this world--in this particular age of this world--it should prove difficult to preserve not only active, but vivid and dominant, the perception of the everywhere determining hand of God, the sense of absolute dependence on Him, the conviction of utter inability to do even the least thing to rescue ourselves from sin--at the height of its conception? Is it not enough to account for whatever depression Calvinism may be suffering in the world today, to point to the natural difficulty--in this materialistic age, conscious of its newly realized powers over against the forces of nature and filled with the pride of achievement and of material well-being--of guarding our perception of the governing hand of God in all things, in its perfection; of maintaining our sense of dependence on a higher power in full force; of preserving our feeling of sin, unworthiness, and helplessness in its profundity? Is not the depression of Calvinism, so far as it is real, significant merely of this--that to our age the vision of God has become somewhat obscured in the midst of abounding triumphs, that the religious emotion has in some measure ceased to be the determining force in life, and that the evangelical attitude of complete dependence on God for salvation does not readily commend itself to men who are accustomed to lay forceful hands on everything else they wish, and who do not quite see why they may not take heaven also by storm?" [165]

Yet there is no occasion for Calvinists to feel discouraged. The easy going religion of today, with its emphasis on social problems rather than on doctrine, has brought into the Church multitudes which in other ages would have remained outside; and the mere fact that Calvinists are not so conspicuous in the congregation does not necessarily mean that their actual numbers have decreased. "There are very likely more Calvinists in the world today than ever before," says Dr. Warfield. "Even relatively, the professedly Calvinistic Churches are, no doubt, holding their own. There are important tendencies of modern thought which play into the hands of this or that Calvinistic conception. Above all, there are to be found everywhere humble souls, who, in the quiet of retired lives, have caught a vision of God in His glory and are cherishing in their hearts that vital flame of complete dependence on Him which is the very essence of Calvinism." [166] And again, "I fully believe that Calvinism, as it has supplied the sinews of evangelical Christianity in the past, so is its strength in the present, and is its hope for the future."

And in close conformity with this Dr. F. W. Loetscher, has said: "It is no wonder that our age, distraught by its very knowledge, irreverent of antiquity, impatient of creeds and dogmas, intolerant alike of human and divine authority, overborne by the currents of atheistic Naturalism and pantheistic Evolution, is directing its heaviest artillery of unbelief against Calvinism as the strongest citadel of supernatural revelation and redemption. And as Professor Henry B. Smith prophesied a generation ago: 'One thing is certain--that infidel science will rout everything excepting a thorough-going Christian orthodoxy.' Let us, then, resolutely accept this challenge. And let us be of good cheer; for Calvinism can no more perish from the earth than sinful man can utterly lose his sense of dependence upon God, or the Almighty can abdicate the throne of His universal dominion."

James Anthony Froude, the distinguished professor of Church History in Oxford University, England, said of the rather lifeless religion which had become so common in his day: "This was not the religion of your fathers; this was not the Calvinism which overthrew spiritual wickedness, and hurled kings from their thrones, and purged England and Scotland, for a time at least, of lies and charlatanry. Calvinism is the spirit which rises in revolt against untruth, the spirit which, as I have shown you, has appeared and reappeared, and in due time will appear again, unless God be a delusion and man be as the beasts that perish."

It may be proper at this point to say that the author of this book was not reared in a Calvinistic Church, and he well remembers how revolutionary these doctrines seemed when he first came in contact with them. During one Christmas vacation of his College course he happened to read the first volume of Charles Hodge's "Systematic Theology," which contains a chapter on "The Decrees of God," and which stated these truths with such compelling force that he was never able to get away from them. Furthermore, he takes some pride in the fact that he has reached this position only after a rather severe mental and spiritual struggle, and he feels deeply sympathetic toward others who may be called upon to go through a somewhat similar experience. He knows the sacrifice required to withdraw from the church of his youth when he became convinced that that church taught a system which contained much error. Most of his closest relatives and friends belonged to that church, and he will perhaps be pardoned if he betrays a bit of intolerance toward those "born Presbyterians" who remain members of the Presbyterian Church while openly opposing or ridiculing these doctrines.

Footnotes:

    152. Calvin's Calvinism, p. 29.
    153. God Sovereign and Man Free, p. 46.
    154. The Creed of Presbyterians, pp. 53, 94.
    155. Christianity and Liberalism, p. 51.
    156. Article, Calvin as a Theologian and Calvinism Today, pp. 23, 24.
    157. The Fundamental Principle of Calvinism, p. 25.
    158. Calvin's Calvinism, p. 30.
    159. Systematic Theology, I., p. 535.
    160. Article printed in Christianity Today, Sept., 1930, p. 7.
    161. Predestination, p. 124.
    162. Predestination, p. 124.
    163. Systematic Theology, p. 368.
    164. Shedd, Calvinism, Pure and Mixed, p. 160.
    165. Article, Calvinism Today, p. 7.
    166. Article, The Theology of Calvin, p. 8.

Chapter XXVIII – Calvinism in History

1. Before the Reformation. 2. The Reformation. 3. Calvinism in England. 4. Calvinism in Scotland. 5. Calvinism in France. 6. Calvinism in Holland. 7. Calvinism in America. 8. Calvinism and Representative Government. 9. Calvinism and Education. 10. John Calvin. 11. Conclusion.

1. BEFORE THE REFORMATION

It may occasion some surprise to discover that the doctrine of Predestination was not made a matter of special study until near the end of the fourth century. The earlier church fathers placed chief emphasis on good works such as faith, repentance, almsgiving, prayers, submission to baptism, etc., as the basis of salvation. They of course taught that salvation was through Christ; yet they assumed that man had full power to accept or reject the gospel. Some of their writings contain passages in which the sovereignty of God is recognized; yet along side of those are others which teach the absolute freedom of the human will. Since they could not reconcile the two they would have denied the doctrine of Predestination and perhaps also that of God's absolute Foreknowledge. They taught a kind of synergism in which there was a co-operation between grace and free will. It was hard for man to give up the idea that he could work out his own salvation. But at last, as a result of a long, slow process, he came to the great truth that salvation is a sovereign gift which has been bestowed irrespective of merit; that it was fixed in eternity; and that God is the author in all of its stages. This cardinal truth of Christianity was first clearly seen by Augustine, the great Spirit-filled theologian of the West. In his doctrines of sin and grace, he went far beyond the earlier theologians, taught an unconditional election of grace, and restricted the purposes of redemption to the definite circle of the elect. It will not be denied by anyone acquainted with Church History that Augustine was an eminently great and good man, and that his labors and writings contributed more to the promotion of sound doctrine and the revival of true religion than did those of any other man between Paul and Luther.

Prior to Augustine's day the time had been largely taken up in correcting heresies within the Church and in refuting attacks from the pagan world in which it found itself. Consequently but little emphasis had been placed on the systematic development of doctrine. And that the doctrine of Predestination received such little attention in this age was no doubt partly due to the tendency to confuse it with the Pagan doctrine of Fatalism which was so prevalent throughout the Roman Empire. But in the fourth century a more settled time had been reached, a new era in theology had dawned, and the theologians came to place more emphasis on the doctrinal content of their message. Augustine was led to develop his doctrines of sin and grace partly through his own personal experience in being converted to Christianity from a worldly life, and partly through the necessity of refuting the teaching of Pelagius, who taught that man in his natural state had full ability to work out his own salvation, that Adam's fall had but little effect on the race except that it set a bad example which is perpetuated, that Christ's life is of value to men mainly by way of example, that in His death Christ was little more than the first Christian martyr, and that we are not under any special providence of God. Against these views Augustine developed the very opposite. He taught that the whole race fell in Adam, that all men by nature are depraved and spiritually dead, that the will is free to sin but not free to do good toward God, that Christ suffered vicariously for His people, that God elects whom He will irrespective of their merits, and that saving grace is efficaciously applied to the elect by the Holy Spirit. He thus became the first true interpreter of Paul and was successful in securing the acceptance of his doctrine by the Church.

Following Augustine there was retrogression rather than progress. Clouds of ignorance blinded the people. The Church became more and more ritualistic and salvation was thought to be through the external Church. The system of merit grew until it reached its climax in the "indulgences." The papacy came to exert great power, political as well as ecclesiastical, and throughout Catholic Europe the state of morals came to be almost intolerable. Even the priesthood became desperately corrupt and in the whole catalogue of human sins and vices none are more corrupt or more offensive than those which soiled the lives of such popes as John XXIII and Alexander VI.

From the time of Augustine until the time of the Reformation very little emphasis was placed on the doctrine of Predestination. We shall mention only two names from this period: Gottschalk, who was imprisoned and condemned for teaching Predestination; and Wycliffe, "The Morning Star of the Reformation," who lived in England. Wycliffe was a reformer of the Calvinistic type, proclaiming the absolute sovereignty of God and the Foreordination of all things. His system of belief was very similar to that which was later taught by Luther and Calvin. The Waldensians also might be mentioned for they were in a sense "Calvinists" before the Reformation, one of their tenets being that of Predestination.

2. THE REFORMATION

The Reformation was essentially a revival of Augustinianism and through it evangelical Christianity again came into its own. It is to be remembered that Luther, the first leader in the Reformation, was an Augustinian monk and that it was from this rigorous theology that he formulated his great principle of justification by faith alone. Luther, Calvin, Zwingli and all the other outstanding reformers of that period were thorough-going predestinarians. In his work, "The Bondage of the Will," Luther stated the doctrine as emphatically and in a form quite as extreme as can be found among any of the reformed theologians. Melanchthon in his earlier writings designated the principle of Predestination as the fundamental principle of Christianity. He later modified this position, however, and brought in a kind of "synergism" in which God and man were supposed to co-operate in the process of salvation. The position taken by the early Lutheran Church was gradually modified. Later Lutherans let go the doctrine altogether, denounced it in its Calvinistic form, and came to hold a doctrine of universal grace and universal atonement, which doctrine has since become the accepted doctrine of the Lutheran Church. In regard to this doctrine Luther's position in the Lutheran Church is similar to that of Augustine in the Roman Catholic Church,--that is, he is a heretic of such unimpeachable authority that he is more admired than censured.

To a great extent Calvin built upon the foundation which Luther laid. His clearer insight into the basic principles of the Reformation enabled him to work them out more fully and to apply them more broadly. And it may be further pointed out that Luther stressed salvation by faith and that his fundamental principle was more or less subjective and anthropological, while Calvin stressed the principle of the sovereignty of God, and developed a principle which was more objective and theological. Lutheranism was more the religion of a man who after a long and painful search had found salvation and who was content simply to bask in the sunshine of God's presence, while Calvinism, not content to stop there, pressed on to ask how and why God had saved man.

"The Lutheran congregations," says Froude, "were but half emancipated from superstition, and shrank from pressing the struggle to extremes; and half measures meant half-heartedness, convictions which were half convictions, and truth with an alloy of falsehood. Half measures, however, could not quench the bonfires of Philip of Spain or raise men in France or Scotland who would meet crest to crest the princes of the house of Lorraine. The Reformers required a position more sharply defined and a sterner leader, and that leader they found in John Calvin . . . For hard times hard men are needed, and intellects which can pierce to the roots where truth and lies part company. It fares ill with the soldiers of religion when 'the accursed thing' is in the camp. And this is to be said of Calvin, that so far as the state of knowledge permitted, no eye could have detected more keenly the unsound spots in the creed of the Church, nor was there a Reformer in Europe so resolute to exercise, tear out and destroy what was distinctly seen to be false--so resolute to establish what was true in its place, and make truth, to the last fibre of it, the rule of practical life." [167]

This is the testimony of the famous historian from Oxford University. Froude's writings make it plain that he had no particular love for Calvinism; and in fact he is often called a critic of Calvinism. These words just quoted simply express the impartial conclusions of a great scholar who looks at the system and the man whose name it bears from the vantage ground of learned investigation.

In another connection Froude says: "The Calvinists have been called intolerant. Intolerance of an enemy who is trying to kill you seems to me a pardonable state of mind . . . The Catholics chose to add to their already incredible creed a fresh article, that they were entitled to hang and burn those who differed from them; and in this quarrel the Calvinists, Bible in hand, appealed to the God of battles. They grew harsher, fiercer,--if you please, more fanatical. It was extremely natural that they should. They dwelt, as pious men are apt to dwell in suffering and sorrow, on the all-disposing power of Providence. Their burden grew lighter as they considered that God had so determined that they must bear it. But they attracted to their ranks almost every man in Western Europe that ' hated a lie.' They were crushed down, but they rose again. They were splintered and torn, but no power could bend or melt them. They abhorred as no body of men ever more abhorred all conscious mendacity, all impurity, all moral wrong of every kind so far as they could recognize it. Whatever exists at this moment in England and Scotland of conscious fear of doing evil is the remnant of the convictions which were branded by the Calvinists into the people's hearts. Though they failed to destroy Romanism, though it survives and may survive long as an opinion, they drew its fangs; they forced it to abandon that detestable principle, that it was entitled to murder those who dissented from it. Nay, it may be said that by having shamed Romanism out of its practical corruption the Calvinists enabled it to revive." [168]

At the time of the Reformation the Lutheran Church did not make such a complete break with the Catholic Church as did the Reformed. In fact some Lutherans point out with pride that Lutheranism was a "moderate Reformation." While all protestants appealed to the Bible as a final authority, the tendency in Lutheranism was to keep as much of the old system as did not have to be thrown out, while the tendency in the Reformed Church was to throw out all that did not have to be kept. And in regard to the relationship which existed between the Church and the State, the Lutherans were content to allow the local princes great influence in the Church or even to allow them to determine the religion within their bounds--a tendency leading toward the establishment of a State Church--while the Reformed soon came to demand complete separation between Church and State.

As stated before, the Reformation was essentially a revival of Augustinianism. The early Lutheran and Reformed Churches held the same views in regard to Original Sin, Election, Efficacious Grace, Perseverance, etc. This, then, was the true Protestantism. "The principle of Absolute Predestination," says Hastie, "was the very Hercules-might of the young Reformation, by which no less in Germany than elsewhere, it strangled the serpents of superstition and idolatry; and when it lost its energy in its first home, it still continued to be the very marrow and backbone of the faith in the Reformed Church, and the power that carried it victoriously through all its struggles and trials." [169] "It is a fact that speaks volumes for Calvinism," says Rice, "that the most glorious revolution recorded in the history of the Church and of the world, since the days of the Apostles, was effected by the blessings of God upon its doctrines." [170] Needless to say, Arminianism as a system was unknown in Reformation times; and not until 1784, some 260 years later, was it championed by an organized church. As in the fifth century there had been two contending systems, known as Augustinianism and Pelagianism, with the later rise of the compromised system of Semi-Pelagianism, so at the Reformation there were two systems, Protestantism and Roman Catholicism, with the later rise of Arminianism, or what we might call Semi-Protestantism. In each case there were two strongly opposite systems with the subsequent rise of a compromised system.

3. CALVINISM IN ENGLAND

A glance at English history readily shows us that it was Calvinism which made Protestantism triumphant in that land. Many of the leading Protestants who fled to Geneva during the reign of Queen Mary afterward obtained high positions in the Church under Queen Elizabeth. Among them were the translators of the Geneva version of the Bible, which owes much to Calvin and Beza, and which continued to be the most popular English version till the middle of the seventeenth century when it was superseded by the King James version. The influence of Calvin is shown in the Thirty-Nine Articles of the Church of England, especially in Article XVII which states the doctrine of Predestination. Cunningham has shown that all of the great theologians of the Established Church during the reigns of Henry VIII, Edward VI and Elizabeth were thorough-going predestinarians and that the Arminianism of Laud and his successors was a deviation from that original position.

If we search for the true heroes of England, we shall find them in that noble body of English Calvinists whose insistence upon a purer form of worship and a purer life won for them the nickname, "Puritans," to whom Macaulay refers as "perhaps the most remarkable body of men which the world has ever produced." "That the English people became Protestant," says Bancroft, "is due to the Puritans." Smith tells us: "The significance of this fact is beyond computation. English Protestantism, with its open Bible, its spiritual and intellectual freedom, meant the Protestantism not only of the American colonies, but of the virile and multiplying race which for three centuries has been carrying the Anglo-Saxon language, religion, and institutions into all the world. [171]

Cromwell, the great Calvinistic leader and commoner, planted himself upon the solid rock of Calvinism and called to himself soldiers who had planted themselves upon that same rock. The result was an army which for purity and heroism surpassed anything the world had ever seen. "It never found," says Macaulay, "either in the British Isles or on the Continent, an enemy who could stand its onset. In England, Scotland, Ireland, Flanders, the Puritan warriors, often surrounded by difficulties, sometimes contending against threefold odds, not only never failed to conquer, but never failed to destroy and break in pieces whatever force was opposed to them. They at length came to regard the day of battle as a day of certain triumph, and marched against the most renowned battalions of Europe with disdainful confidence. Even the banished Cavaliers felt an emotion of national pride when they saw a brigade of their countrymen, outnumbered by foes and abandoned by friends, drive before it in headlong rout the finest infantry of Spain, and force a passage into a counterscarp which had just been pronounced impregnable by the ablest of the marshals of France." And again, "That which chiefly distinguished the army of Cromwell from other armies, was the austere morality and the fear of God which pervaded the ranks. It is acknowledged by the most zealous Royalists that, in that singular camp, no oath was heard, no drunkenness or gambling was seen, and that, during the long dominion of soldiery, the property of the peaceable citizens and the honor of woman were held sacred. No servant girl complained of the rough gallantry of the redcoats. Not an ounce of plate was taken from the shops of the goldsmiths" [172]

Prof. John Fiske, who has been ranked as one of the two greatest American historians, says, "It is not too much to say that in the seventeenth century the entire political future of mankind was staked upon the questions that were at issue in England. Had it not been for the Puritans, political liberty would probably have disappeared from the world. If ever there were men who laid down their lives in the cause of all mankind, it was those grim old Ironsides, whose watch-words were texts of Holy Writ, whose battle-cries were hymns of praise." [173]

On three different occasions Cromwell was offered, and was urged to accept, the Crown of England, but each time he refused. Doctrinally we find that the Puritans were the literal and lineal descendants of John Calvin; and they and they alone kept alive the precious spark of English liberty. In view of these facts no one can rashly deny the justice of Fiske's conclusion that "It would be hard to over-rate the debt which mankind owes to John Calvin."

McFetridge in his splendid little book, "Calvinism in History," says, "If we ask again, Who brought the final great deliverance to English liberty? we are answered by history, The Illustrious Calvinist, William, Prince of Orange, who, as Macaulay says, found in the strong and sharp logic of the Geneva school something that suited his intellect and his temper; the keystone of whose religion was the doctrine of Predestination; and who, with his keen logical vision, declared that if he were to abandon the doctrine of Predestination he must abandon with it all his belief in a superintending Providence, and must become a mere Epicurean. And he was right, for Predestination and an overruling Providence are one and the same thing. If we accept the one, we are in consistency bound to accept the other," (P. 52).

4. CALVINISM IN SCOTLAND

The best way to discover the practical fruits of a system of religion is to examine a people or a country in which for generations that system has held undisputed sway. In making such a test of Roman Catholicism we turn to some country like Spain, Italy, Colombia, or Mexico. There, in the religious and political life of the people, we see the effects of the system. Applying the same test to Calvinism we are able to point to one country in which Calvinism has long been practically the only religion, and that country is Scotland. McFetridge tells us that before Calvinism reached Scotland, "gross darkness covered the land and brooded like an eternal nightmare upon all the faculties of the people." [174] "When Calvinism reached the Scotch people," says Smith, "they were vassals of the Romish church, priest-ridden, ignorant, wretched, degraded in body, mind, and morals. Buckle describes them as 'filthy in their persons and in their homes,' 'poor and miserable,' 'excessively ignorant and exceedingly superstitious,'-- 'with superstition ingrained into their characters.' Marvelous was the transformation when the great doctrines learned by Knox from the Bible in Scotland and more thoroughly at Geneva while sitting at the feet of Calvin, flashed in upon their minds. It was like the sun arising at midnight . . . Knox made Calvinism the religion of Scotland, and Calvinism made Scotland the moral standard for the world. It is certainly a significant fact that in that country where there is the most of Calvinism there should be the least of crime; that of all the people of the world today that nation which is confessedly the most moral is also the most thoroughly Calvinistic; that in that land where Calvinism has had supremest sway individual and national morality has reached its loftiest level." [175] Says Carlyle, "This that Knox did for his nation we may really call a resurrection as from death." "John Knox," says Froude, "was the one man without whom Scotland as the modern world has known it, would have had no existence."

In a very real sense the Presbyterian Church of Scotland is the daughter of the Reformed Church of Geneva. The Reformation in Scotland, though coming some time later, was far more consistent and radical than in England, and it resulted in the establishment of a Calvinistic Presbyterianism in which Christ alone was recognized as the head of the Church.

It is, of course, an easy matter to pick out the one man who in the hands of Providence was the principal instrument in the reformation of Scotland. That man was John Knox. It was he who planted the germs of religious and civil liberty and who revolutionized society. To him the Scotch owe their national existence. "Knox was the greatest of Scotsmen, as Luther the greatest of Germans," says Philip Schaff. "The hero of the Scotch Reformation," says Schaff, "though four years older than Calvin, sat humbly at his feet and became more Calvinistic than Calvin. John Knox spent the five years of his exile (1554-1559), during the reign of Bloody Mary, mostly at Geneva, and found there 'the most perfect school of Christ that ever was since the days of the Apostles.' After that model he led the Scotch people, with dauntless courage and energy, from mediaeval semi-barbarism into the light of modern civilization, and acquired a name which, next to those of Luther, Zwingli, and Calvin, is the greatest in the history of the Protestant Reformation." [176]

"No grander figure," says Froude, "can be found in the entire history of the Reformation in this island than that of Knox. . . . The time has come when English history may do justice to one but for whom the Reformation would have been overthrown among ourselves; for the spirit which Knox created saved Scotland; and if Scotland had been Catholic again, neither the wisdom of Elizabeth's ministers, nor the teaching of her bishops, nor her own chicaneries, would have preserved England from revolution. He was the voice which taught the peasant of the Lothians that he was a free man, the equal in the sight of God with the proudest peer or prelate that had trampled on his forefathers. He was the antagonist whom Mary Stuart could not soften nor Maitland deceive; he it was that raised the poor

The Reformed Doctrine Of Predestination

commons of his country into a stern and rugged people, who might be hard, narrow, superstitious and fanatical, but who nevertheless, were men whom neither king, noble nor priest could force again to submit to tyranny. And his reward has been the ingratitude of those who should most have done honor to his memory." [177]

The early Scotch reformed theology was based on the predestinarian principle. Knox had gotten his theology directly from Calvin in Geneva, and his chief theological work was his treatise on Predestination, which was a keen, forcible and unflinching polemic against loose views which were becoming widespread in England and elsewhere. During the seventeenth and eighteenth centuries topics such as predestination, election, reprobation, the extent and value of the atonement, the perseverance of the saints, were the absorbing interest of the Scotch peasantry. From that land those doctrines spread southward into parts of England and Ireland and across the Atlantic to the west. In a very real sense Scotland can be called the "Mother Country of modern Presbyterianism."

5. CALVINISM IN FRANCE

France, too, at that time, was all aglow with the free, bounding, restless spirit of Calvinism. "In France the Calvinists were called Huguenots. The character of the Huguenots the world knows. Their moral purity and heroism, whether persecuted at home or exiled abroad, has been the wonder of both friend and foe." [178] "Their history," says the Encyclopaedia Britannica, "is a standing marvel, illustrating the abiding power of strong religious conviction. The account of their endurance is amongst the most remarkable and heroic records of religious history." The Huguenots made up the industrious artisan class of France and to be "honest as a Huguenot" became a proverb, denoting the highest degree of integrity.

On St. Bartholomew's Day, Sunday, August 24, 1572, a great many Protestants were treacherously murdered in Paris, and for days thereafter the shocking scenes were repeated in different parts of France. The total number of those who lost their lives in the St. Bartholomew massacre has been variously estimated at from 10,000 to 50,000. Schaff estimates it at 30,000. These furious persecutions caused hundreds of thousands of the French Protestants to flee to Holland, Germany, England, and America. The loss to France was irreparable. Macaulay the English historian writes as follows of those who settled in England: "The humblest of the refugees were intellectually and morally above the average of the common people of any kingdom in Europe." The great historian Lecky, who himself was a cold-blooded rationalist, wrote: "The destruction of the Huguenots by the Revocation of the Edict of Nantes was the destruction of the most solid, the most modest, the most virtuous, the most generally enlightened element in the French nation, and it prepared the way for the inevitable degradation of the national character, and the last serious bulwark was removed that might have broken the force of that torrent of skepticism and vice which, a century later, laid prostrate, in merited ruin, both the altar and the throne." [179]

"If you have read their history," says Warburton, "you must know how cruel and unjust were the persecutions instigated against them. The best blood of France deluged the battlefield, the brightest genius of France was suffered to lie neglected and starving in prison, and the noblest characters which France ever possessed were hunted like wild beasts of the forest, and slain with as little pity." And again, "In every respect they stood immeasurably superior to all the rest of their fellow-countrymen. The strict sobriety of their lives, the purity of their moral actions, their industrious habits, and their entire separation from the foul sensuality which corrupted the whole of the national life of France at this period, were always effectual means of betraying the principles which they held, and were so regarded by their enemies." [180]

The debauchery of the kings had descended through the aristocracy to the common people; religion had become a mass of corruption, consistent only with its cruelty; the monasteries had become breeding places of iniquity; celibacy had proved to be a foul fountain of unchastity and uncleanness; immorality, licentiousness, despotism and extortion in State and Church were indescribable; the forgiveness of sins could be purchased for money, and a shameful traffic in indulgences was carried on under the pope's sanction; some of the popes were monsters of iniquity; ignorance was appalling; education was confined to the clergy and the nobles; many even of the priests were unable to read or write; and society in general had fallen to pieces.

This is a one-sided, but not an exaggerated, description. It is true as far as it goes, and needs only to be supplemented by the brighter side, which was that many honest Roman Catholics were earnestly working for reform from within the Church. The Church, however, was in an irreformable condition. Any change, if it was to come at all, had to come from without. Either there would be no reformation or it would be in opposition to Rome.

But gradually Protestant ideas were filtering into France from Germany. Calvin began his work in Paris and was soon recognized as one of the leaders of the new movement in France. His zeal aroused the opposition of Church authorities and it became necessary for him to flee for his life. And although Calvin never returned to France after his settlement in Geneva, he remained the leader of the French

Reformation and was consulted at every step. He gave the Huguenots their creed and form of government. Throughout the following period it was, according to the unanimous testimony of history, the system of faith which we call Calvinism that inspired the French Protestants in their struggle with the papacy and its royal supporters.

What the Puritan was in England, the Covenanter was in Scotland, and the Huguenot was in France. That Calvinism developed the same type of men in each of these several countries is a most remarkable proof of its power in the formation of character.

So rapidly did Calvinism spread throughout France that Fisher in his History of the Reformation tells us that in 1561 the Calvinists numbered one-fourth of the entire population. McFetridge places the number even higher. "In less than half a century," says he, "this so-called harsh system of belief had penetrated every part of the land, and had gained to its standards almost one-half of the population and almost every great mind in the nation. So numerous and powerful had its adherents become that for a time it appeared as if the entire nation would be swept over to their views." [181] Smiles, in his "Huguenots in France," writes: "It is curious to speculate on the influence which the religion of Calvin, himself a Frenchman, might have exercised on the history of France, as well as on the individual character of the Frenchman, had the balance of forces carried the nation bodily over to Protestantism, as was very nearly the case, toward the end of the sixteenth century," (p. 100). Certainly the history of the nation would have been very different from that which it has been.

6. CALVINISM IN HOLLAND

In the struggle which freed the Netherlands from the dominating power of the Papacy and from the cruel yoke of Spain we have another glorious chapter in the history of Calvinism and humanity. The tortures of the Inquisition were applied here as in few other places. The Duke of Alva boasted that within the short space of five years he had delivered 18,600 heretics to the executioner.

"The scaffold," says Motley, "had its daily victims, but did not make a single convert. . . . There were men who dared and suffered as much as men can dare and suffer in this world, and for the noblest cause that can inspire humanity." He pictures to us "the heroism with which men took each other by the hand and walked into the flames, or with which women sang a song of triumph while the grave-digger was shoveling the earth upon their living faces." And in another place he says: "The number of Netherlanders who were burned, strangled, beheaded, or buried alive, in obedience to the edicts of Charles V., and for the offence of reading the Scriptures, of looking askance at a graven image, or ridiculing the actual presence of the body and blood of Christ in a wafer, have been placed as high as one hundred thousand by distinguished authorities, and have never been put at a lower mark than fifty thousand." [182] During that memorable struggle of eighty years, more Protestants were put to death for their conscientious belief by the Spaniards than Christians suffered martyrdom under the Roman Emperors in the first three centuries. Certainly in Holland history crowns Calvinism as the creed of martyrs, saints and heroes.

For nearly three generations Spain, the strongest nation in Europe at that time, labored to stamp out Protestantism and political liberty in these Calvinistic Netherlands, but failed. Because they sought to worship God according to the dictates of their conscience and not under the galling chains of a corrupt priesthood their country was invaded and the people were subjected to the cruelest tortures the Spaniards could invent. And if it be asked who effected the deliverance, the answer is, it was the Calvinistic Prince of Orange, known in history as William the Silent, together with those who held the same creed. Says Dr. Abraham Kuyper, "If the power of Satan at that time had not been broken by the heroism of the Calvinistic spirit, the history of the Netherlands, of Europe and of the world would have been as painfully sad and dark as now, thanks to Calvinism, it is bright and inspiring." [183]

If the spirit of Calvinism had not arisen in Western Europe following the outbreak of the Reformation, the spirit of half-heartedness would have gained the day in England, Scotland and Holland. Protestantism in these countries could not have maintained itself; and, through the compromising measures of a Romanized Protestantism, Germany would in all probability have been again brought under the sway of the Roman Catholic Church. Had Protestantism failed in any one of these countries it is probable that the result would have been fatal in the others also, so intimately were their fortunes bound together. In a very real sense the future destiny of nations was dependent on the outcome of that struggle in the Netherlands. Had Spain been victorious in the Netherlands, it is probable that the Catholic Church would have been so strengthened that it would have subdued Protestantism in England also. And, even as things were, it looked for a time as though England would be turned back to Romanism. In that case the development of America would automatically have been prevented and in all probability the whole American continent would have remained under the control of Spain.

Let us remember further that practically all of the martyrs in these various countries were Calvinists,--the Lutherans and Arminians being only a handful in comparison. As Professor Fruin justly remarks, "In Switzerland, in France, in the Netherlands, in Scotland and in England, and wherever Protestantism has had to establish itself at the point of the sword, it was Calvinism that gained the day."

The Reformed Doctrine Of Predestination

However the fact is to be explained it is true that the Calvinists were the only fighting Protestants.

There is also one other service which Holland has rendered and which we must not overlook. The Pilgrims, after being driven out of England by religious persecutions and before their coming to America, went to Holland and there came into contact with a religious life which from the Calvinistic point of view was beneficial in the extreme. Their most important leaders were Clyfton, Robinson, and Brewster, three Cambridge University men, who form a noble and heroic trio as can be found in the history of any nation. They were staunch Calvinists holding all the fundamental views that the Reformer of Geneva had propounded. The American historian Bancroft is right when he simply calls the Pilgrim-fathers, "men of the same faith with Calvin."

J. C. Monsma, in his book, "What Calvinism Has Done For America," gives us the following summary of their life in Holland: "When the Pilgrims left Amsterdam for Leyden, the Rev. Clyfton, their chief leader, decided to stay where he was, and so the Rev. John Robinson, Clyfton's chief assistant hitherto," was elected leader, or pastor by the people. Robinson was a convinced Calvinist and opposed the teachings of Arminius whenever opportunity was afforded him. "We have the indisputable testimony of Edward Winslow, that Robinson, at the time when Arminianism was fast gaining ground in Holland, was asked by Polyander, Festus Homilus, and other Dutch theologians, to take part in the disputes with Episcopius, the new leader of the Arminians, which were daily held in the academy at Leyden. Robinson complied with their request and was soon looked upon as one of the greatest of Gomarian theologians. In 1624 the Pilgrim pastor wrote a masterful treatise, entitled, "A Defense of the Doctrine Propounded by the Synod of Dort, etc.' As the Synod of Dordrecht, of international fame was characterized by a strict Calvinism in all its decisions, no more need be said of Robinson's religious tendencies.

"The Pilgrims were perfectly at one with the Reformed (Calvinistic) churches in the Netherlands and elsewhere. In his Apology, published in 1619, one year before the Pilgrims left Holland, Robinson wrote in a most solemn way, 'We do profess before God and men that such is our accord, in case of religion, with the Dutch Reformed Churches, as that we are ready to subscribe to all and every article of faith in the same Church, as they are laid down in the Harmony of Confessions of Faith, published in that name.'" (p. 72, 73.)

7. CALVINISM IN AMERICA

When we come to study the influence of Calvinism as a political force in the history of the United States we come to one of the brightest pages of all Calvinistic history. Calvinism came to America in the Mayflower, and Bancroft, the greatest of American historians, pronounces the Pilgrim Fathers "Calvinists in their faith according to the straightest system." [184] John Endicott, the first governor of the Massachusetts Bay Colony; John Winthrop, the second governor of that Colony; Thomas Hooker, the founder of Connecticut; John Davenport, the founder of the New Haven Colony; and Roger Williams, the founder of the Rhode Island Colony, were all Calvinists. William Penn was a disciple of the Huguenots. It is estimated that of the 3,000,000 Americans at the time of the American Revolution, 900,000 were of Scotch or Scotch-Irish origin, 600,000 were Puritan English, and 400,000 were German or Dutch Reformed. In addition to this the Episcopalians had a Calvinistic confession in their Thirty-nine Articles; and many French Huguenots also had come to this western world. Thus we see that about two-thirds of the colonial population had been trained in the school of Calvin. Never in the world's history had a nation been founded by such people as these. Furthermore these people came to America not primarily for commercial gain or advantage, but because of deep religious convictions. It seems that the religious persecutions in various European countries had been providentially used to select out the most progressive and enlightened people for the colonization of America. At any rate it is quite generally admitted that the English, Scotch, Germans, and Dutch have been the most masterful people of Europe. Let it be especially remembered that the Puritans, who formed the great bulk of the settlers in New England, brought with them a Calvinistic Protestantism, that they were truly devoted to the doctrines of the great Reformers, that they had an aversion for formalism and oppression whether in the Church or in the State, and that in New England Calvinism remained the ruling theology throughout the entire Colonial period.

With this background we shall not be surprised to find that the Presbyterians took a very prominent part in the American Revolution. Our own historian Bancroft says: "The Revolution of 1776, so far as it was affected by religion, was a Presbyterian measure. It was the natural outgrowth of the principles which the Presbyterianism of the Old World planted in her sons, the English Puritans, the Scotch Covenanters, the French Huguenots, the Dutch Calvinists, and the Presbyterians of Ulster." So intense, universal, and aggressive were the Presbyterians in their zeal for liberty that the war was spoken of in England as "The Presbyterian Rebellion." An ardent colonial supporter of King George III wrote home: "I fix all the blame for these extraordinary proceedings upon the Presbyterians. They have been the chief and principal instruments in all these flaming measures. They always do and ever will act against government from that restless and turbulent anti-monarchial spirit which has always distinguished them everywhere." [185] When the news of "these extraordinary proceedings" reached England, Prime Minister Horace Walpole said in Parliament, "Cousin America has run off with a Presbyterian parson."

"The Rev. Dr. John Witherspoon, a native of Scotland and a lineal descendant of John Knox, was, in the revolutionary time, president of Princeton College, and was the only clerical member of the Revolutionary Congress. He, as might be expected, earnestly and eloquently supported every measure adopted by Congress for securing independence. When the important moment came for signing the Declaration, and some of the members were hesitating to affix their names to it, he delivered an eloquent appeal, in which he said: 'That noble instrument upon your table, which insures immortality to its author, should be subscribed this very morning by every pen in the house. He that will not respond to its accents, and strain every nerve to carry into effect its provisions, is unworthy the name of a freeman. For my own part, of property I have some, of reputation more. That reputation is staked, that property is pledged, on the issue of this contest. And although these gray hairs must soon descend into the sepulchre, I would infinitely rather they should descend thither by the hand of the public executioner than desert at this crisis the sacred cause of my country.'" [186]

History is eloquent in declaring that American democracy was born of Christianity and that that Christianity was Calvinism. The great Revolutionary conflict which resulted in the formation of the American nation, was carried out mainly by Calvinists, many of whom had been trained in the rigidly Presbyterian College at Princeton, and this nation is their gift to all liberty loving people.

"The Principles of the Republic of the United States," says Schaff," can be traced through the intervening link of Puritanism to Calvinism, which, with all its theological rigor, has been the chief educator of manly character and promoter of constitutional freedom in modern times." [187]

The testimony of Emilio Castelar, the famous Spanish statesman, orator and scholar, is interesting and valuable. Castelar had been professor of Philosophy in the University of Madrid before he entered politics, and he was made president of the republic which was set up by the Liberals in 1873. As a Roman Catholic he hated Calvin and Calvinism. Says he: "It was necessary for the republican movement that there should come a morality more austere than Luther's, the morality of Calvin, and a Church more democratic than the German, the Church of Geneva. The Anglo-Saxon democracy has for its lineage a book of a primitive society--the Bible. It is the product of a severe theology learned by the few Christian fugitives in the gloomy cities of Holland and Switzerland, where the morose shade of Calvin still wanders . . . And it remains serenely in its grandeur, forming the most dignified, most moral and most enlightened portion of the human race." [188] We feel like asking Castelar how a fountain so bitter could send forth such sweet waters.

Says Motley: "In England the seeds of liberty, wrapped up in Calvinism and hoarded through many trying years, were at last destined to float over land and sea, and to bear the largest harvests of temperate freedom for great commonwealths that were still unborn." [189] "The Calvinists founded the commonwealths of England, of Holland, and America." And again, "To Calvinists more than to any other class of men, the political liberties of England, Holland and America are due." [190]

The testimony of another famous historian, the Frenchman Taine, who himself held no religious faith, is worthy of consideration. Concerning the Calvinists he said: "These men are the true heroes of England. They founded England, in spite of the corruption of the Stuarts, by the exercise of duty, by the practice of justice, by obstinate toil, by vindication of right, by resistance to oppression, by the conquest of liberty, by the repression of vice. They founded Scotland; they founded the United States; at this day they are, by their descendants, founding Australia and colonizing the world." [191]

In his book, "The Creed of Presbyterians," E. W. Smith asks concerning the American colonists, "Where learned they those immortal principles of the rights of man, of human liberty, equality and self-government, on which they based their Republic, and which form today the distinctive glory of our American civilization? In the school of Calvin they learned them. There the modern world learned them. So history teaches," (p. 121).

We shall now pass on to consider the influence which the Presbyterian Church as a Church exerted in the formation of the Republic. "The Presbyterian Church," said Dr. W. H. Roberts in an address before the General Assembly, "was for three-quarters of a century the sole representative upon this continent of republican government as now organized in the nation." And then he continues: "From 1706 to the opening of the revolutionary struggle the only body in existence which stood for our present national political organization was the General Synod of the American Presbyterian Church. It alone among ecclesiastical and political colonial organizations exercised authority, derived from the colonists themselves, over bodies of Americans scattered through all the colonies from New England to Georgia. The colonies in the seventeenth and eighteenth centuries, it is to be remembered, while all dependent upon Great Britain, were independent of each other. Such a body as the Continental Congress did not exist until 1774. The religious condition of the country was similar to the political. The Congregational Churches of New England had no connection with each other, and had no power apart from the civil government. The Episcopal Church was without organization in the colonies, was dependent for support

The Reformed Doctrine Of Predestination

and a ministry on the Established Church of England, and was filled with an intense loyalty to the British monarchy. The Reformed Dutch Church did not become an efficient and independent organization until 1771, and the German Reformed Church did not attain to that condition until 1793. The Baptist Churches were separate organizations, the Methodists were practically unknown, and the Quakers were non-combatants."

Delegates met every year in the General Synod, and as Dr. Roberts tells us, the Church became "a bond of union and correspondence between large elements in the population of the divided colonies." "Is it any wonder," he continues, "that under its fostering influence the sentiments of true liberty, as well as the tenets of a sound gospel, were preached throughout the territory from Long Island to South Carolina, and that above all a feeling of unity between the Colonies began slowly but surely to assert itself? Too much emphasis cannot be laid, in connection with the origin of the nation, upon the influence of that ecclesiastical republic, which from 1706 to 1774 was the only representative on this continent of fully developed federal republican institutions. The United States of America owes much to that oldest of American Republics, the Presbyterian Church." [192]

It is, of course, not claimed that the Presbyterian Church was the only source from which sprang the principles upon which this republic is founded, but it is claimed that the principles found in the Westminster Standards were the chief basis for the republic, and that "The Presbyterian Church taught, practiced, and maintained in fulness, first in this land that form of government in accordance with which the Republic has been organized." (Roberts).

The opening of the Revolutionary struggle found the Presbyterian ministers and churches lined up solidly on the side of the colonists, and Bancroft accredits them with having made the first bold move toward independence. [193] The synod which assembled in Philadelphia in 1775 was the first religious body to declare openly and publicly for a separation from England. It urged the people under its jurisdiction to leave nothing undone that would promote the end in view, and called upon them to pray for the Congress which was then in session.

The Episcopalian Church was then still united with the Church of England, and it opposed the Revolution. A considerable number of individuals within that Church, however, labored earnestly for independence and gave of their wealth and influence to secure it. It is to be remembered also that the Commander-in-Chief of the American armies, "the father of our country," was a member of her household. Washington himself attended, and ordered all of his men to attend the services of his chaplains, who were clergymen from the various churches. He gave forty thousand dollars to establish a Presbyterian College in his native state, which took his name in honor of the gift and became Washington College.

N. S. McFetridge has thrown light upon another major development of the Revolutionary period. For the sake of accuracy and completeness we shall take the privilege of quoting him rather extensively. "Another important factor in the independent movement," says he, "was what is known as the 'Mecklenburg Declaration,' proclaimed by the Scotch-Irish Presbyterians of North Carolina, May 20, 1775, more than a year before the Declaration (of Independence) of Congress. It was the fresh, hearty greeting of the Scotch-Irish to their struggling brethren in the North, and their bold challenge to the power of England. They had been keenly watching the progress of the contest between the colonies and the Crown, and when they heard of the address presented by the Congress to the King, declaring the colonies in actual rebellion, they deemed it time for patriots to speak. Accordingly, they called a representative body together in Charlotte, N. C., which by unanimous resolution declared the people free and independent, and that all laws and commissions from the king were henceforth null and void. In their Declaration were such resolutions as these: 'We do hereby dissolve the political bands which have connected us with the mother-country, and hereby absolve ourselves from all allegiance to the British crown. . . . 'We hereby declare ourselves a free and independent people; are, and of right ought to be, a sovereign and self-governing association, under control of no power other than that of our God and the general government of Congress; to the maintenance of which we solemnly pledge to each other our mutual cooperation and our lives, our fortunes and our most sacred honor.' . . . That assembly was composed of twenty-seven staunch Calvinists, just one-third of whom were ruling elders in the Presbyterian Church, including the president and secretary; and one was a Presbyterian clergyman. The man who drew up that famous and important document was the secretary, Ephraim Brevard, a ruling elder of the Presbyterian Church and a graduate of Princeton College. Bancroft says of it that it was, 'in effect, a declaration as well as a complete system of government.' (U.S. Hist. VIII, 40). It was sent by special messenger to the Congress in Philadelphia, and was published in the Cape Fear Mercury, and was widely distributed throughout the land. Of course it was speedily transmitted to England, where it became the cause of intense excitement.

"The identity of sentiment and similarity of expression in this Declaration and the great Declaration written by Jefferson could not escape the eye of the historian; hence Tucker, in his Life of Jefferson, says: 'Everyone must be persuaded that one of these papers must have been borrowed from the other.' But it is certain that Brevard could not have 'borrowed' from Jefferson, for he wrote more than a year before Jefferson; hence Jefferson, according to his biographer, must have 'borrowed' from Brevard. But it was a happy plagiarism, for which the world will freely forgive him. In correcting his first draft of the Declaration it can be seen, in at least a few places, that Jefferson has erased the original words and inserted those which are first found in the Mecklenberg Declaration. No one can doubt that Jefferson had Brevard's resolutions before him when he was writing his immortal Declaration." [194]

This striking similarity between the principles set forth in the Form of Government of the Presbyterian Church and those set forth in the Constitution of the United States has caused much comment. "When the fathers of our Republic sat down to frame a system of representative and popular government," says Dr. E. W. Smith, "their task was not so difficult as some have imagined. They had a model to work by." [195]

"If the average American citizen were asked, who was the founder of America, the true author of our great Republic, he might be puzzled to answer. We can imagine his amazement at hearing the answer given to this question by the famous German historian, Ranke, one of the profoundest scholars of modern times. Says Ranke, 'John Calvin was the virtual founder of America.'" [196]

D'Aubigne, whose history of the Reformation is a classic, writes: "Calvin was the founder of the greatest of republics. The Pilgrims who left their country in the reign of James I, and landing on the barren soil of New England, founded populous and mighty colonies, were his sons, his direct and legitimate sons; and that American nation which we have seen growing so rapidly boasts as its father the humble Reformer on the shore of Lake Leman." [197]

Dr. E. W. Smith says, "These revolutionary principles of republican liberty and self-government, taught and embodied in the system of Calvin, were brought to America, and in this new land where they have borne so mighty a harvest were planted, by whose hands?--the hands of the Calvinists. The vital relation of Calvin and Calvinism to the founding of the free institutions of America, however strange in some ears the statement of Ranke may have sounded, is recognized and affirmed by historians of all lands and creeds." [198]

All this has been thoroughly understood and candidly acknowledged by such penetrating and philosophic historians as Bancroft, who far though he was from being Calvinistic in his own personal convictions, simply calls Calvin "the father of America," and adds: "He who will not honor the memory and respect the influence of Calvin knows but little of the origin of American liberty."

When we remember that two-thirds of the population at the time of the Revolution had been trained in the school of Calvin, and when we remember how unitedly and enthusiastically the Calvinists labored for the cause of independence, we readily see how true are the above testimonies.

There were practically no Methodists in America at the time of the Revolution; and, in fact, the Methodist Church was not officially organized as such in England until the year 1784, which was three years after the American Revolution closed. John Wesley, great and good man though he was, was a Tory and a believer in political non-resistance. He wrote against the American "rebellion," but accepted the providential result. McFetridge tells us: "The Methodists had hardly a foothold in the colonies when the war began. In 1773 they claimed about one hundred and sixty members. Their ministers were almost all, if not all, from England, and were staunch supporters of the Crown against American Independence. Hence, when the war broke out they were compelled to fly from the country. Their political views were naturally in accord with those of their great leader, John Wesley, who wielded all the power of his eloquence and influence against the independence of the colonies. (Bancroft, Hist. U.S., Vol. VII, p. 261.) He did not foresee that independent America was to be the field on which his noble Church was to reap her largest harvests, and that in that Declaration which he so earnestly opposed lay the security of the liberties of his followers." [199]

In England and America the great struggles for civil and religious liberty were nursed in Calvinism, inspired by Calvinism, and carried out largely by men who were Calvinists. And because the majority of historians have never made a serious study of Calvinism they have never been able to give us a truthful and complete account of what it has done in these countries. Only the light of historical investigation is needed to show us how our forefathers believed in it and were controlled by it. We live in a day when the services of the Calvinists in the founding of this country have been largely forgotten, and one can hardly treat of this subject without appearing to be a mere eulogizer of Calvinism. We may well do honor to that Creed which has borne such sweet fruits and to which America owes so much.

8. CALVINISM AND REPRESENTATIVE GOVERNMENT

While religious and civil liberty have no organic connection, they nevertheless have a very strong affinity for each other; and where one is lacking the other will not long endure. History is eloquent in declaring that on a people's religion ever depends their freedom or their bondage. It is a matter of supreme importance what doctrines they believe, what principles they adopt: for these must serve as the basis upon which the superstructure of their lives and their government rests. Calvinism was revolutionary. It taught the natural equality of men, and its essential tendency was to destroy all distinctions of rank and all claims to superiority which rested upon wealth or vested privilege. The

The Reformed Doctrine Of Predestination

liberty-loving soul of the Calvinist has made him a crusader against those artificial distinctions which raise some men above others.

Politically, Calvinism has been the chief source of modern republican government. Calvinism and republicanism are related to each other as cause and effect; and where a people are possessed of the former, the latter will soon be developed. Calvin himself held that the Church, under God, was a spiritual republic; and certainly he was a republican in theory. James I was well aware of the effects of Calvinism when he said: "Presbytery agreeth as well with the monarchy as God with the Devil." Bancroft speaks of "the political character of Calvinism, which with one consent and with instinctive judgment the monarchs of that day feared as republicanism." Another American historian, John Fiske, has written, "It would be hard to overrate the debt which mankind owes to Calvin. The spiritual father of Coligny, of William the Silent, and of Cromwell, must occupy a foremost rank among the champions of modern democracy .... The promulgation of this theology was one of the longest steps that mankind has ever taken toward personal freedom." [200] Emilio Castelar, the leader of the Spanish Liberals, says that "Anglo-Saxon democracy is the product of a severe theology, learned in the cities of Holland and Switzerland." Buckle, in his History of Civilization says, "Calvinism is essentially democratic," (I, 669). And de Tocqueville, an able political writer, calls it "A democratic and republican religion." [201]

The system not only imbued its converts with the spirit of liberty, but it gave them practical training in the rights and duties as freemen. Each congregation was left to elect its own officers and to conduct its own affairs. Fiske pronounces it, "one of the most effective schools that has ever existed for training men in local serf-government." [202] Spiritual freedom is the source and strength of all other freedom, and it need cause no surprise when we are told that the principles which governed them in ecclesiastical affairs gave shape to their political views. Instinctively they preferred a representative government and stubbornly resisted all unjust rulers. After religious despotism is overthrown, civil despotism cannot long continue.

We may say that the spiritual republic which was founded by Calvin rests upon four basic principles. These have been summed up by an eminent English statesman and jurist, Sir James Stephen, as follows: "These principles were, firstly that the will of the people was the one legitimate source of the power of the rulers; secondly, that the power was most properly delegated by the people, to their rulers, by means of elections, in which every adult man might exercise the right of suffrage; thirdly, that in ecclesiastical government, the clergy and laity were entitled to an equal and co-ordinate authority; and fourthly that between the Church and State, no alliance, or mutual dependence, or other definite relation, necessarily or properly existed." [203]

The principle of the sovereignty of God when applied to the affairs of government proved to be very important. God as the supreme Ruler, was vested with sovereignty; and whatever sovereignty was found in man had been graciously granted to him. The scriptures were taken as the final authority, as containing eternal principles which were regulative for all ages and on all peoples. In the following words the Scriptures declared the State to be a divinely established institution: "Let every soul be in subjection to the higher powers: for there is no power but of God; and the powers that be are ordained of God. Therefore he that resisteth the power, withstandeth the ordinance of God; and they that withstand shall receive to themselves judgment. For rulers are not a terror to the good work, but to the evil. And wouldst thou have no fear of the power? do that which is good, and thou shalt have praise for the same: for he is a minister of God to thee for good. But if thou do that which is evil, be afraid; for he beareth not the sword in vain: for he is a minister of God, an avenger for wrath to him that doeth evil. Wherefore ye must needs be in subjection, not only because of the wrath, but also for conscience sake. For this cause ye pay tribute also; for they are ministers of God's service, attending continually upon this very thing. Render to all their dues; custom to whom custom; fear to whom fear; honor to whom honor," Romans 13:1-7.

No one type of government, however, whether democracy, republic, or monarchy, was thought to be divinely ordained for any certain age or people, although Calvinism showed a preference for the republican type. "Whatever the system of government," says Meeter, "be it monarchy or democracy or any other form, in each case the ruler (or rulers) was to act as God's representative, and to administer the affairs of government in accordance with God's law. The fundamental principle supplied at the same time the very highest incentive for the preservation of law and order among its citizens. Subjects were for God's sake to render obedience to the higher powers, whichever these might be. Hence Calvinism made for highly stabilized governments.

"On the other hand this very principle of the sovereignty of God operated as a mighty defense of the liberties of the subject citizens against tyrannical rulers. Whenever sovereigns ignored the Will of God, trampled upon the rights of the governed and became tyrannical, it became the privilege and the duty of the subjects, in view of the higher responsibility of the supreme Sovereign, God, to refuse obedience and even, if necessary, to depose the tyrant, through the lesser authorities appointed by God for the defense of the rights of the governed." [204]

The Calvinistic ideas concerning governments and rulers have been ably expressed by J. C.

Monsma in the following lucid paragraph: "Governments are instituted by God through the instrumentality of the people. No kaiser or president has any power inherent in himself; whatever power he possesses, whatever sovereignty he exercises, is power and sovereignty derived from the great Source above. No might, but right, and right springing from the eternal Fountain of justice. For the Calvinist it is extremely easy to respect the laws and ordinances of the government. If the government were nothing but a group of men, bound to carry out the wishes of a popular majority, his freedom-loving soul would rebel. But now, to his mind, and according to his fixed belief,--back of the government stands God, and before Him he kneels in deepest reverence. Here also lies the fundamental reason for that profound and almost fanatical love of freedom, also the political freedom, which has always been a characteristic of the genuine Calvinist. The government is God's servant. That means that AS MEN all government officials stand on an equal footing with their subordinates; have no claim to superiority in any sense whatever For exactly the same reason the Calvinist gives preference to a republican form of government over any other type. In no other form of government does the sovereignty of God, the derivative character of government powers and the equality of men as men, find a clearer and more eloquent expression." [205]

The theology of the Calvinist exalted one Sovereign and humbled all other sovereigns before His awful majesty. The divine right of kings and the infallible decrees of popes could not long endure amid a people who place sovereignty in God alone. But while this theology infinitely exalted God as the Almighty Ruler of heaven and earth and humbled all men before Him, it enhanced the dignity of the individual and taught him that all men as men were equal. The Calvinist feared God; and fearing God he feared nobody else. Knowing himself to have been chosen in the counsels of eternity and marked for the glories of heaven, he possessed something which dissipated the feeling of personal homage for men and which dulled the lustre of all earthly grandeur. If a proud aristocracy traced its lineage through generations of highborn ancestry, the Calvinists, with a loftier pride, invaded the invisible world, and from the book of life brought down the record of the noblest enfranchisement, decreed from eternity by the King of kings. By a higher than any earthly lineage they were heaven's noblemen because God's sons and priests, joint heirs with Christ, kings and priests unto God, by a divine anointing and consecration. Put the truth of the sovereignty of God into a man's mind and heart, and you put iron in his blood. The Reformed Faith has rendered a most valuable service in teaching the individual his rights.

In striking contrast with these democratic and republican tendencies which are found to be inherent in the Reformed Faith we find that Arminianism has a very pronounced aristocratic tendency. In the Presbyterian and Reformed Churches the elder votes in Presbytery or Synod or General Assembly on full equality with his pastor; but in Arminian churches the power is largely in the hands of the clergy, and the laymen have very little real authority. Episcopacy stresses rule by the hierarchy. Arminianism and Roman Catholicism (which is practically Arminian) thrive under a monarchy, but there Calvinism finds its life cramped. On the other hand Romanism especially does not thrive in a republic, but there Calvinism finds itself most at home. An aristocratic form of church government tends toward monarchy in civil affairs, while a republican form of church government tends toward democracy in civil affairs. Says McFetridge, "Arminianism is unfavorable to civil liberty, and Calvinism is unfavorable to despotism. The despotic rulers of former days were not slow to observe the correctness of these propositions, and, claiming the divine right of kings, feared Calvinism as republicanism itself." [206]

9. CALVINISM AND EDUCATION

Again, history bears very clear testimony that Calvinism and education have been intimately associated. Wherever Calvinism has gone it has carried the school with it and has given a powerful impulse to popular education. It is a system which demands intellectual manhood. In fact, we may say that its very existence is tied up with the education of the people. Mental training is required to master the system and to trace out all that it involves. It makes the strongest possible appeal to the human reason and insists that man must love God not only with his whole heart but also with his whole mind. Calvin held that "a true faith must be an intelligent faith"; and experience has shown that piety without learning is in the long run about as dangerous as learning without piety. He saw clearly that the acceptance and diffusion of his scheme of doctrine was dependent not only upon the training of the men who were to expound it, but also upon the intelligence of the great masses of humanity who were to accept it. Calvin crowned his work in Geneva in the establishment of the Academy. Thousands of pilgrim pupils from Continental Europe and from the British Isles sat at his feet and then carried his doctrines into every corner of Christendom. Knox returned from Geneva fully convinced that the education of the masses was the strongest bulwark of Protestantism and the surest foundation of the State. "With Romanism goes the priest; with Calvinism goes the teacher," is an old saying, the truthfulness of which will not be denied by anyone who has examined the facts.

This Calvinistic love for learning, putting mind above money, has inspired countless numbers of Calvinistic families in Scotland, in England, in Holland, and in America, to pinch themselves to the bone in order to educate their children. The famous dictum of Carlyle, "That any being with capacity for knowledge should die ignorant, this I call a tragedy," expresses an idea which is Calvinistic to the core. Wherever Calvinism has gone, there knowledge and learning have been encouraged and there a sturdy race of thinkers has been trained. Calvinists have not been the builders of great cathedrals, but they have been the builders of schools, colleges, and universities. When the Puritans from England, the Covenanters from Scotland, and the Reformed from Holland and Germany, came to America they brought with them not only the Bible and the Westminster Confession but also the school. And that is why our American Calvinism never

> *"Dreads the skeptic's puny hands,*
> *While near her school the church spire stands,*
> *Nor fears the blinded bigot's rule,*
> *While near her church spire stands a school."*

Our three American universities of greatest historical importance, Harvard, Yale, and Princeton, were originally founded by Calvinists, as strong Calvinistic schools, designed to give students a sound basis in theology as well as in other branches of learning. Harvard, established in 1636, was intended primarily to be a training school for ministers, and more than half of its first graduating classes went into the ministry. Yale, sometimes referred to as "the mother of Colleges," was for a considerable period a rigid Puritan institution. And Princeton, founded by the Scotch Presbyterians, had a thoroughly Calvinistic foundation.

"We boast," says Bancroft, "of our common schools; Calvin was the father of popular education--the inventor of the system of free schools." [207] "Wherever Calvinism gained dominion," he says again, "it invoked intelligence for the people and in every parish planted the common school." [208]

"Our boasted common-school system," says Smith, "is indebted for its existence to that stream of influences which followed from the Geneva of Calvin, through Scotland and Holland to America; and, for the first two hundred years of our history almost every college and seminary of learning and almost every academy and common school was built and sustained by Calvinists." [209]

The relationship which Calvinism bears to education has been well stated in the two following paragraphs by Prof. H. H. Meeter, of Calvin College: "Science and art were the gifts of God's common grace, and were to be used and developed as such. Nature was looked upon as God's handiwork, the embodiment of His ideas, in its pure form the reflection of His virtues. God was the unifying thought of all science, since all was the unfolding of His plan. But along with such theoretical reasons there are very practical reasons why the Calvinist has always been intensely interested in education, and why grade schools for children as well as schools of higher learning sprang up side by side with Calvinistic churches, and why Calvinists were in so large measure the vanguard of the modern universal education movement. These practical reasons are closely associated with their religion. The Roman Catholics might conveniently do without the education of the masses. For them the clergy--in distinction from the laity--were the ones who were to decide upon matters of church government and doctrine. Hence these interests did not require the training of the masses. For salvation, all that the layman needed was an implied faith in what the church believed. It was not necessary to be able to give an intelligent account of the tenets of his faith. At the services not the sermon but the sacrament was the important conveyor of the blessings of salvation, the sermon was less needed. And this sacrament again did not require intelligence, since it operated ex opere operato.

"For the Calvinist matters were just reversed. The government of the church was placed in the hands of the elders, laymen, and these had to decide upon the matters of church policy and the weighty matters of doctrine. Furthermore, the layman himself had the grave duty, without the intermediation of a sacerdotal order, to work out his own salvation, and could not suffice with an implied faith in what the church believed. He must read his Bible. He must know his creed. And it was a highly intellectual erred at that. Even for the Lutheran, education of the masses was not as urgent as for the Calvinist. It is true, the Lutheran also placed every man before the personal responsibility to work out his own salvation. But the laity were in the Lutheran circles excluded from the office of church government and hence also from the duty of deciding upon matters of doctrine. From these considerations it is evident why the Calvinist must be a staunch advocate of education. If on the one hand God was to be owned as sovereign in the field of science, and if the Calvinist's very religious system required the education of the masses for its existence, it need not surprise us that the Calvinist pressed learning to the limit. Education is a question of to be or not to be for the Calvinist." [210]

The traditionally high standards of the Presbyterian and Reformed Churches for ministerial training are worthy of notice. While many other churches ordain men as ministers and missionaries and allow them to preach with very little education, the Presbyterian and Reformed Churches insist that the candidate for the ministry shall be a college graduate and that he shall have studied for at least two years under some approved professor of theology. (See Form of Government, Ch. XIV, sec. III & VI). As a result a larger proportion of these ministers have been capable of managing the affairs of the influential city churches. This may mean fewer ministers but it also means a better prepared and a better paid ministry.

10. JOHN CALVIN

John Calvin was born July 10, 1509, at Noyon, France, an ancient cathedral city about seventy miles northeast of Paris. His father, a man of rather hard and severe character, held the position as apostolic secretary to the bishop of Noyon, and was intimate with the best families of the neighborhood. His mother was noted for her beauty and piety, but died in his early youth.

He received the best education which France at that time could give, studying successively at the three leading universities of Orleans, Bourges, and Paris, from 1528 to 1533. His father intended to prepare him for the legal profession since that commonly raised those who followed it to positions of wealth and influence. But not feeling any particular calling to that field, young Calvin turned to the study of Theology and there found the sphere of labor for which he was particularly fitted by natural endowment and personal choice. He is described as having been of a shy and retiring nature, very studious and punctual in his work, animated by a strict sense of duty, and exceedingly religious. He early showed himself possessed of an intellect capable of clear, convincing argument and logical analysis. Through excessive industry he stored his mind with valuable information, but undermined his health. He advanced so rapidly that he was occasionally asked to take the place of the professors, and was considered by the other students as a doctor rather than an auditor. He was, at this time, a devout Catholic of unblemished character. A brilliant career as a humanist, or lawyer, or churchman, was opening before him when he was suddenly converted to Protestantism, and cast in his lot with the poor persecuted sect.

Without any intention on his part, and even against his own desire, Calvin became the head of the evangelical party in Paris in less than a year after his conversion. His depth of knowledge and earnestness of speech were such that no one could hear him without being forcibly impressed. For the present he remained in the Catholic Church, hoping to reform it from within rather than from without. Schaff reminds us that "all the Reformers were born, baptized, confirmed, and educated in the historic Catholic Church, which cast them out; as the Apostles were circumcised and trained in the Synagogue, which cast them out." [211]

The zeal and earnestness of the new Reformer did not long go unchallenged and it soon became necessary for Calvin to escape for his life. The following account of his flight from Pads is given by the Church historian, Philip Schaff: "Nicholas Cop, the son of a distinguished royal physician (William Cop of Basel), and a friend of Calvin was elected Rector of the University, Oct. 10, 1533, and delivered the usual inaugural oration on All Saints' Day, Nov. 1, before a large assembly in the Church of the Mathurins. This oration, at the request of the new Rector, had been prepared by Calvin. It was a plea for a reformation on the basis of the New Testament, and a bold attack on the scholastic theologians of the day, who were represented as a set of sophists, ignorant of the Gospel .... The Sorbonne and the Parliament regarded this academic oration as a manifesto of war upon the Catholic Church, and condemned it to the flames. Cop was warned and fled to his relatives in Basel. (Three hundred crowns were offered for his capture, dead or alive.) Calvin, the real author of the mischief, is said to have descended from a window by means of sheets, and escaped from Paris in the garb of a vine-dresser with a hoe upon his shoulder. His rooms were searched and his books and papers were seized by the police .... Twenty-four innocent Protestants were burned alive in public places of the city from Nov. 10, 1534, till May 5, 1535....Many more were fined, imprisoned, and tortured, and a considerable number, among them Calvin and Du Tillet, fled to Strassburg . . . For nearly three years Calvin wandered as a fugitive evangelist under assumed names from place to place in southern France, Switzerland, and Italy, till he reached Geneva as his final destination." [212]

Shortly after, if not before, the first edition of his Institutes appeared, in March, 1536, Calvin and Louis Du Tillet crossed the Alps into Italy where the literary and artistic Renaissance had its origin. There he labored as an evangelist until the Inquisition began its work of crushing out both the Renaissance and the Reformation as two kindred serpents. He then bent his way, probably through Asota and over the Great St. Bernard, to Switzerland. From Basel he made a last visit to his native town of Noyon in order to make a final settlement of certain family affairs. Then, with his younger brother Antoine and his sister Marie, he left France forever, hoping to settle in Basel or Strassburg and to lead there the quiet life of a scholar and author. Owing to the fact that a state of war existed between Charles V. and Francis I., the direct route through Lorraine was closed, so he made a circuitous journey through Geneva.

Calvin intended to stop only a night in Geneva, but Providence had decreed otherwise. His presence was made known to Farel, the Genevan reformer, who instinctively felt that Calvin was the man to complete and save the Reformation in Geneva. A fine description of this meeting of Calvin and Farel is given by Schaff. Says he: "Farel at once called on Calvin and held him fast, as by divine command. Calvin protested, pleading his youth, his inexperience, his need of further study, his natural timidity and bashfulness, which unfitted him for public action. But all in vain. Farel, 'who burned of a marvelous zeal to advance the Gospel,' threatened him with the curse of Almighty God if he preferred his studies to the work of the Lord, and his own interest to the cause of Christ. Calvin was terrified and shaken by these words of the fearless evangelist, and felt 'as if God from on high had stretched out His hand.' He submitted, and accepted the call to the ministry, as teacher and pastor of the evangelical Church of Geneva." [213]

Calvin was twenty-five years younger than Luther and Zwingli, and had the great advantage of building on the foundation which they had laid. The first ten years of Calvin's public career were contemporary with the last ten of Luther's although the two never met personally. Calvin was intimate with Melanchthon, however, and kept up a correspondence with him until his death.

At the time Calvin came upon the scene it had not yet been determined whether Luther was to be the hero of a great success or the victim of a great failure. Luther had produced new ideas; Calvin's work was to construct them into a system, to preserve and develop what had been so nobly begun. The Protestant movement lacked unity and was in danger of being sunk in the quicksand of doctrinal dispute, but was saved from that fate chiefly by the new :impulse which was given to it by the Reformer in Geneva. The Catholic Church worked as one mighty unit and was seeking to stamp out, by fair means or foul, the different Protestant groups which had arisen in the North. Zwingli had seen this danger and had tried to unite the Protestants against their common foe. At Marburg, after pleadings and with tears in his eyes, he extended to Luther the hand of fellowship regardless of their difference of opinion as to the mode of Christ's presence in the Lord's Supper; but Luther refused it under the restraint of a narrow dogmatic conscience. Calvin also, working in Switzerland with abundant opportunity to realize the closeness of the Italian Church, saw the need for union and labored to keep Protestantism together. To Cranmer, in England, he wrote, "I long for one holy communion of the members of Christ. As for me, if I can be of service, I would gladly cross ten seas in order to bring about this unity." His influence as exerted through his books, letters, and students, was powerfully felt throughout the various countries, and the statement that he saved the Protestant movement from destruction seems to be no exaggeration.

For thirty years Calvin's one absorbing interest was the advancement of the Reformation. Reed says, "He toiled for it to the utmost limit of his strength, fought for it with a courage that never quailed, suffered for it with a fortitude that never wavered, and was ready at any moment to die for it. He literally poured every drop of his life into it, unhesitatingly, unsparingly. History will be searched in vain to find a man who gave himself to one definite purpose with more unalterable persistence, and with more lavish serf-abandon than Calvin gave himself to the Reformation of the 16th century." [214]

Probably no servant of Christ since the days of the Apostles has been at the same time so much loved and hated, admired and abhorred, praised and blamed, blessed and cursed, as the faithful, fearless, and immortal Calvin. Living in a fiercely polemic age, and standing on the watchtower of the reform movement in Western Europe, he was the observed of all observers, and was exposed to attacks from every quarter. Religious and sectarian passions are the deepest and strongest, and in view of the good and the bad which is known to exist in human nature in this world we need not be surprised at the reception given Calvin's teachings and writings.

When only twenty-six years of age Calvin published in Latin his "Institutes of the Christian Religion." The first edition contained in brief outline all the essential elements of his system, and, considering the youthfulness of the author, was a marvel of intellectual precocity. It was later enlarged to five times the size of the original and published in French, but never did he make any radical departure from any of the doctrines set forth in the first edition. Almost immediately the Institutes took first place as the best exhibition and defense of the Protestant cause. Other writings bad dealt with certain phases of the movement but here was one that treated it as a unit. "The value of such a gift to the Reformation," says Reed, "cannot easily be exaggerated. Protestants and Romanists bore equal testimony to its worth. The one hailed it as the greatest boon; the other execrated it with the bitterest curses. It was burnt by order of the Sorbonne at Paris and other places, and everywhere it called forth the fiercest assaults of tongue and pen. Florimond de Raemond, a Roman Catholic theologian, calls it 'the Koran, the Talmud of heresy, the foremost cause of our downfall.' Kampachulte, another Roman Catholic, testifies that 'it was the common arsenal from which the opponents of the Old Church borrowed their keenest weapons,' and that 'no writing of the Reformation era was more feared by Roman Catholics, more zealously fought against, and more bitterly pursued than Calvin's Institutes.' Its popularity was evidenced by the fact that edition followed edition in quick succession; it was translated into most of the languages of western Europe; it became the common text-book in the schools of the Reformed Churches, and furnished the material out of which their creeds were made." [215]

"Of all the services which Calvin rendered to humanity," says Dr. Warfield,"--and they were neither few nor small--the greatest was undoubtedly his gift to it afresh of this system of religious thought, quickened into new life by the forces of his genius." [216]

The Institutes were at once greeted by the Protestants with enthusiastic praise as the clearest, strongest, most logical, and most convincing defense of Christian doctrines since the days of the

Apostles. Schaff characterizes them well when he says that in them "Calvin gave a systematic exposition of the Christian religion in general, and a vindication of the evangelical faith in particular, with the apologetic and practical aim of defending the Protestant believers against calumny and persecution to which they were then exposed, especially in France." [217] The work is pervaded by an intense earnestness and by fearless and severe argumentation which properly subordinates reason and tradition to the supreme authority of the Scriptures. It is admittedly the greatest book of the century, and through it the Calvinistic principles were propagated on an immense scale. Albrecht Ritschl calls it "the masterpiece of Protestant theology." Dr. Warfield tells us that "after three centuries and a half it retains its unquestioned preeminence as the greatest and most influential of all dogmatic treatises." And again he says, "Even from the point of mere literature, it holds a position so supreme in its class that every one who would fain know the world's best books, must make himself familiar with it. What Thucydides is among Greek, or Gibbon among eighteenth-century English historians, what Plato is among philosophers, or the Iliad among epics, or Shakespeare among dramatists, that Calvin's 'Institutes' is among theological treatises." [218] It threw consternation into the Roman Church and was a powerful unifying force among Protestants. It showed Calvin to be the ablest controversialist in Protestantism and as the most formidable antagonist with which the Romanists had to contend. In England the Institutes enjoyed an almost unrivaled popularity, and was used as a text book in the universities. It was soon translated into nine different European languages; and it is simply due to a serious lack in the majority of historical accounts that its importance has not been appreciated in recent years.

A few weeks after the publication of the Institutes, Bucer, who ranks third among the Reformers in Germany, wrote to Calvin: "It is evident that the Lord had elected you as His organ for the bestowment of the richest fulness of blessing to His Church." Luther wrote no systematic theology. Although his writings were voluminous, they were on scattered subjects and many of them deal with the practical problems of his day. It was thus left to Calvin to give a systematic exhibition of the evangelical faith.

Calvin was, first of all, a theologian. He and Augustine easily rank as the two outstanding systematic expounders of the Christian system since St. Paul. Melanchthon, who was himself the prince of Lutheran theologians, and who, after the death of Luther, was recognized as the "Preceptor of Germany," called Calvin preeminently "the theologian."

If the language of the Institutes seems harsh in places we should remember that this was the mark and weakness of theological controversy in that age. The times in which Calvin lived were polemic. The Protestants were engaged in a life and death struggle with Rome and the provocations to impatience were numerous and grievous. Calvin, however, was surpassed by Luther in the use of harsh language as will readily be seen by an examination of the latter's work, The Bondage of the Will, which was a polemic written against the free-will ideas of Erasmus. And furthermore, none of the Protestant writings of the period were so harsh and abusive as were the Roman Catholic decrees of excommunication, anathemas, etc., which were directed against the Protestants.

In addition to the Institutes, Calvin wrote commentaries on nearly all of the books of both the Old and New Testaments. These commentaries in the English translation comprise fifty-five large volumes, and, taken in connection with his other works, are nothing less than marvelous. The quality of these writings was such that they soon took first place among exegetical works on the Scriptures; and among all the older commentators no one is more frequently quoted by the best modern scholars than is Calvin. He was beyond all question the greatest exegete of the Reformation period. As Luther was the prince of translators, so Calvin was the prince of commentators.

Furthermore, in order to estimate the true value of Calvin's commentaries, it must be borne in mind that they were based on principles of exegesis which were rare in his day. "He led the way," says R. C. Reed, "in discarding the custom of allegorizing the Scriptures, a custom which had come down from the earliest centuries of Christianity and which had been sanctioned by the greatest names of the Church, from Origen to Luther, a custom which converts the Bible into a nose of wax, and makes a lively fancy the prime qualification of an exegete." [219] Calvin adhered strictly to the spirit and letter of the author and assumed that the writer had one definite thought which was expressed in natural everyday language. He mercilessly exposed the corrupt doctrines and practices of the Roman Catholic Church. His writings inspired the friends of reform and furnished them with most of their deadly ammunition. We can hardly overestimate the influence of Calvin in furthering and safeguarding the Reformation.

Calvin was a master of patristic and scholastic learning. Having been educated in the leading universities of his time, he possessed a thorough knowledge of Latin and French, and a good knowledge of Greek and Hebrew. His principal commentaries appeared in both French and Latin versions and are works of great thoroughness. They are eminently fair and frank, and show the author to have been possessed of a singular balance and moderation in judgment. Calvin's works had a further effect in giving form and permanence to the then unstablized French language in much the same way that Luther's translation of the Bible moulded the German language.

The Reformed Doctrine Of Predestination

One other testimony which we should not omit is that of Arminius, the originator of the rival system. Certainly here we have testimony from an unbiased source. "Next to the study of the Scriptures," he says, "I exhort my pupils to pursue Calvin's commentaries, which I extol in loftier terms than Helmick himself (Helmick was a Dutch theologian); for I affirm that he excels beyond comparison in the interpretation of Scripture, and that his commentaries ought to be more highly valued than all that is handed down to us by the library of the fathers; so that I acknowledge him to have possessed above most others, as rather above all other men, what may be called an eminent gift of prophecy." [220]

The influence of Calvin was further spread through a voluminous correspondence which he carried on with church leaders, princes, and nobles throughout Protestant Christendom. More than 300 of these letters are still preserved today, and as a rule they are not brief friendship exchanges but lengthy and carefully prepared treatises setting forth in a masterly way his views of perplexing ecclesiastical and theological questions. In this manner also his influence in guiding the Reformation throughout Europe was profound.

Due to an attempt of Calvin and Farel to enforce a too severe system of discipline in Geneva, it became necessary for them to leave the city temporarily. This was two years after Calvin's coming. Calvin went to Strassburg, in southwestern Germany, where he was warmly received by Bucer and the leading men of the German Reformation. There he spent the next three years in quiet and useful labors as professor, pastor, and author, and came into contact with Lutheranism at first hand. He had a great appreciation for the Luthern leaders and felt closely allied to the Lutheran Church, although he was unfavorably impressed with the lack of discipline and with the dependence of the clergy upon the secular rulers. He later followed the progress of the Reformation in Germany step by step with the warmest interest, as is shown in his correspondence and various writings. During his absence from Geneva affairs reached such a crisis that it seemed that the fruits of the Reformation would be lost and he was urgently requested to return. After repeated urgings from various sources he did so and took up the work where he had left off before.

The city of Geneva, located on the shores of a lake which bears the same name, was Calvin's home. There, among the snow-capped Alps, he spent most of his adult life, and from there the Reformed Church has spread out through Europe and America. In the affairs of the Church, as well as in the affairs of the State, the little country of Switzerland has exerted an influence far out of proportion to its size.

Calvin's influence in Geneva gives us a fair sample of the transforming power of his system. "The Genevese," says the eminent church historian, Philip Schaff, "were a light-hearted, joyous people, fond of public amusements, dancing, singing, masquerades, and revelries. Recklessness, gambling, drunkenness, adultery, blasphemy, and all sorts of vice abounded. Prostitution was sanctioned by the authority of the State, and superintended by a woman called the Reine de bordel. The people were ignorant. The priest had taken no pains to instruct them, and had set them a bad example." From a study of contemporary history we find that shortly before Calvin went to Geneva the monks and even the bishop were guilty of crimes which today are punishable with the death penalty. The result of Calvin's work in Geneva was that the city became more famed for the quiet, orderly lives of its citizens than it had previously been for their wickedness. John Knox, like thousands of others who came to sit as admiring students at Calvin's feet, found there what he termed "the most perfect school of Christ that ever was on the earth since the days of the Apostles."

Through Calvin's work Geneva became an asylum for the persecuted, and a training school for the Reformed Faith. Refugees from all the countries of Europe fled to this retreat, and from it they carried back with them the clearly taught principles of the Reformation. It thus acted as a center emanating spiritual power and educational forces which guided and moulded the Reformation in the surrounding countries. Says Bancroft, "More truly benevolent to the human race than Solon, more self-denying than Lycurgus, the genius of Calvin infused enduring elements into the institutions of Geneva and made it for the modern world the impregnable fortress of popular liberty, the fertile seed-plot of democracy."[221]

Witness as to the effectiveness of the influences which emanated from Geneva is found in one of the letters of the Roman Catholic Francis de Sales to the duke of Savoy, urging the suppression of Geneva as the capital of what the Romish Church calls heresy. "All the heretics," said he, "respect Geneva as the asylum of their religion.... There is not a city in Europe which offers more facilities for the encouragement of heresy, for it is the gate of France, of Italy, and of Germany, so that one finds there people of all nations--Italians, French, Germans, Poles, Spaniards, English, and of countries still more remote. Besides, every one knows the great number of ministers bred there. Last year it furnished twenty to France. Even England obtains ministers from Geneva. What shall I say of its magnificent printing establishments, by means of which the city floods the world with its wicked books, and even goes the length of distributing them at the public expense? ....All the enterprises undertaken against the Holy See and the Catholic princes have their beginnings at Geneva. No city in Europe receives more apostates of all grades, secular and regular. From thence I conclude that Geneva being destroyed would naturally lead to the dissipation of heresy." [222]

Another testimony is that of one of the most bitter foes of Protestantism, Philip II of Spain. He wrote to the king of France: "This city is the source of all mischief for France, the most formidable enemy of Rome. At any time, I am ready to assist with all the power of my realm in its overthrow." And when the Duke of Alva was expected to pass near Geneva with his army, Pope Pius V asked him to turn aside and "destroy that nest of devils and apostates."

The famous academy of Geneva was opened in 1558. With Calvin there were associated ten able and experienced professors who gave instruction in grammar, logic, mathematics, physics, music, and the ancient languages. The school was remarkably successful. During the first year more than nine hundred students, mostly refugees from the various European countries, were enrolled, and almost as many more attended his theological lectures preparing themselves to be evangelists and teachers in their native countries and to establish churches after the model which they had seen in Geneva. For more than two hundred years it remained the principal school of Reformed Theology and literary culture.

Calvin was the first of the Reformers to demand complete separation between Church and State, and thus he advanced another principle which has been of inestimable value. The German Reformation was decided by the will of the princes; the Swiss Reformation, by the will of the people; although in each case there was a sympathy between the rulers and the majority of the population. The Swiss Reformers, however, living in the republic at Geneva, developed a free Church in a free State, while Luther and Melanchthon, with their native reverence for monarchial institutions and the German Empire, taught passive obedience in politics and brought the Church under bondage to the civil authority.

Calvin died in the year 1564, at the early age of fifty-five. Beza, his close friend and successor, describes his death as having come quietly as sleep, and then adds: "Thus withdrew into heaven, at the same time with the setting sun, that most brilliant luminary, which was the lamp of the Church. On the following night and day there was intense grief and lamentation in the whole city; for the Republic had lost its wisest citizen, the Church its faithful shepherd, and the Academy an incomparable teacher."

Schaff describes Calvin as "one of those characters that command respect and admiration rather than affection, and forbid familiar approach, but gain upon closer acquaintance. The better he is known, the more he is admired and esteemed." And concerning his death Schaff says: "Calvin had expressly forbidden all pomp at his funeral and the erection of any monument over his grave. He wished to be buried, like Moses, out of reach of idolatry. This was consistent, with his theology, which humbles man and exalts God." [223] Even the spot of his grave in the cemetery at Geneva is unknown. A plain stone, with the initials "J. C.," is pointed out to strangers as marking his resting-place, but it is not known on what authority. He himself requested that no monument should mark his grave. His real monument, however, says S. L. Morris, is "every republican government on earth, the public school system of all nations, and 'The Reformed Churches throughout the world holding the Presbyterian System.'"

We must now consider an event in the life of Calvin which to a certain extent has cast a shadow over his fair name and which has exposed him to the charge of intolerance and persecution. We refer to the death of Servetus which occurred in Geneva during the period of Calvin's work there. That it was a mistake is admitted by all. History knows only one spotless being--the Savior of sinners. All others have marks of infirmity written which forbid idolatry.

Calvin has, however, often been criticized with undue severity as though the responsibility rested upon him alone, when as a matter of fact Servetus was given a court trial lasting over two months and was sentenced by the full session of the civil Council, and that in accordance with the laws which were then recognized throughout Christendom. And, far from urging that the sentence be made more severe, Calvin urged that the sword be substituted for the fire, but was overruled. Calvin and the men of his time are not to be judged strictly and solely by the advanced standards of our twentieth century, but must to a certain extent be considered in the light of their own sixteenth century. We have seen great developments in regard to civil and religious toleration, prison reform, abolition of slavery and the slave trade, feudalism, witch burning, improvement of the conditions of the poor, etc., which are the late but genuine results of Christian teachings. The error of those who advocated and practiced what would be considered intolerance today, was the general error of the age. It should not, in fairness, be permitted to give an unfavorable impression of their character and motives, and much less should it be allowed to prejudice us against their doctrines on other and more important subjects.

The Protestants had just thrown off the yoke of Rome and in their struggle to defend themselves they were often forced to fight intolerance with intolerance. Throughout the sixteenth and seventeenth centuries public opinion in all European countries justified the right and duty of civil governments to protect and support orthodoxy and to punish heresy, holding that obstinate heretics and blasphemers should be made harmless by death if necessary. Protestants differed from Romanists mainly in their definition of heresy, and by greater moderation in its punishment. Heresy was considered a sin against society, and in some cases as worse than murder; for while murder only destroyed the body, heresy destroyed the soul. Today we have swung to the other extreme and public opinion manifests a latitudinarian indifference toward truth or error. During the eighteenth century the reign of intolerance was gradually undermined. Protestant England and Holland took the lead in extending civil and

The Reformed Doctrine Of Predestination

religious liberty, and the Constitution of the United States completed the theory by putting all Christian denominations on a parity before the law and guaranteeing them the full enjoyment of equal rights.

Calvin's course in regard to Servetus was fully approved by all the leading Reformers of the time. Melanchthon, the theological head of the Lutheran Church, fully and repeatedly justified the course of Calvin and the Council of Geneva, and even held them up as models for imitation. Nearly a year after the death of Servetus he wrote to Calvin: "I have read your book, in which you dearly refuted the horrid blasphemies of Servetus .... To you the Church owes gratitude at the present moment, and will owe it to the latest posterity. I perfectly assent to your opinion. I affirm also that your. magistrates did right in punishing, after regular trial, this blasphemous man." Bucer, who ranks third among the Reformers in Germany, Bullinger, the close friend and worthy successor of Zwingli, as well as Farel and Beza in Switzerland, supported Calvin. Luther and Zwingli were dead at this time and it may be questioned whether they would have approved this execution or not, although Luther and the theologians of Wittenberg had approved of death sentences for some Anabaptists in Germany whom they considered dangerous heretics,--adding that it was cruel to punish them, but more cruel to allow them to damn the ministry of the Word and destroy the kingdom of the world; and Zwingli had not objected to a death sentence against a group of six Anabaptists in Switzerland. Public opinion has undergone a great change in regard to this event, and the execution of Servetus which was fully approved by the best men in the sixteenth century is as fully condemned in the nineteenth century.

As stated before, the Roman Catholic Church in this period was desperately intolerant toward Protestants; and the Protestants, to a certain extent and in self-defense, were forced to follow their example. In regard to Catholic persecutions Philip Schaff writes as follows: "We need only refer to crusades against the Albigenses and Waldenses, which were sanctioned by Innocent III, one of the best and greatest of popes; the tortures and autos-da-fé of the Spanish Inquisition, which were celebrated with religious festivities; and fifty thousand or more Protestants who were executed during the reign of the Duke of Alva in the Netherlands (1567-1573); the several hundred martyrs who were burned in Smithfield under the reign of bloody Mary; and the repeated wholesale persecutions of the innocent Waldenses in France and Piedmont, which cried to heaven for vengeance. It is vain to shift the responsibility upon the civil government. Pope Gregory XIII commemorated the massacre of St. Bartholomew not only by a Te Deum in the churches of Rome, but more deliberately and permanently by a medal which represents 'The Slaughter of the Huguenots' by an angel of wrath." [224]

And then Dr. Schaff continues: "The Roman Church has lost the power, and to a large extent also the disposition, to persecute by fire and sword. Some of her highest dignitaries frankly disown the principle of persecution, especially in America, where they enjoy the full benefits of religious freedom. But the Roman curia has never officially disowned the theory on which the practice of persecution is based. On the contrary, several popes since the Reformation have indorsed it .... Pope Pius IX., in the Syllabus of 1864, expressly condemned, among the errors of this age, the doctrine of religious toleration and liberty. And this pope has been declared to be officially infallible by the Vatican decree of 1870, which embraces all of his predecessors (notwithstanding the stubborn case of Honorius I) and all his successors in the chair of St. Peter," (p. 669). And in another place Dr. Schaff adds, "If Romanists condemned Calvin, they did it from hatred of the man, and condemned him for following their own example even in this particular case."

Servetus was a Spaniard and opposed Christianity, whether in its Roman Catholic or Protestant form. Schaff refers to him as "a restless fanatic, a pantheistic pseudo-reformer, and the most audacious and even blasphemous heretic of the sixteenth century." [225] And in another instance Schaff declares that Servetus was "proud, defiant, quarrelsome, revengeful, irreverent in the use of language, deceitful, and mendacious"; and adds that he abused popery and the Reformers alike with unreasonable language. [226] Bullinger declares that if Satan himself should come out of hell, he could use no more blasphemous language against the Trinity than this Spaniard. The Roman Catholic Bolsec, in his work on Calvin, calls Servetus "a very arrogant and insolent man," "a monstrous heretic," who deserved to be exterminated.

Servetus had fled to Geneva from Vienne, France; and while the trial at Geneva was in progress the Council received a message from the Catholic judges in Vienne together with a copy of the sentence of death which had been passed against him there, asking that he be sent back in order that the sentence might be executed on him as it had already been executed on his effigy and books. This request the Council refused but promised to do full justice. Servetus himself preferred to be tried in Geneva, since he could see only a burning funeral pyre for himself in Vienne. The communication from Vienne probably made the Council in Geneva more zealous for orthodoxy since they did not wish to be behind the Roman Church in that respect.

Before going to Geneva Servetus had urged himself upon the attention of Calvin through a long series of letters. For a time Calvin replied to these in considerable detail, but finding no satisfactory results were being accomplished he ceased. Servetus, however, continued writing and his letters took on a more arrogant and even insulting tone. He regarded Calvin as the pope of orthodox Protestantism, whom he was determined to convert or overthrow. At the time Servetus came to Geneva the Libertine party, which was in opposition to Calvin, was in control of the city Council. Servetus apparently planned to join this party and thus drive Calvin out. Calvin apparently sensed this danger and was in no mood to permit Servetus to propagate his errors in Geneva. Hence he considered it his duty to make so dangerous a man harmless, and determined to bring him either to recantation or to deserved punishment. Servetus was promptly arrested and brought to trial. Calvin conducted the theological part of the trial and Servetus was convicted of fundamental heresy, falsehood and blasphemy. During the long trial Servetus became emboldened and attempted to overwhelm Calvin by pouring upon him the coarsest kind of abuse. [227] The outcome of the trial was left to the civil court, which pronounced the sentence of death by fire. Calvin made an ineffectual plea that the sword be substituted for the fire; hence the final responsibility for the burning rests with the Council.

Dr. Emile Doumergue, the author of Jean Calvin, which is beyond comparison the most exhaustive and authoritative work ever published on Calvin, has the following to say about the death of Servetus: "Calvin had Servetus arrested when he came to Geneva, and appeared as his accuser. He wanted him to be condemned to death, but not to death by burning. On August 20, 1553, Calvin wrote to Farel: 'I hope that Servetus will be condemned to death, but I desire that he should be spared the cruelty of the punishment'--he means that of fire. Farel replied to him on September 8th: 'I do not greatly approve that tenderness of heart,' and he goes on to warn him to be careful that 'in wishing that the cruelty of the punishment of Servetus be mitigated, thou art acting as a friend towards a man who is thy greatest enemy. But I pray thee to conduct thyself in such a manner that, in future, no one will have the boldness to publish such doctrines, and to give trouble with impunity for so long a time as this man has done.'

"Calvin did not, on this account, modify his own opinion, but he could not make it prevail. On October 26th he wrote again to Farel: 'Tomorrow Servetus will be led out to execution. We have done our best to change the kind of death, but in vain. I shall tell thee when we meet why we had no success.' (Opera, XIV, pp. 590, 613-657).

"Thus, what Calvin is most of all reproached with--the burning of Servetus--Calvin was quite opposed to. He is not responsible for it. He did what he could to save Servetus from mounting the pyre. But, what reprimands, more or less eloquent, has this pyre with its flames and smoke given rise to, made room for! The fact is that without the pyre the death of Servetus would have passed almost unnoticed."

Doumergue goes on to tell us that the death of Servetus was "the error of the time, an error for which Calvin was not particularly responsible. The sentence of condemnation to death was pronounced only after consultation with the Swiss Churches, several of which were far from being on good terms with Calvin (but all of which gave their consent) .... Besides, the judgment was pronounced by a Council in which the inveterate enemies of Calvin, the free thinkers, were in the majority." [228]

That Calvin himself rejected the responsibility is clear from his later writings. "From the time that Servetus was convicted of his heresy," said he, "I have not uttered a word about his punishment, as all honest men will bear witness." [229] And in one of his later replies to an attack which had been made upon him, he says: "For what particular act of mine you accuse me of cruelty I am anxious to know. I myself know not that act, unless it be with reference to the death of your great master, Servetus. But that I myself earnestly entreated that he might not be put to death his judges themselves are witnesses, in the number of whom at that time two were his staunch favorites and defenders." [230]

Before the arrest of Servetus and during the earlier stages of the trial Calvin advocated the death penalty, basing his argument mainly on the Mosaic law, which was, "He that blasphemeth the name of Jehovah, he shall surely be put to death," Lev. 24:16--a law which Calvin considered as binding as the decalogue and applicable to heresy as well. Yet he left the passing of sentence wholly to the civil council. tie considered Servetus the greatest enemy of the Reformation and honestly believed it to be the right and duty of the State to punish those who offended against the Church. He also felt himself providentially called to purify the Church of all corruptions, and to his dying day he never changed his views nor regretted his conduct toward Servetus.

Dr. Abraham Kuyper, the statesman-theologian from Holland, in speaking to an American audience not many years ago expressed some thoughts in this connection which are worth repeating. Said he: "The duty of the government to extirpate every form of false religion and idolatry was not a find of Calvinism, but dates from Constantine the Great and was the reaction against the horrible persecutions which his pagan predecessors on the Imperial throne had inflicted upon the sect of the Nazarene. Since that day this system had been defended by all Romish theologians and applied by all Christian princes. In the time of Luther and Calvin, it was a universal conviction that that system was the true one. Every famous theologian of the period, Melanchton first of all, approved of the death by fire of Servetus; and the scaffold, which was erected by the Lutherans, at Leipzig for Kreel, the thorough Calvinist, was infinitely more reprehensible when looked at from a Protestant standpoint.

"But whilst the Calvinists, in the age of the Reformation, yielded up themselves as martyrs, by tens of thousands, to the scaffold and the stake (those of the Lutherans and Roman Catholics being

The Reformed Doctrine Of Predestination

hardly worth counting), history has been guilty of the great and far-reaching unfairness of ever casting in their teeth this one execution by fire of Servetus as a crimen nefandum.

"Notwithstanding all this I not only deplore that one stake, but I unconditionally disapprove of it; yet not as if it were the expression of a special characteristic of Calvinism, but on the contrary as the fatal after-effect of a system, grey with age, which Calvinism found in existence, under which it had grown up, and from which it had not yet been able entirely to liberate itself." [231]

Hence when we view this affair in the light of the sixteenth century and consider these different aspects of the case,--namely, the approval of the other reformers, a public opinion which abhorred toleration as involving indifference to truth and which justified the death penalty for obstinate heresy and blasphemy, the sentence also passed on Servetus by the Roman Catholic authorities, the character of Servetus and his attitude toward Calvin, his going to Geneva for the purpose of causing trouble, the passing of sentence by a civil court not under Calvin's control, and Calvin's appeal for a lighter form of punishment,--we come to the conclusion that Calvin, in so far as he is chargeable with the affair, acted from a strict sense of duty, and that his responsibility is much less than has been commonly assumed. Furthermore, we are glad to say that while there was only one instance of this kind there was only one with which Calvin was in any way connected.

11. CONCLUSION

We have now examined the Calvinistic system in considerable detail, and have seen its influence in the Church, in the State, in society, and in education. We have also considered the objections which are commonly brought against it, and have considered the practical importance of the system. It now remains for us to make a few general observations in regard to the system as a whole.

A sure test of the character of individuals or of systems is found in Christ's own words: "By their fruits ye shall know them." By that test Calvinists and Calvinism will gladly be judged. The lives and the influences of those who have held the Reformed Faith is one of the best and most conclusive arguments in its favor. Smith refers to "that divinely vital and exuberant Calvinism, the creator of the modern world, the mother of heroes, saints and martyrs in number without number, which history, judging the tree by its fruits, crowns as the greatest creed of Christendom." [232] The impartial verdict of history is that as a character builder and as a proclaimer of liberty to men and nations Calvinism stands supreme among all the religious systems of the world. In calling the roll of the great men of our own country the number of Presbyterian presidents, legislators, jurists, authors, editors, teachers and business men is vastly disproportionate to the membership of the Church. Every impartial historian will admit that it was the Protestant revolt against Rome which gave the modern world its first taste of genuine religious and civil liberty, and that the nations which have achieved and enjoyed the greatest freedom have been those which were most fully brought under the influence of Calvinism. Furthermore that great life-giving stream of religious and civil liberty has been made by Calvinism to flow over all the broad plains of modern history. When we compare countries such as England, Scotland and America, with countries such as France, Spain and Italy, which never came under the influences of Calvinism, we readily see what the practical results are. The economic and moral depression in Roman Catholic countries has brought about such a decrease even in the birth rate that the population in those countries hah become almost stationary, while the population in these other countries has steadily increased.

A brief examination of Church history, or of the historic creeds of Protestantism, readily shows that the doctrines which today are known as Calvinism were the ones which brought about the Reformation and preserved its benefits. He who is most familiar with the history of Europe and America will readily agree with the startling statement of Dr. Cunningham that, "next to Paul, John Calvin has done most for the world." And Dr. Smith has well said: "Surely it should stop the mouths of the detractors of Calvinism to remember that from men of that creed we inherit, as the fruits of their blood and toil, their prayers and teachings, our civil liberty, our Protestant faith, our Christian homes. The thoughtful reader, noting that these three blessings lie at the root of all that is best and greatest in the modern world, may be startled at the implied claim that our present Christian civilization is but the fruitage of Calvinism." [233]

We do but repeat the very clear testimony of history when we say that Calvinism has been the creed of saints and heroes. "Whatever the cause," says Froude, "the Calvinists were the only fighting Protestants. It was they whose faith gave them courage to stand up for the Reformation, and but for them the Reformation would have been lost." During those centuries in which spiritual tyranny was numbering its victims by the thousands; when in England, Scotland, Holland and Switzerland, Protestantism had to maintain itself with the sword, Calvinism proved itself the only system able to cope with and destroy the great powers of the Romish Church. Its unequalled array of martyrs is one of its crowns of glory. In the address of the Methodist Conference to the Presbyterian Alliance of 1896 it was graciously said: "Your Church has furnished the memorable and inspiring spectacle, not simply of a solitary heroic soul here and there, but of generations of faithful souls ready for the sake of Christ and His truth to go cheerfully to prison and to death. This rare honor you rightly esteem as the most precious part of your priceless heritage." "There is no other system of religion in the world," says McFetridge, which has such a glorious array of martyrs to the faith. "Almost every man and woman who walked to the flames rather than deny the faith or leave a stain on conscience was the devout follower, not only, and first of all, of the Son of God, but also of that minister of God who made Geneva the light of Europe, John Calvin." [234] To the Divine vitality and fruitfulness of this system the modern world owes a debt of gratitude which in recent years it is slowly beginning to recognize but can never pay.

We have said that Calvinistic theology develops a liberty loving people. Where it flourishes despotism cannot abide. As might have been expected, it early gave rise to a revolutionary form of Church government, in which the people of the Church were to be governed and ministered to, not by the appointees of any one man or set of men placed over them, but by pastors and officers elected by themselves. Religion was then with the people, not over them. Testimony from a remarkable source as to the efficiency of this government is that of the distinguished Roman Catholic, Archbishop Hughes of New York: "Though it is my privilege to regard the authority exercised by the General Assembly as usurpation, still I must say, with every man acquainted with the mode in which it is organized, that for the purpose of popular and political government its structure is little inferior to that of Congress itself. It acts on the principle of a radiating center, and is without an equal or a rival among the other denominations of the country." [235]

From freedom and responsibility in the Church it was only a step to freedom and responsibility in the State; and historically the cause of freedom has found no braver nor more resolute champions than the followers of Calvin.

"Calvinism," says Warburton, "is no dreamy, theoretical creed. It does not,--despite all the assertions of its adversaries,--encourage a man to fold his arms in a spirit of fatalistic indifference, and ignore the needs of those around him, together with the crying evils which lie, like putrifying sores, upon the open face of society." [236] Wherever it has gone marvelous moral transformations have followed in its wake. For purity of life, for temperance, industry, and charity, the Calvinists have stood without superiors.

James Anthony Froude has been recognized as one of England's most able historians and men of letters. For a number of years he was professor of History at Oxford, England's greatest university. While he accepted another system for himself, and while his writings are such that he is often spoken of as an opponent of Calvinism, he was free from prejudice, and the ignorant attacks upon Calvinism which have been so common in recent years aroused in him the learned scholar's just impatience.

"I am going to ask you," says Froude, "to consider how it came to pass that if Calvinism is indeed the hard and unreasonable creed which modern enlightenment declares it to be, it has possessed such singular attractions in past times for some of the greatest men that ever lived; and how--being as we are told, fatal to morality, because it denies free will--the first symptom of its operation, wherever it established itself, was to obliterate the distinction between sins and crimes, and to make the moral law the rule of life for States as well as persons. I shall ask you, again, why, if it be a creed of intellectual servitude, it was able to inspire and sustain the bravest efforts ever made by man to break the yoke of unjust authority. When all else has failed,--when patriotism has covered its face and human courage has broken down,--when intellect has yielded, as Gibbon says, 'with a smile or a sigh,' content to philosophize in the closet, and abroad worship with the vulgar,--when emotion, and sentiment, and tender imaginative piety have become the handmaids of superstition, and have dreamt themselves into forgetfulness that there is any difference between lies and truth,--the slavish form of belief called Calvinism, in one or other of its many forms, has borne ever an inflexible front to illusion and mendacity, and has preferred rather to be ground to powder like flint than to bend before violence or melt under enervating temptation." [237]

To illustrate this Froude mentions William the Silent, Luther, Calvin, Knox, Coligny, Cromwell, Milton, and Bunyan, and says of them: "These men are possessed of all the qualities which give nobility and grandeur to human nature,--men whose life was as upright as their intellect was commanding and their public aims untainted with selfishness; unalterably just where duty required them to be stern, but with the tenderness of a woman in their hearts; frank, true, cheerful, humorous, as unlike sour fanatics as it is possible to imagine anyone, and able in some way to sound the key-note to which every brave and faithful heart in Europe instinctively vibrated." [238]

We shall now turn our attention to Calvinism as an evangelizing force. A very practical test for any system of religious doctrine is, "Has it, in comparison with other systems, proved itself a success in the evangelization of the world?" To save sinners and convert them to practical godliness is the chief purpose of the Church in this world; and the system which will not measure up to this test must be set aside, no matter how popular it may be in other respects.

The first great Christian revival, in which three thousand people were converted, occurred under the preaching of Peter in Jerusalem, who employed such language as this: "Him being delivered up by the determinate council and foreknowledge of God, ye by the hands of lawless men did crucify and slay," Acts 2:23. And the company of disciples, when in earnest prayer shortly afterward, spoke in these

The Reformed Doctrine Of Predestination

words: "For of a truth in this city against thy holy servant Jesus, whom thou didst anoint, both Herod and Pontius Pilate, with the Gentiles and the peoples of Israel, were gathered together, to do whatsoever thy hand and thy counsel foreordained to come to pass," Acts 4:27, 28. That is Calvinism rigid enough.

The next great revival in the Church, which occurred in the fourth century through the influence of Augustine, was based on these doctrines, as is readily seen by anyone who reads the literature on that period. The Reformation, which is admitted by all to have been incomparably the greatest revival of true religion since New Testament times, occurred under the soundly predestinarian preaching of Luther, Zwingli, and Calvin. To Calvin and Admiral Coligny belongs the credit of having inspired the first Protestant foreign missionary enterprise, the expedition to Brazil in 1555. True, the venture proved unsuccessful, and the religious wars in Europe prevented the renewal of the enterprise for a considerable period.

McFetridge has given us some interesting and comparatively unknown facts about the rise of the Methodist Church. Says he: "We speak of the Methodist Church beginning in a revival. And so it did. But the first and chief actor in that revival was not Wesley, but Whitefield (an uncompromising Calvinist). Though a younger man than Wesley, it was he who first went forth preaching in the fields and gathering multitudes of followers, and raising money and building chapels. It was Whitefield who invoked the two Wesleys to his aid. And he had to employ much argument and persuasion to overcome their prejudices against the movement. Whitefield began the great work at Bristol and Kingswood, and had found thousands flocking to his side, ready to be organized into churches, when he appealed to Wesley for assistance. Wesley, with all his zeal, had been quite a High-Churchman in many of his views. He believed in immersing even the infants, and demanded that dissenters should be rebaptized before being taken into the Church. He could not think of preaching in any place but in a church. 'He should have thought,' as he said, 'the saving of souls almost a sin if it had not been done in a church.' Hence when Whitefield called on John Wesley to engage with him in the popular movement, he shrank back. Finally, he yielded to Whitefield's persuasions, but, he allowed himself to be governed in the decision by what many would rate as a superstition. He and Charles first opened their Bibles at random to see if their eyes should fall on a text which might decide them. But the texts were all foreign to the subject. Then he had recourse to sortilege, and cast lots to decide the matter. The lot drawn was the one marked for him to consent, and so he consented. Thus he was led to undertake the work with which his name has been so intimately and honorably associated ever since.

"So largely was the Methodist movement owing to Whitefield that he was called 'the Calvinistic establisher of Methodism,' and to the end of his life he remained the representative of it in the eyes of the learned world. Walpole, in his Letters, speaks only once of Wesley in connection with the rise of Methodism, while he frequently speaks of Whitefield in connection with it. Mant, in his course of lectures against Methodism, speaks of it as an entirely Calvinistic affair. Neither the mechanism nor the force which gave rise to it originated with Wesley. Field-preaching, which gave the whole movement its aggressive character, and fitted and enabled it to cope with the powerful agencies which were armed against it, was begun by Whitefield, whilst 'Wesley was dragged into it reluctantly.' In the polite language of the day 'Calvinism' and 'Methodism' were synonymous terms, and the Methodists were called 'another sect of Presbyterians.' ....

"It was Calvinism, and not Arminianism, which originated (so far as any system of doctrine originated) the great religious movement in which the Methodist Church was born.

"While, therefore, Wesley is to be honored for his work in behalf of that Church, we should not fail to remember the great Calvinist, George Whitefield, who gave that Church her first beginnings and her most distinctive character. Had he lived longer, and not shrunk from the thought of being the founder of a Church, far different would have been the results of his labors. As it was, he gathered congregations for others to form into Churches, and built chapels for others to preach in."[239]

Furthermore, when we come to a study of foreign missions we find that this system of belief has been the most important agency in carrying the Gospel to the heathen nations. St. Paul, whom the more liberal opponents of Calvinism admit to have been responsible for the Calvinistic cast of the theological thought of the Church, was the greatest and most influential of missionaries. If we call the roll of the heroes of Protestant Missions we find that almost without exception they have been disciples of Calvin. We find Carey and Martyn in India, Linvingstone and Moffat in Africa, Morrison in China, Paton in the South Seas, and a great host of others. These men professed and possessed a Calvinism which was not static but dynamic; it was not their creed only, but their conduct.

And in regard to foreign missions, Dr. F. W. Loetscher has said: "Though like all our sister Churches we have reason, in view of our unprecedented resources and the appalling needs of heathen lands, to lament that we have not accomplished more, we may at least thank God that our venerated fathers made so good a beginning in establishing missions all over the world; that the Calvinistic Churches today surpass all others in their gifts to this cause; and in particular that our own denomination has the unique honor and privilege of discharging her far-reaching responsibilities by actually confronting every one of the great non-Christian religions, and preaching the gospel on more continents, and among more nations, peoples, and tongues, than any other evangelical Church in the world." [240]

Although to some it may sound like an unwarranted exaggeration, we have no hesitation in saying that through the centuries Calvinism, fearlessly and ringingly polemic in its insistence upon, and defense of, sound doctrine, has been the real strength of the Christian Church. The traditionally high standards of the Calvinistic Churches in regard to ministerial training and culture have borne a great harvest in bringing multitudes to the feet of Jesus, not in temporary excitement, but in perpetual covenant. Judged by its fruits Calvinism has proven itself incomparably the greatest evangelizing force in the world.

The enemies of Calvinism are not able honestly to confront the testimony of history. Certainly a glorious record belongs to this system in the history of modern civilization. None more noble can be found anywhere. "It has ever been a mystery to the so-called liberals," says Henry Ward Beecher, "that the Calvinists, with what they have considered their harshly despotic and rigid views and doctrines, should always have been the staunchest and bravest defenders of freedom. The working for liberty of these severe principles in the minds of those that adopted them has been a puzzle. But the truth lies here: Calvinism has done what no other religion has ever been able to do. It presents the highest human ideal to the world, and sweeps the whole road to destruction with the most appalling battery that can be imagined.

"It intensifies, beyond all example, the individuality of man, and shows in a clear and overpowering light his responsibility to God and his relations to eternity. It points out man as entering life under the weight of a tremendous responsibility, having on his march toward the grave, this one sole solace--of securing heaven and of escaping hell.

"Thus the Calvinist sees man pressed, burdened, urged on, by the most mighty influencing forces. He is on the march for eternity, and is soon to stand crowned in heaven or to lie sweltering in hell, thus to continue for ever and ever. Who shall dare to fetter such a being? Get out of his way! Hinder him not, or do it at the peril of your own soul. Leave him free to find his way to God. Meddle not with him or with his rights. Let him work out his own salvation as he can. No hand must be laid crushingly upon a creature who is on such a race as this--a race whose end is to be eternal glory or unutterable woe for ever and ever." [241]

"This tree," to adopt the eloquent paragraph of another, "may have, to prejudiced eyes, a rough bark, a gnarled stem, and boughs twisted often into knotted shapes of ungraceful strength. But, remember, it is not a willow-wand of yesterday. These boughs have wrestled with the storms of a thousand years; this stem has been wreathed with the red lightning and scarred by the thunderbolt; and all over its rough rind are the marks of the battle-axe and the bullet. This old oak has not the pliant grace and silky softness of a greenhouse plant, but it has a majesty above grace, and a grandeur beyond beauty. Its roots may be strangely contorted, but some of them are rich with the blood of glorious battlefields, some of them are clasped around the stakes of martyrs; some of them hidden in solitary cells and lonely libraries, where deep thinkers have mused and prayed, as in some apocalyptic Patmos; and its great tap-root runs back, until it twines in living and loving embrace around the cross of Calvary. Its boughs may be gnarled, but they hang clad with all that is richest and strongest in the civilization and Christianity of human history." [242]

This is no vain and empty eulogy of Calvinism. With the above facts and observations every enlightened and impartial reader of history will agree. Furthermore, the author would say of this book what Dr. E. W. Smith in his book, "The Creed of Presbyterians," said at the close of the chapter on, "The Creed Tested By Its Fruits,"--namely that these facts and observations are "set forth, not to stimulate denominational vanity, but to fill us with gratitude to God for that past history and that present eminence which should be to every one of us

'A vantage-ground for nobleness';

and above all to kindle in our hearts a holy enthusiasm for that Divine system of truth, which, under God, has been the foremost factor in the making of America and the modern world."

In conclusion we would say that in this book the reader has found some very old-fashioned divinity--divinity as old as the Bible, as old and older than the world itself, since this plan of redemption was hidden in the eternal counsels of God. No attempt has been made to cloak the fact that the doctrines advocated and defended in these pages are really wonderful and startling. They are enough to electrify the sleepy sinner who has taken it for granted all his life long that he can square matters with God any time he pleases, and they are sufficient to horrify the sleepy "saint" who has been deluding himself in the deadening repose of a carnal religion. But why should they not cause astonishment? Does not nature teem with wonders? Why should not revelation? One needs to read but little to become aware that Science brings to light many astonishing truths which an uneducated man finds it hard, if not impossible, to believe; and why should it not be so with the truths of Revelation and the spiritually uneducated? If the Gospel does not startle and terrify and amaze a man when presented to him, it is not the true Gospel. But who was ever amazed at Arminianism with its doctrine that every man carves out

The Reformed Doctrine Of Predestination

his own destiny? It will not suffice merely to ignore or ridicule these doctrines as many are inclined to do. The question is, Are these doctrines true? If they are true, why ridicule them? If they are not true, disprove them. We close with the statement that this great system of religious thought which bears Calvin's name is nothing more or less than the hope of the world.

Footnotes:

167. Calvinism, p. 42.
168. Calvinism, p. 44.
169. History of the Reformation, p. 224.
170. God Sovereign and Man Free, p. 14.
171. The Creed of Presbyterians, p. 72.
172. Macaulay, History of England, I., p. 119.
173. The Beginnings of New England, pp. 37, 51.
174. Calvinism in History, p. 124.
175. The Creed of Presbyterians, pp. 98, 99.
176. The Swiss Reformation, II., p. 818.
177. Hist. Eng. X. 437.
178. Smith, The Creed of Presbyterians, p. 83.
179. Eng. Hist. Eighteenth Century, I., pp. 264, 265.
180. Calvinism, pp. 84, 92.
181. Calvinism in History, p. 144.
182. Rise of the Dutch Republic, I., p. 114.
183. Lectures on Calvinism, p. 44.
184. Hist. U. S., I., p. 463.
185. Presbyterians and the Revolution, p. 49.
186. Scotch and Irish Seeds in American Soil, p. 334.
187. Creeds of Christendom, p. 219.
188. Harper's Monthly, June and July, 1872.
189. The United Netherlands, III., p. 121.
190. The United Netherlands, IV., pp. 548, 547.
191. English Literature, II., p. 472.
192. Address on, "The Westminster Standards and the Formation of the American Republic.
193. Hist. U. S., X., p. 77.
194. Calvinism in History, pp. 85-88.
195. The Creed of Presbyterians, p. 142.
196. Id. p. 119.
197. Reformation in the Time of Calvin, I., p. 5.
198. The Creed of Presbyterians, p. 132.
199. Calvinism in History, p. 74.
200. Beginnings of New England, p. 58.
201. Democracy, I., p. 384.
202. The Beginnings of New England, p. 59.
203. Lectures on the History of France, p. 415.
204. The Fundamental Principles of Calvinism, H. H. Meeter, p. 92.
205. What Calvinism Has Done for America, p. 6.
206. Calvinism in History, p. 21.
207. Miscellanies, p. 406.
208. Hist. Of U. S., II., p. 463.
209. The Creed of Presbyterians, p. 148.
210. The Fundamental Principles of Calvinism, p. 96-99.
211. The Swiss Reformation, p. 312.
212. Schaff, The Swiss Reformation, p. 322.
213. The Swiss Reformation, p. 348.
214. Calvin Memorial Addresses, p. 34.
215. Calvin Memorial Addresses, p. 20.
216. Article, The Theology of Calvin, p. 1.
217. The Swiss Reformation, p. 330.
218. Calvin and Calvinism, pp. 8, 374.
219. Calvin Memorial Addresses, p. 22.
220. Quoted by James Orr, Calvin Memorial Addresses, p. 92.
221. Miscellanies, p. 406.

222. Vie de ste. Francois de Sales, par son neveu, p. 20.
223. The Swiss Reformation, p. 826.
224. History of the Swiss Reformation, II, p. 698.
225. The Creeds of Christendom, I., p. 464.
226. The Swiss Reformation, II., p. 787.
227. See Schaff, The Swiss Reformation, II., p. 778.
228. Doumergue, Article, What Ought to be Known About Calvin, in the Evangelical Quarterly, Jan. 1929.
229. Opera, VIII., p. 461.
230. Calvin's Calvinism, p. 346.
231. Lectures on Calvinism, p. 129.
232. The Creed of Presbyterians, p. vii.
233. The Creed of Presbyterians, p. 74.
234. Calvinism in History, p. 113.
235. Presbyterians and the Revolution, p. 140.
236. Calvinism, p. 78.
237. Calvinism, p. 7.
238. Calvinism, p. 8.
239. Calvinism in History, pp. 151-153.
240. Address before the General Assembly of the Presbyterian Church, U.S.A., 1929.
241. Plymouth Pulpit, article, Calvinism.
242. Power and Claims of a Calvinistic Literature, p. 35, quoted from Smith, The Creed of Presbyterians, p. 105.

www.ingramcontent.com/pod-product-compliance
Lightning Source LLC
Chambersburg PA
CBHW030234170426
43201CB00006B/216